A *Publishers Weekly* Best Book of 2006

"An outstanding and often hilarious memoir of one man's interaction with the saints of the Roman Catholic tradition."

Winner of a 2007 Christopher Award

For books that "affirm the highest values of the human spirit"

First Place Hard Cover Spirituality, 2007 Catholic Press Association Award

"In a cross between Holden Caulfield and Thomas Merton, James Martin has written one of the best spiritual memoirs in years. With help from the saints who have inspired and guided his way, he recounts a journey that is as entertaining as it is profound."
—Robert Ellsberg, author of *All Saints*

"It isn't often that a new and noteworthy book comes along in this genre, but we have reason to celebrate *My Life with the Saints*. It is earmarked for longevity. It will endure as an important and uncommon contribution to religious writing."
—Doris Donnelly, *America*

"In a volume that is part spiritual memoir, part inspirational guide, Martin, a Jesuit priest and associate editor at *America*, applies the teachings of great saints to everyday life. Martin is interested in holding up the saints not as paragons but as exemplars of holy struggle. All the saints, he writes, struggled in one way or another. . . . Martin's final word for us is as Jungian as it is Catholic: God does not want us to be like Mother Teresa or Dorothy Day. God wants us to be most fully ourselves."
—*The Washington Post Book World*

"Martin takes a splendid idea and develops it masterfully by weaving stories from his life into those of his favorite saints. Martin's animated style and wide-ranging experiences will make this a book readers of diverse backgrounds will enjoy."
—*Publishers Weekly* (starred review)

"A wonderful new book . . . both deeply spiritual and profoundly human. . . . What's delightful about this book is its sheer unpredictability. You never know where Fr. Martin's journey will take you, and what saints, icons, and plain old human beings you'll meet along the way. . . . [And] there are places in the book where you will laugh out loud."
—Terry Golway, *The Irish Echo*

"What a wonderful book this is! Charming, enthralling, intimate, full of wisdom and self-effacing humor, it supplies not just a biographical overview of a wide variety of holy women and men throughout history, but in their powerfully affective influence on Martin's life we see how useful it is to continually turn to the saints for encouragement and guidance."
—Ron Hansen, author of *Mariette in Ecstasy*

"With wit and candor, Martin brings [the saints] and his other seemingly distant role models down to earth, citing instances from their biographies and, with deepest effectiveness, revealing his personal connection to each and how each has assisted with his life."
—*Booklist*

"An account of spiritual peregrination that is as delightful as it is instructive. . . . He succeeds in making 'the cloud of witnesses' persuasively present."
—*First Things*

"This new account by Jesuit Fr. James Martin stands out because it weaves the author's personal struggles and doubts together with colorful portraits of the holy people who have inspired him. . . . This splendid book might prompt readers to look deeper into the lives of the saints whose stories speak to them."
—*National Catholic Reporter*

"Perhaps the most significant contribution Martin's memoir offers is the multiple examples of how to appropriate the wisdom of the saints into one's own life. . . . Martin's accessible writing fuels the imagination such that one is inspired to give the saints a second look."
—Renee LaReau, Bustedhalo.com

Other Books by James Martin, SJ

*Seven Last Words: An Invitation to a Deeper
Friendship with Jesus*

The Abbey

Jesus: A Pilgrimage

*Between Heaven and Mirth: Why Joy, Humor, and Laughter
Are at the Heart of the Spiritual Life*

The Jesuit Guide to (Almost) Everything

*A Jesuit Off-Broadway: Behind the Scenes with Faith, Doubt,
Forgiveness, and More*

*Becoming Who You Are: Insights on the True Self from
Thomas Merton and Other Saints*

Lourdes Diary: Seven Days at the Grotto of Massabieille

Searching for God at Ground Zero

*This Our Exile: A Spiritual Journey with the Refugees
of East Africa*

*In Good Company: The Fast Track from the Corporate World
to Poverty, Chastity and Obedience*

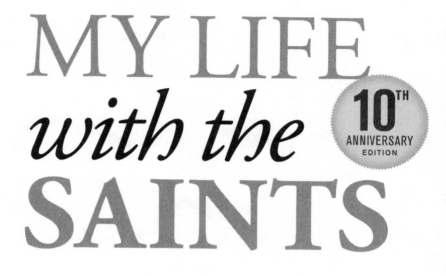

WITH A NEW EPILOGUE BY THE AUTHOR

MY LIFE
with the 10TH ANNIVERSARY EDITION
SAINTS

JAMES MARTIN, SJ

Foreword by John L. Allen, Jr.

LOYOLA PRESS.
A JESUIT MINISTRY
Chicago

LOYOLA PRESS.
A JESUIT MINISTRY

3441 N. Ashland Avenue
Chicago, Illinois 60657
(800) 621-1008
www.loyolapress.com

Imprimi Potest: Very Rev. Thomas J. Regan, SJ

ISBN-13: 978-0-8294-4452-0
ISBN-10: 0-8294-4452-1
Library of Congress Control Number: 2016943245

Printed in the United States of America.
16 17 18 19 20 21 22 23 24 RRD 10 9 8 7 6 5 4 3 2 1

Fratribus carissimis in Societate Jesu.

For me to be a saint means to be myself.
—Thomas Merton

CONTENTS

Foreword xi

1 The Saint of the Sock Drawer
 An Introduction... 1

2 Child of God
 Joan of Arc.. 11

3 Inward Drama
 Thérèse of Lisieux 27

4 The True Self
 Thomas Merton 41

5 *Ad Majorem Dei Gloriam*
 Ignatius of Loyola 71

6 More Than Ever
 Pedro Arrupe 101

7 In the Grotto of Massabieille
 Bernadette Soubirous... 123

8 Share This Joy with All You Meet
 Mother Teresa 149

9 Vicar of Christ
 Pope John XXIII 175

10 Living in Her World
 Dorothy Day 203

11 For I Am a Sinful Man
 Peter 223

12 *Fides Quaerens Intellectum*
    Thomas Aquinas.. 245

13 Fools for Christ
    Francis of Assisi... 261

14 Hidden Lives
    Joseph.. 287

15 Who Trusts in God
    The Ugandan Martyrs.. 303

16 The Most Precious Thing I Possess
    Aloysius Gonzaga.. 319

17 Full of Grace
    Mary.. 333

18 Holy in a Different Way
    A Conclusion.. 359

19 Still Trying to Become a Saint
    An Epilogue.. 379

For Further Reading.. 395

Acknowledgments... 409

A Guide for Reading Groups... 413

About the Author... 417

Foreword

Like countless numbers of people, I was captivated by Fr. James Martin's *My Life with the Saints* when it appeared ten years ago. I was reasonably familiar with the usual sorts of hagiography, but this was the most human, honest, warm, and even humorous treatment of the stories of the saints I had ever encountered. A reviewer once described the book as an invitation to friendship not only with the saints, but with the author, and I can report from personal experience that that's true. I first met Jim in person a few years after the book's publication, but I told him I felt we had been friends for a long time because I got to know him, and to cherish him, through the book.

Since then, of course, Jim has gone on to become far more than the author of this one book—the official chaplain of *The Colbert Report*, a *New York Times* best-selling author, a regular contributor to the Jesuit-run *America* magazine, and a ubiquitous presence in the media whenever there's a breaking story about Catholicism. In effect, he's become one of the leading public voices on Catholicism in America, and those of us in the Church should feel we won the lottery with that outcome because few people are better at putting an appealing public face on the faith than Jim.

I do a fair number of public appearances myself, largely because I'm a journalist, and it often seems that the only times I get to see

Jim in person these days are on TV platforms or when we're sharing space at a book-signing table at a Catholic gathering. (For the record, his lines are always substantially longer than mine.) And though Jim has become a celebrity, he has remained recognizably Jim: grounded, humble, able to acknowledge his flaws and struggles, and always seeking to identify the good in others. Perhaps his study of the saints has had some transfer effect, because he often seems a bit of a saint-in-the-making himself.

We live in a media-saturated world, in which there's a bevy of talking heads on every conceivable subject—and thank God for it, because otherwise I'd be forced to find a real job to pay the bills! As a result, Jim is hardly the only Catholic commentator out there, but he fills a niche relatively few others do. It's not that he's the smartest of the lot, although he's an extremely bright guy, or that he's always the best informed and most connected, although he knows his stuff. And it's not that Jim is the most effective defender or critic of the hierarchy, because he's too balanced to be reliably in either camp, or that he's the most pious cleric you'll ever find on television.

What makes Jim unique, I would say, is his rare ability to be a truly successful public figure in an age of hyperbolic rage and partisan acrimony without ever succumbing to those temptations. His prominence makes the point that you don't have to fume and smolder to get attention, and you don't have to demonize people with whom you disagree in order to be persuasive. Instead, the Jim Martin experiment in American public life shows that a generous and calm personality, one based on treating people with respect and civility, actually can win hearts and minds, as Jim has been doing for a full decade since the appearance of *My Life with the Saints*.

A further illustration of Jim's success comes with the fact that most of my conservative Catholic friends see him as a definite liberal, while most of my friends on the left think he's not nearly liberal

enough. Perhaps he leans a little bit to the liberal side of some argu-
ments, but the fundamental truth is that Jim is far too wise to suc-
cumb to the illusion that ideology should ever prevail over concrete
experience and flesh-and-blood people in shaping perceptions.

Jim has one final quality that's perennially in short supply, especially when talk turns to religion: a great sense of humor. The Catholic
poet and writer Hilaire Belloc once said, "Wherever the Catholic sun
doth shine, there's laughter and good red wine," and I have to say that
twenty years of covering the Catholic Church day in and day out have
taught me that that's true.

Here's an example from an unexpected quarter. In 2005, I published a book about the election of Pope Benedict XVI, who isn't
most people's idea of a stand-up comic. The book was divided into
three parts, including the final days of St. John Paul II, the inside
story of Benedict's election, and then my projections on where his
papacy would go. Later, Benedict had an aide call to deliver the following message: "Please thank Herr Doktor Allen for having written
this book . . . especially the last part, about the future of my papacy,
because it has saved me the trouble of thinking about it for myself!"

Yes, Catholics know how to laugh and let the good times roll, but
we aren't always as skilled at projecting that quality in public. In terms
of its image, Catholicism often comes off as a scold, something like
the Doctor No character from the old James Bond films. Not so with
Jim, who always has a smile on his face and a laugh-line on his tongue.
Sure, his humor is generally a prelude to a serious point or spiritual
insight, but it's the laughter that gets people listening. They are open
to the Christian message that Jim presents in large part because they
like the messenger.

On this tenth anniversary of *My Life with the Saints*, I encourage
you to read the book if you haven't done so yet. Once you're done,
seek out as much of Jim's other work as you can, follow him in the

media, and tell your friends and neighbors to do the same. His balanced, civil, and deeply funny voice is a balm to much of what ails this culture (and this Church), and those of us who are Catholics ought to be proud that this voice is coming from one of us.

John L. Allen Jr. is the editor of Crux, an
independent Catholic news site, and the author of
many books, including *The Future Church*.

1

The Saint of the Sock Drawer

An Introduction

When I was nine, my greatest pleasure was ordering things through the mail. The cereal boxes that filled our kitchen shelves all boasted small order forms on the back, which I would clip out, fill in with my address and send away, along with a dollar bill or two. A few weeks later a brown paper package addressed to me would arrive in our mailbox. Nothing filled me with more excitement.

While the most attractive offers typically appeared in comic books, these advertisements rarely represented what the postman eventually delivered. The "Terrifying Flying Ghost" on the inside back cover of a *Spider-Man* comic book turned out to be a cheap plastic ball, a rubber band, and a piece of white tissue paper. The "Fake Vomit" looked nothing like the real stuff, and the "Monster Tarantula" was not monstrous at all.

Worst of all were the "Sea Monkeys." The colorful advertisement depicted smiling aquatic figures (the largest one wearing a golden crown) happily cavorting in a sort of sea city. Unfortunately, my six-week wait for them had a disappointing end: the Sea Monkeys turned out to be a packet of shrimp eggs. And while the Sea Monkeys did eventually hatch in a fishbowl on a chair in my bedroom, they were so small as to be nearly invisible, and none, as far as I could tell, wore a crown. (Sea Monkey City was nearly decimated when I accidentally sneezed on it during my annual winter cold.)

Other purchases were more successful. My "Swimming Tony the Tiger" toy, whose purchase required eating my way through several boxes of Sugar Frosted Flakes to earn sufficient box tops, amazed even my parents with his swimming skills. The orange and black plastic tiger had arms that rotated and legs that kicked maniacally, and he was able to churn his way through the choppy waters of the stopped-up kitchen sink. One day, Tony, fresh from a dip, slipped from my fingers and fell on the linoleum floor. Both of his arms fell off, marking the end of his short swimming career. I put the armless tiger in the fishbowl with the Sea Monkeys, who seemed not to mind the company.

But even with my predilection for mail-order purchases, I would be hard-pressed to explain what led me to focus my childish desires on a plastic statue of St. Jude that I had spied in a magazine. I can't imagine what magazine this might have been, since my parents weren't in the habit of leaving Catholic publications lying around the house, but apparently the photo of the statue was sufficiently appealing to convince me to drop $3.50 into an envelope. That sum represented not only an excess of three weeks' allowance but also the forgoing of an *Archie* comic book—a real sacrifice at the time.

It certainly wasn't any interest on the part of my family, or any knowledge about St. Jude, that drew me to his statue. I knew nothing about him, other than what the magazine ad told me: he was the patron saint of hopeless causes. Even if I had been interested in reading about him, there would have been little to read; for all his current popularity, Jude remains a mysterious figure. Though he is named as one of the twelve apostles of Jesus, there are only three brief mentions of Jude in the entire New Testament. In fact, two lists of the apostles don't include him at all. Instead they mention a certain "Thaddeus," giving rise to the name "St. Jude Thaddeus." To confuse matters more, there is also a Jude listed as the brother of Jesus in the Gospel of Mark. And though some ancient legends mention his work in Mesopotamia, the *Encyclopedia of Catholicism* says candidly, "We have no reliable information about this obscure figure."

But Jude's story didn't concern me. What appealed to me most was that he was patron of hopeless causes. Who knew what help someone like that could give me? A tiger that could swim in the kitchen sink was one thing, but a saint who could help me get what I wanted was quite another. It was worth at least $3.50.

In a few weeks, I received a little package containing a nine-inch beige plastic statue, along with a booklet of prayers to be used for praying to my new patron. St. Jude the Beige, who held a staff and carried a sort of plate emblazoned with the image of a face (which I supposed was Jesus, though this was difficult to discern), was immediately given pride of place on top of the dresser in my bedroom.

At the time, I prayed to God only intermittently and then mainly to ask for things, such as: "Please let me get an A on my next test." "Please let me do well in Little League this year." "Please let my skin clear up for the school picture." I used to envision God as the Great Problem Solver, the one who would fix everything if I just prayed hard enough, used the correct prayers, and prayed in precisely the right way. But when God couldn't fix things (which seemed more frequent than I would have liked), I would turn to St. Jude. I figured that if it was beyond the capacity of God to do something, then *surely* it must be a lost cause, and it was time to call on St. Jude.

Fortunately, the booklet that accompanied the St. Jude statue included plenty of good prayers and even featured one in Latin that began "Tantum ergo sacramentum . . ." I saved the Latin prayer for the most important hopeless causes—final exams and the like. When

I *really* wanted something, I would say the "Tantum ergo sacramentum" prayer three times on my knees.

St. Jude stood patiently atop my dresser until high school. My high school friends, when visiting my house, often asked to see my bedroom (we were all inordinately curious about what each other's bedroom looked like). And though I was by now fond of St. Jude, I was afraid of what my friends would think if they spotted the strange plastic statue standing on my dresser. So St. Jude was relegated to inside my sock drawer and brought out only on special occasions.

My faith was another thing, you could say, that was relegated to the sock drawer for the next several years. During high school, I made it to Mass more or less weekly; but later, in college, I became just an occasional churchgoer (though I still prayed to the Great Problem Solver). And as my faith grew thinner and thinner, my affinity for St. Jude began to seem a little childish: silly, superstitious, and faintly embarrassing.

That changed for me at age twenty-six. Dissatisfied with my life in the business world, I began to consider doing something else, though at the time I had little idea of what that something else would be. All I knew was that after five years in corporate America, I was miserable and wanted out. From that rather banal sentiment, however, God was able to work. The Great Problem Solver was at work on a problem that I only dimly comprehended. In time, God would give me an answer to a question that I hadn't even asked.

One evening, after a long day's work, I came home and flipped on the television set. The local PBS station was airing a documentary about a Catholic priest named Thomas Merton. Though I had never heard of Merton, all sorts of famous talking heads appeared on screen to testify to his enormous influence on their lives. In just a few minutes of watching the program, I got the idea that Thomas Merton was bright, funny, holy, and altogether unique. The documentary was so interesting that it prompted me to track down, purchase, and read his autobiography, _The Seven Storey Mountain_, which told the story of his journey from an aimless youth to a Trappist monk. It captivated me as few books ever have.

Over the next two years, whenever I thought seriously about the future, the only thing that seemed to make any sense was entering a religious order. There were, of course, some doubts, some false starts, some hesitations, and some worries about embarrassing myself, but eventually I decided to quit my job and, at age twenty-eight, enter the Society of Jesus, the religious order more commonly known as the Jesuits. It was certainly the best decision I've ever made.

Upon entering the Jesuit novitiate, I was surprised to learn that most of my fellow novices had strong "devotions," as they called them, to one saint or another. They spoke with obvious affection for their favorite saints—almost as if they knew them personally. One novice, for example, was especially fond of Dorothy Day, quoting her liberally during our weekly community meetings. Another talked a great deal about St. Thérèse of Lisieux. But though my brother novices were sincere in their devotions, and they patiently related the lives of their heroes and heroines to me, I now found the idea of praying to the saints wholly superstitious. What was the point? If God hears your prayers, why do you need the saints?

These questions were answered when I discovered the collection of saints' biographies that filled the creaky wooden bookcases in the novitiate library.

I pulled my first selection from the shelves as a result of some serious prompting from one novice: "You've got to read _The Story of a Soul_," he kept telling me (badgering me was more like it). "Then you'll understand why I like Thérèse so much."

At this point, I knew little about the "Little Flower," as she is known, and imagined Thérèse of Lisieux as a sort of shrinking violet:

timid, skittish, and dull. So I was astonished when her autobiography revealed instead a lively, intelligent, and strong-willed woman, someone I might like to have known. Reading her story led me to track down biographies of other saints—some well-known, some obscure—in our library: St. Stanislaus Kostka, who, despite vigorous protests from his family, walked 450 miles to enter the Jesuit novitiate; St. Thomas More, whose fine intellect and love of country did not blind him to the centrality of God in his life; St. Teresa of Ávila, who decided, to the surprise of most and the dismay of many, to overhaul her Carmelite Order; and Pope John XXIII, who, I was happy to discover, was not only compassionate and innovative but also witty.

Gradually, I found myself growing fonder of these saints and developing a tenderness toward them. I began to see them as models of holiness relevant to contemporary believers, and to understand the remarkable ways that God works in the lives of individuals. Each saint was holy in his or her unique way, revealing how God celebrates individuality. As C. S. Lewis writes in *Mere Christianity*: "How monotonously alike all the great tyrants and conquerors have been: how gloriously different are the saints."

This gave me enormous consolation, for I realized that none of us are meant to be Thérèse of Lisieux or Pope John XXIII or Thomas More. We're meant to be ourselves, and meant to allow God to work in and through our own individuality, our own humanity. As St. Thomas Aquinas said, grace builds on nature.

Moreover, I found companions among the saints—friends to turn to when I needed a helping hand. My novice director told me that he thought of the saints as older brothers and sisters to whom one could look for advice and counsel. The Catholic theologian Lawrence S. Cunningham, in his book *The Meaning of Saints*, suggests that the saints also serve as our "prophetic witnesses," spurring us to live more fully as Christian disciples. Of course some might argue (and some do argue) that all you need is Jesus. And that's true: Jesus is everything, and the saints understood this more than anyone.

But God in his wisdom has also given us these companions of Jesus to accompany us along the way, so why not accept the gift of their friendship and encouragement? And there's no reason to feel as if devotion to the saints somehow takes away from your devotion to Jesus: everything the saints say and do is centered on Christ and points us in his direction. One day at Mass in the novitiate chapel, I heard—as if for the first time—a prayer of thanksgiving to God for the saints: "You renew the Church in every age by raising up men and women outstanding in holiness, living witnesses of your unchanging love. They inspire us by their heroic lives, and help us by their constant prayers to be the living sign of your saving power."

And I thought, *Yes.*

In reading the lives of the saints, I also discovered that I could easily recognize myself, or at least parts of myself, in their stories. This was the aspect of their lives that I most appreciated: they had struggled with the same human foibles that everyone does. Knowing this, in turn, encouraged me to pray to them for help during particular times and for particular needs. I knew that Thomas Merton had struggled greatly with pride and egotism, so when combating the same I would pray for his intercession. When sick I would pray to Thérèse of Lisieux; she understood what it was to battle self-pity and boredom during an illness. For courage, I prayed to Joan of Arc. For compassion, to Aloysius Gonzaga. For a better sense of humor and an appreciation of the absurdities of life, to Pope John XXIII.

Quite by surprise, then, I went from someone embarrassed by my affection for the saints to someone who counted it as one of the joys of my life. Even after the novitiate, as my Jesuit training continued, I read about the saints and took special pleasure in meeting new ones. You can never have too many friends.

Now I find myself introducing others to favorite saints and, likewise, being introduced. It's funny—the way you discover a new saint is often similar to the way in which you meet a new friend. Maybe you hear an admiring comment about someone and think, *I'd like to get to know that person*, such as when I started reading about English Catholic history and knew that I wanted to meet Thomas More. Perhaps you're introduced to a person by someone else who knows you'll enjoy that person's company, just as that novice introduced me to Thérèse. Or perhaps you run across someone, totally by accident, during your day-to-day life. It wasn't until my philosophy studies as a Jesuit that I read St. Augustine's *Confessions* and fell in love with his writings and his way of speaking of God.

That's what this book is: a personal introduction to some of my favorite saints, holy persons, and companions. (Technically, a "saint" is someone who has been canonized, or officially recognized by the Church as a person who has lived a holy life, enjoys life in heaven with God, and is worthy of public veneration by the faithful.) Over the past few years, whenever I've felt particularly close to a saint, I've spent some time writing down what drew me to him or her. Some of these essays reflect a devotion based on the public actions and well-known writings of a saint; others are rooted in a more personal response to a hidden part of a saint's life—a small, almost unnoticed, piece of his or her story that has affected me in a deep way.

This memoir is organized chronologically, so that the saints are introduced more or less in the sequence in which I first encountered them. In this way, I hope that you might be able to follow the progress of my own spiritual journey as you read about their lives. But a single chapter may range over years and even decades. For example, I first met St. Bernadette when I was a Jesuit novice, but it wasn't until some fifteen years later that I made a pilgrimage to Lourdes, where I came to know her story more intimately.

These reflections are not meant to be exhaustive, scholarly biographies of the lives of these spiritual heroes and heroines. Instead, they are meditations on the way that one Christian relates to these holy persons: how I came to know them, what inspires me about their stories, and what they've meant to me in my own life.

At the beginning of this essay, I said that I wasn't sure what led me to my affinity for St. Jude. But as I think about it, I know it was God who did so. God works in some very weird ways, and moving a boy to begin a life of devotion to the saints through a magazine advertisement is just one of them. Yet grace is grace, and when I look back over my life, I give thanks that I've met so many wonderful saints—who pray for me, offer me comfort, give me examples of discipleship, and help me along the way.

All of this, I like to think, is thanks to St. Jude. For all those years stuck inside the sock drawer, he prayed for a boy who didn't even know that he was being prayed for.

2

Child of God

Joan of Arc

Q. How do you know that it is Saint Margaret and Saint
Catherine who speak to you?
A. I have told you often enough that they are Saint
Margaret and Saint Catherine—believe me if you like.
—Transcript of the trial of Joan of Arc

I had a big decision to make when I was twelve: French or Spanish? Our junior high school language program started in seventh grade; the idea was that students would continue with one language until senior year in high school, leaving them if not completely fluent then at least able to move easily from a seat on the student council to a job at the United Nations. Today it would be an easier decision, but in the 1970s Spanish had not yet become a kind of second language in the United States. It was a tough call, my first real "adult" choice and one that I thought could possibly have drastic, even life-changing consequences.

"It's up to you," said my mother, a former French teacher, who used to sing French songs to my sister and me while she was cooking. (I knew where her sympathies lay.) My father, on the other hand, spoke Spanish fluently and around the time of my big decision started dropping references to all the people at his office with whom he could converse *en español*.

I would like to say that I chose French because it seemed more mysterious, or more elegant, or more international, or—better yet—because I had an intuition that so many of the saints I would come to love would be French, and that even as an adolescent I harbored hopes to travel someday to Lourdes or read the autobiography of Thérèse of Lisieux in her native language. But that would be a lie. I chose French because I saw one of the French textbooks, and it looked skinnier and therefore easier than the Spanish one.

So I spent the next three years at Plymouth Junior High School with Mr. Sherman, our rail-thin, nattily dressed French teacher, who had a goatee and who insisted that we always call him "Monsieur Sherman."

On the first day of class, we seventh graders received our French names. Monsieur Sherman sailed up and down the aisles asking us our names and baptizing us with new ones. Most were direct translations. I became Jacques Martin, and my friend Peggy became Marguerite. My friend Jeanne stayed Jeanne, but with a nicer pronunciation. She was now *Zhaann*, instead of *Jeenee*.

Learning a new language was a joy. Screwing up my lips for *u* and swallowing my tongue for *r* was new and different, and fun. And at age twelve, my mind was still capable of memorizing footlong columns of *vocabulaire* and page after page of verb conjugations. My classmates and I breezed through the next three years with Monsieur Sherman, taking dictation, doing drills to improve our *vocabulaire*, completing sentences, comprehending essays, putting on playlets, giving speeches, and watching ancient (that is, 1950s) filmstrips and movies about France and French culture.

Our textbooks and movies, however, made me wonder why French people had nothing but conversations like the following:

Margot: Hello.

Le professeur: Hello.

Margot: How are you?

Le professeur: I am fine.

Margot: Where is the book?

Le professeur: The book is in the library.

Margot: Thank you.

Le professeur: You're welcome.

Margot: Good-bye.

Le professeur: Good-bye.

France sounded like a dull place. People there had apparently little to talk about. "Where is the book?" was a real conversation stopper. It did not surprise me that Margot decided to take her leave. Margot, by the way, was the star of our textbook, *Je Parle Français*, and spent the bulk of her days asking for books, commenting at length on the weather, and listing for her friends in numbing detail every item of clothing that she was taking with her on a vacation. "Here is my shirt!" she would exclaim. "And here is my hat!"

As do many who study foreign languages, I still remember a surprising number of the stilted conversations from our books and films with near-perfect recall, as these were the very first ones imprinted on my twelve-year-old mind.

At the end of the first year, M. Sherman screened his prized collection of slides for us, which he had taken on his last trip to his beloved France. As I recall, he spent a lot of time around the Louvre and going in and out of the subway in Paris. One slide showed a statue of a young woman astride a gleaming golden horse in another French town.

"Jeanne d'Arc," he said. But before I could ask who she was—*click*—we were in Chartres.

After three years of Monsieur Sherman, my classmates and I graduated to high school, and the same cohort took classes with Madame Paulos and Madame Ramsey. Madame Paulos had a particular interest in French philosophy, so her tenth-grade charges read plenty of Jean-Paul Sartre, and we became probably the only fifteen-year-old existentialists in the area. Thanks to her efforts, when I arrived in college not only could I conjugate the *plus-que-parfait* (which I was unable to do in English), but I could also, when my freshman-year roommate told me proudly that he was reading Sartre, say haughtily but quite truthfully, "Yeah, I read that in tenth grade. In the original!"

As an undergraduate at the University of Pennsylvania, I studied business at the Wharton School. And though there was little room on our schedules for electives, I knew that I wanted to continue my French. During freshman year, I signed up for a course entitled "Intermediate French Grammar." But the class included things I had already mastered in high school, and I decided I wanted more of a challenge. So instead I took "Advanced French Conversation," confident that I could more than hold my own in any conversation about books, libraries, or items of clothing.

Unfortunately, I failed to realize that in a conversational French class at a large university, there is a good chance that people will have learned the language not in their suburban Philadelphia high school, like you, but in France, where they grew up. My class was entirely populated with French natives, whose conversation proved indeed advanced.

After all this French, I was itching to try it out beyond the classroom. So following graduation from college, I decided to take a trip to Europe.

Even in the wake of my college expenses, I had saved up some cash. To clinch the deal, my parents had given me a perfect graduation gift: enough money to buy a one-month Eurail pass. And, happily, one of my high school friends, Jeanne, or *Zhaann*, wanted to join me for a sprint around the continent.

It was a freewheeling trip—the first time I had ever been overseas—that took us from London to Paris to Rome to Florence to Venice to Vienna and back to London. We visited all the must-see sites, including a great number of cathedrals. Jeanne had been raised a Philadelphia Quaker, so I could act as if I knew everything about Catholic churches (which I certainly didn't). During our stay in Florence I was furious when we were turned out of the city's gorgeous Renaissance cathedral for wearing inappropriate attire: cutoff denim shorts and T-shirts. Filled with unrighteous indignation, I said to Jeanne (in words I recall with embarrassment): "Look, I give the church a dollar every time I go to Mass. I *deserve* to be let in!"

Despite our years of French, Jeanne and I had a tough time making ourselves understood in Paris. In one café, we mustered up our best pronunciation, with *r*'s and *u*'s that would make Monsieur Sherman proud, and asked for a plate of *fruits*, ending up instead with a steaming plate of greasy *frites*. Still, we were able to negotiate the city and take in most of the important sights. At Notre Dame, I spent as much time in the gift shop as I did in the cathedral itself, purchasing an expensive set of black rosary beads.

At one point, we passed a gilt statue of St. Joan of Arc, mounted on a horse, dazzling in the morning sunlight at the Place des Pyramides. "Your patron saint," I said to Jeanne. Ironically, it reminded us of home: there is a copy of the statue in Philadelphia, not far from the city's art museum. There the proud and resolute Joan sits astride her golden charger, defiantly holding a banner aloft as cars and buses rush past on their way into the city.

As we snapped photos of the statue, Jeanne asked what I knew about Joan of Arc. Embarrassed, I admitted that I knew little. I vaguely remembered Monsieur Sherman mentioning her in French class. She was a young girl (how young?) who heard voices (from whom?), led the French army to victory (against whom?), was burned at the stake (why, exactly?), and was declared a saint (when?).

As soon as I got home from Europe, I decided to return. There was so much more I wanted to see. I had used up all my savings, but I wanted to go back as soon as I could save enough money from my new job at General Electric.

Three years later and three years richer, I contacted another high school friend, Peggy, or Marguerite, about a return trip. At the time, Peggy and I were engrossed in literature from the First World War. We were fans of a fascinating book called *The Great War and Modern Memory*, written by Paul Fussell, one of our professors at Penn. His book, a study of how that war had influenced a generation of writers, launched me on a reading tour that included Robert Graves's autobiographical *Good-Bye to All That*, Siegfried Sassoon's *Memoirs of George Sherston*, and poetry by Edmund Blunden, Rupert Brooke, and Wilfred Owen.

Admittedly, it was not an interest Peggy and I could easily share with many others: World War I literature is not the sort of thing that pops up at cocktail gatherings or tailgate parties.

In any event, Peggy suggested we take a two-week trip to visit the major World War I battlefields in western Belgium and northern France: Ypres, Passendale, and Verdun.

One night, at my parents' house, with a crinkly Michelin map spread out on the kitchen table, Peggy and I discussed our plans. Yet the more we thought about the trip, the more morbid our little odyssey seemed. And the longer we considered our tour through the ghostly battlefields (and, after all, cemeteries) the more our attention was drawn to some very different sights nearby, namely, the cathedrals of Chartres and Reims, the Champagne region of France, and, most of all, the storied castles of the Loire Valley.

Which is where we ended up. We set aside our interest in learning more about the horrors of the First World War for another, equally ardent desire—to see the beauties of the ancient vineyards, medieval cathedrals, and Renaissance châteaux of France.

Like the first trip, it was a joyful few weeks. Peggy and I rented a teeny car in Paris and drove south—from town to town and castle to castle in a leisurely fashion, stopping where and when we wanted. Our proficiency in French seemed miraculously to return, and the residents of the Loire Valley were more forgiving of our high school pronunciation than had been the Parisians.

Still, there were linguistic glitches. One evening I decided to travel to Chartres on the train, while Peggy stayed behind with our car in Paris. On her way out of the city, Peggy got hopelessly lost and pulled over to ask directions.

Unfortunately, she confused the verb *chercher* (to seek) with *trouver* (to find). She drove around Paris, rolling down her window every few minutes to say, "Je trouve la rue à Chartres": "I find the road to Chartres." Needless to say, many Parisians greeted this news of Peggy's discovery with a mild shrug. One man said, "Congratulations."

"Monsieur Sherman would have been horrified," she said the next day.

Near the middle of our trip, on November 1, the Feast of All Saints, Peggy and I arrived in Orléans. The town sat squarely in the middle of the château towns that interested us: Chenonceaux, Chambord, and Chinon. Dog-tired, we arrived late in the afternoon and found ourselves rooms and a hearty supper in a small pension called Hôtel de Berry, close to the center of town. We would spend the next day touring the nearby châteaux before moving on to Reims.

In the morning, we opened our *Baedeker's* and flipped to the section on Orléans. I knew almost nothing about the town, except for some vague connection to Joan of Arc. The travel guide laid out Joan's story.

❦

Born during the Hundred Years' War, at the time of the conflict between the houses of Orléans and Burgundy, Joan, a young peasant girl, heard the voices of three saints—Michael, Margaret, and Catherine—who instructed her to save France. In the beginning, few people paid attention to Joan's claims about her mission. But after she successfully predicted defeats, met the crown prince (known as the dauphin), and was vetted by a group of prominent theologians, it was decided that she should be put to use in the fight against the English.

In April 1429, Joan requested and received military assistance to free the captured Orléans, which had been besieged by the English since October 1428. After convincing the dauphin to provide her with troops, she led the army into battle in a suit of white armor, holding aloft a banner that bore an image of the Trinity and the legend "Jesus, Maria." Despite being shot in the shoulder with an English arrow, Joan and her army freed the city on May 8. The English troops left the city, and the nearby English forts were captured. Since 1430 an annual commemoration of the victory has taken place in Orléans. And so Joan's title: "Maid of Orléans."

After another military campaign, Joan watched proudly as the dauphin was crowned King Charles VII at the cathedral in Reims. However, Joan was rudely shunted aside by royal courtiers as well as by the increasingly jealous (all-male) army. In a subsequent battle the Maid was captured by Burgundian troops, who then sold her to their allies, the English. The new king, significantly, failed to intervene.

Joan was imprisoned for a year and questioned by a church court sympathetic to her enemies, and an English ecclesiastical court sought to convict her on charges of witchcraft and heresy. (Her refusal to wear women's attire also infuriated the judges.)

On February 21, 1431, Joan appeared before an ecclesiastical court presided over by the bishop of Beauvais, a man named Cauchon, who was in thrall to the English. After a lengthy questioning in Rouen that stretched over six public and nine private sessions, an inaccurate summary of Joan's statements was drawn up and submitted to the judges and to officials at the University of Paris. Joan had firmly adhered to her story of voices and divine guidance, but, as Richard McBrien writes in his *Lives of the Saints*, "her lack of theological sophistication led her into damaging mistakes." She was denounced as a heretic.

Though threatened with torture, Joan refused to retract any of her statements. But later, brought before a huge crowd to be sentenced, she was intimidated into making some sort of retraction (the details of which are still disputed). Back in her jail cell, however, she regained her confidence and reversed her claim: she once again appeared in male clothing and declared her conviction that it was in fact God who had sent her. On May 29, she was condemned as a relapsed heretic and handed over to secular authorities. Joan was burned at the stake on the following day. Her last words were "Jesus, Jesus."

Joan's ashes, as Butler's *Lives of the Saints* puts it, "were contemptuously cast into the Seine."

Reading the spare entry from the guidebook, spending time in the town she delivered, and seeing the simple bronze statue of Joan in the plaza before the Hôtel Groslot in Orléans—she stands with head bowed, a mournful look on her rust-streaked face—made me anxious to find out more about her.

Once I returned home, I decided to learn more about Joan's life. As a result, she would become the first saint to be more for me than an image in stained glass or a name over a church door. After scouting around, I tracked down a copy of Vita Sackville-West's beautifully written 1936 biography, *Saint Joan of Arc*, which offered a sympathetic look at the saint and the complicated times in which she lived.

Soon after finishing the book, I noticed that Victor Fleming's film *Joan of Arc* was airing on TV. For a while, then, my mental image of the sad-faced Joan standing in the plaza in Orléans was replaced by Ingrid Bergman: clad in brilliant silver armor, astride her white charger, silhouetted against an impossibly blue Hollywood backlot sky. Or kneeling before the dauphin, played by José Ferrer, who peers haughtily at the star over his prodigious nose. Or bound with rope to the stake, a slim wooden cross raised to her lips for a last kiss. This Joan was beautiful, luminous, romantic.

It is likely an idealized picture. She was, after all, only sixteen when she presented herself to the dauphin. After surveying the evidence, Vita Sackville-West says, "We can presume her, then, to be a strong, healthy, plain, sturdy girl." Sackville-West implies a plainness that may have enabled Joan to avoid the sexual desire of her fellow soldiers during their campaigns. Yet Donald Spoto's scholarly biography, *Joan*, quotes several companions-at-arms who describe her as beautiful. Not long ago, the discovery of Joan's suit of armor (pierced in all the correct places, corresponding to her wounds) showed her to be a small woman. In any event, she was probably no Ingrid Bergman. Perhaps in stature more like another movie actress, *Saint Joan*'s Jean Seberg.

There is a late-nineteenth-century painting of Joan by Jules Bastien-Lepage hanging in the Metropolitan Museum of Art in New

York City. The Met was only a few blocks away from my new apartment in Manhattan, and after my trip to Orléans I began to visit it frequently.

Increasingly I found myself drawn to this great painting. Joan listens attentively to the voices of the saints, who are depicted as twining through a dense green thicket of trees in her parents' garden at Domrémy. St. Michael, in armor, floats in a tree, holding a sword. St. Catherine, with a garland of white blossoms woven through her hair, prays. St. Margaret is barely visible. Joan stands on the right side of the painting, her wide gray eyes glowing, her left arm held out before her as if awaiting directions. This dark-haired Joan is statuesque, earthy, magnificent.

But it was not these potent visual images as much as the marvelous illogic of her story that beguiled me. Jehanne la Pucelle, a young peasant (who could not read and, later, could not sign her name to her confession—she instead scrawled a cross), hears the voices of not one but three saints, who command her to lead the French army to victory over the English. The saints instruct her to dress as a man, a soldier. She does. She travels to meet the dauphin and, confronting an annoying demonstration of royal persiflage, promptly picks him out of the crowd at court, kneels at his feet, and tells him a certain secret, a secret so profound (and still unknown) that it immediately convinces the young, weak prince of the righteousness of Joan's cause. Then—added as an afterthought in some blasé accounts of her life—she *does* lead the army to victory. She prays to St. Catherine for the wind to change during the battle at Orléans. It does. The dauphin is crowned King Charles VII in Reims. All as Joan has said.

But the wind changes again. The new king proves fickle and decides not to lengthen Joan's incredible string of military victories. For her accomplishments, she is excommunicated by the Church, which has always been suspicious of her reliance on "voices." The

English burn the Maid as a heretic. (Legend has it, though, that her strong heart was not consumed by the flames.)

Each saint holds a particular appeal for believers. What is Joan's? Her youth? Her military valor? Her courage in facing her critics and her executioners? For many, it is her willingness to be, in the words of St. Paul, a "fool for Christ." The audacity of her plan, based on directives from heavenly voices, is, centuries later, still breathtaking, no matter how many times we have heard the story.

⁂

Twenty years after my discovery of Joan, I found myself leading a monthly book club for young adults at a Jesuit parish in New York City. The group consisted of twenty or so twentysomethings, men and women, who gathered to discuss books of interest to Catholic adults. One evening each month we would meet for a simple meal of pizza and soda, followed by an hour's conversation about a book we had read over the past four weeks.

I quickly grew fond of these gatherings. They served as an easy way for the young adults in the parish to be introduced to all kinds of books and writers. We read works of spirituality, theology, fiction, biography, history, and autobiography and—every year at Christmas—one of the four Gospels. Over the years we read Thomas Merton, Walker Percy, Willa Cather, Flannery O'Connor, Henri Nouwen, Dorothy Day, Andre Dubus, Ron Hansen, and Kathleen Norris, as well as writers lesser known but no less talented. The meetings were also a natural place for people to find a sense of community in an often lonely city. As for me, it was fun just being with the group, occasionally offering my own perspectives on the books but more often listening to the group discuss what being Catholic meant in their own lives.

The meetings also provided some unintentional humor. After a long discussion on the Gospel of Mark, I noticed that one woman, usually chatty, had remained silent. When I asked how she had liked Mark's Gospel, she said that she would rather not say anything, for fear of offending me.

Though I assured her that there was little she could say that would offend me, she still demurred. "Don't worry," I said, "I'm sure I've heard it all by now. What did you think of the Gospel?"

"Well," she said. "I didn't like *Jesus* very much!"

Everyone laughed (some out of shock). But after I assured her that it was natural to have strong reactions to Jesus (she had found him overly harsh in places), her blunt comments led to an honest discussion about the responses that Jesus' contemporaries may have had to him.

One month I assigned the short biography *Joan of Arc* by the Catholic novelist Mary Gordon. Her book portrayed Joan as a kind of feminist saint. For many participants it was their first serious introduction to Joan. I sensed that they knew as little about her as I had when I spied her statue in Paris.

During the discussion the same young woman seemed fidgety. Finally she spoke.

"Let me get this straight," she said. "Joan of Arc was a soldier who led people into battle. So why is she a saint?"

Her question deserved a careful reply. I wanted to explain that Joan was devoted to Jesus Christ, to prayer, to the sacraments, to the Church, and to its saints. That she believed in God even when God asked her to accomplish the seemingly impossible. That she persevered during the direst of circumstances and eventually *did* achieve the impossible. That she inspired the confidence of princes, soldiers, and peasants alike. That she suffered physical deprivations in the name of her cause: to set captives free. That she continued to love the Church even as she was persecuted by it. That she was human enough to falter before her judges, but strong (and humble) enough to recant. That she died a martyr's death with the name of Jesus on her lips.

Before I could offer my explanation, one young man offered a different answer—at once simpler and wiser. It satisfied the questioner and quieted me in a way that I imagine Joan might have silenced her judges five centuries ago.

"Joan was holy," he said, "because she trusted."

An excellent answer. But for me, Joan is a saint whose mysterious appeal goes beyond even her remarkable trust. I often wonder why I have been so drawn to her. One reason might be that she is the first saint I really "met," and her story imprinted itself as indelibly on my soul as those French vocabulary words did on my seventh-grade mind. And like my introduction to French in junior high school, Joan's story also introduced me to a new language: the special language of the saints, made up of verbs like *believe, pray, witness* and the nouns of their actions, *humility, charity, ardor.* So Joan of Arc holds a unique place in my spiritual life as the first saint I came to know. Often what you remember best is what you learned first.

Yet Joan confuses me as much as she attracts me. She acts like a crazy young girl, hearing voices, leaving her family, going to war, and dying for an unseen person. Her story is more profoundly *other* than the story of almost any other saint in this book. (And that's saying a lot, as you'll see.) Even St. Francis of Assisi would seem more at home in our world than Joan. To many people today Francis would seem attractive and compelling, much like Mother Teresa. Joan, however, would probably just seem crazy.

But my desire to follow God was just starting to take root when I saw the statue of Joan in Orléans. At that time, I was going to church more regularly and paying more attention to the Gospel stories. My life seemed a little nuts, and I felt a little like Joan—not hearing voices, of course, but feeling that my attraction to religion was a crazy thing that had to be trusted anyway. Faith was something that seemed sensible and nonsensical at the same time. Joan found her way to God by learning a language that no one else could hear, and so she is the perfect model for someone on the beginning of a faith journey. She had no idea what path to take to reach her destination, and neither did I.

But, as my friend Peggy discovered, lost on the road to Chartres, the road that we seek is often the road we have already found.

3

Inward Drama

Thérèse of Lisieux

> For me, prayer is the heart's impulse, a simple gaze
> toward heaven. It is a cry of gratitude and love, from the
> depths of trial as well as the heights of joy. Finally, it is
> something great, supernatural, that expands my soul and
> unites me to Jesus.
> —THÉRÈSE OF LISIEUX, *THE STORY OF A SOUL*

For as long as I can remember, I've been a movie nut. My favorite gift from my parents for my First Holy Communion was being taken to see *The Sound of Music*. (This seemed more than justly deserved in light of all the time I had spent in Sunday school memorizing the Act of Contrition.) When I was in high school, Friday and Saturday nights meant one thing for me and my friends: movies. So the summer after my junior year in high school I was overjoyed to get a job as usher at our local movie theater, whose name betokened a double helping of suburban fun: Cinema on the Mall.

My job involved opening up the theaters in the afternoons, locking them up at night, and standing around tearing tickets, but I quickly added other responsibilities. These included talking incessantly to the girls who worked the candy counter, eating candy with them (that is, opening up Good 'n' Fruity boxes and draining them of their contents before carefully closing them up and replacing them under the counter), letting all of my high school friends in for free, eating more candy, and talking some more.

Sadly, the assistant manager of the Cinema on the Mall, a sour-faced man named Donald, sized up my job performance and saddled me with one other responsibility: making popcorn in a tiny unventi-lated room located in the attic above the theater. While the popcorn at the Cinema on the Mall was advertised at our candy counter as "Fresh!" it was actually popped in a huge bathtub-sized metal bin sev-eral weeks before. It was my weekly job to heat the "butter" (animal fat, if you're interested) in a small oven, mix in a heavy bag of ker-nels, stir in a fluorescent yellow powder, pop the corn, dump the fluffy new corn into the metal bathtub, strain the unpopped seeds through a screen, and funnel the finished product into a clear plastic trash bag.

This I did in ten-hour shifts. The only thing that kept me from insanity in the little whitewashed cinder-block room was a radio; I still know the words to every hit song from the summer of that year. Once, on a lunch break, I went into a McDonald's in the mall and stood there slack jawed and brain fried, trying to decide which greasy entrée to order. My T-shirt and jeans were completely covered with oil and coated with the pungent popcorn seasoning. Next to me a woman exclaimed to her friend, "Helen, do you smell *popcorn*?" She snuffled. "Yes!" said her friend. "Where's it coming from? It's like we're in the *movies!*"

But even the extended popcorn-making shifts could not depress my spirits. For I was relieved that I was no longer dealing with the challenges of my previous summer jobs: washing dishes, busing tables, caddying, and mowing lawns. Mainly I was delighted that I could see movies for free whenever I wanted. The selections, of course, were severely limited, since in the late 1970s movies ran for weeks, even months, at a time. And one's appreciation of, say, *The Cat from Outer Space* is not something that deepens over repeated viewings.

My love for movies continued through college. When my weekend finances were low (which was always), there was usually a classic movie playing for a few bucks somewhere on Penn's campus. It was during college that I was introduced to what would later be called "independent" films, as well as to foreign-language films. Reading subtitles made me feel immensely sophisticated and grateful that I had finally found another use for my high school French. My freshman-year roommate, Brad, was an energetic and enthusiastic communications major who dragged me to dozens of films. (Not movies, said Brad, *films*). There were films I would never have chosen to see on my own—*Jules et Jim, The 400 Blows, Un Chien Andalou, The Battleship Potemkin, The Cabinet of Dr. Caligari, Rashomon*—but to which I was delighted to have been introduced.

Following graduation, and after three years of working with General Electric in New York, I took a job in their office in Stamford, Connecticut. And though I was sad leaving a city where there seemed to be a cinema on every corner, I was happy to learn about a newly opened theater near Stamford specializing in experimental, independent, and classic films.

One week an unusual advertisement in the theater's schedule caught my attention. It was a haunting black-and-white photograph of a woman's face floating above a single word: *Thérèse*. Though I wasn't sure what the film was about—something about the ad seemed vaguely religious—I convinced a coworker to accompany me to the screening.

The film, directed by Alain Cavalier, was a bold, spare look at the life of Thérèse of Lisieux, the nineteenth-century French saint, about whom I knew absolutely nothing. The almost complete absence of physical scenery meant that the film focused on the quiet interactions of the few characters. The narrative progressed through a series of simple vignettes: Thérèse entering a monastery; Thérèse being "clothed" with her religious habit; Thérèse working at her simple tasks in the community; Thérèse suffering humiliations from the other sisters; Thérèse growing ill; Thérèse dying.

I found the film, in its simplicity and power, utterly captivating and its main character fascinating. Toward the end of the film my eyes were filling with tears.

On the way out of the theater, I brushed away the tears, worried that my friend would notice.

Suddenly he turned to me. "What a waste of a life!" he snapped. "All that suffering for nothing!"

His comments shocked me. It was the first time I realized that my feelings toward religion might be the opposite of what others experienced.

What also surprised me was feeling duty-bound to defend Thérèse. I engaged my coworker in a heated, if inarticulate, discussion about religion, suffering, the value of sacrifice, the role of faith, and the example of the person whose life we had just seen played out before us. I didn't understand why I felt so strongly about the movie. I only knew that I did.

As a movie buff, I am not surprised that my introduction to Thérèse of Lisieux was through a film rather than an academic biography. In their occasional depictions of the lives of the saints, movies can serve the same purpose that murals or frescoes did in prior centuries: painting the story of the saint in broad strokes, amplifying some details, avoiding others, and in general communicating the essence of the life. The cycle of frescoes of St. Francis in the basilica of Assisi, which portrays his casting off his clothing, his efforts to rebuild the church, his preaching to the birds, and his death, looks like nothing so much as a storyboard for a filmed version of his life. In the case of a few saints, I prefer the movie version of their lives to any biographies I've read. The best way to come to know St. Thomas More, I believe, is to watch *A Man for All Seasons*. The filmed biography *Romero* is likewise a beautiful window into the life of the martyred archbishop of San Salvador, Oscar Romero.

Two years after seeing *Thérèse*, I met up with her again. At the beginning of my second year as a Jesuit, our novitiate community in Boston welcomed three first-year novices (our "primi," as they were called), one of whom was named David. Articulate and energetic, David had spent a few years working as an architect in Boston before entering the Jesuits. He had also been raised in a large and strongly Catholic family and so entered the novitiate with an impressive religious background and an educated affection for prayer, the Mass, and the saints.

Since I had spent little time around devout Catholics prior to entering the Jesuits, I knew few people like David. He was the first person I had ever met who could be fairly described as "pious." Though his way of looking at life was new to me, I found his spirituality engaging and inviting, and our friendship grew naturally.

One day David told me about his "devotion" to Thérèse of Lisieux: how he enjoyed reading about her, found encouragement from her example, and asked for her intercession in prayer. He spoke about her with great enthusiasm and, occasionally, some emotion. Unfortunately, I had no clue who David was talking about.

As he talked, I kept thinking, *Thérèse of Lisieux . . . Thérèse of Lisieux . . . Which one is she?*

Dumbfounded, I stared at him. In response, he took a Bible off his nightstand, opened it, and pulled out a prayer card. On the front was a small black-and-white photograph of a young nun kneeling in her habit.

Something about the image looked familiar.

"Oh yeah," I said. "I think I saw a movie about her once."

David directed me to a dog-eared copy of *The Story of a Soul* in the novitiate library. "Read this," he said. "Then you'll understand why I like Thérèse so much." His devotion and my dimly remembered reaction to the movie led me to begin her book that night. And thus began my second introduction to the woman popularly known as the "Little Flower."

On January 2, 1873, Marie-Françoise-Thérèse Martin was born in Alençon, France, to Louis and Zélie Martin, two devout Catholics. Louis, a watchmaker, had earlier in life presented himself to a monastery but had been refused admission because of his lack of knowledge of Latin. Zélie had been similarly rejected by a local order of nuns called the Sisters of the Hôtel Dieu; she became, instead, a lacemaker. But the couple's intense love for Catholicism and for religious life was passed on to their children.

When Thérèse was four, her mother died. Shortly afterward, the family moved from Alençon to Lisieux. As a young girl, Thérèse led a cosseted existence, living under the loving care of her devoted father and treated with great tenderness by her four older sisters. By most accounts, Thérèse was her father's favorite daughter. Many biographies portray the young Thérèse as a spoiled little girl.

Perhaps because of this supportive environment, Thérèse was a cheerful girl and a naturally religious one as well. "I loved God very much," she would write later, "and offered my heart to him very often." She was attracted to almost any expression of religiosity: she described the first communion of her sister Céline as "one of the most beautiful days in my life."

As early as age nine, Thérèse discovered within herself the desire to be a nun. When two of her sisters entered the Carmelite monastery in Lisieux, it only intensified her desire to enter a religious order. Faced with the prospect of having to wait until age sixteen to enter the monastery, an adolescent Thérèse took advantage of a providentially planned trip. She accompanied her father on a parish pilgrimage to Rome, and while there petitioned Pope Leo XIII for a special dispensation to enter the Carmelite Order before she turned sixteen. Presented with the enthusiastic French girl, the pope was noncommittal. "You will enter if God wills it," he said blandly.

But her single-mindedness did not go unnoticed by officials at home. Her request was granted a few months later by the local bishop, and Thérèse entered the Carmelite monastery, or the Carmel, on April 9, 1888, at age fifteen.

Her life within the monastery walls was short and uneventful, "lacking in outward drama," as Robert Ellsberg says in his book *All Saints*. Within a year of entrance she received her habit. The next year she officially entered the novitiate and was assigned to care for the refectory and to sweep the corridors. In 1890, she made her profession of the vows of poverty, chastity, and obedience. In 1891, she was named aid to the sacristan. In 1893, she painted a fresco in the oratory and was named "second portress," that is, assistant doorkeeper.

In 1896, on the morning of Good Friday, Thérèse awoke to find her mouth full of blood. And though she had been praying ardently that she would be accepted for missionary service in Vietnam, Thérèse rejoiced that she would soon be in heaven.

Yet it proved not to be a quick and painless journey. A year of intense suffering followed.

The same year she contracted tuberculosis, she was asked by her superior to write what would become her spiritual testimony. She titled it "Springtime Story of a Little White Flower Written by Herself and Dedicated to Reverend Mother Mary Agnes of Jesus."

It was this remarkable book that would ultimately draw millions of believers to Jesus. The life lacking in outward drama was revealed to be full of inward drama. Surprisingly, Thérèse described a powerful call to the priesthood: "I would like to perform the most heroic deeds. I feel I have the courage of a Crusader. I should like to die on the battlefield in defense of the church. If only I were a priest!" Thérèse devoted herself to prayer and to the service of God in the monastery. She prayed for missionary priests in particular; as a result, this cloistered nun is one of the two patron saints of missionaries, along with the peripatetic St. Francis Xavier.

Her autobiography also shows how convent life led Thérèse to become what one biographer, Kathryn Harrison, calls a "genius of secret mortification." Believing that she could never live up to the high standards of her saintly heroes, Thérèse embraced small, daily hardships as both a test and a gift from God. This would be her personal path to holiness. "I applied myself to practicing little virtues, not having the capability of practicing the great." She suffered small indignities at the hands of her sisters and strove to be as generous as possible even during her illness. The sisters in her convent who showed the least kindness to Thérèse were the ones she tried to love the most; the most vexing and disagreeable sister was the one she chose to sit beside during recreation.

Sr. Thérèse did all this without hope of reward in the convent. "Because of my lack of virtue," she wrote, "these little practices cost me very much and I had to console myself with the thought that at the Last Judgment everything would be revealed. I noticed this: when one performs her duty, never excusing herself, no one knows it; on the contrary, imperfections appear immediately."

Throughout her life, Thérèse aimed to offer these "little" efforts to the God with whom she had fallen in love as a little girl. Her autobiography is a testimony to both the joy and the pain that accompany a life of faith. As Thérèse continued writing, her physical condition deteriorated. The last few chapters were written during a period of extreme suffering. On September 30, 1897, at age twenty-four, she died. Her last words were "Oh, I love Him . . . My God . . . I love you."

But even at her death, the hardworking disciple considered her work unfinished. There was so much more to do, by way of intercession for those she left behind: "After my death I will let fall a shower of roses. I will spend my heaven doing good on earth."

A year after her death, her spiritual autobiography was published in a sanitized version by her sisters under the title *The Story of a Soul.* The work was first passed privately among Carmelite convents, but it eventually reached the outside world, where its success surprised almost everyone. As a result of her "Springtime Story," Thérèse became one of the most popular saints in the Church—her story captivating, her example inspiring, and her "Little Way" accessible to countless believers.

In 1925, only twenty-eight years after her death, Thérèse was declared a saint. And in 1997, Pope John Paul II declared her a doctor of the church, that is, an eminent teacher of the faith. She is one of only three women to have been so named (along with Catherine of Siena and Teresa of Ávila).

In her autobiography, *The Story of a Soul,* Thérèse frequently speaks of her lifelong love of flowers and gardens. Here, she employs the image of the garden to illustrate her idea of the Little Way to God.

Jesus deigned to teach me this mystery. He set before me the book of nature; I understood how all the flowers he has created are beautiful, how the splendor of the rose and the whiteness of the lily do not take away the perfume of the little violet or the delightful simplicity of the daisy. I understood that if all flowers wanted to be roses, nature would lose her springtime beauty, and the fields would no longer be decked out with little wildflowers.

And so it is in the world of souls, Jesus' garden. He willed to create great souls comparable to lilies and roses, but he has created smaller ones and these must be content to be daisies or violets destined to give joy to God's glances when He looks down at His feet. Perfection consists in doing His will, in being what He wills us to be. . . .

Just as the sun shines simultaneously on the tall cedars and on each little flower as though it were alone on the earth, so Our Lord is occupied particularly with each soul as though there were no others like it. And just as in nature all the seasons are arranged in such a way as to make the humblest daisy bloom on a set day, in the same way, everything works out for the good of each soul.

It was her deep humility that rendered Thérèse of Lisieux a potent and accessible model for Christians worldwide. After all, who hasn't been humbled by life? Who hasn't experienced personal limitations? Who hasn't felt "little" compared to others? Who hasn't suffered? Thérèse is a saint who many feel would understand their problems. Thérèse is someone an ordinary person can talk to. People feel comfortable with the Little Flower.

That saintly nickname is taken from the original title of her autobiography. Thérèse protested that in the garden of God she was only a "little flower," a small daisy compared to the more magnificent roses that she saw around her. She called herself "la petite Thérèse" in order to distinguish herself from Teresa of Ávila, her Carmelite predecessor. What has become known as her "Little Way" is a pliable and durable spirituality that consists of doing small things with love for God, a way of discipleship that stresses a cheerful humility before the Creator and a willingness to accept suffering.

But to think of Thérèse of Lisieux as simply a delicate hothouse flower is to overlook the considerable resolve that lay beneath the fragile petals. Albino Luciani, Pope John Paul I, once called her "a steel bar." This was, after all, a person who at age fifteen refused to let something as minor as church law stand in the way of her entrance into the monastery: she simply took her case to the Vatican. Even in the face of a painful terminal illness, she continued to pray and to believe.

In her Christian resolve and calm confidence, she resembles no one so much as her great hero and countrywoman Joan of Arc, whom Thérèse once portrayed in a pageant during her time in Carmel, dressing up as the Maid of Orléans in makeshift paper armor. One of her Carmelite sisters photographed her in costume. A sad-eyed Thérèse, dark tresses framing her face, stares at the viewer. In her hand is a sword upon which she appears to lean, as if on a crutch.

The spirituality of Thérèse of Lisieux is typically illustrated by her self-denial and willingness to accept the slights of her sisters in the convent. But this is too narrow a view of Thérèse, who became a saint not because of the sufferings of her body but because of the activities of her heart. "Neither do I desire any longer suffering or death, and still I love them both; it is *love* that attracts me," she writes in *The Story of a Soul.*

Taking her inspiration from St. Paul, who compared the Christian community to a body with many parts, Thérèse boldly declared that she would be the heart. Her ascetic spirituality, particularly her approach to illness, may seem odd to modern readers. (When her illness prompted her to think that she might die, her soul, she said, was "flooded with joy.") But her austerities flowed from a consuming love for God and a desire to offer herself to Jesus.

A word about her response to her illness: around the time of its onset, Thérèse, who had been filled with a sense of God's presence since her childhood, began to experience a crushing sense of God's absence in her prayer, what St. John of the Cross calls the "dark night." She hid this from her sisters, lest she burden them with her torment. Only to a few did she confess her state of mind. "If you only knew what darkness I am plunged into!" she admitted to one sister. At times she flirted with suicide—pointedly telling her Carmelite sisters that medicines should not be kept near the bed of a sick person.

Steven Payne, a Carmelite priest and scholar, notes that many experts believe that Thérèse's spiritual trial primarily concerned her confidence in heaven and an afterlife, rather than doubts about the existence of God. "Of course," he wrote in a letter to me, "it's hard to tell from what she says, because she may not have thought it through completely and in any case was trying to protect the other sisters from the burden. But if you read the text closely, what she talks about is that sense that there is sheer nothingness on the other side of death. That would be a particularly acute trial for Thérèse, since her confidence in the reality of heaven had always been so strong and powerful."

Yet though she struggled, wept, and raged, she continued to *believe*—drawing from a deep well of trust filled from the springs of a lifelong friendship with God. As Kathryn Harrison writes in *Saint Thérèse of Lisieux*, Thérèse's "dark night" may be the most compelling aspect of her life, the point where many lives intersect with hers. "At last she has taken her place among us," writes Harrison, "not so much revealed herself as human as given birth to her naked self, plummeting to earth, wet and new and terrified. If we allow her to become a saint, if we believe in her, it's because here, finally, she has achieved mortality."

St. Thérèse of Lisieux, or, to use the name she chose on the occasion of her profession of vows, Thérèse de l'Enfant Jésus et de la Sainte Face, is now found on small holy cards, staring out frankly at the viewer, clad in a brown and white Carmelite robe, typically holding a bouquet of multicolored roses and a crucifix. She can be found in churches large and small around the world, standing silently in the identical pose as a polychromed plaster statue, a figure in brilliant stained glass, or a portrait in a faded fresco. She can be found in the millions of copies of her autobiography, in countless languages and editions, scattered among homes, apartments, rectories, and religious communities. And she can be found in the hearts of those who feel that, above almost all the saints, she is the one who most understands what it means to be a human being who suffers *and* rejoices in everyday life.

Her life—at once simple and complex, clear and opaque, childlike and mature, humble and bold, joyful and sorrowful—has spoken to millions of people. It spoke to my friend David. And it spoke to me, from the first moment I met her, in that little movie theater in Connecticut.

Though there are parts of her story that I find difficult to accept (her childhood religiosity can sound pretentious, precious, and even a little neurotic, and her efforts at self-denial sometimes are close to masochistic), and though it is embarrassing to admit that one of my favorite saints is one of the most girlish and cloying, it is finally the woman herself who appeals to me. Like every other saint, Thérèse Martin was a product of her times, raised in the overheated environment of a super-religious family and formed in pious nineteenth-century French convent life. So it is hardly surprising that some of her words and actions occasionally baffle us. But shining through the nineteenth-century piety, like a pale green shoot bursting through dark soil, is a stunningly original personality, a person who, despite the difficulties of life, holds out to us her Little Way and says to us one thing: *Love.*

I find Thérèse to be a companionable presence, a cheerful sister, a patient woman, and a lifelong believer. She is joyful, patient, and generous. She is someone whose company, had I known her, would have made me a better Christian. Most of all, she reminds me of those men and women I have met over the course of my life who are—to use an underused word—kind. So Thérèse is someone I like to read about, pray with, and pray to.

⁂

Some days when I pray to Thérèse, I remember my original introduction to her life, and I think about my friend's biting comments. They still shock me. "A waste of a life," he said. "All that suffering for nothing." And I am almost embarrassed for her.

But Thérèse Martin heard similarly harsh comments in the monastery, from sisters jealous of her youth, confused by her sanctity, and baffled by her charity. Such misunderstanding was part of her life.

And I imagine Thérèse in heaven, smiling at this misunderstanding. Smiling at those who still see her as too naive, too humble, or too pious. Smiling at those who underestimate the power of her Little Way. Smiling at all of these people. And praying for them, too.

4

The True Self

Thomas Merton

> For me to be a saint means to be myself. Therefore the
> problem of sanctity and salvation is in fact the problem of
> finding out who I am and of discovering my true self.
> —THOMAS MERTON, *NEW SEEDS OF CONTEMPLATION*

During an American Poetry course in college, I was introduced to Walt Whitman. Our young professor was something of a Whitman devotee and scholar: she had written a well-received biography of the poet. One day she said that if we were ever accused of contradicting ourselves we should quote the following lines from "Song of Myself":

> Do I contradict myself?
> Very well then I contradict myself,
> (I am large, I contain multitudes.)

With those lines, Whitman could easily have been speaking about Thomas Merton—another poet, as well as a mystic, a monk, an artist, a peace activist, a priest, a spiritual master, an ecumenist, a Zen practitioner, and a saint.

Merton's contradictions are his most endearing features. A man in love with the world around him who chooses to become a cloistered monk: a Trappist, Fr. M. Louis, OCSO (for the Order of Cistercians of the Strict Observance). A peripatetic man and an inveterate traveler who takes a vow of stability, choosing to remain at the Abbey of Our Lady of Gethsemani, in the secluded hills of Kentucky. A man who freely takes a vow of obedience but who spends much of his religious life butting heads with his order's superiors. A man in love with his vocation but constantly questioning it. A devout Catholic convert fascinated by Eastern religions. A famous writer who professes to hate (or tries to convince himself that he hates) the trappings and "business" of fame. A man who could write one day of his desire never to write another sentence, only to write a few days later of his joy in seeing another of his books published. (In one memorable journal entry, he reveals a barely hidden satisfaction that the burlap covering his new book is the same fabric used in the chic Manhattan supper clubs of the day.)

These paradoxes, these Whitmanesque multitudes, helped make Thomas Merton one of the protean figures of twentieth-century Catholicism. His open and honest 1948 memoir, *The Seven Storey Mountain*, which details his journey to the Trappist monastery, was a publishing phenomenon that even the savvy Merton was unable to foresee. It introduced contemplative prayer to millions of readers and heralded a postwar renewal in monastic life in the United States. His writings on peace presaged Pope John XXIII's encyclical *Pacem in Terris* ("Peace on Earth"). His continuing zest for life helped recast Christianity for a jaded America.

His book helped recast me as well.

It's not a stretch to say that *The Seven Storey Mountain* changed my life. But to understand how, you might have to understand something about my life before I encountered Thomas Merton.

At seventeen, I began undergraduate studies at the University of Pennsylvania's Wharton School of Business. Why I decided to study business is difficult to explain and, at this writing, difficult even for me to understand.

The simplest explanation is this: during my junior and senior years in high school, I wasn't sure what I wanted to do in life. Certainly there were plenty of subjects I enjoyed studying in high school—English, French, history, art—but none seemed practical enough for a career. I loved French, for example, but I couldn't figure out what to do with it.

Enter the idea of studying business. At the time, I had a vague idea that a business major would enable me to land a job in the "business end" of any number of fields, such as the "business end" of English (publishing) or the "business end" of art (managing a museum or gallery). At the very least, a business degree would likely lead to a high-paying job after graduation, and this, I reasoned, would make me happy.

On this point, everyone—my family, my friends, my high school guidance counselor—agreed.

The problem was that whenever I considered "earning a living," I thought mostly about the "earning" and nothing about the "living." I hadn't the slightest notion what living in the business world would mean. Would I find it fulfilling? Enjoyable? Would it be a good use of my skills? Was it something that I wanted to do? These were questions that—perhaps not surprisingly at age seventeen—I failed to reflect upon.

Ultimately, I decided to study business in college—finance, to be exact.

While I can't say I enjoyed the courses at Wharton in the same way that I enjoyed seeing a good movie or downing beers with friends, there were some courses that I was able to master—accounting, for one. Besides having some excellent accounting professors, I appreciated the way that everything fit together in accounting: like a difficult but ultimately satisfying puzzle whose individual pieces locked together neatly and sensibly. Still, tallying up balance sheets, reviewing income statements, and poring over cash-flow reports weren't activities I wanted to do in my spare time.

On the other hand, there were a few courses at Wharton that I loathed. My Probability and Statistics professor, certainly the dullest teacher I've ever had, employed the same example throughout one entire semester to illustrate each of his probability theorems: "Imagine two urns," he would say in a nasal monotone, facing a class of one hundred glassy-eyed business students. "One contains green balls and one contains red balls. We will select a ball from each urn and . . ."

I am unable to remember the pedagogical point of the urns and balls, since I was usually passed out on my desk, catching up on sleep and drooling on my notebook. For much of the semester, I simply had no idea what was going on in Probability. So after years of landing at the top of my class through elementary school, junior high school, and high school and evincing horror at even a B, I received my first-ever C. This time I couldn't be horrified. Upon opening my report card, I confessed to my roommate, "I deserved this C. Actually, I deserved a D." I made a mental note not to apply for a job in the probability industry.

Fortunately, Probability marked the exception, and I did well overall in school. And when interviewing season rolled around in the fall of senior year, I looked forward to plucking some attractive fruits off the job tree.

Wharton's reputation in the corporate world made finding a job ridiculously easy. At the beginning of senior year, hundreds of corporate recruiters flocked to the school to conduct interviews: in a few months I had received a number of excellent offers. After narrowing them down to three or four, I settled on a corporate training program at General Electric in New York City.

Once again, almost no reflection was involved in my decision. To use some accounting terminology, I simply went along with "generally accepted principles." For example, what should you do at the end of business school? Interview for jobs. Which job offer should you accept? The one with the highest salary. The more important questions were the ones that no one asked me, or rather, that I failed to ask myself: What do you desire in life? And what does God desire for you?

It's difficult to say when, exactly, I understood that I was in the wrong place. Looking back, I can say that the realization dawned gradually, as the joy was slowly leeched out of my life. After a few years in the corporate world, I found myself working almost around the clock, witnessing daily examples of callous behavior from management, and finding myself on a tedious path that seemed to have a single goal: making money.

Eventually I realized that my life at work had no real meaning. But there was an even bigger problem—I couldn't see a way out.

One night, after a long day, I came home and turned on the TV. I remember the evening vividly. At the time, I was sharing a house with two other GE employees. It was around 9:00, and I was dead tired after a miserable day. I had just thrown some leftover pasta into the microwave and plopped down on the ratty beige couch in front of our TV.

Flipping through the channels aimlessly—past stale sitcoms, dull movies, and boring reruns—I stumbled across a public-television documentary called *Merton: A Film Biography*. On the screen appeared a variety of people, some of whom I recognized, some of whom I didn't, who spoke about the effect that one man had had on their lives. Apparently, he was a Catholic monk, or, more specifically, a "Trappist" (I had no idea what that meant), who had left his previous life (whatever that had been), and had written an influential biography (that I had never heard of). Though I caught only the last few minutes of the program, something about their comments made me want to know more about Thomas Merton. I was drawn by something else, too: the look on his face in the still photographs. It seemed to radiate peace.

The next day, I tracked down his autobiography, *The Seven Storey Mountain*, in a local bookstore. Late that night, I began reading. In just a few pages, it captivated me as no other book had before, or has since. Thomas Merton struck me as someone I might like to have known—bright, funny, creative, a fellow who would have made a good friend. He struggled with some of the same things I did—pride, ambition, selfishness. And he struggled with the same questions I was wondering about: What are we made for? Who is God? What is the purpose of our lives? Merton seemed full of wonderful contradictions—a man who sought humility while struggling with an overweening ego, a man in love with the world who decided to, in a sense, flee it. To me Merton's contradictions, his "multitudes," as Whitman would say, revealed his deep humanity. As I read the book, his search became my search, and I longed to know where his life would lead.

⚜

On January 31, 1915, in a small town in the French Pyrenees called Prades, Thomas Merton was born. His father, Owen, a New Zealander, was a painter of some renown. "My father painted like Cézanne," wrote Merton with evident pride, "and understood the southern French landscape the way Cézanne did." Ruth, Merton's American-born mother, was also something of an artist: his parents met while studying at a studio in Paris.

Merton enjoyed a lifelong appreciation of French art, language, and culture. He wrote feelingly about France in the early pages of *The Seven Storey Mountain* as "a setting for the best of the cathedrals, the most interesting towns, . . . and the greatest universities."

In many ways, France would always represent home for the rootless young Merton. Years after he left the country he returned in a roundabout way: by joining the Trappists, the Order of Cistercians of the Strict Observance, a religious order founded in Cîteaux, France. (The word *Cistercian* is a version of the town's original Latin name, Cistercium.) His background had practical applications, too: as a young monk at Gethsemani, Merton was asked to translate numerous documents from the order's headquarters in France.

But for most of his early life Thomas Merton found himself without a real home: his childhood was, by almost all accounts, sad. Tom's mother died when he was six. Thereafter his father moved the family from place to place, town to town, and country to country while he pursued his artistic career. For a time the family (which included Tom's younger brother, John Paul) lived with Ruth's family in Douglaston, New York, and then, for a while, in Bermuda. During their stay in Bermuda, Owen, hoping to sell some of his paintings in New York, left Tom in the care of a woman author he had just met. (His father's casual passing off of his child to a recent acquaintance still seems shocking to me.) Later, Tom, Owen, and John Paul returned to France, taking up residence in a town called Saint-Antonin, where Merton enrolled in a nearby secondary school.

One summer, with his father traveling once again, Merton boarded with the Privats, a Catholic family in Murat. This proved a "great grace" for the boy. Tom Merton was moved by the affection shown him by this elderly couple and their young nephew, who became his friend. The passages in his autobiography describing his stay with the Privats are among the tenderest he ever set down on paper. "I owe many graces to their prayers," he writes, "and perhaps ultimately the grace of my conversion and even of my religious vocation. Who shall say? But one day I shall know, and it is good to be able to be confident that I will see them again and be able to thank them."

In 1929, Merton was sent off to a boarding school called Oakham, in Rutland, England. He hated it. (The chapter relating his experiences at this time is entitled "The Harrowing of Hell.") Around this time, his father fell ill, suffering from the effects of a brain tumor. Visiting Owen during a summer holiday, Tom was startled to find his father's London hospital bed covered with drawings "unlike anything he had ever done before—pictures of little, irate Byzantine-looking saints with beards and great halos." In 1931, a few days before Tom's sixteenth birthday, his father died.

A bright and articulate young man, Merton won a scholarship to Clare College, at Cambridge, and began his university studies. But it was an even less congenial place for Merton than Oakham had been; he referred in his autobiography to the university's "dark, sinister atmosphere." Tom spent much of his day carousing with, as he described them, "a pack of hearties who wore multicolored scarves around their necks and who would have barked all night long . . . if they had not been forced to go home to bed at a certain time."

While in England, according to some later biographers, a dissolute Tom fathered a child. Many years later, when Merton was about to enter the Trappists, his guardian undertook an unsuccessful search for the woman and her child. The mother and child, it seems, were killed in the Blitz during the Second World War. Some sources contend that the Trappist censors responsible for vetting Merton's manuscripts removed this episode from *The Seven Storey Mountain* so as not to offend the presumably delicate sensibilities of the time. As I read Merton's biography, unaware of this part of his life, I was puzzled by his frequent expressions of self-disgust and his oft-stated fear that his past would be an impediment to his entrance into religious life. Later biographers would provide a fuller account of this difficult chapter in Merton's life.

The childhood and adolescence described in *The Seven Storey Mountain* were lonely and aimless, as Tom failed to make close friends. He suffered separation from his only brother, missed his parents deeply, and behaved in ways that disgusted him—drinking, smoking, partying, and always showing off. Tom seemed forever to be searching for something, while remaining unaware of what he was searching for. One thinks of both St. Augustine's rambunctious youth as described in his *Confessions* and Dorothy Day's description many centuries later of her "long loneliness."

After considering Tom's experiences in England, Tom's guardian suggested that he return to the States to continue his education. Merton accepted this advice with alacrity: "It did not take me five minutes to come around to agreeing with him."

Columbia University and New York City proved more agreeable for Merton. He met many companionable young men (though it would be some time before he established healthy relationships with women) who remained his friends for life. He found his studies enjoyable. Tom also came under the influence of the popular English professor Mark Van Doren, whom Merton admired for his sense of "vocation," and his "profoundly scholastic" mind, which helped prepare Merton to receive "the good seed of scholastic philosophy." With characteristic self-absorption Merton concluded, "I can see that Providence was using him as an instrument more directly than he realized." Of course this was true, but as described it sounds as if the sole reason that Professor Van Doren was placed on earth was to help Thomas Merton understand Thomas Aquinas.

One passage in the autobiography about Merton's college years stopped me cold. Almost as an aside, Merton notes that he became a cartoonist and, later, art editor of the university's humor magazine, the *Jester*. I had to read this twice to make sure I hadn't misunderstood. As it happened, my only extracurricular activity during college (other than smoking pot and drinking beer) was being a cartoonist and, later, art editor of the university's humor magazine, the *Punch Bowl*. This was a small coincidence, but how many art editors of Ivy League humor magazines are there? Reading that passage cemented for me my connection to Tom Merton: for the rest of his story, I was with him, on his side.

His autobiography made it clear that Merton cut a wide figure at Columbia. Just a few years ago I was given confirmation of this. I was running a book club at a Jesuit parish in New York, and one month we read *The Seven Storey Mountain*. After our meeting an elderly woman, who had remained silent during the evening's lively discussion, asked to speak with me. She told me that her husband had known Merton at Columbia. "My husband was so surprised when he read his book," she said. "All he could remember of Merton was that he was always ready to go out drinking or to a party. My husband said he couldn't believe what was going on inside of Merton."

The first paragraph of this excerpt from Merton's book *No Man Is an Island* changed my life. When I first read it, at age twenty-six, it stopped me in my tracks and then started me on the path that would lead to the Jesuits:

> Why do we have to spend our lives striving to be something that we would never want to be, if we only knew what we wanted? Why do we waste our time doing things which, if we only stopped to think about them, are just the opposite of what we were made for?
>
> We cannot be ourselves unless we know ourselves. But self-knowledge is impossible when thoughtless and automatic activity keeps our souls in confusion. In order to know ourselves it is not necessary to cease all activity in order to think about ourselves. That would be useless, and would probably do most of us a great deal of harm. But we have to cut down our activity to the point where we can think calmly and reasonably about our actions. We cannot begin to know ourselves until we can see the real reasons why we do the things we do, and we cannot be ourselves until our actions correspond to our intentions, and our intentions are appropriate to our own situation. But that is enough. It is not necessary that we succeed in everything. A man can be perfect and still reap no fruit from his work, and it may happen that a man who is able to accomplish very little is much more of a person than another who seems to accomplish very much.

What was going on inside of Merton was the slow process of conversion: from an old way of life to a new one, or, more specifically, from no particular religious affiliation to a wholehearted embrace of Roman Catholicism. His autobiography reveals that his transformation happened in a number of ways. The first way was through a sort of gradual intellectual progression, as Merton searched for a system of beliefs to satisfy his natural curiosity. Professor Van Doren really did prepare his mind for scholasticism, so that when Merton came across a text called *The Spirit of Medieval Philosophy*, by Étienne Gilson, its scholastic approach to the question of God's existence made a "profound impression" on him. So Merton's first way to God was through the intellect.

Merton's second path to conversion was through the senses and, especially, through art. This too happened gradually. The son of two artists, Merton was acutely aware of his surroundings, and during Merton's early life God spoke to him through the physical world—and Merton gradually became *aware* that God was doing so. As a boy, for example, Merton flipped through a picture book of monasteries and, captivated by their beauty, was "filled with a kind of longing." Years later, during an extended trip through Europe, he was "fascinated" by the Byzantine mosaics and religious art in Rome. God drew him closer in this way as well. "And thus without knowing anything about it," he wrote, "I became a pilgrim. I was unconsciously and unintentionally visiting all the great shrines of Rome, and seeking out their sanctuaries with some of the eagerness and avidity and desire of a true pilgrim, though not quite for the right reason."

Finally, God drew Merton in through his emotions. From his relationship with the Privats, to his stolen prayers in a church in Rome, to a surprising moment beside the bed of his dying grandfather, when he felt the urge to fall to his knees and pray, Merton was drawn inexorably closer to God through the intimate workings of his emotional life.

Thomas Merton's conversion occurred gradually, yet in my first reading of his book it seemed to happen all at once: Merton discovered Scholastic philosophy; he attended a Mass at a nearby church; and—bang!—a few pages later, he was baptized as a Roman

Catholic at Corpus Christi Church near Columbia University. In what I saw as his straightforward approach to changing his life, Merton appealed to me immensely. Desperate at the time to escape the bonds of my life in corporate America, I found in Merton someone who knew what to do and was able to do it quickly.

His life changed even more rapidly and decisively in the years after his baptism. Once Merton graduated from Columbia and began working on a master's degree in English, he also began considering a vocation to the priesthood. He quickly ran through a number of religious orders: the Dominicans were rejected because they slept in common dormitories. The Benedictines were rejected because "it might just mean being nailed down to a desk in an expensive prep school in New Hampshire for the rest of my life." The Jesuits were "geared to a pitch of active intensity and military routine which were alien to my own needs." The irony in these rejections is that his eventual entrance into the Trappists would require sleeping in common dormitories more primitive than those in Dominican houses, being "nailed down" to one place for longer than most Benedictines, and living a "pitch of active intensity and military routine" far outstripping that of most Jesuits.

Only the Rule of St. Francis of Assisi appealed to Tom. Providentially, his friend Dan Walsh was familiar with the Franciscans at St. Bonaventure College in Olean, a town in upstate New York. So after finishing his master's degree at Columbia, Tom took a teaching position at the college, and in November 1939, he applied to enter the Franciscans. The following June, however, his application was rejected.

In Michael Mott's superb biography, *The Seven Mountains of Thomas Merton*, Mott conjectures that Merton's rejection by the Franciscans might have stemmed from several factors: Merton's fathering of a child, his recent conversion, and perhaps "his sense of his own unfitness." Whatever the reason, a disconsolate Tom sought solace in the confessional of a Capuchin church in Manhattan.

His confessor was unduly harsh. "The priest, probably judging that I was some emotional and unstable and stupid character, began to tell me in very strong terms that I certainly did not belong in the monastery, still less the priesthood and, in fact, gave me to understand that I was simply wasting his time and insulting the Sacrament of Penance by indulging my self-pity in his confessional." Merton emerged from this ordeal in tears.

Yet with surprising equanimity and uncharacteristic freedom, Merton accepted the decision of the Franciscans and decided to return to St. Bonaventure to work with the friars. He settled into life as a teacher and, despite the Franciscans' rejection, was increasingly drawn to living as if he were in a religious order: he prayed regularly, taught classes, and lived simply. A few months later, casting about for a place to make an Easter retreat, Tom recalled Dan Walsh's comment about a Trappist monastery in the Kentucky hills, called Our Lady of Gethsemani.

At this point in his tale, my pulse quickened: I had to keep myself from racing ahead in the book. Merton seemed on the brink of finding what he had long been searching for. I wondered why I felt that I had done the same.

Merton arrived at Gethsemani late one night and was greeted by the monastery's porter, or doorkeeper. "Have you come here to stay?" asked the blunt Trappist brother.

"The question terrified me," wrote Merton. "It sounded too much like the voice of my own conscience."

"What's the matter?" answered the porter. "Why can't you stay? Are you married or something?"

"No," answered Merton, "I have a job."

But as soon as Merton stepped into the halls of the monastery it was clear where he had arrived. "I felt the deep, deep silence of the night," he wrote,

> and of peace, and of holiness enfold me like love, like safety.
>
> The embrace of it, the silence! I had entered into a solitude that was an impregnable fortress. And the silence that enfolded me, spoke to me, and spoke louder and more eloquently than any voice, and in the middle of the quiet, clean-smelling room, with the moon pouring its peacefulness in through the open window, with the warm night air, I realized truly whose house that was, O glorious Mother of God!

Merton had come home.

It took Merton a few months before he decided to enter the order. For him the monastery was the "center of all the vitality that is in America," and it exerted on him an immediate and irresistible pull.

He returned to St. Bonaventure, stunned by the force of his visit to Gethsemani, and began leading a life patterned even more closely on that of a religious community. He rose early in the morning, prayed for three-quarters of an hour, attended Mass, and did a great deal of "spiritual reading." Around this time he received a "big present . . . in the order of grace." He met, through her writings, St. Thérèse of Lisieux. And he discovered that "the Little Flower really was a saint, and not just a mute pious little doll in the imaginations of a lot of sentimental old women. And not only was she a saint, but a great saint, one of the greatest: tremendous! I owe her all kinds of public apologies and reparation for having ignored her greatness."

In a burst of enthusiasm he added: "It is a wonderful experience to discover a new saint. For God is greatly magnified and marvelous in each one of His saints: differently in each individual one."

It was almost comical to read this as I was discovering Merton.

By this point, Merton had little doubt about what he had to do. But there was a final consideration. Some months earlier Merton had been rejected by the draft board for health reasons (as a young man he had had numerous problems with his teeth). With war approaching, however, the rules were relaxed, and Merton received another letter from the draft board. He made a decision. As Michael Mott puts it in his biography, "If Gethsemani will not have him, Merton is resigned to go into the army. He is firm on one point: he will not kill, but he will serve." Merton was also resigned to doing God's will. If God wished for him to enter religious life, he would enter. If not, he would join the army. Merton had given up trying to run his life according to his own plan, preferring to let God do so instead.

In the end, to the wonder of his friends, he resigned from his position at St. Bonaventure and entered the Trappists on December 10, 1941.

The remainder of *The Seven Storey Mountain* details his life in the monastery. In short order, Merton received his novice's habit; learned about the Trappist Rule; made his temporary profession of the vows of poverty, chastity, and obedience; wrote poetry; participated in the rich liturgical life of the monastery; began his exploration of the world of contemplative prayer; and, in the process, discovered the peace he had desired all his life. "The months have gone by," he writes to God toward the end of the book, "and You have not lessened any of those desires, but You have given me peace, and I am beginning to see what it is all about. I am beginning to understand."

The Seven Storey Mountain is a beautiful book, and near the end of it I began to taste some of the peace Merton had felt. Without leaving anything behind, or leaving anything at all, I felt as if I had come home. When I finished the book late one night and set it on my nightstand, I knew with certainty that this was what I wanted to do with my life—maybe not exactly what Merton had done, and maybe not as a Trappist monk or even in a monastery, but something very nearly like it.

For me, Thomas Merton's description of religious life was an invitation to a new life. The monastic world seemed such a perfect place—peaceful and serene, full of purpose and prayer. Even then, I suspected that that was an idealized picture. (Merton later admitted as much.) And I realized that since I was desperately searching for an escape route from my current situation, any alternative would have held some appeal. Yet I also knew that, for some reason, the life that Merton described exerted a clear pull on my heart.

That's what the "call" was for me. Today many people, even believers, think that a call to the priesthood or religious life is something of an otherworldly experience—hearing voices, seeing visions. But for me it was merely a simple attraction, a heartfelt desire, a sort of emotional pull—and the happy inability to think of anything else. And once I started down that road and allowed myself to ask questions that I should have asked years ago, everything changed.

Considering those questions, which had long lain dormant in my soul, led to some surprising answers, and within two years of reading *The Seven Storey Mountain*, I entered the Jesuit novitiate.

When I feel a sense of despair creeping into my days (a sure sign that one needs help in the spiritual life), I often turn to this beautiful passage from *No Man Is an Island*, from a chapter entitled "Mercy."

How close God is to us when we come to recognize and to accept our abjection and to cast our care entirely upon Him!

Against all human expectation He sustains us when we need to be sustained, helping us to do what seemed impossible. We learn to know Him, now, not in the "presence" that is found in abstract consideration—a presence in which we dress Him in our own finery—but in the emptiness of a hope that may come close to despair. For perfect hope is achieved on the brink of despair when, instead of falling over the edge, we find ourselves walking on the air. Hope is always just about to turn into despair, but never does so, for at the moment of supreme crisis God's power is suddenly made perfect in our infirmity. So we learn to expect His mercy most calmly when all is most dangerous, to seek Him quietly in the face of peril, certain that He cannot fail us though we may be upbraided by the just and rejected by those who claim to hold the evidence of His love.

I discovered the contours of the next several years of Merton's life in his book *The Sign of Jonas.* In some ways it is a more enjoyable work than *The Seven Storey Mountain*, since his starry-eyed fervor had worn off and he could more clearly describe the reality of religious life. The excerpts from his journals tell the tale of the first years after his entrance into the monastery until the time of his ordination, which he described as the "one great secret for which I had been born."

For the rest of his life Thomas Merton (now Father M. Louis, OCSO) wrote numerous books on the contemplative life, on nonviolence, on Cistercian life, on Christian doctrine, and on Zen, serving as a spiritual guide for millions around the world. He filled volumes with his poetry. He maintained an extensive correspondence with writers, activists, and religious leaders of almost every stripe. He served as master of students and, later, master of novices for his abbey. He was visited at Gethsemani by peace activists, writers, poets, artists, musicians, priests, sisters, brothers, and those who simply appreciated his outlook on the modern world. He fell deeply in love with a woman—a nurse he met while recuperating in a local hospital—but chose to break off the relationship and remain a monk. Eventually he was given permission to become a hermit and live in a small house on the grounds of the monastery.

And, of course, he continually explored his inner life and deepened his relationship with God.

Thomas Merton continued to be a man of contradictions, and it was these contradictions that drew me to him. One can stand back and say, "Yes, this man of opposites, this proud and boastful monk, who was sometimes unwilling to listen to advice, sometimes overly self-absorbed, sometimes overly spiteful, was also holy. He was dedicated to God and to the Church; he was helpful to so many; he was generous with his talent, time, and prayers; and he wished peace to all he met." Seeing that someone so human could be holy gives me great hope. Especially with Merton one sees both the sins and the sanctity. And I wonder if this isn't something like the way God sees us.

❧

A final paradox: in 1968, after years of butting heads with his religious superiors, Merton was granted permission to leave the monastery for an extended trip to Asia. On his way he stopped in a place called Polonnaruwa, in Ceylon (now Sri Lanka), where he paused before immense statues of the Buddha. He was overwhelmed by a feeling of grace, of contentment, unlike any he had ever known. "Looking at these figures," he wrote, "I was suddenly, almost forcibly, jerked clean of the habitual, half-tired vision of things, and an inner clearness, clarity, as if exploding from the robes themselves, became evident and obvious." The devout Catholic monk had enjoyed a mystical experience in front of a statue of the Buddha.

A few weeks later, on December 10, 1968, in Bangkok for an ecumenical conference, Merton was taking a bath when he slipped in the bathroom, grabbed an electric fan, and was electrocuted.

And so the man who took a vow of stability in a Kentucky monastery died miles and miles away in Bangkok, called home by the One he sought in contradictions.

❧

Since first reading *The Seven Storey Mountain*, I had hoped to visit the Abbey of Gethsemani one day. Just a few summers ago the opportunity presented itself, through an unexpected turn of events.

In May, a Jesuit friend named Kevin mentioned that he would be spending his summer at an internship program for spiritual directors. The five-week program, at a retreat house in Ohio, sounded ideal: an opportunity to direct retreatants through the Spiritual Exercises of St. Ignatius of Loyola. "Why don't you check it out?" he said.

The following morning I called Bill, a Jesuit and one of the program's directors, who said that there was still room. Even better, Bill said that another good friend of mine, Dave, had been accepted into the program. After completing a brief application, I was accepted, too. It seemed that God wanted me to go; at the very least, God was making it easy to do so.

Boarding the plane to Cincinnati, I realized I would be spending the summer somewhere near Kentucky. But how near? At the airport, I was met by Dave and Sr. Martha, an Ursuline nun and the program's codirector. Martha said that she was a Louisville native, and though I didn't know exactly where that was, I knew it was in Kentucky, and possibly near Gethsemani.

"Are we anywhere near, um . . . Kentucky?" I asked.

Martha laughed. "We're *in* Kentucky!" she said as we passed a sign: Cincinnati and Northern Kentucky Airport.

The next two weeks at the Jesuit retreat house in Milford, Ohio, were busy ones. Kevin, Dave, and I spent the mornings with Martha and Bill in classes focusing on the Spiritual Exercises, retreat ministry, and spiritual direction. "Team meetings" with the other directors on the retreat took place at noon. Afterward came a hurried lunch of traditionally lousy retreat-house fare, then three or four hours of giving spiritual direction. Mass was at 5:00 p.m., where we were sometimes expected to preach.

After dinner, we were left to ourselves, and Kevin, Dave, and I happily spent the time seeing movies (we saw everything that summer, no matter how cheesy), renting videos, and consuming an inordinate amount of ice cream at a Cincinnati hangout called Graeter's, which was justly renowned for its product. All in all, Kevin and Dave were the perfect companions for the summer: bright, prayerful, hardworking, and fun.

If the nights were relaxing, the days proved to be a riot of activity. One morning Bill said, in a solemn tone, that if we were to be good spiritual directors, we needed to be contemplative. Later that day, after we choked down our lunch, Kevin, Dave, and I ran to meet with our retreatants. As we sprinted down the hallway of the retreat house, Kevin laughed. "This is so *contemplative!*"

The next morning I half jokingly told Bill that I was looking forward to returning to New York, where life was more relaxed.

Midway through the Spiritual Exercises, our retreatants were given a "break day," something that St. Ignatius built into the retreat, knowing that thirty straight days of silent prayer is strenuous even for the most dedicated spiritual athletes. Happily, this meant that we interns would get a break, too. So Kevin, Dave, and I decided to take a road trip to nearby Gethsemani. After we settled on an overnight visit, I offered to make the arrangements.

The guest master at the abbey, however, said that staying for only one night during a weekend was impossible. The monastery was sponsoring a three-day retreat, and we would be taking away rooms from people who might want to stay the entire weekend. Did we, he asked, want to sign up for the entire three days? That would be a lot simpler.

"Well, what does *that* mean? Are we going to be on retreat? Will we be able to *talk*?" asked Dave, giving voice to the same worry that Kevin and I had.

Our break from the retreat was seeming more and more like *another* retreat. In the end we decided to go anyway and trusted that whatever awaited us at Gethsemani—retreat, break, weekend getaway—would be what God intended for us.

This is my favorite prayer by Merton, taken from his book *Thoughts in Solitude,* and one that I have found anyone can pray:

> My Lord God, I have no idea where I am going. I do not see the road ahead of me. I cannot know for certain where it will end. Nor do I really know myself, and the fact that I think I am following your will does not mean that I am actually doing so. But I believe that the desire to please you does in fact please you. And I hope I have that desire in all that I am doing. I hope that I will never do anything apart from that desire. And I know that if I do this you will lead me by the right road, though I may know nothing about it. Therefore I will trust you always though I may seem to be lost and in the shadow of death. I will not fear, for you are ever with me, and you will never leave me to face my perils alone.

A week later, we piled into Bill's beat-up car and said a prayer to Our Lady of the Way before starting out. (Our piety seemed to increase each day of the retreat.) The ride took us past Louisville and through the bluegrass horse country of Kentucky. In a few hours we were wending our way through what is known as the "knob" country of Kentucky because of the small round hills dotting the landscape.

A few miles after Bardstown, the tall steeple of the Abbey of Our Lady of Gethsemani came into view, rising over the grassy country-side like a ship's mast over a green ocean. The abbey was surrounded by a low gray wall, which was in turn surrounded by lush fields that stretched toward the horizon.

When we emerged from the car, we were bowled over by the heat. I remembered a passage in *The Sign of Jonas* where Thomas Merton talks about the summer in the monastery. It is an entry from August 8, 1947: "Hot, sticky weather. Prickly heat. Red lumps all over your neck and shoulders. Everything clammy. *Paenitentiam agite!* It is better than a hairshirt."

We carried our luggage into the monastery's guesthouse. Over the doorway was a single word, in big block letters, carved into the stone lintel: *Pax.* Opposite the entrance, across a plaza, was the entrance to the monastery cloister. It too had a legend engraved above the doorway: "God Alone." The guesthouse interior was refreshingly cool; there seemed little danger that anyone inside would get prickly heat. Seated at the desk was the porter, in the traditional Trappist habit of a white alb and black scapular, which is a kind of relic for me. For no matter how many times I see it, it fills me with a kind of joy, as if I am closer to the possibility of a life of pure contemplation and more connected to the real-life Thomas Merton.

The monastery's porter pulled out a guest list. "Let's see," he said, "Fr. Martin, you're in this room." He pointed to a room on the top floor of the monastery residence and handed me a key.

"Fr. Dave," he said. Dave made a face at Kevin and me. He was not ordained but was too polite to correct the porter. "You're here, also in the monastery."

"And Fr. Kevin," he said. "There was no more room in the monastery proper, so we put you in the guesthouse, which is just next door. There's air conditioning there."

Dave and I looked at each other. That meant there was *no* air conditioning in our rooms. "It's very pleasant in the guesthouse," said the porter. "You have your own bathroom, too."

"Vespers is at 5:30," he said, "followed by supper at 6:00. The rest of the schedule is posted outside the chapel. Would any of you like to concelebrate at Mass?" At this point, Kevin and Dave informed the porter that I was the only priest in the bunch. I said that I would love to concelebrate tomorrow.

"Mass is at 6:15 in the morning," he said. "Just fill out a card in the dining room, and an alb and stole will be waiting for you tomorrow." Kevin, Dave, and I decided to drop off our bags in our rooms and meet at the guesthouse a few minutes later.

My spartan quarters were like most other retreat-house rooms—there was a bed, a wooden desk, and a sink—with one exception. Owing to the oppressive heat, a large overhead fan seemed stuck in overdrive: it was spinning madly, like an airplane propeller, and a blast of hot air greeted me when I opened the door.

Downstairs, in the guesthouse, Kevin surprised me. "I want you to have my room," he said. "It's really nice and it has air conditioning. You've been wanting to come here for so long, so you should have it."

I was touched by Kevin's offer and reminded of how grateful I was to have so many generous friends. But immediately I thought, *Hmm . . . what would Thomas Merton do?* The most charitable thing would be to let Kevin have it. And maybe God wanted me to have the room I had been given for some special but as yet unforeseen reason. So I decided I would give up Kevin's room, as an ascetic test.

"No, you keep it," I said, feeling super-holy.

"No, *you* should have it."

"No, you take it."

Dave rolled his eyes. "If one of you doesn't stop being so damn holy, *I'll* take it!"

In the end, Kevin kept his room. (Weeks after the trip Kevin confessed that while Dave and I were kept awake by the heat, he didn't sleep because he was unable to adjust the air conditioning and was actually too cold.)

After our extended room discernment, we visited the chapel. It was a long, narrow building with a simple design and an impressively high ceiling. The abbey's original chapel had been an ornate affair, but after the Second Vatican Council the community hired the architect William Schickel to simplify its look. Schickel stripped away the decorative columns and cornices to reveal the bare brick, now painted white, and dark wooden beams that crisscrossed the ceiling and supported the walls behind the altar.

Near the entrance of the chapel was a small area for guests to sit, marked off by a low metal gate. Beyond the gate, wooden stalls for the monks lined the walls. At the far end of the pebbly floor, simple metal chairs surrounded a plain wood altar. Wonderfully cool, the chapel smelled like incense and, improbably, new carpeting. I peered down the aisle toward the sanctuary and imagined Thomas Merton kneeling before his abbot and pronouncing his vows, or lying prostrate on the floor, during the long ordination ceremony.

After our visit to the chapel, we wandered around the side of the guesthouse to the cemetery. Row after row of low metal crosses, painted white, punctuated the green grass. After a few minutes we found what I had hoped to see. The bronze plaque read: "Fr. Louis Merton, Died Dec. 10, 1968."

As I stood in the broiling sun, I thought of all the monks who had gathered decades ago around this spot, probably pondering Merton's contradictory life and his strange, almost literary, death. (The accidentally electrocuted Merton had ended *The Seven Storey Mountain* with the words "That you may become the brother of God and learn to know the Christ of the burnt men.") I thought also about how my vocation to the Jesuits really began here at Gethsemani.

It was nearing the time for Vespers, so we filed into the chapel, picking up a small booklet with the hour's prayers. Presently twenty or so people took their places on the metal chairs beside us. A bell sounded, and in a few moments the monks silently filed in from side doors. As they entered, they dipped their fingers in the stone holy water fonts and slowly made the sign of the cross. The sight of so many Trappist monks in their distinctive habit, in the church in which Merton spent so much time, was surprisingly moving. After having read so much about his life and this place, I had a difficult time believing that I was there.

The prayers were a surprise. I had expected something out of a Gregorian chant CD—lush polyphony and well-trained voices, perhaps accompanied by the deep tones of an organ. Instead we heard something simpler: the sound of sixty-six men, many elderly, singing the psalms plainly. ("Oh yes," said Martha when we returned, "the Benedictines are much better singers than the Trappists.") But it was still lovely, and I marveled that monks had been praying like this since long before I was born, and would do so long after I was gone.

In the courtyard outside the chapel we checked out the schedule for Saturday prayers:

Vigils	3:15 a.m.
Lauds	5:45 a.m.
Terce	7:30 a.m.
Sext	12:15 p.m.
None	2:15 p.m.
Vespers	5:30 p.m.
Compline	7:30 p.m.
Mass	6:15 a.m.

Supper followed Vespers. There were two dining rooms for the retreatants: the main room, where silence was kept, and a smaller room where people were allowed to speak. We three spiritual athletes chose the silent room. After the bland fare of the Jesuit retreat house, I was delighted by the abbey's fantastic cooking—fresh vegetables, wonderful bread, and, since it was Friday, plenty of fish. And the best cheese I had ever eaten: fresh from the farm. In his journals, Thomas Merton mocked the "cheese industry" at Gethsemani. For once I disagreed with him.

There was a conference after dinner for retreatants, where we were surprised and pleased to hear an elderly monk declaim verses from the Jesuit poet Gerard Manley Hopkins and speak feelingly about his poetry and life. Then it was time for Compline, the final prayer of the day (so named because it "completes" the day). Compline closed with both monks and retreatants filing up the aisle to receive the abbot's blessing for the night. Afterward, Kevin, Dave, and I gathered outside the chapel and teased one another about who would make it to tomorrow's first prayer, Vigils, at 3:15 a.m. (Only Dave, as it turned out—and mainly, he said, because it was too hot to sleep.)

After a shower (to cool off) and my own prayers, I decided to visit the chapel again. As my eyes adjusted to the darkness, I was happy to find it empty—and completely silent. Kneeling at the visitors' gate, I wanted to offer some quick prayers before bed. I was beat after a long day. But suddenly I thought about the course of my life. How was it that I had been drawn into religious life? Looking back, it seemed that I had been forcibly pulled from a life of unhappiness and placed into one of joy. I wondered over the amazing way God had worked in my life, leading me to places that I couldn't have seen for myself. I thought of how happy I was to be there, to be spending the summer doing something I loved, with great Jesuit friends who kept me honest, prayed with me, and made me laugh. I was filled with gratitude for being a Jesuit. This happiness seemed almost too much for my heart to contain, and I wept for a time in the chapel, grateful yet unable to express this gratitude completely.

In the early morning, after Lauds, I wandered into the spacious sacristy, where a monk handed me a soft white alb and a gold stole made of crinkly raw silk. At Mass, when I was not listening to the priest, my eyes wandered to the spot where Merton was ordained. I knew it well from old photographs.

Saturday breakfast was wonderful. Along with the best cheese I've ever eaten, the abbey also boasts the best oatmeal I've ever eaten. Kevin, Dave, and I walked through the fields across the street after breakfast. I told them how much I was enjoying myself. Kevin laughed. "Are we going to have to leave you here?"

That day we played hooky from our retreat and drove into nearby Bardstown, where many Catholics settled in the early 1800s, fleeing religious persecution in the East. Consequently, in the middle of Kentucky, towns have improbably Catholic names: St. Mary, St. Francis, Loreto. Even the Jesuits made it to Bardstown, founding St. Joseph College in the middle of town. (Those same Jesuits later moved to New York to begin Fordham University.)

We raced back in time for Vespers and supper. We decided to eat in the "speaking" dining room that night, although we worried that by doing so we would make the Jesuits look bad. "Who's going to know?" I asked.

Along with my meal I ate my words. Two of the monks were hosting guests in that dining room. "Great," whispered Kevin. "Now they'll tell the other monks how the Jesuits couldn't keep silent for two days." After dinner came another conference, this time on the gift of silence, and then Compline.

At the end of our three days, having followed the rhythm of the Trappists, I was starting to feel that perhaps the life of a monk would not suit me. It seemed as if we were in the chapel constantly (which was, of course, the point). As was customary on many of my retreats, my appreciation for the value of the "active" life had grown.

The next morning after Lauds at 5:45, we dragged our bags down to the guesthouse. Before we left, I remembered one more thing I had to do, or rather, say. Something I had forgotten. I hurried over to Merton's grave, around the side of the monastery.

I looked down at the bright green grass and thought about Merton's strange, complicated, and contradictory life. And about my favorite lines from Walt Whitman, which come near the end of "Song of Myself":

> I bequeath myself to the dirt to grow from the
>   grass I love.
> If you want me again look for me under your
>   boot-soles.

I thought of everything I would like to say to Thomas Merton: That there was probably no other person other than Jesus so responsible for my vocation. That, thanks to his writings, I still carried within myself the pull toward the monastic life in the midst of an active world. That his life of contradictions and complexities helped me see that all of us, no matter how crazy our lives seem, can be holy. That he helped me understand what he called my "true self," the person I am before God, and the person I am meant to be. And that, though obviously flawed, he remained one of my great heroes.

But nothing seemed right. So I said simply, "Thanks," trusting that he knew all that I meant. And then I ran off to join my friends.

5

Ad Majorem Dei Gloriam

Ignatius of Loyola

*Until the age of twenty-six he was a man given over to
the vanities of the world.*
—*The Autobiography of St. Ignatius Loyola*

For me, chief among the joys of leaving the corporate world and
entering the Jesuit novitiate in Boston was the slowing down of
my life. I had spent six years working days, nights, and weekends, so
my introduction to the daily schedule, or *ordo*, of the novitiate was a
welcome change.

That's not to say that the life of a Jesuit novice was not full and
active in its own way. First-year novices were expected to spend fifteen
hours a week at our "ministries" outside the novitiate—I worked in
a local Catholic hospital that cared for the seriously ill. Novices were
also expected to cook once a week for the community (which consisted of fifteen Jesuits), to attend Mass every day (including Sundays,
of course), to pray at least an hour a day (not including community
prayer, at 7:00 a.m.), to complete our "house jobs" (mine was cleaning the kitchen), to participate in weekly spiritual direction (that is,
discussing your prayer with one of the novitiate staff), and to attend
Sunday evening "faith sharing" meetings (where you were to describe

your spiritual life to the other novices). Finally, we were expected to join in the weekly *manualia*, a sort of Saturday morning community housecleaning. I always seemed to get stuck with toilet duty.

But while there was a lot to do, it was a more reasonable life than the one I had led at General Electric. More humane. For this I was instantly grateful to God.

Another requirement for novices was the daily "conference," an hour-long class presided over by the novice director and his assistant. At 8:00 a.m. every day we gathered around a huge oak trestle table in the library for an introduction to the history and spirituality of the Society of Jesus. An important part of our first year of training was learning about the founder of the Jesuits, St. Ignatius of Loyola; about the early Jesuits; and about both Jesuit and Ignatian spirituality. ("Ignatian spirituality" refers to the saint's overall spiritual outlook, whereas "Jesuit spirituality" also includes the spirituality of the Jesuit Order itself, based on its constitutions, its governance, and what is called its "way of proceeding.")

Given these educational goals, I was not surprised when the novice director asked us to read *The First Jesuit*, a biography of St. Ignatius written by the historian Mary Purcell, as well as *The Autobiography of St. Ignatius Loyola*.

What did surprise me was that after finishing those two books (which seemed, at least to my novice mind, rather comprehensive), we were asked to read another biography: *St. Ignatius Loyola: The Pilgrim Years*, by James Brodrick, SJ.

Then another: *Ignatius of Loyola: Founder of the Jesuits*, by Cándido de Dalmases, SJ.

Finally—apparently in case we weren't paying attention to the first four books—we were assigned *Friends in the Lord*, by Javier Osuna, SJ, focusing on St. Ignatius and the original Jesuits.

We were also strongly encouraged (should we have any free time) to plow through *Ignatius of Loyola and the Founding of the Society of Jesus,* by André Ravier, SJ, and *The Jesuits: Their Spiritual Doctrine and Practice,* by Joseph de Guibert, SJ. Nor were novices to neglect *Letters of St. Ignatius of Loyola,* selected and translated by William J. Young, SJ.

Fortunately, that last volume, while weighing in at a hefty 450 pages, nonetheless represented only a small fraction of the saint's 6,813 letters. The book's dust jacket proudly calls Ignatius "one of the most assiduous letter writers of his own or any other age." In number, his letters are double the extant letters of Erasmus, Luther, and "almost" (said the dust jacket with a faint air of disappointment) John Calvin.

In any event, you will not be surprised to learn that by the end of the first year of the novitiate, I could recite the story of St. Ignatius by heart.

❧

Iñigo of Loyola was born in 1491 in the Basque Country of northern Spain. As a boy, he served as a page in the court of a local nobleman, and later distinguished himself as a valiant soldier. He describes himself in his short autobiography as "a man given over to the vanities of the world," particularly concerning his physical appearance. He seems also to have been a ladies' man. At least that's how he fancied himself. He was definitely a rake. It was rumored that he fathered an illegitimate child. (There is some evidence to support this, but it is inconclusive.) And he may be the only canonized saint with a notarized police record, for nighttime brawling with intent to inflict serious harm.

During Iñigo's soldiering career, his leg was struck by a cannonball in a battle at Pamplona in 1521. This pivotal incident, which might have been merely tragic to another person, marked the beginning of a new life for Iñigo. It is also one of the scenes most often depicted in murals and mosaics of the saint's life. At St. Ignatius Loyola Church in New York City, high over the main altar is a brightly colored mosaic of the battle at Pamplona. Atop the parapets of a medieval castle, the injured Iñigo, still clad in a suit of gray armor over a sky blue doublet, reclines in the arms of his fellow soldiers. As the battle rages about him and soldiers scale the castle walls on rickety wooden ladders, Iñigo gazes placidly heavenward, as if already anticipating something new from God.

After the battle, he was brought to his elder brother's home, the family's ancestral castle of Loyola, to recuperate. The bone in his leg was set poorly, and Iñigo, "given over to the vanities of the world," wanted the leg to look smart in his courtier's tights. He therefore submitted to a series of gruesome and painful operations. The leg never healed properly, and he was left with a lifelong limp.

Confined to his sickbed, Iñigo asked a relative for some books. All she could offer was pious reading, which he took grumpily and grudgingly. To his great surprise, the soldier found himself attracted to the lives of the saints and began thinking, *If St. Francis or St. Dominic could do such-and-such, maybe I could do great things.* He also noticed that after thinking about doing great deeds for God, he was left with a feeling of peace—what he termed "consolation." On the other hand, after imagining success as a soldier or impressing a particular woman, though he was initially filled with great enthusiasm, he would later be left feeling "dry."

Slowly, he recognized that these feelings of dryness and consolation were God's ways of leading him to follow a path of service. He perceived the peaceful feeling as God's way of drawing him closer. This realization also marked the beginning of his understanding of "discernment" in the spiritual life, a way of striving to seek God's will in one's life, a key concept in Ignatian spirituality.

Iñigo decided after his recovery that he would become a pilgrim and tramp to the Holy Land to see what he might do there in God's service. First he made a pilgrimage to a well-known monastery in Spain, in Montserrat, where he confessed his sins, laid aside his knightly armor, and put on the homespun garb of a pilgrim. From Montserrat, Iñigo journeyed to a nearby small town called Manresa, where he lived the life of a poor pilgrim: praying, fasting continually, and begging for alms.

During his time in Manresa, his prayer intensified and he experienced great emotional variances in his spiritual life, as he moved from a desolation that was nearly suicidal to a mystical sense of union with God. In the end, his prayer made him more certain that he was being called to follow God more closely. Iñigo spent several months in seclusion in Manresa, experiencing prayer that grew ever deeper, and then commenced his journey to Jerusalem.

After a series of mishaps in Jerusalem and elsewhere, he decided that to accomplish anything noteworthy in the church of his time, he would need more education and perhaps even to become a priest. So the former soldier vowed to recommence his education, an arduous process that took him to the university cities of Alcalá, Salamanca, and, finally, Paris. And since he had little knowledge of Latin, he had to sit in class—at age thirty—with small boys learning their Latin lessons.

Even in my third or fourth reading of the saint's story, I found this chapter of Ignatius's life impressive and touching. It always called to mind the image of the middle-aged man seated at a too-small desk, hunched over his books. The proud courtier who had hoped to win the attraction of influential men and highborn women nonetheless found the humility necessary to admit that in many ways he was no more advanced than a schoolboy.

While studying in Paris, Iñigo attracted attention as a result of his ascetic penchant for dressing in the poorest clothes, begging for alms, helping the poor, and assisting other students in prayer. In Paris he also completed what later become known as *The Spiritual Exercises,* a handbook of practices on prayer, on the human condition, on God's love, and on the life of Jesus, all designed to help people draw closer to God. Iñigo also led his new roommate, Francisco Javier, through these exercises. His friend would later become better known, of course, as St. Francis Xavier, one of the Church's great missionaries. Around this time in Paris, Iñigo, for reasons still unknown, changed his own name to the more familiar-sounding Ignatius.

Gradually, Ignatius gathered around him a tight-knit group of six men, who decided they would work together in the service of God.

But doing what? Initially, they decided to go to Jerusalem, as so many Christians before them had done. If that was not possible, they would present themselves directly to the pope, who, by virtue of his knowledge of the needs of the universal church, would be better able to discern a direction for the group. Eventually, the men decided to form the Company of Jesus, or *Societas Jesu* in Latin, for the purpose of "helping souls."

At first, Ignatius had a tough time winning formal acceptance for his society. For one thing, some in the church hierarchy were disturbed that he was not founding a more traditional religious order, with an emphasis on common prayer and a stricter, even cloistered, community life. But Ignatius's men (derisively called "Jesuits" by their critics) wanted to work *in the world*. Ignatius, ever resourceful, shrewdly enlisted the help of powerful churchmen to speak on the society's behalf.

From these humble efforts began the Society of Jesus. After settling in Rome and receiving papal approval for his new order, Ignatius began the difficult task of writing the Jesuits' constitutions and mapping out plans for the work of its members. In all of these efforts Ignatius proved both ambitious and persistent. At the same time, he was flexible and ready to do whatever might be God's will. He fought for the Society whenever a church official raised another objection about his new order. Yet he used to say that if the pope ever ordered the Jesuits to disband, he would need only fifteen minutes in prayer to compose himself and be on his way.

In my novitiate, St. Ignatius was presented as the model Jesuit: intelligent, prayerful, and *disponible*—available, disposed to do God's will. He was ambitious to do great things *ad majorem Dei gloriam*, for the greater glory of God. Another way of expressing this is the Jesuit tradition of *magis*, the best, the highest, the most for God. It has often been noted how fortunate it was for the Catholic Church that Ignatius transformed his worldly ambitions into ambitions for the Church. His courtier's charm, his soldier's tenacity, and his stalwart temperament combined to make him a formidable first superior of the Jesuits. (I remember thinking in the novitiate that Ignatius would not have done so poorly in the corporate world.)

Despite his remarkably compelling and undeniably inspiring life, St. Ignatius doesn't elicit the kind of widespread affection afforded to saints such as Thérèse of Lisieux or Francis of Assisi. Descriptions of Ignatius often use such terms as *intellectual, serious, austere, mystical*—making the saint, while respected, a rather distant figure.

And while Jesuits revere their founder, more than a few hold "Fr. Ignatius" at arm's length. An elderly Jesuit at Boston College once said to me, regarding the prospect of his judgment in heaven: "I have no problem with Jesus judging me. It's St. Ignatius I'm worried about!"

It is true that, unlike Francis of Assisi, Ignatius is rarely characterized as endearingly silly (though he liked to perform impromptu Basque dances for melancholy Jesuits) or foolish (though early in his postconversion life he asked his mule to decide, by choosing which fork in the road to take, if he should pursue a man who had just insulted the Virgin Mary). And true, he was not a gifted writer with an instinct for the well-turned phrase, as was his compatriot St. Teresa of Ávila or St. Benedict.

His *Autobiography*—which he dictated only after being asked, and then grudgingly—is occasionally moving in its frank descriptions of his mystical experiences but is sometimes awfully dry. Even Ignatius's greatest contribution to Christian spirituality, *The Spiritual Exercises*, is not a compendium of warm reflections on the love of God. It is instead a series of clear, practical instructions—a how-to manual for retreat directors—that is appreciated more in the doing than the reading. The young Thomas Merton once "made" the Spiritual Exercises on his own, sitting cross-legged on the floor of his apartment in Greenwich Village in the late 1930s. It was a mixed experience for Merton, somewhat akin to attempting to psychoanalyze oneself.

But the two writings into which Ignatius poured his heart and soul—*The Spiritual Exercises* and the *Constitutions* of the Society of Jesus—do work, and have worked well for more than 450 years. For Ignatius of Loyola was nothing if not practical. After discerning God's will for himself, he resolutely set out to do it. He amended his life. Left his military career. Returned to school. Gathered his friends together. Put himself at the disposal of God and the pope. He organized, led, and inspired what he called his "least" Society of Jesus. He wrote their constitutions, opened schools, and sent out missionaries.

Yet at the heart of what can seem like frenetic activity was an intimate relationship with God, which Ignatius often found difficult to put into words. His private journals show minuscule notations crowded beside his entries for daily Mass. As scholars have concluded, these indicate, among other things, those times when he wept during Mass, overwhelmed by love for God. Ignatius found God *everywhere*: in the poor, in prayer, in the Mass, in his fellow Jesuits, in his work, and, most touchingly, on a balcony of the Jesuit house in Rome, where he loved to gaze up silently at the stars at night. During these times he would shed tears in wonder and adoration. His emotional responses to the presence of God in his life gives the lie to the stereotype of the cold saint.

Ignatius was a mystic who loved God with an intensity rare even for saints. He wasn't a renowned scholar like Augustine or Aquinas, not a martyr like Peter or Paul, not a great writer like Teresa or Benedict, and perhaps not a beloved personality like Francis or Thérèse. But he loved God and loved the world, and those two things he did quite well.

The best spiritual directors are those who can help you discern where God is at work in your life, and where you might be tempted to act against God's will. In his *Autobiography*, Ignatius describes the first time he came to understand the way God was working within him, gently drawing him closer through his emotions and desires. This key insight would later form the basis of *The Spiritual Exercises*.

In this passage, Ignatius is lying on a sickbed, convalescing after receiving a serious wound in battle, not long before he decides to devote himself to the service of God. In his autobiography, dictated to his friend Luis Gonçalves da Câmara, Ignatius always refers to himself as "him" or "the pilgrim."

While reading the life of Our Lord and of the saints, he stopped to think, reasoning within himself, "What if I should do what Saint Francis did, what Saint Dominic did?" So he pondered over many things that he found to be good, always proposing to himself what was difficult and serious, and as he proposed them, they seemed to him easy enough to accomplish. But his every thought was to say to himself, "Saint Dominic did this, therefore, I have to do it. Saint Francis did this, therefore, I have to do it." These thoughts also lasted a good while, but when other matters intervened, the worldly thoughts . . . returned, and he also spent much time on them. This succession of such diverse thoughts, either of the worldly deeds he wished to achieve or of the deeds of God that came to his imagination, lasted a long time, and he always dwelt at length on the thought before him, until he tired of it and put it aside and turned to other matters.

Yet there was a difference. When he was thinking about the things of the world, he took much delight in them, but afterwards, when he was tired and put them aside, he found that he was dry and discontented. But when he thought of going to Jerusalem, barefoot and eating nothing but herbs and undergoing all the other rigors that he saw the saints had endured, not only was he consoled when he had these thoughts, but even after putting them aside, he remained content and happy. He did not wonder, however, at this: nor did he stop to ponder the difference until one time his eyes were opened a little, and he began to marvel at the difference and to reflect upon it, realizing from experience that some thoughts left him sad and others happy. Little by little he came to recognize the difference between the spirits that agitated him, one from the enemy, the other from God.

My own affinity to St. Ignatius is not one of great personal affection. Even after many years as a Jesuit, I see Ignatius as a sympathetic but somewhat distant figure, removed from the plane of average men and women. Demanding. Even severe. Still, my gratitude toward him has deepened over the course of my Jesuit life, to the point where he is one of my favorite saints. It's the kind of gratitude you might have for a thrifty and taciturn uncle who has secretly provided the funds for your education without you knowing it. In essence, my gratitude is for his spirituality and for his way of looking at the world and at God. It is his brand of spirituality that changed my life and frames the way I see the world today.

At heart, Ignatian spirituality flows from the saint's most famous work, *The Spiritual Exercises*, which Ignatius wrote over many years; it was the fruit of his prayer and his experience in helping others pray. Any understanding of the spirituality of St. Ignatius and of his Jesuit Order begins with this short work. What has been called his greatest gift to the Church has enabled thousands of men and women—Jesuits, priests, sisters, brothers, laypersons—from almost every Christian denomination to experience a deep intimacy with God. It is no stretch to say that *The Spiritual Exercises* has transformed lives.

Essentially, *The Spiritual Exercises* is a manual for retreat directors that maps out a retreat designed to fit into four weeks. During that time retreatants ponder the love of God, pray over the decision to follow Christ, contemplate events from the life of Jesus of Nazareth, and experience God's creative activity in all things. The Exercises are intended to help one know Jesus more intimately, experience a growing freedom, and understand how to make decisions in accord with God's grace.

Though the Exercises are traditionally divided into four "Weeks," in actual practice it usually takes more than seven days to complete each "Week." To add to the confusion, Jesuits also refer to the Exercises as the "thirty-day retreat" or, for obvious reasons, the "long retreat." A Jesuit will make the long retreat twice in his life, once as a novice, and once after the final stage of Jesuit formation, called "tertianship."

⚜

The Spiritual Exercises begins, after some preliminary observations, with Ignatius's famous "Principle and Foundation," which lays out in broad strokes his religious worldview: "Human beings are created to praise, reverence, and serve God our Lord, and by this means to save their souls." As such, we should make use of things on earth that enable us to do this, and free ourselves of anything that prevents us from doing so. We should be, to use a favorite Ignatian expression, "indifferent to all created things."

Thanks in part to the word that he chose, indifference, as Ignatius uses it, is a commonly misunderstood concept. It does not mean that we should set aside things (or people) as worthless. Rather, we should not be so attached to any thing or person or state of life that it prevents us from loving God. The Exercises invite us to embrace a radical freedom: "On our part," Ignatius writes, "we want not health rather than sickness, riches rather than poverty, long rather than short life, and so in all the rest; desiring and choosing only that which is most conducive for us to the end for which we are created."

One young woman, after hearing those lines, said to me, "I'm not supposed to prefer health over sickness? That's *insane!*"

Of course no one wants to be sick. But in Ignatius's worldview, health should not be something clung to so tightly that the fear of illness prevents you from following God. As in "Well, I'm not going to visit my friend in the hospital, because I might get sick." Ignatius would say that in that case you may not be "indifferent" enough; health has become a sort of god, preventing you from doing good.

The goal is not choosing sickness for its own sake, but moving toward the freedom of knowing that the highest good is not your own physical well-being. For most of us, this kind of complete freedom will remain a lifetime goal.

In my own life, indifference has proven to be a durable spiritual concept. Whenever I find myself overly attached to something—my physical well-being, my plans for worldly success, my popularity among friends, and so on—I remember the need for indifference.

When I was working with refugees in Kenya, for example, immediately before I was set to begin theology studies, my provincial asked me to wait another year before moving on to this next stage of training. He didn't think I was ready yet for theology studies.

I was crushed. Most of my peers were on the same timetable, and now I was being asked to wait.

The more I thought about it, the more I became consumed with concerns for my reputation, for how things would appear. What would everyone else think? That I was a failure. A bad Jesuit. Damaged goods. I was angry with my provincial and told him so.

When I confessed these feelings to my spiritual director in Nairobi, he counseled not only patience but a prayer for, as he called it, the grace of indifference. "Can you be indifferent to your need to have things happen on your own timetable?" he asked. "Are you more concerned with how things appear rather than what is really best for you? Might God's timetable be a better one than yours?"

His reminder about indifference helped me weather a short but intense spiritual storm. As it turned out, that extra year, spent working at *America* magazine, was a wonderful period in my life—one that helped me dream about a new career as a writer—and also helped to better prepare me for theology studies.

A few years later I said to my provincial, "You know, I finally realize that I did have to wait that extra year. You were right."

"I know I was!" he laughed.

But indifference can be a costly grace. Ignatius and the early Jesuits understood this well. In 1539, when a Jesuit whom Ignatius had hoped to send to the Portuguese colony in India fell ill, Ignatius's best friend, Francis Xavier, volunteered. Faced with the decision of keeping his friend at his side or sending him away "for the greater glory of God," Ignatius chose the latter.

It must have been a painful step, one he was able to take only with true indifference. It was this radical kind of freedom that enabled Ignatius to let his friend go, and it was the same freedom that enabled Xavier to become one of the world's greatest Christian missionaries. But the two men, best friends since their university days, would never again see each another. After spreading the message of the gospel in India and Japan, Francis Xavier died off the coast of China in 1552.

Before his departure for India, Francis wrote his best friend a letter from Lisbon, in 1541. To my mind, it is the most moving thing he ever wrote, as it captures both his love for Ignatius as well as his dedication to his new mission:

> There is nothing more to tell you except that we are about to embark. We close by asking Christ our Lord for the grace of seeing each other joined together in the next life; for I do not know if we shall ever see each other again in this, because of the great distance between Rome and India, and the great harvest to be found.

❦

Retreatants usually spend a few days praying over the "Principle and Foundation" not just as a way of thinking about indifference but also as a means of meditating on their relationship with God. This stage of the Exercises allows people to experience gratitude by contemplating God's creative activity in their lives. For many, it may mean pondering the beauty of nature, or the blessings they have received from God, or any of the ways in which they've experienced God throughout their lives.

At this point Ignatius introduces a simple but powerful form of prayer called the "examination of conscience," a way of noticing where God is active in your life. It's also called the "Examen," the Spanish word Ignatius used in the Exercises, or "examination of conscious-ness," another way of translating the Latin, *conscientia.*

There are five steps in the Examen. First, you ask God to be with you. Next, you recall the events of the day for which you feel grateful. Your gratitude need not be for anything extraordinary: it can be for a phone call from a friend, an enjoyable meal, a tough job finally completed. Small things are important, too: a sunny day, a refreshing nap, a baby's smile. Offering gratitude helps you recognize God's presence in these moments.

The third step is a review of the day. Here you try to notice God's presence in the day, seeking an awareness of where you accepted (or did not accept) God's grace. I like to think of this as a movie of the day being replayed. When you recall someone offering you a kind word, you might say to yourself, "Yes, there was God." Conversely, when you recall treating someone with disrespect, you might say, "Yes, there I turned away from God." This leads naturally to the fourth step: asking forgiveness for any sins. The fifth step is asking for the grace to fol-low God more closely during the following day. Ignatius recommends closing the Examen with an Our Father.

The Examen is a simple prayer of awareness. It's about noticing God's presence in the everyday events of life. Prayer, as the Jesuit Walter Burghardt once wrote, is a "long, loving look at the real." And the Examen is just that: a way of seeing God in the reality of everyday life.

"Finding God in all things" is a succinct summary of Ignatian spirituality, and the Examen is a good way of starting to live this ideal.

❦

Besides these everyday graces, at this point in the Exercises retreatants may also recall moments of particular grace, those times when God's presence felt especially near, when we encountered what Sebastian Moore, OSB, has called the desire for "I know not what."

These "peak" experiences are not simply the province of mystics. Many, if not most, people encounter them—though often they are not recognized. Let's say that you are alone on the beach during a beautiful sunset and are overwhelmed by the beauty of creation. Or you are in the midst of an intimate encounter with your spouse or partner and are made aware of a deep connectedness to the Source of all love. In each of these experiences you are encountering God in a profound and personal way—whether you know it or not.

There are a number of descriptions of such experiences in contemporary novels and autobiographies. In my late twenties, when I was first thinking about religious life, I stumbled across a lovely passage in *Surprised by Joy*, by C. S. Lewis. Early in his autobiography, the author recounts a moment when he was standing before a currant bush in a garden and recalled a fond memory from childhood. Lewis was overcome by a desire "from a depth not of years but of centuries." He writes:

> It is difficult to find words strong enough for the sensation that came over me. . . . It was a sensation, of course, of desire, but a desire for what? . . . And before I knew what I desired, the desire itself was gone, the whole glimpse withdrawn, and the world turned

commonplace again, or only stirred by a longing for the longing which had just ceased.

In my own life, such moments have occurred only a few times. Each time I failed to recognize their importance at the time. Only in retrospect did I understand their meaning.

When I was a young boy, for example, I used to ride my bike to the elementary school located a few miles from our house. The twenty-minute ride was wonderfully downhill to school and miserably uphill home. The ride to school took me over the new sidewalks of our neighborhood and past familiar houses to a hidden sidewalk, sandwiched between two houses. At the end of this sidewalk was a steep set of concrete stairs, whose climb warranted dismounting the bike and dragging it up the six steps.

From the top of the steps, I could see my school in the distance. And between the steps and the school lay one of my favorite spots: a broad meadow, bordered on the left by tall oak trees and on the right by our school's vast baseball fields. On cold fall mornings, clad in a corduroy jacket, I would pedal my bike down the bumpy dirt path through a meadow full of crunchy brown leaves, desiccated grasses, and dried milkweed plants powdered in frost. In the winter (when I would not ride but walk to school), the field was an open landscape of white snow that rose wetly over the tops of my black galoshes as my breath made clouds before me.

In the spring, though, the meadow exploded with life. It felt as if I were biking through a science experiment. Fat grasshoppers jumped among the daisies and black-eyed Susans, bees hummed above the Queen Anne's lace, little brown crickets sang underneath pale blue thistles, and cardinals and robins darted from branch to branch. The air was fresh, and the field sang the words of creation.

One warm spring morning, I stopped to catch my breath in the middle of the field. I must have been ten or eleven years old. My schoolbooks, heavy in the bike's metal basket, swung violently to the side, and I almost lost my math homework to the grasshoppers and crickets. Standing astride my bike, I could see much going on around me—so much color, so much activity, so much *life*. Looking toward my school on the horizon, I felt so happy to be alive. And I wanted both to possess and to be a part of all I saw around me. I can still see myself in this meadow, in the warm air, surrounded by creation, more clearly than any other memory from childhood.

Looking back, I believe that I was feeling a sense of God's *promise*: an invitation to limitless joy. It was this memory that came to me at the beginning of the Spiritual Exercises.

⁂

After reflecting on such moments, retreatants begin to see their unwillingness to respond to God's goodness—in other words, their sinfulness. One director explained that the more we recognize God's love, the more we see how, like the sun, it begins to throw a shadow, revealing our own sinful nature.

During the First Week, then, retreatants consider their own sinfulness. Ignatius reminds believers always to ask for what they want in prayer, especially during the Exercises. In the First Week, writes Ignatius, we are to "beg for the grace for a great and intense sorrow for my sins." Over time, retreatants find themselves grateful that though they have sinned often, they are nevertheless loved by God: they are "loved sinners." Gratitude for God's unconditional love usually, and naturally, prompts a desire to respond to it.

To begin the Second Week, Ignatius offers a powerful meditation entitled "The Call of Christ the King." He asks retreatants to imagine serving a charismatic human leader. We are to imagine our hero bidding us to follow him in his lifework, and "to be content to eat as I; also to drink, dress, etc." This is often a deeply moving experience—wouldn't it be fantastic if your own hero called you by name to follow him?

But after meditating on what it would mean for us, we are asked to consider something more important—"how much more worthy" it would be to follow Jesus Christ. This meditation offers a double invitation: to be with Christ and to work for a world of justice, love, and peace.

Now aware of the desire to follow Christ, the retreatant is invited to contemplate the life of Jesus. And Ignatius starts at the beginning of Christ's life—the very beginning—with a meditation that imagines the Holy Trinity gazing down on the earth and deciding to "send" Christ. In one of the loveliest meditations in the Exercises, we are encouraged to see things as God sees them. We are asked to consider all of humanity and "to see the various persons . . . in such variety, in dress as in actions: some white and others black, some at peace and others in war; some weeping and others laughing; some well, others ill; some being born and some dying."

How beautiful it was for me, during my own long retreat, to imagine the Trinity looking on the world in compassion. The meditation not only helped me see the world in a new way, but it also helped me appreciate God's desire to send his Son to this world.

Thus begins the part of the Exercises that appealed most to me: the meditations on the life of Jesus. I was introduced to a type of prayer that goes by many names: "Ignatian contemplation," "contemplative prayer," "composition of place," or simply "imaginative prayer." It is a form of prayer that uses the imagination as a way of encountering God. The method also enables the retreatant to experience the characteristic grace of the Second Week: the desire to know Jesus more fully.

In an Ignatian contemplation we attempt to place ourselves in a particular scene, often from the Gospels. In the story of the Nativity, for example, Ignatius asks us to imagine ourselves with Mary and Joseph on their way to Bethlehem: "to see with the sight of the imagination the road from Nazareth to Bethlehem, considering the length and breadth, and whether the road is level or through valleys and hills; likewise looking at the place or the cave of the Nativity, how large, how small, how low, how high, and how it was prepared."

As we journey with Mary and Joseph, we might ask other questions, beyond those suggested by Ignatius. What do Mary and Joseph look like? What clothes are they wearing? We use the other senses imaginatively as well. What do I hear? (Crunching gravel under the donkey's feet . . . a bird crying in the distance.) What do I smell? (The food we have brought . . . the fresh wind off the grassy fields.)

It may also help to envision being a particular person. Perhaps you are a friend of Joseph, come along to help the couple. In that case, you might think about what you feel. Is your clothing rough or soft? Do you feel the warmth of the sun? Are you fatigued? Through these small details you recreate a Gospel passage in order to more completely enter into it.

As a novice, I had problems with Ignatian contemplation. At the beginning of the long retreat, my spiritual director, named David, gave me a brief introduction to contemplative prayer—using your imagination, placing yourself in the scene, and so on.

It sounded like just about the dumbest thing I had ever heard.

"Let me get this straight," I said. "You want me to make up a picture of the Gospel story in my head?"

David nodded.

"That's ridiculous," I said.

"What's ridiculous?"

"Isn't it all just in my head?" I asked. "Won't I just make the people in my fantasy do what I want them to do?"

"Not necessarily," he said.

I sat there, confused.

"Let me ask you something," David said. "Do you believe that God gave you your imagination?"

"Sure," I said.

"Don't you think that God could use your imagination to draw you closer to him in prayer?"

I had to admit that made sense. God communicates with us through every other part of our lives, so why not through our imagination? David's gentle questioning freed me from my doubts and allowed me to enjoy a new kind of prayer.

When I set aside my suspicions the results amazed me. Sometimes the prayer was difficult or dry, but many times I felt as if I actually *was* in the story. I was right there with the apostles or in the crowds, seeing a miracle, hearing Jesus preach, witnessing the Crucifixion. And I was astonished at the emotions evoked and the insights received. Until entering the Jesuits and experiencing this form of prayer, I doubted that God would ever, or could ever, communicate with me in such an intimate way. Today this type of meditation is the primary way I encounter God in prayer.

One example: during a recent eight-day retreat I was asked to pray over that same passage, the journey of Mary and Joseph to Bethlehem. The previous few months had been difficult ones, focusing on the challenge of chastity in my Jesuit life. I was beginning to think that chastity was sort of a "second-best" kind of life, with its own rewards, to be sure, but not as satisfying as married life.

The first few times I prayed over the passage were largely fruitless. Gradually, though, I was able to imagine myself as a friend of the family. As Mary and Joseph readied themselves for the arduous trip, I decided to help as much as I could. So I went into Nazareth to buy some food for the journey—a few loaves of flat bread, which I bound up in a clean cloth. At the well in the town square, I used an animal skin to collect fresh water. From a vendor I bought a few dates, which I stuffed in my pocket. It felt good to be doing something for the couple—something simple and useful.

When I returned to their house, I found that they were nearly ready to go. Mary was hugely pregnant; I saw how difficult it was for her to move. I realized that she couldn't do everything herself and needed help from Joseph and me.

Once outside, Joseph packed the supplies on his little donkey and helped Mary up. In the meantime I realized I had forgotten a flint for the fire, and I rushed inside to retrieve it. Outside again I watered the donkey, and we were off. Then I heard Joseph say to me, "You're a big help."

It dawned on me that though I was not a member of their family, I enjoyed helping them, walking alongside them. I was part of their life. And I thought of all the people who had invited me into their lives. As a celibate priest, I am welcomed into people's lives not just in baptisms, marriages, and funerals, but also in the most intimate of ways—in hearing their struggles, celebrating their successes, breaking bread with them, seeing their children grow up. As I prayed, I was filled with an overpowering feeling of gratitude for my chastity and my way of life. For the first time as a Jesuit, I no longer saw it as second-best at all. The celibate life is different, but it's a wonderful way for me to live.

All this from a meditation on a simple passage from Scripture.

During the Third Week, after retreatants have meditated on the ministry of Jesus, Ignatius invites us into each painful stage of the passion and death of Jesus—from the Last Supper to his burial. The grace that one requests during the Third Week is to have compassion for and to suffer with Jesus. And as we place ourselves in these scenes, we begin to see Christ's suffering as a sign of his love, as well as the inevitability of hardships for those who follow Christ.

At this stage, retreatants are often drawn to meditate on Christ's self-sacrificing love for humanity and to recall times of suffering in their own lives. Often they also find themselves invited to "die to" different parts of themselves that prevent them from following Christ more fully.

Seeking this grace means moving toward an important kind of indifference—the freedom to set aside aspects of your life that prevent you from following Christ: the freedom of "dying to self." For me, this has often centered on pride: my desire to be popular, admired, and even desired. Those feelings, while not bad in themselves, can often prevent us from following Jesus wholeheartedly. It's easy to see how an overriding concern for "popularity," for example, would be an obstacle to preaching the gospel in situations where doing so would challenge the status quo. Jesus was frequently "unpopular," and so was his message. Following Jesus may mean accepting the ridicule, the contempt, and sometimes the persecution that comes with preaching his message.

The Spiritual Exercises, then, invite us to cross the threshold of self-interest and become united with Christ in his mission—even to the point of accepting hardships and personal suffering. Experience with the Exercises was one thing that enabled dozens of Jesuit martyrs—from St. Edmund Campion (England, 1581) to St. Paul Miki (Japan, 1597) to St. Isaac Jogues (Canada, 1646) to Blessed Miguel

Pro (Mexico, 1927) to the six Jesuits martyred in El Salvador in 1989—to understand the call to follow Christ in this radical way.

When I finally reached the last stage of the Spiritual Exercises, I was surprised to discover that the Fourth Week was relatively short. Ignatius recommends only one meditation on the Resurrection. And the grace that one asks for is easy to request: "to rejoice and be glad intensely."

Once again in the Exercises, this grace usually leads to a desire to respond. After spending thirty days meditating on God's love, being with Jesus in his ministry, witnessing the Passion, and experiencing the Resurrection, one wants to respond. By now the retreatant recognizes God's loving action everywhere. So the Exercises draw to a close with a meditation on how God's love works in our life and, finally, a prayer offering ourselves to God, positioning us to live out the fruits of the retreat.

❊

St. Ignatius of Loyola intended the Exercises not simply for Jesuits, but for all Christians—no matter what their state of life. For Ignatius believed that God desires to be in relationship with every person. Out of this belief flowed his broad-minded and life-affirming spirituality.

Theologians often describe Ignatian spirituality as "incarnational." In other words, while it recognizes the transcendence of God, it is also grounded in the real-life experiences of people living out their daily lives.

It is a spirituality that reminds us that God speaks to us through prayer—but also through our emotions, our minds, and our bodies. God can communicate through sexual intimacy, romantic love, and friendship. God can be found in Scripture and in the sacraments. God can show his love through your sister, your coworker, your spouse, your next-door neighbor, a teacher, a priest, a stranger, or a homeless person. Finding God in all things. And all people.

The path of St. Ignatius means searching for signs of God's presence in the stuff of the everyday. And it means committing yourself to regular prayer in order to contemplate these signs. For without the discipline of prayer we tend to overlook and forget those moments of God's presence. We are to balance, therefore, a life of activity and of prayer. The goal of Ignatian spirituality can be summed up in another succinct expression: desiring to become a "contemplative in action," a person who maintains a contemplative stance in an active life.

It was this spirituality—both practical and mystical, earthy and otherworldly—that, during the first year of my novitiate, drew me close to God for the first time in my life. And it all made sense! Ignatian spirituality helped me meet God in new ways, opened my mind to new ways of prayer, fostered trust in God's presence, and liberated me from the alienation I had experienced for so many years. For the first time ever I felt and believed that God was close to me.

But when I pray to St. Ignatius of Loyola, I don't feel the same affection that I do for, say, Thérèse of Lisieux or Thomas Merton. I don't linger over passages from the letters and journals of Ignatius the way I might reread *The Seven Storey Mountain* or *The Story of a Soul*. And I admit that, like that elderly Jesuit from Boston College who feared his encounter with Ignatius in heaven, I haven't felt as close as I would like to the founder of the Society of Jesus.

§◊§

Not long ago, however, I made a very short pilgrimage to Loyola, the birthplace of Ignatius, with a Jesuit friend, which helped me to see Ignatius anew. And along the way, I received a sort of spiritual gift.

I had been invited on a week-long trip to Lourdes with a Jesuit friend named George, who I had known since the novitiate. We were to serve as chaplains on a pilgrimage organized by the Order of Malta, an international Catholic group that sponsors an annual trip for the sick and their companions (and their chaplains) to the famous shrine in southern France where the Virgin Mary is said to have appeared to a young girl in 1858. This would be our second trip with the group.

Since we had one free day and had already seen much of Lourdes during our first trip, George and I decided to see if we could visit Loyola, located just across the Spanish border. So after a few days of celebrating Masses, walking in Eucharistic processions, visiting the baths with sick and ailing pilgrims, and hearing dozens of confessions, we rented a car for our pilgrimage within a pilgrimage. Secretly I wondered whether we would get lost. Plus I wondered if we would be able to procure any "Loyola water," which supposedly helps women get pregnant, and which had been requested by some of our fellow pilgrims.

Our pilgrimage took us along the coast of Southern France, past Biarritz, the fabled resort where I imagined the moneyed gentry still living in Cole Porter-like style. Surprisingly, George and I arrived in Loyola in just three hours, and here is where it began to seem almost comically easy to see God's hand in our little journey.

When we walked into the ornate basilica in the center of town, we discovered that a Mass in Basque (St. Ignatius's mother tongue) was to begin in just a few minutes. After the Mass (which George said might as well have been in Navajo, for all we understood) we toured Loyola Castle, located within the basilica complex.

On the lowest floor there was a small diorama that showed small plaster statues, no more than a foot high, enacting scenes from the life of Ignatius. One little scene, frozen behind the dust-covered glass, was surprisingly moving: a depiction of a youthful Ignatius taking leave of his family at Loyola Castle, in order to begin his new life. Rarely did I think of Ignatius as a young man, but suddenly, thanks to these tiny, cheesy, dusty sculptures, I began to get a glimmer of what it must have meant for him to give up everything for God.

On the uppermost floor, we stumbled on a room enclosed by a glass partition. I asked a tour guide about the room. "Eso es la capilla de la conversión," he said blandly. This is the chapel of the conversion.

I was stunned: this was the room in which Ignatius experienced his first conversion while recuperating from his injuries. I had no idea that anyone would know exactly which room it had been, but there it was. On the far side of the room was a polychromed statue of the saint lying on his sick bed, clutching a book and looking heavenward, caught in the moment of his decision to change his life. Above his room, painted in gold on a wooden beam, were the words: *Aquí Se Entrego à Dios Iñigo de Loyola*. Here Iñigo of Loyola surrendered him-self to God.

In that glassed-in room a priest was about to celebrate Mass before an ornate wooden altar. Sadly, I said to George, "Well, I guess we won't be able to go inside." But, as if overhearing us, the priest smiled and waved us in. A Frenchman, he invited us to join a group of French pilgrims just beginning their pilgrimage to Santiago de Compostela in Spain. He was overjoyed when he discovered that we were Jesuits, and told his group how providential this was. We celebrated Mass with the group and even proclaimed the readings in our high-school French. Afterward the priest asked us what we did back home. I'm a writer, I said, and George is a prison chaplain.

He put his arms around us and smiled broadly. Then he said to the other pilgrims in French, "These two vocations began in this room."

Okay God, I thought, I guess I'm seeing you pretty clearly now.

Immediately afterward, in the gift shop, George and I met a cheerful Jesuit brother, who, as it happened, knew someone in my community back home in the States. He invited us to lunch in the Jesuit residence, just about to begin, ushering us through the vast corridors and into a colossal granite-walled refectory. Using what Spanish we remembered from summer classes as novices, we asked about the history of the complex of buildings at Loyola and the work of the Jesuits in the community. The meal was all the more delightful as I was down to my very last euro.

Afterward, one of our lunchtime partners, a kind elderly Jesuit, gave us an extensive tour of their main ministry, which was, appropriately enough, a colossal retreat house located on immaculately kept grounds, called the *Centro de Espiritualidad*. Each of the five floors boasted its own chapel, each appealing to a different style of prayer: one ornate, one spare, and so on. One even looked very Zen, though I knew neither the Spanish nor the French for that word. We left the retreat house with just enough time to return to Lourdes.

The absolute ease with which all these things happened, and just at the right time, made it easy to experience God throughout the entire trip. On the other hand, we failed miserably in our attempt to get Loyola water. (The sacristan shrugged when we asked whether they had it in the house.) But no matter. George filled a bottle of water from a fountain outside the basilica and said triumphantly, "Loyola water!" We returned to Lourdes just in time for dinner with our friends. When I described how perfectly our trip to Loyola had gone, one of the young women on our trip said, "Like a confirmation of your Jesuit vocation!"

Sometimes God is not merely quietly present but almost shouts his presence at you.

But none of these insights, and none of this attentiveness to God's presence in my life, would ever have been possible had I not been exposed to Ignatian spirituality, a spirituality that encourages actively looking for God in one's life. And all of this of course was thanks to Ignatius of Loyola.

So even though I may not feel especially close to Ignatius, what I do feel is gratitude—a deep and lasting gratitude for one of the greatest gifts I've ever received: the gift of a spirituality that enables me to see God in all things.

6

More Than Ever

Pedro Arrupe

> I am quite happy to be called an optimist, but my
> optimism is not of the utopian variety. It is based on
> hope. What is an optimist? I can answer for myself in a
> very simple fashion: He or she is a person who has the
> conviction that God knows, can do, and will do what is
> best for mankind.
> —PEDRO ARRUPE, SJ, ONE JESUIT'S
> SPIRITUAL JOURNEY

The first time I called the Jesuit novitiate in Boston, one of the novices picked up the phone. "Arrupe House!" he said brightly.

"Oh . . . sorry," I said, somewhat confused. "I guess I have the wrong number. I wanted the, um, Jesuit novitiate?"

"Yeah," he said, and I could almost hear him rolling his eyes. "That's us. Arrupe House."

Before entering the Society of Jesus, I hadn't a clue as to who (or what) Arrupe was. Paradoxically, now that I've been a Jesuit for some time, it continually surprises me that the name of Pedro Arrupe, superior general of the Jesuits between 1965 and 1983, isn't more widely known.

It's not that I believe that someone should be well known simply by virtue of having been superior of the Jesuit Order. Rather, Pedro Arrupe's life, character, and example are so compelling, and so relevant to contemporary believers, that I am always surprised that more people aren't familiar with his story.

Pedro Arrupe's life can, I think, be seen as a microcosm of the life of the twentieth-century church. He was born in Bilbao, in the Basque Country of Spain, in 1907, to a devout Catholic family. After completing his secondary studies, Arrupe began his medical training first in Valladolid, Spain, and later at the University of Madrid Medical School. But after a visit to Lourdes, where he witnessed a spontaneous healing (a polio-stricken boy was able to walk after seeing a procession of the Blessed Sacrament), his life took a dramatic turn. Thanks to his few years of medical training, Arrupe was permitted to be present at the medical verification of the healing, and he concluded that he had seen a miracle.

"It is impossible to tell you what my feelings and the state of my soul were at that moment," he later said of his experiences at Lourdes. "I had the impression of being near Jesus, and as I felt his all-powerful strength, the world around me began to seem extremely small." After he returned to Madrid he said, "The books kept falling from my hands; those lessons; those experiments about which I was so excited before seemed then so empty. . . . I was dazed with the memory which upset me more every day: only the image of the Sacred Host raised in blessing and the paralyzed boy jumping up from his chair remained fixed in my memory and heart."

Shortly afterward, Pedro Arrupe, age nineteen, gave up his medical career to enter the Jesuit novitiate in Loyola, Spain—the hometown of St. Ignatius, the founder of the Society of Jesus. His medical school professors were horrified.

In 1932, along with all the other Jesuits in Spain, Arrupe was expelled from the country by the Spanish Republic and was forced to complete his studies abroad. After studying in Belgium, Holland, and the United States, he was ordained in 1936. Two years later he was sent by his Jesuit superiors to work in Japan as a parish priest in Yamaguchi.

The young priest immediately immersed himself in Japanese culture in order to better understand the country in which he was living. Arrupe studied the Japanese language as well as its customs—the tea ceremony, flower arranging, calligraphy. He also adopted the Japanese style of praying—sitting cross-legged on a simple mat—which he employed for the rest of his life. (During his time as superior general in Rome, his unusual position at prayer would surprise a few traditionally minded Jesuits.)

While in Yamaguchi, he was suspected (falsely) of espionage for "Western powers" and was arrested and thrown into solitary confinement for thirty-five days. Arrupe endured the December cold with nothing but a sleeping mat in his cell. He later said of this period: "Many were the things I learned during this time: the science of silence, of solitude, of severe and austere poverty, of inner dialogue with the 'guest of my soul.' I believe this was the most instructive month of my entire life."

In 1942, Fr. Arrupe was appointed novice director for the Japanese Jesuits and took up residence at the novitiate outside the town of Hiroshima. When the atomic bomb was dropped on the city on August 6, 1945, Arrupe and his novices cared for the sick and wounded, converting the novitiate into a makeshift hospital. Using his medical training, he performed simple surgery on scores of victims. Arrupe spent the next thirteen years in Japan and in 1959 was appointed superior of the Jesuits' Japanese Province.

Six years later he was elected superior general of the Society of Jesus, during the latter part of the Second Vatican Council and at the beginning of a period of volcanic change in the Church. The Spanish director of novices in Japan seemed to be the perfect man for the times: a person with international vision and experience, a priest who had lived and worked in both the East and the West, and a Jesuit who understood that the Church's center of gravity was moving inexorably away from Europe and to Asia and Africa. Overall, Arrupe understood the meaning of the word *inculturation* long before it became popular.

Heeding the call of the council for religious orders to rediscover their roots, the new "Father General," as he is traditionally called, encouraged his brother Jesuits to adjust the Spiritual Exercises for the current world, to redouble their work with the poor and marginalized, and to promote the "faith that does justice," in accord with the wishes of the Jesuit General Congregation, the order's ultimate governing body. This emphasis on justice as an essential component of the gospel was what Arrupe would become most known for. Long before the martyrdom of many Jesuits who worked with the poor (among them the six priests killed in El Salvador in 1989), Arrupe instinctively grasped the importance of such a project, as well as the risks involved in facing down the forces that oppress the poor. To one of the congregations of Jesuits discussing the matter, he said, in essence, If we choose this path, some will pay with their lives.

"Is our General Congregation," he asked, "ready to take up this responsibility and to carry it out to its ultimate consequence? Is it ready to enter upon the more severe way of the cross? If we are not ready for this, what other use would these discussions have, except perhaps merely an academic one?"

Fr. Arrupe's term as superior general was remarkably fruitful. "Don Pedro," as he was affectionately known, visited Jesuit scholastics, brothers, and priests in high schools and parishes, in the slums and the countryside, in universities and retreat houses, and in their novitiates and infirmaries. Arrupe traveled to every corner of the globe and was invited to address major gatherings of church leaders, social leaders, and lay leaders. His writings and speeches focused not only on the promotion of justice and work with the poor but also on such varied topics as the renewal of religious life, ecumenism, inculturation, secularism and unbelief, evangelization and catechesis, the intellectual life, and the Church's need to reach out to youth.

This is my favorite passage from a book of interviews with Pedro Arrupe called *One Jesuit's Spiritual Journey: Autobiographical Conversations with Jean-Claude Dietsch, SJ*. Here Arrupe tells of visiting his brother Jesuits who were working in a desperately poor slum in Latin America. During his visit he celebrated Mass for the local people in a small, decrepit building; cats and dogs wandered in and out during the Mass. Afterward, Fr. Arrupe was invited to the house of one of the members of the congregation and received an unexpected gift:

When it was over, a big devil whose hang-dog look made me almost afraid said, "Come to my place. I have something to give you." I was undecided; I didn't know whether to accept or not, but the priest who was with me said, "Accept, Father, they are good people." I went to his place; his house was a hovel nearly on the point of collapsing. He had me sit down on a rickety old chair. From there I could see the sunset. The big man said to me, "Look, sir, how beautiful it is!" We sat in silence for several minutes. The sun disappeared. The man then said, "I didn't know how to thank you for all you have done for us. I have nothing to give you, but I thought you would like to see this sunset. You liked it, didn't you? Good evening." And then he shook my hand.

As I walked away I thought, "I have seldom met such a kindhearted person." I was strolling along that lane when a

> poorly dressed woman came up to me; she kissed my hand, looked at me, and with a voice filled with emotion said, "Father, pray for me and my children. I was at that beautiful Mass you celebrated. I must hurry home. But I have nothing to give my children. Pray to the Lord for me; he's the one who must help us." And she disappeared running in the direction of her home.
>
> Many indeed are the things I learned thanks to that Mass among the poor. What a contrast with the great gatherings of the powerful of this world.

One of his most important initiatives on behalf of the poor was the founding, in 1980, of the Jesuit Refugee Service, which he began in response to the worldwide refugee crisis. Four years after I entered the Jesuits, I began working with the Jesuit Refugee Service in East Africa, and I heard the simple logic that prompted Arrupe to found the group: There are Jesuits everywhere in the world, and there are refugees everywhere in the world. Why not bring the two groups together?

During his time as superior general, Arrupe came to exemplify the Jesuit ideal of the "contemplative in action." Vincent O'Keefe, an American Jesuit who was one of Arrupe's chief assistants in Rome, later remarked: "At home or on the road visiting his brothers, Fr. Arrupe radiated a deep inner serenity that enabled him to move from situation to situation, from crisis to crisis, and from language to language." The contemplative. At the same time, noted Fr. O'Keefe, "it was easy to tell when Don Pedro was in residence in Rome, for then the Jesuit headquarters was bustling with visitors from all over the world, while the staff did its best to contend with the drafting of letters and speeches." The contemplative in action.

Even among other religious orders, Arrupe was seen as an inspired and inspiring leader. As a result, he was elected to five consecutive three-year terms as the president of the Union of Superiors General. Arrupe was increasingly seen as a leader within the universal church as well. He attended all the international synods of bishops from 1967 to 1980 and spoke at each one on behalf of both men and women religious orders. Among many he was seen as the "second founder" of the Society of Jesus. Indeed, Arrupe's appearance—slight build, hawklike nose, intelligent eyes, bald pate—prompted many comments about his uncanny resemblance to his fellow Basque, St. Ignatius of Loyola.

It is difficult to communicate how admired Fr. Arrupe was by so many Jesuits, particularly in the United States and especially among younger Jesuits, for whom his commitment to social justice was so important and inspiring. One obvious sign of that affection is the number of Arrupe Houses in the United States. Both my novitiate and my philosophy community were so named, causing no end of confusion to my non-Jesuit friends. "Is every Jesuit community called Arrupe House?" asked a friend after he received a note on house stationery.

Don Pedro was by all accounts highly intelligent, consistently warm, and typically witty. A friend who worked closely with him told me the story of two American novices passing through Rome on their way to India, in order to work with the poor there.

"They're going all the way to India?" asked Arrupe. "It certainly costs a lot of money to teach our men about the poor!"

As comfortable as he was with his brother Jesuits, he was equally at home with laypersons, no matter what their background. The Vatican historian Peter Hebblethwaite, himself a former Jesuit, told of running into Arrupe in Rome when Arrupe's car had been involved in a minor accident. At the time, Hebblethwaite's wife, Margaret, was meeting a certain Jesuit for spiritual direction. Hebblethwaite described the scene in an article for *America* magazine:

His driver was expostulating with the other driver. We stopped. "This is my wife, Margaret," I said. His eyes lit up: "Margaret," he said, "you are doing a retreat with Father Herbie Alfonso?" She was. So the wife of an ex-Jesuit discussed the Spiritual Exercises with the Father General, while I twiddled my thumbs. I suspect it was a unique moment in Jesuit history.

But Pedro Arrupe was not popular everywhere. Because his efforts on behalf of social justice seemed to carry the whiff of socialism or, worse, communism, Arrupe earned the displeasure of some in the Vatican. Within some Roman circles (and even some Jesuit circles), he was thought naive, not so much charismatic as impractical, and even dangerous. This misunderstanding greatly pained Arrupe. As Vatican officials complained, as denunciations from segments of the Catholic press rolled in, and as bishops cornered him at various meetings to bitterly bemoan "socialist" Jesuits in their dioceses, Don Pedro would typically defend his men loyally. (At the same time, he used to say to those Jesuits in question, "Please make it easier to defend you!")

But in case any Jesuits misunderstood Arrupe's stance toward the Church, he pointedly mailed a photo of himself to Jesuit communities around the world showing him in his black cassock kneeling at the feet of Pope John Paul II. The caption, taken from one of the founding documents of the Society of Jesus, reads *Soli Domino ac Ecclesiae Ipsius sponsae, sub Romano Pontifice, Christi in terris Vicario servire* ("To serve the Lord alone and the Church, his spouse, under the Roman Pontiff, the vicar of Christ on earth").

In 1981, at age seventy-four, Arrupe suffered an incapacitating stroke. Unable to continue as superior general, he turned over the governance of the society to Vincent O'Keefe, charging him with guiding the order until a General Congregation could be called to elect a successor. But in a move widely seen as a critique of Arrupe's leadership and a stinging personal rebuke, Pope John Paul II replaced Fr. O'Keefe with his own "delegate," another Jesuit, who would lead the Society until the election of the next superior. It was a crushing blow for the ailing Arrupe. In his book *Pedro Arrupe: Essential Writings*, Kevin Burke, SJ, writes, "Overcome with grief when he learned of this extraordinary intervention into the governance of the Society, Arrupe burst into tears. He was embarking on the most difficult decade in his life, a decade of forced inactivity and silence, a season of profound spiritual poverty and surrender."

In response to this move by the Vatican, Arrupe, ever faithful, instructed Jesuits around the world to accept John Paul's decision with loyalty, as he himself had. It was a move that astonished many of his detractors, who thought him essentially disobedient, and won him the favor of the Vatican. In the end, the Jesuits successfully weathered the ecclesial storm—but also continued their work with the poor.

For the next ten years, Don Pedro lay in a hospital bed, crippled by his stroke—partially paralyzed and increasingly unable to communicate—in the Jesuit headquarters in Rome. Pope John Paul II would visit him a few days before his death in 1991.

❦

In Elizabeth Johnson's book *Friends of God and Prophets*, the theologian outlines two models of relating to the saints. The first, perhaps more well known in Catholic circles, she calls the "patronage model," where the faithful request favors from the saints. Since the saints are closer to God in heaven (and now have no needs themselves), it's natural to ask them for help. Though it is always God to whom we pray, we ask the saint to "intercede" for us, much as we might ask an older brother or sister to approach a parent on our behalf.

But, as Johnson points out, this model did not predominate in the early church. There we find something else: the "companionship model," where the saints are our friends, those who have gone ahead of us and are now cheering us along, brothers and sisters in the community of faith, the great "cloud of witnesses." This is a more egalitarian notion of sanctity and sainthood. St. Paul, for example, speaks of all the Christian faithful as saints.

In my own life, I find both models operative. In general, I relate most often to the saints as companions, as models, and certainly as cheerleaders. But there are many times when I feel the need for help in approaching God, and the saints are fine people to turn to.

Thérèse of Lisieux, for example, is the person I think of when feeling dejected or discouraged. She had a deep understanding of the way grace works through the struggles of everyday life, and her example helps me to more peacefully accept what the day places before me. And when I feel overwhelmed by the day's burdens, I turn to her for her prayers. In my office, I have posted a favorite prayer card of Thérèse, given to me by a friend who visited Lisieux. In her Carmelite habit, Thérèse stares at the camera with her typically frank expression. Underneath the photo is her spidery handwriting: *Je suis venue au Carmel pour sauver les âmes, et surtout afin de prier pour les prêtres* ("I have come to Carmel to save souls, and especially in order to pray for priests"). Thérèse of Lisieux acts as both a model for me and an intercessor.

When I am having difficulties with my vocation—say, when I am trying to accept a difficult decision from a superior—I turn to either Ignatius of Loyola or Thomas Merton. I figure Merton knows a little about difficulties with religious superiors (even the briefest glance at his journals shows that he struggled with his vow of obedience almost daily). And I figure Ignatius knows a little about Jesuit obedience. (Though as one Jesuit remarked, "What does *he* know about it? He was always the boss!") I turn to Aloysius Gonzaga when I'm struggling with chastity. To John XXIII when I am struggling with the Church. And to Dorothy Day when I am finding it hard to live as simply as I should.

And for the record, whenever I lose something, I inevitably fall back on one of the first prayers I was taught in childhood, to St. Anthony of Padua, finder of lost things:

> St. Anthony, St. Anthony,
> please come around.
> Something is lost
> and cannot be found.

Frequently, the speed with which I find the lost object after saying that prayer is close to alarming.

Pedro Arrupe has always been a patron for work with the poor and the underprivileged. Since the novitiate, I have found inspiration in his writings to Jesuits, his speeches about social justice, and his constant encouragement to be a "man for others." In one of my favorite passages from a book entitled *Justice with Faith Today*, Arrupe, speaking on Good Friday in 1977, compares the cry of Jesus from the cross to the cry of the poor today:

> "Whatever you do to the least of my brothers and sisters, the poor and powerless, you do to me." These words are strikingly clear and unmistakable. Jesus identifies himself with the poor. The thirst in the throat of Jesus is a real thirst that cries to heaven as it did then on Calvary. And that cry of Jesus at the point of dying is repeated in thousands of throats that today are clamoring for justice and fair play, when they beg for bread, for

respect for the color of their skin, for a minimal medical assistance, for shelter, for education, for freedom.

So it is to Arrupe that I pray when seeking guidance for ministry among the poor, the marginalized, or the hopeless. I prayed for his help, shortly after his death, when I was working in East Africa with refugees. I prayed for his intercession while working as a prison chaplain in Boston during my theology studies. And I prayed to him during one of the most challenging ministries I've ever undertaken.

※

At the time of the terrorist attacks of September 11, 2001, I was living in New York City and working at *America*, a Jesuit magazine. Two days later, I began ministering to the firefighters, police officers, and rescue workers at the site of the former World Trade Center. Almost immediately I was joined in this work by a number of my brother Jesuits.

In the first few days, gaining entrance to the site was easy: all you needed was a Roman collar. But within a week, as security around the area grew tighter and more organized, it became more difficult to pass through the chain-link barricades erected by the police, the National Guard, and the U.S. Army.

One morning a Jesuit friend and I approached two surly-looking police officers manning one of the checkpoints. Sensing that getting in might prove difficult, we decided to pray for some intercession. Turning to Pedro Arrupe immediately came to mind, not only because we felt he would look out for us as Jesuits, but also because we remembered his experience ministering to the victims of the atomic bomb in Hiroshima. We figured he knew something about the type of ministry we were doing: working with confused and sad men and women following a man-made disaster. So Bob and I stood on a crowded street corner in lower Manhattan as fire engines and police cruisers raced past us, sirens blaring, and asked Fr. Arrupe for his intercession: "Help us get into the site and do God's work."

As we drew nearer to the police officers, their faces softened. Smiling and nodding, they greeted us cheerfully: one, it turned out, had gone to a Jesuit university, Boston College. He asked for a blessing. We had no trouble passing through the barricade.

Each time I approached a barricade with my Jesuit friends, we would pray to Pedro Arrupe. And as I began to work with other young Jesuits at the site, the prayer to Arrupe seemed more and more natural—younger Jesuits in particular consider Fr. Arrupe a hero because of his openness, his sense of humor, his dedication to the poor, and his total commitment to Jesus Christ. And each time we asked his intercession, we were able to pass through another barricade.

One morning, a group of five of us walked to the site, hoping to celebrate Mass with the rescue workers. There were plenty of supplies to lug along: chalices, patens, hosts, wine, a stole. Upon arrival, we stumbled upon an unusually long line of volunteers—steelworkers, doctors, counselors, construction workers, psychologists, engineers, sanitation workers—all standing under a hot September sun, patiently waiting to enter the site. When I inquired about the delay, a sanitation worker said, "The FBI has just declared the place a crime scene. It's gonna be impossible to get in, Father."

After waiting for an hour in the broiling sun, I approached a soldier from the National Guard and explained our desire to celebrate Mass.

He was implacable. Get back in line, he said, and wait your turn.

Glumly I returned to my Jesuit friends. "We can't get in," I said. Bob turned to me and smiled.

"Of course we can't," he laughed. "We forgot to pray to Pedro Arrupe!"

This time I said a short prayer to Fr. Arrupe. A few minutes later I ambled over to another police officer and asked for entrance. I told him we'd been waiting for more than an hour.

"Of course you can come in!" he said. "You just have to know who to ask for help."

⁖

In September of 1983, as the Jesuit General Congregation convened in Rome to elect his successor, Fr. Arrupe, by now unable to speak, provided a personal message to be read to the delegates by another Jesuit. "How I wish I were in a better condition for this meeting with you," it began. "As you can see, I cannot even address you directly."

In the message that marked the end of his eighteen years as superior general, Don Pedro first gave thanks to God and then expressed gratitude to his fellow Jesuits. "Had they not been obedient to this poor Superior General, nothing would have been accomplished." He thanked the Jesuits for their obedience "particularly in these last years." He asked that young Jesuits surrender to the will of God. Of those who were at the peak of their apostolic activity, Arrupe said he hoped they would not "burn themselves out." Rather, he said, they should find a proper balance by centering their lives on God, not on their work. To the old and infirm Jesuits, "of my age," he urged openness.

Finally, with many Jesuits weeping in the hall, Arrupe's message ended with some thoughts and a favorite prayer, taken from the conclusion of *The Spiritual Exercises* of St. Ignatius and made more poignant by what he had experienced as superior general and what he now experienced as a human being:

I am full of hope seeing the Society at the service of Our Lord, and of the Church, under the Roman Pontiff, the vicar of Christ on earth. May she keep going along this path, and may God bless us with many good vocations of priests and brothers: for this I offer to the Lord what is left of my life, my prayers and my sufferings imposed by my ailments.

For myself all I want is to repeat from the depths of my heart: "Take, O Lord, and receive: all my liberty, my memory, my understanding, and my entire will. All I have and all I possess are yours, Lord. You have given it all to me. Now I return it to you. Dispose of it according to your will. Give me only your love and your grace, and I want nothing more."

For me, the story of Pedro Arrupe is the story of a dedicated man whose ultimate cross was not only his physical sufferings but also misunderstanding from the Church he loved so much. Even throughout those difficult times, his hope and his faith in the Church and in God remained. He was, as he said often, "an incorrigible optimist."

❧

Initially, what drew me to Pedro Arrupe was a little prayer card I was given during my philosophy studies, shortly after his death. On its front was a black-and-white photograph of Fr. Arrupe at prayer, in his favorite Japanese style. Wearing a cassock, he sits in the Eastern fashion, feet tucked under him, on a bare floor. His scuffed black shoes lie to his side.

But it was not the image that captivated me but what was printed on the back: a prayer written by Arrupe shortly after he had suffered his stroke, and read out during that same address at the 1983 congregation. It was one of the most moving expressions of surrender I had ever read.

"More than ever," he wrote, "I find myself in the hands of God. This is what I have wanted all my life, from my youth. But now there is a difference; the initiative is entirely with God. It is indeed a profound spiritual experience to know and feel myself so totally in God's hands."

For a long while I wondered: What could enable a person to approach life in this way? He wrote these words during a time of public censure after many years of service, and in the middle of a debilitating illness. What could account for his open and trusting attitude? An answer came when I stumbled across the story of an Italian journalist who interviewed Arrupe in the late 1970s. The journalist asked, "Who is Jesus Christ for you?"

One imagines that the seen-it-all journalist probably expected any one of a host of dull responses. The superior general could be counted on to say something like Jesus Christ is my friend, or Jesus Christ is my brother, or Jesus Christ is my leader.

Don Pedro, however, said this: "For me, Jesus Christ is everything!"

This popular meditation from Pedro Arrupe, which has been printed on note cards, posters, and coffee mugs, has a complicated provenance. Though it has been "attributed" to Arrupe, no one has been able to find it in any of Arrupe's official speeches or letters. Fr. Vincent O'Keefe, SJ, one of Arrupe's closest friends and advisers, once told me that it had most likely been copied down by someone at a talk given by Arrupe and circulated from there. And, said Fr. O'Keefe, it's just the kind of thing Arrupe would say:

Nothing is more practical than finding God, that is, than falling in love in a quite absolute, final way. What you are in love with, what seizes your imagination, will affect everything. It will decide what will get you out of bed in the morning, what you will do with your evenings, how you will spend your weekends, what you read, who you know, what breaks your heart, and what amazes you with joy and gratitude.

Fall in love, stay in love, and it will decide everything.

It was this radical stance, this utter dependence on and trust in Jesus Christ, that enabled Pedro Arrupe to fulfill his vow of obedience even during what for him must have been the most difficult situation imaginable: a public rebuke by the Vatican. And it is here that Arrupe inspires me the most and has become an increasingly important figure to me.

Over the centuries, many loyal and devout Catholics have been misunderstood and treated unjustly by the Church. This is not a controversial statement. Think of Galileo, or, more to the point, Joan of Arc. In the past century, too, a number of committed Catholics have suffered mistreatment at the hands of the church they love. Before the Second Vatican Council, for example, many talented theologians, including such towering figures as the Jesuit John Courtney Murray and the Dominican Yves Congar, were "silenced" by Vatican officials and their own religious orders.

Murray, a theology professor at the Jesuits' Woodstock College, had written extensively on the question of church and state, proposing that constitutionally protected religious freedom, that is, the freedom of individuals to worship as they please, was in accord with Catholic teaching. The Vatican, however, disagreed, and in 1954 Murray's superiors ordered him to cease writing on the topic. But almost ten years later, Fr. Murray was asked by the archbishop of New York, Francis Cardinal Spellman, to accompany him as an official *peritus*, or expert, at the Second Vatican Council. It was there that the previously silenced Murray served as one of the architects for the council's *Declaration on Religious Freedom*, which drew on Murray's earlier, banned work and affirmed religious freedom as a right for all people. Toward the end of the council, John Courtney Murray was invited to celebrate Mass with Pope Paul VI, as a public sign of his official "rehabilitation." Murray died a few years later, in 1967.

Yves Congar's story is similar. The French Dominican priest, whom the *Encyclopedia of Catholicism* calls "perhaps the most influential Catholic theologian of this century prior to Vatican II," wrote extensively on the Church, specifically regarding questions of church authority, tradition, the laity, and relations with other Christian churches. Thanks to his groundbreaking work, Congar was a popular teacher, lecturer, and writer. In 1953, however, his book *True and False Reform in the Church* was abruptly withdrawn from circulation. The next year he, too, was ordered to cease teaching, lecturing, and publishing. Like Murray, however, Congar's work proved foundational to the Second Vatican Council. As a participant in the council, Congar made major contributions to two central documents: the *Dogmatic Constitution on the Church* and the *Decree on Ecumenism*, both of which drew from his earlier, banned writings.

Yves Congar's eventual rehabilitation was even more dramatic than John Courtney Murray's: in 1994, he was named a cardinal by Pope John Paul II.

Before the council, many may have looked at the situations of Murray and Congar and said, "How foolish of them to keep silent!" Others might have said, "How absurd to keep their vow of obedience when they know that their writings would help the church!" Or, more simply, "Why don't they just leave their orders and write what they please?" And over the years many who have been silenced or prevented from doing certain kinds of ministries have left the priesthood or their religious orders or even the Church in order to say what they wanted.

What enabled Murray and Congar and other good servants of the Church, as well as Fr. Arrupe, to accept these decisions was their trust that the Holy Spirit was at work through their vow of obedience, and that through their dedication to their religious vows, God would somehow work, even if these decisions seemed illogical or unfair or even dangerous. (Significantly, one of Congar's final works was entitled *I Believe in the Holy Spirit*.) The stance is similar, I think, to the seriousness with which couples take their marriage vows during rocky periods in their relationship. They trust that even though things are rough at the time or their marriage makes little earthly sense, their vows are a sign of God's fidelity to them, a symbol of the rightness of their commitment, and a reason to trust that God will see them through this period.

Murray and Congar were not the only ones silenced or prevented from carrying out their ministries in the twentieth century. During the latter part of his life, Thomas Merton faced growing fears that he would be prevented by the censors of his Trappist Order from publishing any writings on the cold war. In 1962, the publication of his book *Peace in the Post-Christian Era* was forbidden by his Trappist superiors, who also ordered him to cease writing on issues of war and peace. Merton was furious at the decision, saying that it reflected "an astounding incomprehension of the seriousness of the present crisis in its religious aspect." His book, which contains what are by now widely accepted critiques of war and militarism, was finally published in 2004.

In a moving letter to Jim Forest, a fellow peace activist, Merton explained his decision and his understanding of obedience. His letter is quoted in *Peace in the Post-Christian Era*:

I am where I am. I have freely chosen this state, and have freely chosen to stay in it when the question of possible change arose. If I am a disturbing element, that is all right. I am not making a point of being that, but simply of saying what my conscience dictates and doing so without seeking my own interest. This means accepting such limitations as may be placed on me by authority, and not because I may or may not agree with the ostensible reasons why the limitations are imposed, but out of love of God who is using these things to attain ends which I myself cannot at the moment see or comprehend. I know he can and will in his own time take good care of those who impose limitations unjustly or unwisely. This is his affair and not mine. In this dimension I find no contradiction between love and obedience, and as a matter of fact it is the only sure way of transcending the limits and arbitrariness of ill-advised commands.

Pedro Arrupe, of course, having just suffered a stroke, was not able to write as eloquently about his obedience during his own trial. Nor is it likely that the more mild-mannered Arrupe would have used the same words that Merton did. But though he accepted things with greater equanimity than did Merton, the Vatican's decision still pained Arrupe. One need only recall his tears at the news. Yet Arrupe's short prayer about being in God's hands, like Murray's and Congar's assent to their silencing, and like Merton's remarks about knowing that God was at work in ways that he "cannot at the moment see or comprehend," was a way of expressing his commitment to his vows, his belief that God would ultimately bring about good, and the fact that, for him, Jesus Christ was "everything."

When I entered the Jesuits, I expected that obedience would prove to be the easiest of the vows. Poverty—giving up so much and living with so little—seemed obviously difficult. And I knew chastity would be a great challenge, too; it's difficult to live without sexual intimacy and to experience loneliness so frequently. But obedience didn't trouble me as much. After all, you just have to do what you're told, right? Do the job you're asked to do.

But recently, during the course of writing this book, I was asked by my superiors not to write about certain topics that are still too controversial in the Church. So, wanting to remain faithful to my vow of obedience, and bearing in mind the words of Thomas Merton and the example of Pedro Arrupe, I accepted this decision, though I hope and trust that one day I will be able write about these things more freely.

Or perhaps, in the course of events, I will discover that my conscience moves me to speak more openly or explore other avenues of discourse. The longstanding tradition of the Church, after all, is of the primacy, dignity, and inviolability of the informed conscience. St. Thomas Aquinas famously said that he would rather disobey church teaching than sin against his conscience. More recently, the Second Vatican Council, summing up Catholic teaching on the topic, declared, "In all his activity man is bound to follow his conscience faithfully, in order that he may come to know God. . . . It follows that he is not to be forced to act in a manner contrary to his conscience."

"Conscience," wrote the Council, "is the most secret core and sanctuary of a person. There he is alone with God, whose voice echoes in his depths."

There is a long list of saints and holy persons who have felt duty-bound to speak out about matters concerning the good of their church, even at risk to themselves. Their consciences impelled this. During a time of crisis in the Church in the fourteenth century, St. Catherine of Siena, the renowned mystic, wrote to a group of cardinals in Rome saying, "You are flowers that shed no perfume, but a stench that makes the whole world reek." When asked how she could possibly know so much about Rome from her faraway post, she replied that the stench reached all the way to Siena. In 1374, in a letter to Pope Gregory IX, exiled in France, she instructed him to return to Rome. "Be a man! Father, arise!" she wrote. "I am telling you!"

Catherine could not remain silent.

But for Murray, Congar, and Merton, silence was not only what their vow of obedience demanded, but also what their consciences obliged. For their contemporary Pedro Arrupe, the issue was not so much remaining silent as it was patiently accepting mistreatment in the Church and guiding the rest of the Jesuits, through his example, to respond with charity.

Needless to say, I am no Murray or Congar or Merton or Arrupe. But I know that God will somehow work through all of this. And I trust that both my vow of obedience and the desire to rely on my conscience will, together, prove in some mysterious way to be a source of life for me and for others.

I trust in all this because, as Don Pedro said, "For me Jesus Christ is everything."

7

In the Grotto of Massabieille

Bernadette Soubirous

> Apart from the apparitions, nothing before or after
> singled her out for special notice. There are only traces in
> the stories of her interactions and a few letters indicating
> the strength of her personality and the particularity of her
> spirituality, but in these residues Bernadette begins to
> reveal herself to us.
> —RUTH HARRIS, *LOURDES: BODY AND SPIRIT IN THE
> SECULAR AGE*

One Friday evening during my second year as a novice, I wandered into the TV room to see what video was being served up. Television watching was a popular pastime for novices on a thirty-five-dollar monthly stipend. Our TV room consisted of fifteen individual recliners lined up in front of a large television, an admittedly strange setup that once prompted my brother-in-law to ask if we took a vow against sofas.

"What's on?" I asked the other novices as I walked into the TV room.

"*The Song of Bernadette*," said one, barely glancing up from the TV.

"What's it about?" I asked.

Everyone looked up from his chair, aghast.

"You're kidding, right?" said another novice. "Please tell me you're kidding."

I shook my head dumbly.

One thing I realized after joining the Jesuits was how little Catholic culture I had grown up with, or at least absorbed. While the other novices had grown up in families that went to daily Mass, attended novenas, said grace at meals, and knew the difference between the Immaculate Heart and the Sacred Heart, I was still trying to remember how many sacraments there were.

My ignorance extended not just to weightier theological matters but also to Catholic pop culture. In the space of just a few months I had already been teased for not having seen *Going My Way*, *The Nun's Story*, and *The Trouble with Angels*. I feared that this was another instance of my not knowing a movie that everyone else had seen by age ten.

"Sit down," the novice said. "You can't say that you're Catholic and not have seen this movie."

Based on Franz Werfel's best-selling novel of the same name, *The Song of Bernadette* tells the story of the events that occurred in the small French town of Lourdes in 1858. Starring Jennifer Jones as Bernadette and Charles Bickford as her initially doubtful but eventually supportive pastor, the movie is a perennial Catholic favorite. But *The Song of Bernadette* stints a bit with the actual events, and as moving as the film is, the real story is even more so.

❧❖❧

Bernadette Soubirous, age fourteen, was living with her family in appalling poverty in a small town in southern France. Her father's milling business had recently failed, and, desperate for lodgings, the family had taken up residence in a room that until recently had served as the local jail, called the *cachot*. In this cramped hovel, no more than ten by ten feet square, lived Bernadette's parents and their four children. The first few pages of Franz Werfel's novel capture what must have been the misery of Bernadette's parents, especially her once-proud father: "What annoys him more than this wretched room is the two barred windows, one larger, one smaller, these two abject squinting eyes turned on the filthy yard of the Cachot where the dunghill of the whole neighborhood stinks to heaven."

On February 11, 1858, Bernadette went with her sister, Toinette, and a friend to scrounge some firewood for her mother. The family's poverty prevented her mother from buying wood in the town. Only a few months prior, Bernadette had returned to her family after working as a shepherdess in a nearby town to earn a little money.

The girls' destination was a grotto on the outskirts of Lourdes at a place called Massabieille (the name means "old rock" in the local patois), on the banks of the fast-flowing Gave River. In her superb study of the apparitions Bernadette witnessed and their consequences, *Lourdes: Body and Spirit in the Secular Age*, the Oxford historian Ruth Harris reminds readers of the unappealing state of the now-famous grotto. From as early as the seventeenth century, the town's pigs came to forage at Massabieille and eventually took up residence there. Far from the well-tended and even manicured place that pilgrims encounter today, the original site was "a marginal and even filthy place."

While the two other girls crossed the river to gather wood from the opposite bank, Bernadette, a sickly and asthmatic child, lingered behind. Eventually, she began removing her stockings to wade into the river and join her companions. As she did so, she heard the sound of wind, though she saw nothing moving around her. Bending down to remove her other stocking, she looked up again.

This time, the wind swayed a small rosebush in the niche of the grotto, and a "gentle light" emanated from the spot. Bernadette later reported seeing a young girl in that light, dressed in white, smiling at her. (Later misrepresentations of Bernadette's testimony, including those in *The Song of Bernadette*, depict the vision as a mature woman.)

A frightened Bernadette took a rosary from her pocket and tried to make the sign of the cross. Fear got the better of her, and she found herself unable to do so. But when the young girl made the sign of the cross, Bernadette did the same, and began to pray. "When I finished my rosary," said Bernadette, "she signed for me to approach; but I did not dare. Then she disappeared, just like that."

This was the first of several apparitions that Bernadette would report. As was the case with the rest of the apparitions, no one with her had heard, seen, or experienced anything.

On the way home, Bernadette told her sister what she had seen and swore her to secrecy. But upon entering their house, Toinette burst out with the news to her mother: "Bernadette saw a white girl in the Grotto of Massabieille!" Her parents, furious at their daughter's apparent lies, beat Bernadette and forbade her to return.

A few days later, still confused about what had happened at Massabieille, Bernadette told a priest in the confessional about her vision. Astonished by her composure and the clarity with which she related the story, he asked her permission to speak about this to the local pastor, Abbé Peyramale. According to René Laurentin's exhaustive biography, *Bernadette of Lourdes*, all that the stolid Peyramale had to say was "We must wait and see."

Neighbors and friends tried to convince Bernadette's parents to change their minds about not letting Bernadette return to the grotto. One town notable told her father, sensibly, "A lady with a rosary—that can't be anything bad." Eventually her parents relented, and Bernadette returned, this time with a few other children.

Once more the girl in white appeared. Bernadette asked the vision to "stay if she came from God, to leave if not." Hedging her bets, Bernadette threw holy water in the direction of the apparition, who merely smiled and inclined her head. Bernadette's demeanor during the apparition—she was deathly pale and immobile throughout—so frightened her companions that they raced to a nearby mill for help. Eventually, Bernadette's mother, in obvious distress, ran to the grotto from town. Embarrassed by Bernadette's actions, she had to be restrained from beating her daughter.

By the time of the third apparition, on February 18, many in Lourdes had taken a keen interest in Bernadette's tale. Some pressed her to ask the vision who she was. But when Bernadette came to the vision with paper and pen and asked for a name, the vision merely laughed, and spoke for the first time in the local patois: "Would you have the goodness to come here for fifteen days?"

During Bernadette's next two visits, the vision appeared to her, now accompanied by a growing crowd. After the sixth apparition, on February 21, Bernadette was harshly questioned by the doubtful local police commissioner, who tried to ascertain if she was pulling a childish prank. During the investigation, he tried to get her to say that she was seeing the Virgin Mary, but Bernadette persisted in referring to the vision as *aqueró* ("that"). When pressed to elaborate, she described the vision as wearing "a white robe drawn together with a blue sash, a white veil over her head, and a yellow rose on each foot."

The actual police transcripts reveal the honesty, simplicity, and persistence that would later impress Bernadette's supporters. "Stalwart," Ruth Harris calls her.

When the police commissioner took notes, he slyly changed the record before reading it back to her. "The virgin smiles at me," he said.

"I didn't say *the virgin*," said Bernadette, correcting him.

For me, this is the most compelling aspect of Bernadette Soubirous. She was uninterested in impressing anyone. She avoided saying, until almost the final apparition, that the vision she saw was the Virgin Mary (though others in the town claimed this almost from the beginning). She was, despite her family's poverty, unwilling to profit in any way from her experiences, refusing any and all gifts. In all her testimonies, Bernadette simply told of what she saw and what she didn't see, what she heard and didn't hear. In this way she is reminiscent of Joan of Arc, who said, in essence, This is my experience; believe me if you like.

On February 25, after two intervening apparitions, Bernadette returned to the grotto. The assembled crowd saw Bernadette not in an ecstatic state, as in previous visits, but clawing at the ground in the grotto, drinking some muddy water that she had uncovered, and stuffing her mouth with weeds. Bernadette later explained her actions: "She told me to drink of the spring and wash yourself in it. Not seeing any water, I went to the Gave. But she indicated with her finger that I should go under the rock." The eating of the weeds was an act of penance, said Bernadette, for sinners.

But to onlookers Bernadette was merely scratching at the dirt and eating weeds. They were, predictably, horrified. "She's nuts!" someone shouted. Her aunts, who had accompanied her, gave her a smack as they left the grotto.

In the movie *The Song of Bernadette*, Bernadette's humiliation leads to the film's dramatic high point. After the protagonist and the accompanying crowd leave the grotto, a townsman sits down to rest at the site. As the camera focuses on his hand resting on the dry ground, a few drops, then a trickle, and then a little stream flow past. "Look at it!" he shouts to swelling music. In reality, as René Laurentin describes it in *Bernadette of Lourdes*, a small group of townspeople stayed behind to examine the hole Bernadette had begun. The more they dug, the more pure water gushed forth. But even the movie's account underlines the significance of the day: Bernadette had uncovered the fountain that would become the focus of later pilgrimages.

Again Bernadette was questioned, as annoyed officials redoubled their efforts to frighten her into recanting. Again, she stuck to her story. Two days later, Bernadette returned to the grotto and drank from the spring. On March 1, a local woman whose fall from a tree had permanently crippled her arm went to the spring and plunged her arm in the water. In a few moments her bent fingers straightened and the arm was healed. It would be the first of many miracles attributed to the spring at Lourdes.

Interest over Bernadette's vision continued to mount. By the time of the thirteenth apparition, Bernadette was accompanied by more than fifteen hundred people. After this apparition she raced to Abbé Peyramale to tell him what the vision had said to her: "Go, tell the priests to come here in procession and build a chapel here." As René Laurentin notes, the priest was appalled, imagining the opprobrium that would descend on him if he were to authorize a ridiculous request from a poor young girl. So the practical Peyramale demanded some answers from the vision. Ask her for a name, he ordered Bernadette. And, as an added test, ask her to make the wild rosebush in the grotto flower.

During the next apparition, Bernadette did just that. But the vision merely smiled. No rosebushes bloomed and no names were given. The priest told her again, "If the lady really wishes that a chapel be built, she must tell us her name and make the rosebush bloom."

On March 25, the rosebush was still not in bloom, but a name was given. According to Bernadette, the vision clasped its hands and said, "Que soy era Immaculada Concepciou." I am the Immaculate Conception. Bernadette, whose religious training was rudimentary at best, had no idea what this meant. She kept repeating the phrase over and over, lest she forget it, as she ran to Abbé Peyramale.

The film's depiction of her meeting with her pastor corresponds well to what really happened next. Charles Bickford, as Abbé Peyramale, questions Bernadette severely. "The Immaculate Conception. Do you know what that means?" he demands.

Jennifer Jones, as Bernadette, shakes her head.

The priest explains (in reality he wrote this in a letter to the bishop) that the name is nonsensical. Four years earlier, the doctrine of the Immaculate Conception had been proclaimed by the Vatican, holding that the Virgin Mary had been conceived without original sin. But to say, "I am the Immaculate Conception" was ridiculous, akin to saying not "I am white" but "I am whiteness." But both the Hollywood Bernadette and the real one stuck to the story.

Two more apparitions followed. By the final one, the police had boarded up the front of the grotto to prevent the faithful from gathering. On July 16, on the Feast of Our Lady of Mount Carmel, Bernadette was forced to view the grotto from across the Gave River. But no matter: "I saw neither the boards nor the Gave," she said. "It seemed to me that I was in the Grotto, no more distant than the other times. I saw only the Holy Virgin."

With this final apparition, Bernadette's life changed again. Greatly admired, hounded by the faithful, and even pressed to perform miracles in her hometown (she resisted), Bernadette became the object of fascination for increasing numbers of pilgrims. In 1860, partially to escape her growing fame and partially to receive more of a formal education, she entered a small convent school in Lourdes. But her candor and straightforward attitude remained. In 1861, she was photographed for the first time. Urged by the photographer to adopt the precise pose and expression that she had had during the apparitions, Bernadette protested, "But she isn't here."

Five years later, at age twenty-two, she entered the convent of the Sisters of Charity in Nevers, France, hundreds of miles from Lourdes. Before leaving Lourdes, she paid a last visit to her beloved grotto. "My mission in Lourdes is finished," she said.

Even in the convent, Bernadette was reluctant to discuss her experiences. She told the story of the apparitions only twice to her community, hoping in vain to "hide" herself among her sisters. Her superior, too, asked her to avoid the topic, lest others grow jealous. Always sickly from childhood asthma, Bernadette was unable to assume many of the tasks of the convent and even found it difficult to pray. "Oh dear," she said, "I don't know how to meditate."

Nonetheless, she was a cheerful person, even in the face of illness, always teasing and laughing with her sisters. In the infirmary one day, she took to embroidery, favoring patterns of small hearts. "If someone tells you that I have no heart," she joked, "tell them I make them all day long."

Gradually she weakened from tuberculosis, which she probably contracted while still in Lourdes, and was increasingly confined to her bed. A cancerous tumor was discovered on her leg, and she rapidly declined. On her deathbed, Bernadette returned to her experiences at Massabieille. "I have told the events," she told her sister. "Let people abide by what I said the first time. I may have forgotten and so may others. The simpler one writes, the better it will be." At her death, she was thirty-five years old.

For most of her life, Bernadette patiently endured endless questions about her visions, consistently refused gifts, and occasionally faced jealousy from some of her sisters in the convent. Always an obedient person, she tried to do her best in a difficult situation but grew weary of repeating the same details to both the faithful and the doubtful. When one reads her story, with its details of a poor and hungry childhood, constant demands to answer questions about the apparitions, and even a difficult life in the convent, Bernadette seems at peace only when she is in the grotto. As Ruth Harris writes, "Like the photographs that tried to capture her during the apparitions, Bernadette obeyed, but seemed to leave her heart somewhere else."

Here is Bernadette Soubirous, in her own words, recounting her first vision of *aqueró*, as told in René Laurentin's biography:

> I put my hand in my pocket, and I found my rosary there. I wanted to make the Sign of the Cross. . . . I couldn't raise my hand to my forehead. It collapsed on me. Shock got the better of me. My hand was trembling.
>
> The vision made the Sign of the Cross. Then I tried a second time, and I could. As soon as I made the Sign of the Cross, the fearful shock I felt disappeared. I knelt down and I said my rosary in the presence of the beautiful lady. The vision fingered the beads of her own rosary, but she did not move her lips. When I finished my rosary, she signed for me to approach; but I did not dare. Then she disappeared, just like that.

Ten years after I first saw *The Song of Bernadette*, during my theology studies, one of my professors recommended Ruth Harris's book on Lourdes. Except on her feast day every year, I hadn't thought about St. Bernadette since the novitiate, and I remembered her story vaguely. But upon beginning Harris's book, I was as captivated as when I first saw her tale on television. It filled in the blanks left by the movie and introduced me to what you might call the historical Bernadette.

Then, just a few years ago, I received a phone call from a man in Washington, DC, who had read a book I had written and wanted to meet for lunch. Always happy for a free meal, I agreed to meet him during his next trip to New York. Rob was not only a dedicated Catholic, a good father, and an avid reader, but he was also a knight of Malta. "Do you know much about the Order of Malta?" he asked.

My ignorance of Catholic culture again came to the fore. When I shook my head, Rob gave me a brief précis of the history of the worldwide Catholic charitable organization, which dates back to at least the eleventh century. Technically, the august order is a sovereign state: it enjoys diplomatic relationships with other countries and even is afforded "permanent observer" status at the United Nations, much like the Vatican. Today the international group concentrates not only on fostering the spiritual life of its members, but also on performing a great many charitable works, especially in Catholic hospitals.

"One of our biggest works is an annual trip to Lourdes," said Rob. "We stay for seven days. And it's just an amazing experience. Would you ever think about coming along as a chaplain?"

I told him what a coincidence his offer was: I was right in the middle of rereading Harris's book about Lourdes. But, though flattered, I turned down his kind invitation. Too busy, I said. Rob told me he would keep asking until I agreed.

He did. The following summer he called while I was in Ohio directing a retreat—a time when one naturally feels more open and free—and invited me again in earnest to work as a chaplain on the next trip. And would I like to bring along two other Jesuits to work with me? "Sure," I said. "Sign us up."

Finding Jesuits was easy: two friends, Brian, a priest working at a retreat house, and George, who would be ordained a month after our trip, signed on with alacrity.

As the time approached for our departure, I bought a little spiral-bound notebook to keep as a journal of our pilgrimage to Bernadette's city.

Wednesday, April 28

Members of the Order of Malta have asked us to meet them at Baltimore/Washington International Airport three hours before our 7:00 p.m. charter flight direct to Tarbes-Lourdes-Pyrenees International Airport, a few kilometers from Lourdes. We are greeted by a sea of people, mostly middle-aged or elderly, some wearing silver medals dangling from red ribbons denoting the number of pilgrimages made. Many in the group seem to know one another. Scattered in the crowd are men and women seated in wheelchairs or looking painfully thin. Other couples cradle children obviously suffering from illness or birth defects. These are, as I know from Ruth Harris's book, the *malades*—the sick, the main reason for the journey. Their trips have been paid for by the order—a wonderful act of charity. Everyone, including the *malades*, boards the plane cheerfully.

The flight begins unlike any I've been on, with a bishop leading us in the rosary. The in-flight movie, not surprisingly, is *The Song of Bernadette*.

Thursday, April 29

We land after a long flight and a sleepless one for me. The bus ride from the airport through a rainy countryside studded with tall poplars is full of lively conversation, and we quickly arrive at our lodgings, the Hôtel Saint Sauveur. Seemingly all the hotels and shops at Lourdes boast religious names, and it is startling to see a shop selling tacky souvenirs that is named after Charles de Foucauld, who lived in extreme poverty in the desert, or, worse, a knickknack shop under a sign proclaiming "L'Immaculée Conception." After lunch, our group (there are perhaps 250 of us) processes to Mass in what will become our usual style: the *malades* seated in small hand-pulled carts in front, accompanied by companions, followed by the rest of us.

A letter I received prior to departure said, unexpectedly, "Your cassock can be worn anywhere at anytime. It will be useful for the Mass in the grotto if the weather is cold, and of course during all the processions." Rather than risk giving offense, Brian, George, and I have scrounged up some Jesuit cassocks, and we decide to wear them today. Far from being an embarrassment, as I had expected, the black cassock feels right in Lourdes. As we cross the square in front of the basilica, I notice brown-robed Franciscans, white-robed Dominicans, and even a black-and-white Trappist. While the plain Roman collar makes me feel priestly, the cassock somehow helps me feel very Jesuit. And the cassock is still recognized here. A few days later, a pilgrim greets us with "Ah, les jésuites!"

After Mass in the ornate basilica, someone suggests a visit to the grotto, which I had assumed was far-off. But the church is built directly atop the rocky outcropping, and when I go around the corner and pass huge racks of tall white candles for sale, I am shocked to come upon it. In Bernadette's time Massabieille was where garbage washed ashore from the Gave River. Now, under the massive bulk of the gray church lies the scene familiar from holy cards and reproductions in churches around the world: sinuous gray rocks hover over a plain altar before which stands a huge iron candelabra. In a small niche, where the apparitions occurred, a statue of the Virgin is surrounded by the words spoken to Bernadette on March 25, 1858: "Que soy era Immaculada Concepciou."

The area before the grotto is marked off by signs requesting silence, and as I approach I am drawn to the obvious peace of the place: serenity seems to radiate from Massabieille. Hundreds of people are gathered before the space: *malades* in their blue carts, a Polish priest with a group of pilgrims praying the rosary, a young backpacker in jeans kneeling on the ground. Many stand in line to walk through the grotto. Joining them, I run my hand over the smooth damp rock and am astonished to spy the spring uncovered by Bernadette. I am filled with wonder at being here.

As I pass beneath the Virgin's statue, I notice a host of tiny flowering plants of marvelous variety under her feet, and I think of medieval tapestries.

After dinner, feeling dog-tired, I wander back over to the grotto. Purchasing two candles, I pray for my family and place the candles among an array of them huddled under a metal shed whose wall is engraved with the legend "This flame continues my prayer." Standing before the grotto, I take a card from my pocket. It lists the many people who have asked me to pray for them, and I remember their intentions.

Nearby, I notice a large group congregating in time for the evening rosary procession. Presently, thousands of people light their small candles and begin walking together as an announcer declaims the prayers and mysteries of the rosary in French, English, Spanish, Italian, Polish, and German. Each of us carries a slim taper whose flame is surrounded by a white paper lantern that protects it from the wind. Printed on the lantern are the words to a variety of Marian hymns. We slowly process around the huge oval pavement before the basilica. After the first decade of the rosary, the crowd begins to sing the "Lourdes Hymn." The crowd's song seems to give voice to my own love for Mary, and it moves me to be in the midst of this wonderful assembly.

As the first Ave Maria is sung out over the square, tens of thousands of pilgrims lift their orange-flamed candles in unison, and I am overcome by the sight of this profession of faith: *malades* and the able-bodied, of all ages, from across the globe. It seems a vision of what the world could be.

Late that night I finally climb into bed, after almost thirty-six hours awake. I'm sharing a room with Brian, who I discover is a champion snorer. His bed is a foot away from my own. After an hour of sleeplessness, I pull on my cassock and pad downstairs to the lobby, where I reread a bit of Ruth Harris's book. In another hour, I return to the room, where Brian's snoring has increased in volume.

I lie in bed for a few hours trying to arrive at some spiritual interpretation of the situation. Maybe this is part of a spiritual discipline that God is asking me to accept. I say a rosary. I think of all the sick and disabled with us who put up with much worse. And I recall Ruth Harris's comment that the journey to Lourdes for most pilgrims in the early twentieth century was "harrowing." I say another rosary. Then I decide that I won't do anyone any good as a chaplain if I'm walking around like a zombie.

So, exhausted, I walk downstairs to ask if there are any single rooms available. "Non," says the night clerk with a Gallic shrug. "Pas de chambres, mon père." No rooms.

Hoping for a modicum of rest, I leave the hotel in search of another one. Fortunately, there must be ten hotels on our block. It's about 4:00 a.m., and a fine rain comes down in Lourdes, making the streets slick. Almost comatose now, I spot the Hôtel Moderne across the street and begin walking into the lobby, which, oddly, appears to be open to the night air, and then . . .

Wham!

I walk head-on into a plate-glass door that remained invisible in the darkness. The night clerk rushes to open the door. Disoriented, I blurt out something in French about a room and how much. The desk clerk fixes me with a baleful stare, and I am suddenly able to see myself from his vantage point. Doubtless it looks as if I have returned from a long night of partying on the town. In a cassock! Squinting, he suggests the hotel across the street and swiftly ushers me out the door.

It's almost dawn, so I decide to wait until tomorrow, and I say a prayer to St. Bernadette to find me new lodgings. Rubbing the bump on my forehead, I return to our room, where Brian snores contentedly. At dawn I walk over to another hotel and find an inexpensive room. After thanking Bernadette, I take a long nap.

Friday, April 30

A few hours later, I cross the street to my former hotel for a huge breakfast with George and Brian. On my way over, the night clerk at the Hôtel Moderne spies me through the plate-glass window. He smiles slyly and waggles his finger at me as if to say, "I know all about your revelry last night, Father."

By now, Brian, George, and I have met many members of the order, as well as many of the *malades*. The term is not pejorative here. "We're all *malades* in one way or another," says a bishop on pilgrimage with us. The range of illnesses they live with is stunning: cancer, AIDS, Lyme disease, dementia, birth defects. At lunch, I sit with a couple from Philadelphia. She suffers from a disease I have never heard of, and that has left her, in her late thirties, unable to walk easily and prone to a host of painful physical ailments. She and her husband understand the seriousness of her condition, but they are consistently friendly, happy, and solicitous, and I like them immediately. "Oh, I'm *fine*," she says. "I've been laughing since I got here. So many funny things have happened!" As we process to Mass, Brian and George quietly explain the conditions faced by other *malades* they have met.

Lourdes, of course, is famous for its healing waters, though nothing in the visions of Bernadette suggests that the waters can heal. The short guide we receive from the Order of Malta counsels against expecting physical healings. As we would discover, spiritual healing is the more common result for pilgrims. But I pray for actual physical healing for the *malades* anyway, especially the ones I know, here and at home.

In the afternoon, our group's destination is the stations of the cross, located on the side of a steep hill. The life-sized figures are painted a lurid gold. The knights and dames of the order assist many of the *malades* along the rocky terrain in a cold drizzle. We are handed a small booklet called "Everyone's Way of the Cross," and I groan inwardly, expecting banal sentiments. But I am wrong. If the writing is simple, the prayers are affective, particularly as I notice a frail man being helped over the slippery ground by his companion. "Lord, I know what you are telling me," says the text for the fourth station. "To watch the pain of those we love is harder than to bear our own."

Tonight's rosary procession is, if possible, as moving as last night's. Somehow, in the midst of this huge crowd, Brian, George, and I are spotted by one of the officials of the Domaine, that is, the sprawling area surrounding the grotto and the basilica. "Vous êtes prêtres?" he asks. "Are you priests?" When I nod, he pulls us through the crowd to the steps of the basilica. There we join other priests who gaze out at the enormous throng, just then raising their voices in the "Lourdes Hymn" in the damp night air. An English priest turns to me and says, "The universal church looks well tonight, doesn't it?"

Saturday, May 1

This morning I await a turn at the baths. On long wooden benches under a stone portico sit the *malades* along with their companions and other pilgrims. Flanking me are two men from our pilgrimage with the Order of Malta. One, a fortyish red-haired man, is strangely quiet: later I learn that he is suffering from a form of dementia brought on by Lyme disease. His caring wife suffers greatly. Carved in the stone wall are Mary's words to Bernadette: "Go drink of the waters and bathe yourself there." Every few minutes an Ave Maria is sung in another language.

After an hour, the three of us are called into a small room surrounded by blue and white striped curtains. Once inside we strip to our undershorts and wait patiently on plastic chairs. From the other side of another curtain I hear the splashing of someone entering the bath, and in a few seconds he emerges with a wide grin. As I wonder if the legend that Lourdes water dries off "miraculously" is true, another curtain parts. A smiling attendant invites me inside.

Inside a small chamber three men stand around a sunken stone bath. My high school French comes in handy and we chat amiably. One volunteer points to a wooden peg, and after I hang up my undershorts, he quickly wraps a cold wet towel around my waist. ("I think they kept it in the freezer for us!" says one of the *malades* at lunch.) Another carefully guides me to the lip of the bath and asks me to pray for the healing I need. When I cross myself, they bow their heads and pray along with me. Two of them gently take my arm and lead me down the steps into the bath, where the water is cold, but no colder than a swimming pool. "Asseyez-vous," one says, and I sit down while they hold my arms. Here, praying in this dimly lit room, in this spring water, held by two kind people, I feel entirely separated from my daily life. And then—*whoosh*—they stand me up and point to a statue of Mary, whose feet I kiss. Then I'm handed a quick drink of water from a pitcher.

As I emerge from the bath, a volunteer asks for a blessing. Wearing only a towel, I bless the men, who kneel on the wet stone floor and cross themselves. "The first time you've blessed someone without your clothes?" asks one, and we all laugh.

After the bath I dress quickly and rush over to the Grotto at Massabieille, where our group is celebrating Mass. And, yes, the water dries from my skin immediately.

At 5:00, Brian and I walk through a light drizzle to a nearby Carmelite monastery. Their plain white chapel, with low wooden benches for pews, is utterly quiet, and a nice break from the crowds. We sit for a few minutes until a bell rings loudly and a dozen nuns silently file in for Vespers. They sit behind a tall iron grate to the left side of the altar, separating them from the rest of the chapel. Seeing their brown and white habits reminds me of Thérèse of Lisieux. Their chanting is beautiful—done in high, clear, girlish voices—and it dawns on me that their songs are probably close to the ones that Thérèse heard each day of her life in the monastery in Lisieux. As the plainchant fills the chapel, I feel near to Thérèse and overwhelmed with a sense of the holiness of her life.

Sunday, May 2

A gargantuan church called the Basilica of St. Pius X was built underground in 1958 near the Grotto of Massabieille, where the apparitions took place. It seats, unbelievably, twenty thousand people. The concrete structure would resemble an enormous oval parking lot were it not for the huge portraits of saints, perhaps ten feet high, that line the walls. One banner portraying Pope John XXIII reads "Bienheureux Jean XXIII." The French word for "blessed" means, literally, "well-happy" and seems a far better one than our own. In the morning our group processes to the underground church for a solemn Mass for the Order of Malta, whose members are gathered in Lourdes for their annual visit.

There are scores of priests in the sacristy, dozens of bishops, and even three cardinals. The entrance procession, with tens of thousands of *malades*, their companions, knights, dames, pilgrims, students, and everybody else, is almost alarmingly joyful. High above the floor, mammoth screens show the verses of the hymn, which, now in English, now in French, now in Italian, now in Spanish, now in German, are taken up by the throng. At communion I am handed a gold ciborium brimming with hosts and am pointed to a young Italian guard who carries a yellow flag. He has a girlfriend in America, he explains, and maybe she could call me if she needs to talk? With his flag aloft, he leads me into a sea of people, who engulf me and reach their hands out for communion as if it's the most important thing in the world.

Later on, as I am walking with a Franciscan friend, a French pilgrim asks me to hear a confession. We sit on a stone bench in the sun, and when we have finished, I look up. A little line has formed, and I call my Franciscan friend over to help. An Italian man sits down next to me. "Italiano?" he says, and I nod. But my Italian is very poor, and after a few minutes I am completely lost. Before giving him absolution, I tell him that while I might not understand everything he is saying, God does.

In the afternoon I wander through the town searching for little gifts for friends at home. Before I left the States I heard many Jesuits lament the tackiness of the shops here, but I'm not bothered by them. Most shoppers, I imagine, are thinking of people at home, and so it's just another way of remembering people while at Lourdes.

Looking at a rack of rosary beads, I see an exact copy of the rosary I bought twenty years ago at Notre Dame in Paris, right after graduation from college. It has a tiny metal disk attached to the chain with a portrait of Mary on one side and the word *Indécrochable* on the other. When I returned from Paris all those years ago, I looked up the word in a French-English dictionary, which defined it as "strong" or "unable to be defiled." And I thought that was a good title to apply to Mary: *Indécrochable*.

The shopkeeper comes over. "Ah oui," says Madame. "C'est indécrochable." Then in English she says, "That means these beads are unbreakable." She gives them a tug. "See how strong they are?"

I laugh and tell her that I thought the word applied to Mary, not to the beads. That it was sort of a theological title, *Imaculée, Indécrochable*.

The shopkeeper laughs heartily and quickly tells her assistant, who smiles indulgently. "No," she says in English. "This is not a theological title. This is a marketing title!"

Monday, May 3

At 6:30 this morning, thirty of us take a bus to the house of Bernadette. On the way over, we pass dozens of souvenir shops, and George leans over to me. "Bernadette was lucky, wasn't she?" he whispers. "On the way back from the grotto she could stop off and buy some nice souvenirs for herself." Two women, *malades*, sitting in front of us overhear this and giggle.

Her tiny house, located on a narrow side street, is still referred to as the *cachot*, since it had been a jail before her destitute family moved in. Astonishingly, it is even smaller than the horrible room depicted in *The Song of Bernadette*. In René Laurentin's biography, he notes that in this dank hovel, two beds served six people.

Before we arrived, a sister arranged the *cachot* for Mass, which will be celebrated by Theodore Cardinal McCarrick, archbishop of Washington, DC, who has joined our group for a few days. Because of the room's size, only the *malades* and their companions can fit, along with the cardinal, another priest, and us, the three Jesuits.

As the Mass begins, thirty people, many of them seriously ill, turn their expectant faces to the cardinal. He puts them at ease instantly, saying that we all feel like sardines, and not to worry about standing up during the Mass, since sardines don't have to stand. Everyone laughs. Yesterday the cardinal led a huge Eucharistic procession near the grotto; it is a marvel to see a priest who can preach both to thousands and to a handful of people. He offers a short, moving homily on the meaning of suffering. God loves us, he says. God wants to be with us in our suffering. And God tries to give us hope in our suffering through the person of Jesus Christ.

I think of the incongruity of it all: we are here because of a poor fourteen-year-old girl.

During the rainy afternoon I spend a few hours in a vaguely Gothic building with a white and blue sign out front that reads "Confessions." In front of the building is a statue of a kneeling St. John Vianney, the nineteenth-century French priest known for his compassion in the confessional (he was said to spend upwards of eighteen hours a day hearing confessions). In a narrow hallway people sit placidly on benches outside doors that announce confessions in English, Spanish, French, Dutch, German, and Italian. There seem to be far more Germans than anyone else.

Every few minutes someone pops into my English cubicle and asks hopefully, "Deutsch?"

Tuesday, May 4

Tomorrow we will return to the States, so I decide to return to the baths today. By now I have gotten to know some of the attendants who help the pilgrims seated under the stone portico. I ask one how he likes his job. "Oh, it's not a job!" he says cheerfully. "I'm a volunteer, like everyone else here! If it were just a job, then I would be thinking, One euro for each person I help. Or maybe, One euro for each kilo he weighs!" He laughs. "But this way I look at everybody like a person, not a number."

He says that many pilgrims are nervous and worried when they come for the first time. "C'est naturel," he says. "People might be sick, or they might be cold, or they might be afraid of slipping inside." But his first experience, he says, was transforming. He struggles to find the words in English and then switches back to French. "I felt as if a door had opened in my heart." He flings his hands away from his chest to demonstrate. "After that nothing was the same."

Inside, I see a gregarious attendant I have met before. With a broad smile he shouts out, "Mon ami!" The other volunteer notices my cassock and says, "You are a Jesuit? Then you know my family." When I look confused, he says, "I am Polish and my name is Kostka." So I am helped into the bath by *mon ami* and a member of the family of St. Stanislaus Kostka, one of my Jesuit heroes.

In the afternoon, brushing my teeth in the hotel bathroom, I think that if Mary were to appear today, it would probably be in a spot as unlikely as a bathroom. After all, the original apparitions occurred at a filthy place where pigs came to forage. A few minutes later, when I enter the lobby, an elderly man from our group asks to speak with me about something that happened to him in the baths this morning.

This rational and sensible Catholic has come to Lourdes after a long illness. (I've changed some of the details here, but not the essentials.) He weeps when he says that after the bath, in the men's bathroom, he heard a woman's voice say in a few words that his sins were forgiven. The bathroom was entirely empty. There are, obviously, no women anywhere near the men's baths at Lourdes.

Then he remembered something. Before coming to Lourdes, he had prayed for this grace: despite a recent confession he still felt the weight of his sins. In response, I tell him that there are many ways that God communicates with us in prayer—through insights, memories, emotions—and that while people rarely report this type of experience, it is not unheard of. Something similar represented a pivotal event in

Mother Teresa's life. He is surprised when I say that I was just thinking that a bathroom wouldn't be such a bad place for a religious experience. And though it's unexpected, it makes sense: a grace received in
a clear and distinct way while on pilgrimage. Besides, I say, your sins
really are forgiven.

"What did the voice sound like?" I ask.

"Oh," he says. "Very peaceful."

That night the Order of Malta hosts a farewell dinner for everyone, full of speeches, songs, a few hastily arranged skits, and some
jokey awards. I win an award for valorous service (in light of my blessing people without the benefit of clothes). The youngest *malades*, children with scoliosis, cancer, and birth defects, sing a little song, hesitant
and off-key, that leaves most of the crowd near tears.

Over dinner, one knight tells me that the boy with scoliosis, one
of the most cheerful children one could hope to meet, said that his
classmates might be sad when he returned to school. "They thought
that I would be tall and that my back would be straight," he explained.
He had visited the baths just that morning, with no apparent physical
change. "But that's okay," he said. "I'll be tall and my back will be
straight in heaven."

The story told by Bernadette Soubirous is difficult for even
devout Catholics to accept. Of course, it's not essential that a Catholic
believe in this story or in the apparitions at Lourdes, as one needs to
believe in, say, the Resurrection. But the beauty of the story, as well as
Bernadette's character, has always made it easy for me to accept. The
Virgin's messages were simple and sensible: penance, prayer, pilgrimage. And somehow, after visiting Lourdes, I have become even more
convinced, thanks to the place and the people.

Bernadette has become for me a symbol of the need to stay true to
your own personal vision. Beginning with the first apparition in 1858
and continuing through the scoldings of her mother, the ridicule of

friends, the questioning by local authorities, the examinations by the Church, and the lingering doubts that persisted until the end of her life, Bernadette stuck to her story. Even in the face of persecution, she simply told what she had seen. She is a powerful model of fidelity, and a witness to the importance of trusting one's experience, no matter what the consequences. Bernadette is, in her own way, a prophetic figure.

I have thought about Bernadette Soubirous many times since first watching *The Song of Bernadette* on television that night in the novitiate. I think of her when people, and there have been very many, ridicule my choice of entering the Jesuits, saying that religious life is dying or that the Church does more harm than good. I remember her when people, and there have been many, express their contempt because they find the Catholic Church loathsome, or because Catholic priests are now routinely labeled as pedophiles and sexual abusers. I think of her when people, and there are some, tell me to my face that only the gullible, the credulous, or the stupid believe in God. In all these situations, I think of Bernadette, with her eyes fixed on the small niche in the grotto, confident in what she sees, and unwavering in what she believes.

Early on my last morning here, I pay a final visit to the grotto. Even before dawn, a Mass is in progress, and pilgrims are already here, kneeling before the space, running their hands over the rock, praying the rosary, and hoping for healing, as they have been since 1858.

The sun rises over the basilica, and the bells chime the first clear notes of the "Lourdes Hymn" as I cross the square.

8

Share This Joy with All You Meet

Mother Teresa

You can do something I can't do. I can do something you can't do. Together let us do something beautiful for God.

—MOTHER TERESA

I was a big fan, and so was envious of the people I knew who had met her. My father, for example, had shaken her hand.

When I was still in college, my dad found himself in an airport terminal in Japan on the return leg of a business trip. Patiently waiting for his flight home, he noticed a commotion: a crowd of people had gathered for what appeared to be a celebrity arrival. Everyone was in high spirits. Working his way through the crowd, my father suddenly found himself face-to-face with Mother Teresa. He reached out his hand and she grabbed it. "Dad met Mother Teresa!" my mother told me that night on the phone. "He said she was very tiny."

When I next saw him I asked which hand she had touched, and he held it out, reverently.

Later on, as a Jesuit, I would meet a surprising number of people who had met and even worked with her. Her home in Calcutta was a magnet for believers and nonbelievers alike, all desiring to meet the woman who was called, even before her canonization in 2016, the "Saint of the Gutters." Those who met her talked about her obvious holiness, her straightforward attitude, and her dry wit. (Her typical response when given a donation from a wealthy benefactor was "Not enough!") She also had a deserved reputation for stubbornness.

A fellow Jesuit told me a story illustrating this last trait. He was a specialist in public health who had gone to Calcutta to volunteer in her home for the sick. Mother, as everyone called her, took special interest in meeting with priests. During my friend's first meeting with her, he took the opportunity to suggest how to improve the sanitary conditions of her hospices. Your sisters should arrange their medicines this way, not that way; they should treat the patients this way, not that way; they should do things this way, not that way.

Mother smiled and said, That's not our way.

My friend persisted. It really is better, he said, to do things my way. After all, I have a PhD in public health. No, said Mother calmly, that is not our way.

Really, said my friend, his anger increasing at her intransigence, it would be much better. No, Mother repeated, that is not our way, Father.

My friend slammed his hand on the table in frustration. "You are so . . . *unreasonable!*"

He laughed at himself as he related the story. "You told a living saint that she was unreasonable?" said one novice. "That's good for at least a few more days in purgatory!"

My one contact with Mother Teresa came years later, during my theology studies in Cambridge, Massachusetts. I had published a short series of articles in *America* magazine entitled "How Can I Find God?" that included responses to that question from people of many faiths. A few months after the articles appeared, a publisher asked if I might be interested in turning the series into a book. If I did, I would have to ask many more people for responses.

I came up with a wish list and mailed letters to religious leaders, public figures, writers, and so on. In time, my Jesuit housemates grew accustomed to seeing envelopes arrive for me from all over the world. ("Why is someone at the White House writing to you?") I was happy that about half of the people I wrote to responded, and I received essays from people I never dreamed would have the time to write: Elie Wiesel, Joseph Cardinal Bernardin, Robert Coles, Mary Higgins Clark, Kathleen Norris.

Even the rejections were interesting. John Updike typed on the back of a plain white postcard, "I think my reaction is that the question was too mighty to answer offhandedly and I don't have time to answer it any other way." William F. Buckley Jr. wrote this from his offices at the *National Review*: "Sorry I can't cooperate, but I am just finishing a book that seeks to answer that question, and I am temperamentally incapable of the kind of condensation you are requesting." Another favorite came from the astronomer Carl Sagan: "The question *How can I find God?* assumes the answer to the key undecided issue."

Even the pope wrote back, or at least his "assessor" did, whoever that was. The response came on heavy cream stationery that bore the letterhead of the Secretariat of State (First Section, General Affairs):

> His Holiness Pope John Paul II has received your letter and has asked me to thank you. He appreciates the sentiments which prompted you to write to him, but I regret that it will not be possible to comply with your request.

Obviously a form letter, but it was fun imagining the pope saying to some monsignor, "Yes, tell that fellow I appreciate the sentiments which prompted him to write to me!"

But my favorite rejection came in a small white envelope with type that had clearly been produced by some ancient machine. The return address was Missionaries of Charity, 54A A. J. C. Bose Road, Calcutta 700016, India. The scholastic, or seminarian, sorting mail that day, a good friend named Tim, called up the stairs.

"Hey, Jim!" he shouted. "Did you write to Mother Teresa?"

I came tearing down the stairs and carefully opened the envelope, pulling out a half sheet of thin white paper. Inside the letter was a small white card. Tim waited as I read the letter aloud. "Dear Brother James," it started.

After telling me that she had received my letter, she wrote:

> God love you for your beautiful effort to lead people nearer to His truth and love. I will certainly keep this project in my prayers, that Jesus may use this book for the glory of God and the good of His people.
>
> I regret to inform you, however, that I will be unable to contribute to the book as you requested.
>
> Keep the joy of loving Jesus in your heart and share this joy with all you meet. Let us pray.
>
> God bless you,
> M Teresa, mc

"Wow," said Tim. "What's the card say?" I handed it over and he read it to me:

The fruit of SILENCE is Prayer

The fruit of PRAYER is Faith

> The fruit of FAITH is Love
> The fruit of LOVE is Service
> The fruit of SERVICE is Peace
> Mother Teresa

I proudly showed the letter to everyone in my community. Another Jesuit said, "That's as good as an essay. You should just print her letter in your book!"

That was as close as I ever got to one of my great heroes. But in a way I felt almost as close to her when I was in the novitiate and spent four months working with the Missionaries of Charity, Mother Teresa's religious order, in Kingston, Jamaica.

During our first year as novices, we were asked to go on a "third world experiment." ("Experiment" is Jesuit lingo for "experience.") Around Christmas my classmate Bill and I were informed that we would be working in Jamaica, where generations of New England Jesuits had served in small parishes and had run two prestigious high schools in Kingston. The Jesuits were such a part of the island's Catholic culture that the then archbishop of Kingston was himself a Jesuit (and a native-born Jamaican).

The impetus behind sending novices to the developing world was multilayered. First, it was an attempt to expose us to the life of the poor overseas and to offer us an opportunity to become more knowledgeable about the struggles of people in the developing world. This was a way of coming to understand the Church's "preferential option for the poor." Second, it was a way of fostering reliance on God in an unfamiliar situation. Third, it would help us gain an understanding of a different country and culture. Finally, it was a way for us to encounter the works of the Society of Jesus worldwide, to expand our horizon of religious life beyond just the American way of proceeding—a chance, as my novice director explained, to be introduced to the "international Society of Jesus."

An elderly Jesuit who had spent many years in "the missions" smiled slyly when I mentioned the last rationale.

"You know," he said, "part of coming to know the international Society is discovering that Jesuits from other countries can be just as much of a pain in the ass as the American ones!"

But I wasn't thinking about any of these things before I left for Jamaica; I was thinking about myself and what might happen to me. I was frightened about working in the third world. And while I now see clearly that the experience in Jamaica was transformative, reading my journals from the time removes some of the rosy glow of memory and reminds me how terrified I was.

This was to be expected. Not only was I a champion worrier, but the novices in the year ahead had also successfully filled my head with horror stories about their time in Kingston, stories that were partially true, partially designed to show how tough they were, and partially intended to freak me out.

One scholastic told of a parish in a neighborhood so violent and so riven by gang warfare that the gunfire at times kept some of the novices huddled for safety on the floor of the rectory. (True.) Another said that the main Jesuit community, located in a notorious Kingston slum (true, but it was relatively safe for the Jesuits), was surrounded by a high wall topped with broken glass (true also) and patrolled by armed guards (there were guards, but they weren't armed). Another confided that since there were no pharmacies in the city (obviously untrue), he brought an entire shopping bag full of pharmacopoeia with him (true, but this said more about him than about the state of Jamaican medicine).

And though the occasional negative stories were outweighed by the positive ones (the Jamaican people were warm, the countryside stunning, the culture fascinating, the Jesuits welcoming), I was still worried. Most of my fears centered on illness. What if I got sick? Could I drink the water? Eat the food? One scholastic told me how he had contracted dengue fever during his novice experiment there. His description of the disease, an extremely painful mosquito-borne illness (from which he eventually recovered), was memorable.

"During the first week you're afraid you're going to die," he said. "During the second week you're afraid that you're not."

The night before my flight, I sat on the couch in the living room, vainly trying to distract myself by reading another biography about St. Ignatius. An elderly Jesuit named Joe strolled in with a cup of coffee and sat down in a rocking chair. Joe, who had held a variety of jobs during his long career, was now a sought-after spiritual director who resided at the novitiate with us. (Jesuits call these wise men who live with the younger ones "spiritual fathers.") I admired Joe greatly. He seemed about the freest man I knew. Few things seemed to trouble him, and, in his late seventies, he had a great zest for life and an open mind. Joe's refrain when asked if he wanted to experience something new—to visit a new church for Sunday Mass, to work in a new ministry, to change the way we did things in the house, even to learn to cook a new dish—was always "Why not?"

"Ready for Jamaica?" he said to me.

Out came all of my fears. My worries about living in the developing world, my concerns over running into violence, and, most of all, my fear of getting sick.

Joe listened patiently. I can still see him sitting across from me, pulling on his gray beard and rocking in his chair.

Finally he said, "Why not just allow yourself to get sick?"

Sometimes it takes just a few words to open your mind. And those were exactly the words I needed to hear. What Joe was telling me was that I needed to allow myself to be human. And sometimes humans get sick and have to deal with it as best they can. That night I recorded his words in my journal—underlining them in red and highlighting them in yellow so that I would be able to locate them easily in Jamaica. After that I wrote: "I really pray for that kind of acceptance of myself. And also for the ability to be myself, not always putting on a brave face before everyone, particularly when I am depressed, worried, confused, etc."

Joe's insight helped me leave for the four months in Kingston with something resembling peace. But that didn't mean a smooth ride.

My fellow novice Bill and I lived with the community at a Jesuit high school in Kingston, St. George's College. As we had been informed, there was indeed a tall stone fence ringing the school grounds, located in the middle of a dangerous area of the city. As we had been warned, our rooms were spartan: a bed, a desk, plain wooden floors, and windows without screens. (The day I arrived, my ceiling was decorated with a very active wasps' nest.) And as we had been told, sleeping at night was a challenge—what with the whine of mosquitoes, the noise from the nearby bars that blared reggae music, the shouting, and the very rare, but nevertheless worrisome, rounds of gunfire.

But there were plenty of good things that I hadn't expected, which balanced things out. There were, for example, many younger Jesuits working in Kingston at the time. Our house included three "regents," younger Jesuits working full-time before their theology studies: two Jamaicans, one American. A newly ordained priest lived with us as well. A few miles away, a young Canadian regent worked in a desperately poor neighborhood at a church called St. Peter Claver, named after the Jesuit called the "slave to the slaves," a Spanish missionary who had worked with native-born slaves in Colombia. Another American regent worked at a small parish near the University of the West Indies, called St. Thomas Aquinas. These Jesuits, just five or six years ahead of me, listened to my worries, gently reassured me, and when my fears were obviously ridiculous, did me the great favor of getting me to laugh at myself.

Before Bill and I left the States, the novice director said that we were free to choose two kinds of ministry, but that one of them had to be with the Missionaries of Charity. So one of the first things that Bill and I did was visit the hospice run by Mother Teresa's sisters.

To reach the hospice we first had to pass, on foot, through one of the poorest slums in the city, which began nearly at the front gate of the Jesuit high school.

This was my first encounter with the living conditions for hundreds of millions of people, with a world that would become more familiar the longer I worked as a Jesuit. Potholed streets wound their way past small concrete houses with rusty tin roofs. Mangy goats roamed around bleating, bony dogs lazed in the gutters, and the biggest pigs I had ever seen rooted around in stinking piles of garbage. Everywhere I looked were busy people: heavyset women selling fruit at stands, young men laughing and smoking (exactly what I didn't know for sure, but because of my extensive experience in college, I could hazard a guess), and skinny children heading for their schools in neat white shirts and blue trousers or skirts. With such cramped living quarters, most of life seemed to take place on the street. That morning we passed a man brushing his teeth in the street. He expectorated loudly as Bill and I passed.

Somehow everybody knew we were "priests," though we wore nothing distinctive (except our white skin). "Good morning, Fada!" they said politely.

The hospice of the Missionaries of Charity was a two-story concrete building painted a bright white and blue. Small letters painted on the wall announced its name and its patron: Our Lady Queen of Peace. As soon as we entered, I was bowled over by the smell, a combination of bleach, urine, excrement, food, milky tea, and disinfectant that instantly and permanently imprinted itself onto my memory.

We were greeted by a smiling Indian-born sister clad in the distinctive blue and white sari of Mother Teresa's order. Seeing the habit had an immediate effect on me. It was like meeting Mother Teresa herself, and I found myself tongue-tied, as if I were in the presence of some special brand of holiness. (Even now, years after entering the Jesuits and a few years after ordination as a priest, there are still habits—Carmelite, Franciscan, Trappist—that stop me in my tracks, reminding me so much of my heroes who wore them.)

The sisters' mission was to care for the poor, sick, and dying in the slums of Kingston. Each morning they set out to find people too sick to care for themselves. Many times they carried the sick back to the hospice, where they were bathed, clothed, and given food and a place to stay, often to die. The men slept in one wing, the women in another. It was a bright, pleasant place, with a spacious courtyard open to the warm Jamaican sun. Following the afternoon rains, the sick sat in the atrium and watched the sisters wash the soiled linens as the yellow lizards sunned themselves and caught roaches and water bugs.

The Missionaries of Charity were always in motion, even in the hottest weather. Up at dawn for Mass, then out to take care of people in the neighborhood, often helping them clean their small houses, then back to the hospice to prepare lunch for the guests, then work, and then more work, and then more work, and then dinner. But despite their punishing schedule the sisters always seemed full of joy. When you asked how they could be so cheerful, they responded with answers that would have seemed corny coming from anyone else. "We care for Christ in his distressing disguise," one of the sisters told me one day, quoting Mother Teresa.

The sisters quoted Mother Teresa frequently. "Mother says . . ." they would say to explain why we did things in a certain fashion. Her standards and guidelines ran the house. Kathryn Spink notes in her excellent biography *Mother Teresa*: "Theologically and temperamentally Mother Teresa was a firm believer in the strict adherence to regulations, in details of discipline, tidiness in housekeeping, in religious dress, uniformity of forms of prayer and devotions. She liked details to be fixed and adhered to." Like religious men and women in communities of old, a Missionary of Charity could move halfway across the world to another community and still feel at home. Mother was an unseen presence, hovering over all that the sisters did, ordering their time and their activities.

Far more influential than her instructions about, say, how to wash linens was her approach to caring for the Poorest of the Poor. (She would always capitalize that reference in her letters, as she would *Jesus* and *God*.) It was a deeply contemplative stance. Her sisters were to be "professionals in prayer" who sought to serve Christ by serving his poor. And they were not simply social workers. "It is the presence of Christ which guides us," she explained. To a man who once saw her cleaning the wounds of a leper and said, "I wouldn't do that for a million dollars," Mother Teresa replied, "Neither would I. But I would gladly do it for Christ."

In a letter to me, Kathryn Spink emphasized "the absolute centrality" of the words of the Gospel of Matthew in Mother Teresa's mission. "She took literally Jesus' words: 'Whatsoever you do to the least of my brothers, you do to me.'" Ms. Spink continued:

> From this arose the conviction that in touching the bodies of the poor, she and her sisters were actually touching

the body of Christ. It is this mystical vision of Christ crying out for love in the broken bodies of the poor and simultaneously offering himself in the Eucharist as food in order that the poor might be fed that is at the root of everything Mother Teresa did and the manner in which she did it.

Working alongside the sisters helped me see that the spirituality of the Missionaries of Charity was not so far removed from that of the Jesuits. It was at once mystical and practical, active and contemplative, earthly and otherworldly. And just as the spirituality of the Jesuits was rooted in the life and times of St. Ignatius of Loyola, the sisters' spirituality was rooted in the example of the woman now called St. Teresa of Calcutta.

⚜

Agnes Gonxha Bojaxhiu was born in Skopje, Albania, in 1910. Both her parents were devout. Her mother, Drana, used to care for an old woman living nearby who was ravaged by alcoholism and covered with sores. Drana washed and cooked for her. Years later, Mother Teresa would say that the woman suffered as much from her crushing loneliness as from her illnesses. Drana also counseled her daughter that charity should be done silently. "When you do good," she said, "do it quietly, as if you were throwing a stone into the sea."

A Jesuit priest's talk at the local parish about the work of Catholic missionaries worldwide struck a chord in Agnes, who had dreamed of a religious vocation as early as age twelve. In October 1928, at the age of eighteen, she entered the novitiate of the Loreto Sisters in Dublin, Ireland. Three months later, Sr. Mary Teresa, as she was now called (choosing a religious name to honor St. Thérèse of Lisieux), set sail for India. She would spend the rest of her life there.

Her early years in India mirrored the lives of the other Loreto sisters: Sr. Teresa taught in a Catholic school run by the order in Calcutta and elsewhere. The mission of the Loreto Sisters focused on tackling the problems of poverty through education. And it was as a teacher that the young sister had her first experience of the living conditions of the local children and their families. "It is not possible to find worse poverty," she wrote. In 1937, she pronounced her perpetual vows of poverty, chastity, and obedience and, as was the custom for Loreto sisters, was now called "Mother Teresa." A few years later, Mother Teresa made a private vow, with the consent of her spiritual director, to give God anything he may ask and not to refuse him anything.

On September 10, 1946, Mother Teresa began a long, dusty train ride to Darjeeling. Over the previous few months, she had grown exhausted from her work at the school and frequently fell ill. So her superiors sent her away for a short retreat and some relaxation. It was on this train ride that Mother Teresa experienced what she described as a "call within a call."

Though she refrained from speaking directly about the experience during her lifetime (believing that it would focus attention more on her and less on God), after her death, when her "cause" for canonization was begun, what happened to her on that train ride was finally discovered.

Her letters to her spiritual director and her local bishop reveal that she had experienced the rarest of graces, what spiritual writers call a "locution." That is, she reported hearing words addressed to her from God. In a long letter to Ferdinand Périer, SJ, the archbishop of Calcutta, she describes the words she heard, ones that would change the course of her life: "Wouldst thou not help?" In her prayer, Christ asked her plainly to leave the convent and begin her work with the poor.

In response, Mother Teresa poured out her doubts and fears in prayer. She was already happy as a Loreto nun—how could she leave? She would be exposing herself to many sufferings and privations. She would be the "laughingstock of so many." She would experience loneliness, ignominy, and uncertainty. But the voice she heard in prayer was nonetheless firm: "Wouldst thou refuse to do this for me?"

For the next several weeks, Mother Teresa enjoyed a deep intimacy with God in her prayer, what St. Ignatius would call "consolation." After speaking with her Jesuit spiritual director, she decided to approach the archbishop to request his permission to depart from the convent and begin this new venture with the poor. With his approval, Mother Teresa wrote to the Mother General of the Loreto Sisters and, later, to Pope Pius XII, for permission to leave her order. In April of 1948 word arrived from Rome that Mother Teresa's request had been granted.

Thus began her life of total service, familiar to believers and nonbelievers alike. But it was hardly an easy beginning. "To leave Loreto," she wrote, "was the most difficult thing I have ever done. It was much more difficult than to leave my family and country and enter religious life. Loreto, my spiritual training, my work there, meant everything to me."

Added to the mental and emotional challenges were more practical ones. Before beginning her service to the poor, she had to undergo medical training with the Medical Mission Sisters. Next she had to search for a place to stay, finding temporary lodgings in a convent of the Little Sisters of the Poor in Calcutta. Once settled, she began teaching in the slums, dressed in a simple sari of blue and white, scratching letters in the mud with a stick before the poor children who squatted beside her.

In a short while, she located a small house in town, where she began attracting the first of her sisters. Many other helpers, doctors, nurses, and laypeople gathered around the new Missionaries of Charity to aid them in their work with the poor. Eventually, she founded Nirmal Hriday, "Place of the Immaculate Heart," housed in a building that had originally served as a pilgrims' rest home for Hindus visiting the Kali temple next door.

Despite her charitable work and her welcoming of people from all faiths, there was noticeable hostility directed toward this foreign Christian woman and her companions, who appeared to be pushing their way into Hindu territory. People threw stones at them and threatened them, and one man tried to kill Mother Teresa. But their hostility was met with love and, as always, more service. In her biography, Kathryn Spink recounts the story of a leader of a group of young Hindus who entered Nirmal Hriday to turn out Mother Teresa. "Having witnessed, however, the care with which the suffering, emaciated bodies of the poor were tended, he returned to his fellow protesters outside with the directive that he would evict the Sisters but only on one condition: namely that they persuade their mothers and sisters to undertake the same service."

The rest of her life would be characterized by nonstop activity and compassionate service to the poor: an endless procession of opening up new hospices, traveling around the world to meet with the members of her ever-expanding order, and helping found an order of brothers, and then priests, and then "coworkers" under the umbrella of the Missionaries of Charity.

In 1969, the British journalist Malcolm Muggeridge produced a film about Mother Teresa that aired on BBC television entitled *Something Beautiful for God* and later published a book of the same name. At the time of the documentary, Muggeridge was not a believer (under her influence he would be received into the Church many years later) but was deeply attracted to the authenticity of Mother Teresa's work. (In one of the book's more charming passages, Mother Teresa, noting the dedication with which the film crew listens to the director, tells her sisters that they should listen to God with the same attentiveness.) The portrait of a believing woman by a nonbeliever brought Mother Teresa international acclaim and attention.

As Mother Teresa and her order became increasingly well known, honors and accolades were showered on her by governments, universities, religious organizations, and charitable groups around the world. She accepted all of these for the opportunity, typically in the acceptance speeches, to share her message: "It gives me a chance to speak of Christ to people who otherwise may not hear of him." And she cannily used her fame to open doors for the establishment of new convents for her sisters and hospices for the poor around the world.

In 1979, after years of others promoting her candidacy, Mother Teresa was awarded the Nobel Peace Prize. Asked why she had decided to accept the award in person, she replied: "I am myself unworthy of the prize. I do not want it personally. But by this award the Norwegian people have recognized the existence of the poor. It is on their behalf that I have come."

As was her custom at public ceremonies, Mother Teresa spoke extemporaneously, bringing no notes with her to the ceremony in Oslo. Clad in her blue and white sari and an old cardigan, the frail and bent old woman spoke at length about her lifetime of service, telling stories of the poor, detailing her opposition to abortion, and, throughout the speech, returning to the love of God: "Let us keep that joy of loving Jesus in our hearts," she told the audience in the Aula Magna of the University of Oslo, "and share that joy with all we come in touch with. That radiating joy is real, for we have no reason not to be happy because we have Christ with us. Christ in our hearts, Christ in the poor we meet, Christ in the smile we give and the smile we receive."

Unlike her two namesakes, Thérèse of Lisieux and Teresa of Ávila, Mother Teresa is not generally known as an avid writer or great wordsmith. Still, the simplicity of her words takes nothing away from, and may indeed add to, the power of her message.

Today it is very fashionable to talk about the poor. Unfortunately it is very unfashionable to talk with them.

In the developed countries there is a poverty of intimacy, a poverty of spirit, of loneliness, of lack of love. There is no greater sickness in the world than that one.

God does not demand that I be successful. God demands that I be faithful.

In order to be a saint, you have to seriously want to be one.

Throughout her life, Mother Teresa regularly set aside her personal and physical needs, embracing the hardships that came with her ministry as a way of identifying with the hardships of Jesus. During her stay in Norway, it was with difficulty that her sisters convinced her to at least wear woolen socks as protection against the cold Scandinavian winter. And it was only while accompanying another sister on a visit to a physician in the United States that a doctor discovered that Mother Teresa suffered from a weakened heart and needed medical attention.

Occasionally she was tart in her disapproval of those who were not working as diligently as she. Early in the history of her order she wrote with evident frustration to some malingering sisters: "And yet Mother can work till all hours of the night, traveling by night and working by day. Is this not a humiliation for you that I at my age can take a regular meal and do a full day's work—and you live with the name of the poor but enjoy a lazy life?"

Mother Teresa maintained this strenuous schedule even in the midst of failing health, until the end of her life. In 1997, stooped and ill from a hard life of work, she died at age eighty-seven. Before the funeral Mass, the body of Agnes Gonxha Bojaxhiu was carried through the streets of Calcutta by the same gun carriage that had borne the bodies of Mahatma Gandhi and Jawaharlal Nehru, with tens of thousands of Indians lining the route. At her death she was almost universally hailed as a "living saint." That a few detractors would accuse her of accepting money for her beloved poor from some unsavory political leaders and plutocrats did not trouble her admirers, who understood where all the money and all her efforts were directed: to the Poorest of the Poor.

Just six years later—record time—she was declared "Blessed Teresa of Calcutta" by one of her many admirers, Pope John Paul II.

Much of her story is familiar. But there was one facet of her life, revealed only after her death, that astonished even those who knew her well. And it is this hidden part of her life that makes her an even more compelling figure.

The great secret of her life was that shortly after her momentous train ride to Darjeeling, after a time of feeling intensely close to God, Mother Teresa experienced a spiritual darkness for the rest of her life.

Though the months after the train ride were filled with consolation, shortly thereafter and continuing until her death Mother Teresa began to describe an "interior darkness," a feeling of distance from God. To one of her spiritual directors she wrote that God seemed absent, heaven empty, and, most difficult of all, her sufferings meaningless. Mother Teresa confided to Archbishop Périer, "In my soul I feel just that terrible pain of loss, of God not wanting me, of God not being God, of God not really existing."

When I first read about this, just a few years after her death, I was stunned. In an article in the Catholic magazine *First Things* entitled "The Dark Night of Mother Teresa," the author, Carol Zaleski, drew on documents and letters compiled by Fr. Brian Kolodiejchuk, a Missionary of Charity responsible for advancing the process of Mother Teresa's canonization. These letters clearly show Mother Teresa struggling with what St. John of the Cross called the "dark night," that is, a protracted experience of distance from God and an extreme "dryness" in prayer. And for Mother Teresa, who had once felt God to be so close, this distance, this feeling of abandonment, was a source of confusion, bafflement, and pain. "As far as we know," said Fr. Kolodiejchuk, "Mother Teresa remained in that state of 'dark' faith and total surrender till her death." (Years later I asked Fr. Kolodiejchuk specifically: "Did it last for the rest of her life?" "Yes," he said.)

One of Zaleski's comments on these letters captured my own reaction: "We may prefer to think that she spent her days in a state of ecstatic mystical union with God, because that would get us ordinary worldlings off the hook."

It's a fair bet to say that many assumed that the woman often referred to as a "living saint" spent her days blissfully aware of the presence of God. And so Mother Teresa's arduous service to the poor was therefore easier than it would be for the rest of us—because she had the constant comfort and assurance from God that the rest of us lack. As a result, we might conclude that *we* are not meant to do that kind of work. Leave it to those like Mother Teresa, for whom it's easier, for whom it comes more naturally. But, as it turned out, it was not any "easier" for Mother Teresa to work with the poor or to lead a Christian life than it is for any of us. It was harder than anyone could have imagined.

Many of us also believe that it is only we mortals who struggle with our prayer, who can find prayer dull or dry or boring, who wonder if God hears us, if God cares, if it's all worth the effort. How lovely it must be, we think, to be a saint, and to find prayer always easy and sweet and consoling. We're sure that all the saints had to do was close their eyes to be instantly rewarded with warm feelings of God's presence. But the example of Mother Teresa—to say nothing of that of a long line of saints, including Thérèse of Lisieux, who struggled with her own "dark night" during her final illness—shows us that, in the end, the saints really are like the rest of us and struggle in every way that we do, even where we would least suspect it: in the spiritual life. Sometimes they have to struggle even more.

Over time, with the help of her spiritual director, Mother Teresa came to view this painful darkness as the "spiritual side" of her ministry, a way of completely identifying with Christ, even in his feelings of abandonment on the cross. "I have come to love the darkness," she wrote in one letter, "for I believe it is a part, a very, very small part, of Jesus' darkness and pain on earth." Now she, too, would experience what it meant to feel like the old, sick woman whom her mother had cared for years ago in Skopje. She would feel forgotten and unwanted. In this she would be able to identify more with the poor in their suffering.

For the record, however, Kathryn Spink, her official biographer, wonders how pervasive this "dark night" was in Mother Teresa's life. In a letter, Spink wrote: "One only had to be with Mother for a while to know that the joy you so rightly mention was not skin-deep. To watch how she grew in stature following prayer before the Blessed Sacrament and see how she was visibly energized by being among the people in whom she consistently saw Christ was to realize that she was being constantly confirmed in what God was doing through her."

Though Spink expressed the highest respect for those who were responsible for Mother Teresa's cause for canonization, she also pointed out the perils of taking letters and writings belonging to a particular context and creating something "more sustained" from them. So whether this experience continued for the remainder of her life or simply represented long chapters of her life is something only Mother Teresa could have known. Overall, however, her biographer was certain, she said, that Mother Teresa did face interior darkness. "The dark night of the soul is of course part of the spiritual journey and I have no doubt that she experienced it, particularly during the early years when she stepped out into a void, very much alone and on the receiving end of criticism from all kinds of quarters, but also later in her life."

What remains clear is that Mother Teresa struggled intensely in her spiritual life. And this makes what she accomplished even more extraordinary and her example more meaningful to me. Her ministry, based as it was on a singularly intimate encounter with Jesus that would gradually fade into silence, whether lengthy or lifelong, is a remarkable testimony of fidelity.

Nothing so binds me to Mother Teresa as this facet of her life, and I have found, when telling this story to others, whether in articles, in homilies, or on retreats, that nothing so deepens their appreciation of her holiness.

⸙

But I knew none of this when I was working with the Missionaries of Charity in Kingston. All I knew was that Mother Teresa's sisters worked hard, were cheerful with everyone in the hospice, and asked the Jesuit novices only to follow their example.

Our work at Our Lady Queen of Peace was to wash, dress, and care for the men who lived in the hospice. Modesty prevented the sisters from showering and dressing the men (they did so for the women); the sisters employed one elderly Jamaican man for the task. But since he was unable to wash the dozens of men in the hospice by himself, Bill and I were put to work.

Simple tasks, really, but also grim work to which I never grew accustomed. In the early morning, Bill and I would be greeted by a phalanx of poor, elderly Jamaican men seated placidly on cheap plastic seats in the courtyard, awaiting their showers.

Leading them into the steamy bathroom, I first had to help the men out of their clothes. More often than not, their pants were wet with urine or stained from where they had soiled themselves during the night. This made the otherwise straightforward act of undressing them an ordeal, as I struggled to pull the dirty clothes off them while I knelt on the wet tiled floor in the bathroom. Next I guided them into one of the showers. Also a challenge: many of them were infirm and so needed to be led across the slippery tile floor. One man, named Ezekiel, was blind and so needed practically to be lifted into the shower.

Then I would reach around the men, turn on the water, and help them wash themselves. Sometimes during their shower they would ask me to reach places that they couldn't reach, and I would use a rag to wash them. Ezekiel often used this time to blow his nose, blowing snot through one nostril while closing the other with his finger. (I had to be fast on my feet to stay out of firing range.) After drying the men off, I pulled on their new clothes and guided them back to the men's dormitory.

By morning's end I was wiped out but thankful that shower time was over, and happy to help the sisters distribute bread and tea to the men and women. This was an opportunity to chat with everyone, and since the showers were completed I was in a good mood. Bill and I could rest for a few minutes before turning our attention to other duties, the least appealing of which was clipping toenails. "Brother Jim, Brother Jim," some would shout when they saw me doing this for one of the men. "Clip my nails, too!"

As much as I wanted to envision myself as a sort of Jesuit-style Mother Teresa, as much as I desired to find Christ in all the people, and as much as I tried to be mindful during my ministry, at the beginning of my time at the hospice I found the work revolting. Bill seemed to take more easily to the work than I did, which only added to my frustration and sense of failure. I felt that because I was a Jesuit, these most Christian of tasks should somehow be easier for me. Why wasn't God helping me feel more comfortable here? I wondered if I was cut out for working with the poor.

But often just when I was about ready to throw in the towel, one of the sisters would smile and make a joke, or tell me what a great job I was doing, and how Mother would be proud of my work, and how Mother loved the Jesuits, and did I know that Mother liked Jesuits best of all for spiritual directors? And I knew that I couldn't let the sisters down. The sisters got me through the first few weeks, and after that I was gradually able to enter more fully into the work (though I never, ever liked clipping toenails). In time, I grew to know the men at Our Lady Queen of Peace as individuals, not simply as bodies to be washed.

This was a great grace, which would deepen over the course of my novitiate: the understanding that "the poor" and "the sick" and "the homeless" were not categories but individuals. Malcolm Muggeridge speaks about this same realization in his book *Something Beautiful for God*. During the filming of his documentary in Calcutta at Nirmal Hriday, Muggeridge moved through three stages in response to the sick and the dying. The first was horror at the sights, smells, and sounds of the hospice. Second was compassion. And the third, something Muggeridge never had experienced before, was the awareness that the lepers and the sick before him "were not pitiable, repulsive, or forlorn, but rather dear and delightful; as it might be, friends of long-standing, brothers and sisters."

The sisters' cheerfulness, which I had at first assumed was an artful camouflage for disgust at their tasks, was revealed over time as both utterly genuine and wonderfully helpful to me and to the poor with whom they worked. And, as I would later discover, it found its roots in the spirituality of Mother Teresa. It was not a cheerfulness that masked the difficulties of the work—for the sisters were serious about their tasks. They struggled daily in a difficult situation: working long hours in a hot climate with the neediest of people using the simplest of tools. Rather, it was a cheerfulness that communicated the joy of their vocation and the joy of serving Christ.

It had a practical application, too. Their attitude was a gift to those poor who had known mostly misery and rejection in life. "We want to make them feel that they are loved," Mother Teresa told Muggeridge. "If we went to them with a sad face, we would only make them much more depressed."

Plainly, the sisters were happy to be Missionaries of Charity. And they were happy to be serving God in this way. "True holiness," Mother Teresa had written, "consists in doing God's will with a smile." That is a difficult statement for many to accept, since it's so close to the banal "offer it up for God" spirituality. But Mother Teresa, whose interior life was full of darkness, put into practice what she believed to great effect. So did her sisters.

And their joy was contagious. I had no trouble understanding why they attracted so many vocations. It reminded me of a comment by the Jesuit superior general, who visited our Jesuit province just a few months after I entered. During the Father General's presentation at the New England novitiate, one novice tentatively asked him the best way to promote Jesuit vocations. His answer came without hesitation: "Live your own joyfully!"

Toward the end of my time in Kingston, I was grateful not just for having survived my ministry at Our Lady Queen of Peace, not just for meeting some wonderful people among the poor, and not just for never *once* getting sick, as I had feared I would. I was grateful most of all for the chance to come to know the Missionaries of Charity and to encounter firsthand the remarkable spirituality of their order. In the midst of difficult work, they were joyful. And their joy was a great example to me, a singular gift to the poor, and truly, in the words of Mother, "something beautiful for God."

9

Vicar of Christ

Pope John XXIII

Once you have renounced everything, really everything,
then any bold enterprise becomes the simplest and most
natural thing in all the world.
—ANGELO RONCALLI, MAY 5, 1928

In June, after spending four months working with Mother Teresa's sisters, I returned to the States and began my long retreat at the Eastern Point Retreat House in Gloucester, Massachusetts, an easy place to pray.

The retreat complex at Eastern Point is dominated by a sprawling mansion, once called "Blighty" and built by a wealthy Boston couple eager to escape the sultry city summers. Not surprisingly, the rooms are currently used for purposes far different from what the original builders intended. The oak-paneled living room, whose focus is a huge fireplace, is now reserved in the evenings for prayer and meditation. In the autumn and winter, retreatants sit before the fire as they think about the day's prayer, quietly read their Bibles, or pen a few notes in a journal. The marble-floored dining room, whose windows face the horizon, serves as the house chapel; there the Blessed

Sacrament, the consecrated Host, is reserved for private meditation—the devotional practice known by Catholics as "adoration."

Blighty's former solarium is now a small meditation chapel. Two sides are made up of floor-to-ceiling windows that afford a clear view of the retreat house grounds. Terra-cotta tiles cover the floor; blue and pink pillows are pushed up against the wall for one to sit on during prayer. In the middle of the room stands a delicately carved wooden statue of Mary, who cradles the infant Jesus. Sunlight has faded the bright colors of her gown to a pale rose and a paler cornflower blue. Even in winter, with snow swirling outside the windows, the room exudes warmth.

But it is not the mansion that attracts so many to Gloucester (the house is always full); it is what surrounds it. For both the main house and the connecting buildings sit on a windswept promontory overlooking the Atlantic Ocean. Because of the retreat house's position, the sea surrounds it, and you never feel far from the Atlantic. The sea is there as you eat your meals, inescapable as you peer through the large plate-glass windows in the dining room. In the morning sun, with the sea colored a steely blue, the lobstermen drop their traps from their small boats. In the afternoon, plowing the now green-brown water, they return to haul in the day's catch. The sea is there as you brush your teeth or read or pray in your little room. (Even if you don't have an "ocean view" you can still hear the waves.) And it is there, unseen, as you amble around the grounds of the retreat house—through the brambles and the bushes, over the gravel paths, or under the fragrant evergreen trees.

I spent much of the time during those thirty days on the huge rocks that line the beachfront at Eastern Point. Walking directly away from the house, you push through sea grasses and wildflowers on a dirt path leading to cliffs of pinkish gray granite that tower above the ocean. You can stand there for hours watching the pounding waves and feeling the occasional mist of salt spray. You can observe the cormorants, seagulls, swans, and mallards that fly the short distance from the ocean to a freshwater pond on the other side of the retreat house. You can watch the magnificent sunsets, the dense morning fogs, and the dramatic North Atlantic storms that announce their arrival with blue-black clouds on the horizon. And you can think about creation and God's marvelous works.

In my mind, it is the perfect setting for a retreat: the ideal place to pray and to be encouraged to pray.

At the beginning of the thirty days, the assistant novice director, named David, laid out a few simple rules. First, I was to observe complete silence, except for daily meetings with him for spiritual direction. Second, there were to be at least three one-hour-long prayer periods each day. I soon decided that praying after meals worked best: it was an easy schedule to remember, and the torpor that overcame me after meals made it a natural time to sit still. Third, I could not do any reading—except for the lives of the saints, and only before bedtime. Here was another opportunity to meet a new saint; during my time in Gloucester, I plowed through Richard Marius's splendid biography *Thomas More*.

Though I imagined that the silence would be the most difficult requirement (a friend asked if I could remain silent for thirty *minutes*, let alone thirty days), it was the no-reading policy that proved most challenging. While I readily gave myself to prayer, I never lost the desire to read or the tendency—at least occasionally—to find myself bored. Halfway through the retreat, I glumly told David that I felt guilty I was bored. At heart, I was starting to fear that I wouldn't "change" enough as a result of the retreat.

David smiled and counseled patience. "You know," he said, "you brought along all your old habits and desires on retreat, and you'll probably leave with most of them. You're still a human being, after all! It's what God does with those habits and desires that will be important."

One night, around ten o'clock, I was exploring the house library, a small, wood-paneled room with the typically motley jumble of old, used, worn, and downright ugly furniture that characterizes "Jesuit style." (In fairness, the little library at Eastern Point has since been spruced up.) Poking through the shelves, I came upon a book called *Wit and Wisdom of Good Pope John.*

Published in 1964, not long after the pope's death, the book had torn and yellowed pages. Despite David's warning not to lose myself in books, the temptation to peek inside was irresistible. After a few pages I was hooked: who knew John XXIII was so funny? Of course, not all the stories were laugh-out-loud funny. And I had already heard his famous answer to the journalist who asked innocently, "How many people work in the Vatican?"

"About half of them," said His Holiness.

But the passage that made me laugh in the retreat house (and drew pointed glances from more silent retreatants) was one that placed the pope in a Roman hospital called the Hospital of the Holy Spirit. Shortly after entering the building, he was introduced to the sister who ran the hospital.

"Holy Father," she said, "I am the superior of the Holy Spirit."

"You're very lucky," said the pope, delighted. "I'm only the Vicar of Christ!"

It was that somewhat frivolous story that drew me to John XXIII. How wonderful to keep his sense of humor, even while holding a position of such authority, when he could easily have become cold or authoritarian. How wonderful to have a sense of humor at all! A requirement of the Christian life, I think.

It reminded me of a story I had heard from a friend about Fr. Pedro Arrupe, the former superior general of the Jesuits, often called "Father General," or, more simply, "the General." Once, Father General was visiting Xavier High School in New York City, which has, since its founding, sponsored a military cadet corps for its boys, a sort of junior ROTC. For his visit, the school's cadets, in full uniform, lined both sides of the street. When Father General emerged from his car, the phalanx of cadets snapped to attention and saluted crisply.

He turned to my friend. "Now," he said, "I feel like a real general!"

Pope John XXIII had a similarly wry sense of humor, and who couldn't love a pope who had a sense of humor? Who couldn't feel affection for a man who was so comfortable with himself that he constantly made jokes about his height (which was short), his ears (which were big), and his weight (which was considerable). When he once met a little boy named Angelo, he exclaimed, "That was my name, too!" And then, conspiratorially, "But then they made me change it!"

For his humor, his openness, his generosity, and his warmth, many people loved him: Good Pope John.

But to see John XXIII as a sort of papal Santa Claus is to only partly understand him. An experienced diplomat, a veteran of ecumenical dialogue, and a gifted pastor and bishop, he brought a wealth of experience to the office of pope.

⚜

Angelo Giuseppe Roncalli was born in 1881, the third of thirteen children of the Roncalli family, who were poor farmers in the town of Sotto il Monte, Italy, near Bergamo. As a boy, Angelo was devoted to his mother, Marianna, who taught him his first poem, about the Blessed Mother. About his father he wrote in his journal: "My father is a peasant who spends his days digging and hoeing . . . and I am worth much less, for my father is at least simple and good, while I am full of malice."

Angelo was a cheerful and naturally religious boy who was delighted when his normally reserved father hoisted him on his shoulders to get a glimpse of a church procession in a nearby town. He recalled this incident when, as pope, he was first carried into St. Peter's Basilica on his grand *sedia gestatoria*, the portable papal throne. "Once again I am being carried. . . . More than seventy years ago I was carried on the shoulders of my father at Ponte San Pietro. . . . The secret of life is to let oneself be carried by God and so carry Him [to others]."

Not surprisingly, Angelo decided to study for the priesthood and entered the minor seminary in Bergamo at age eleven. His childhood piety continued unabated. The biographer Peter Hebblethwaite, in his book *John XXIII: Pope of the Century*, says simply, "His aim in life was to be a holy priest."

In 1904, Roncalli was ordained in Rome, a few weeks after receiving his doctorate in sacred theology from the Roman College. The next year Don Roncalli was appointed secretary for the new, reform-minded bishop of Bergamo. One day, by chance, he stumbled upon the archive of the papers of St. Charles Borromeo, the Milanese archbishop who was active in the Council of Trent. The project of editing Borromeo's archives took Roncalli almost the rest of his life: the last volume appeared in 1957. As Hebblethwaite notes, Roncalli's familiarity with these papers deepened his understanding that the Council of Trent was not an "anti-Protestant polemic" but a "reforming council." It was a lesson he would put to use many years later.

When the First World War erupted, Don Roncalli was conscripted into the Italian army as a hospital orderly and, later, a military chaplain. The experience affected him profoundly. While he would always maintain that "war is and remains the greatest evil," he experienced a sense of God's presence beside the men with whom he served. A few years after the war, in 1920, Roncalli spoke of ministering to the dying and wounded men: "It often happened—permit me this personal memory—that I had to fall on my knees and cry like a child, alone in my room, unable to contain the emotion I felt at the simple and holy deaths of so many of the poor sons of our people."

After the war, Pope Benedict XV appointed Roncalli as the national director of the Congregation for the Propagation of the Faith, known by its Latin name, Propaganda Fide. In this role he was to provide for the needs of the Church in what were called "mission territories." Besides collecting funds for overseas dioceses, Roncalli was asked to promote the ordination of clergy in the mission territories, encourage missionary orders to set aside any nationalist tendencies, and exhort Italian Catholics to pray for the needs of the mission church. In his extensive travels around the Italian dioceses and his work with various missionary orders, he began to acquire an understanding of the worldwide church, another resource upon which he would draw in later life.

Because of Roncalli's success at Propaganda Fide—and his interest in Charles Borromeo, the former archbishop of Milan—he came to the attention of the archbishop of Milan, Achille Ratti. In 1922, Ratti was elected pope, taking the name Pius XI. Their friendship began Roncalli's career in the Vatican; in 1925, he was told that he had been named "apostolic visitor" to Bulgaria.

Roncalli objected, saying (truthfully) that he had no diplomatic experience and, worse, the assignment would take him away from his beloved family. (His two unmarried sisters, who looked after him in Rome, were deeply attached to their brother.) But after meeting with his family and spending time in prayer, he agreed. Before Roncalli departed, Pius XI commented that when he himself had served as a Vatican diplomat in Poland, working with other bishops without being one himself had proved awkward. So Roncalli was consecrated archbishop and took up his residence in Sofia, where he would stay for the next ten years.

The position turned out to be an arduous one. "Bulgaria is my cross," he wrote candidly. But Roncalli accepted it freely, and with an open heart he tried to do his best. (He chose for his bishop's motto *Obedientia et Pax*—"Obedience and Peace.") "I'm sincerely ready to stay here until I die, if obedience wants it. I let others waste their time dreaming about what might happen to me. . . . The idea that one would be better off somewhere else is an illusion."

During his assignment he cared for the sixty-two thousand Bulgarian Catholics, often reaching their poor villages by mule or on horseback. At the same time he dealt deftly with the variety of Christian denominations in the country: the Bulgarian Catholics were a minority in a country where the official church was the Bulgarian Orthodox one. By the time he left the country, Archbishop Roncalli was widely admired for his perseverance, good humor, and patience.

His next diplomatic role called on his ecumenical skills: having earned the reputation as an expert on the Balkan region, Roncalli was appointed apostolic delegate in Istanbul.

Here, too, the archbishop dealt with a wide variety of Christian denominations. First, of course, were the Catholics in his region—about thirty-five thousand living around Istanbul: Latin Catholics from France, Italy, Germany, and Austria, as well as Uniate Catholics, including Armenians, Chaldeans, Syrians, Maronites, Melkites, Bulgarians, and Greeks. In addition, Archbishop Roncalli was responsible for fostering good relations with the one hundred thousand Orthodox Christians in the area and negotiating with the often suspicious Turkish government as the world was consumed once again by war. During the Second World War he did what he could to prevent the deportation of Jews from German-occupied Greece. Indeed, his journals show his special concern for the Jews, whom he called "children of the promise." Once again Roncalli's deft diplomacy earned him favor in the Vatican. In 1944, he received word of his appointment as apostolic ambassador to France.

Postwar France called on all of Roncalli's diplomatic skills. An initial challenge was treating the delicate issue of "collaborationist" bishops, that is, those bishops who cooperated with the pro-Nazi Vichy regime. (In the end they were discreetly removed.) He skillfully handled the new worker-priest movement. His time in France also coincided with the flowering of *la nouvelle théologie*, championed by such French Catholic scholars as the Jesuit Henri de Lubac and the Dominican Yves Congar. Their theology emphasized a return to Scripture and to the early church fathers; it also provoked condemnations from many in the Vatican. Archbishop Roncalli handled all of these concerns with charity and tact.

The ambassador, or "nuncio" in Vaticanese, also became a fixture in the larger French cultural world. His French, however, was far from fluent. After a microphone malfunctioned during one of his Masses, he said, "Dear children, you have heard nothing of what I was saying. Don't worry. It wasn't very interesting. I don't speak French very well. My saintly mother, who was a peasant, didn't make me learn it early enough!"

Archbishop Roncalli was especially popular with the diplomatic corps in France, of whom, by long-standing protocol, the Vatican nuncio was the head. Their respect may have been a tribute to his diplomatic skills, but their affection was a tribute to his personality, his warmth, and, often, his wit. During a dinner party in Paris, he was asked, "Aren't you embarrassed, Monseigneur, when there are women present who wear very low-cut dresses? It's often a scandal."

"A scandal? Why no," the nuncio replied. "When there's a woman with a plunging neckline, they don't look at her. They look at the apostolic nuncio to see how he's taking it!"

Roncalli kept a journal during his days as a seminarian and continued the practice faithfully throughout his life. Published after his death as *Journal of a Soul*, it is a remarkable document that gives the reader a sense of the sweep of Catholic history from 1895 through 1961. Yet when I first read it, shortly after my long retreat at Gloucester, it seemed remarkable less for its historical interest than for its spiritual value: it offers a window into the soul of one of the great religious figures of our time. Moreover, it shows that Roncalli's spiritual stance scarcely changed over his lifetime. Paradoxically, his spiritual "growth" consisted in his maintaining the simple piety of his youth in the face of his increasing authority and power.

It is a piety consistently based on humility, obedience, and a reliance on God that only deepened as Roncalli moved up in Vatican circles. A few weeks after a seminary retreat in 1898, he wrote in his journal: "A month has already gone by since I came out from the holy Exercises. Where have I got to now in the way of virtue? Oh poor me!" In preparation for consecration as bishop in 1925, he writes, "I have not sought or desired this new ministry: the Lord has chosen me, making it so clear that it is his will that it would be a grave sin for me to refuse. So it will be for him to cover up my failings and supply my insufficiencies. This comforts me and gives me tranquillity and confidence." And three years after taking over as nuncio in Paris, in 1947, he writes: "The sense of my unworthiness keeps me good company: it makes me put all my trust in God."

The constant thread woven through his journals is that of a desire for humility and reliance on God, to be "carried by God," as he would say later.

He would need all his humility in the coming years. In 1952, Archbishop Roncalli was informed that he would soon be named a cardinal and that he should prepare to become patriarch of Venice. Before departing Paris he invited to dinner eight of the men who had served as prime minister during his term as nuncio. Only under the nuncio's roof, said Parisians, could so many French politicians with such diverse views meet in such a friendly way.

When he assumed leadership of the archdiocese of Venice in a grand ceremony (the city's gondoliers had repainted their gondolas in preparation), he was seventy-one. Over the door to his study he placed the motto *Pastor et Pater*—"Pastor and Father"—to remind him of the nature of his new job, which he expected would be his last. He enjoyed Venice, its people, and its history. Even the rumors of his being *papabile*, that is, possible papal material, he dismissed. "Who wants to be more than a cardinal?" he wrote to his sister Maria.

But in 1958, at the conclave to select a successor to Pius XII, Roncalli became one of the early favorites. And after eleven ballots, at 4:50 in the afternoon of October 28, Cardinal Roncalli was elected pope. He had feared this, had wished that it would not be so, but in the end his lifelong trust in God didn't fail him.

"Listening to your voice," he told the conclave, "I tremble and am seized with fear. What I know of my poverty and smallness is enough to cover me with confusion. But seeing the sign of God's will in the votes of my brother cardinals in the Holy Roman Church, I accept the decision they have made."

The dean of the College of Cardinals asked the new pope what name he would be called by. As many of his biographers have noted, his choice would be the first of many innovations: "I will be called John," he said, resurrecting a name that had been thought unsalvageable, thanks to the militaristic "antipope" John XXII, who reigned in the fifteenth century. This was of little matter to Roncalli: "The name of John is dear to me," he explained to the assembled cardinals, "because it is the name of my father, because it is the name of the humble parish church where we were baptized, and because it is the name of innumerable cathedrals throughout the world." It had taken him only a few minutes to begin to change things.

Immediately after his election, Roncalli was escorted into an anteroom where a Roman tailor had at the ready two white papal cassocks—one for a thin pope and one for a fat one. But even the larger cassock did not fit the 205-pound pontiff. In the end the tailor used safety pins and covered John's ample girth with a surplice, successfully hiding the handiwork from the television cameras. And so, in contrast with his gaunt, ascetic, taciturn predecessor, Pius XII, a portly, jovial, and garrulous Pope John XXIII walked onto the balcony overlooking St. Peter's Square with a smile for the overjoyed crowds.

Even on this day he recorded an entry in his diary. His thoughts went back to his early life. "Today the entire world writes and talks of nothing but me: the person and the name. O my dear parents, O mother, O my father and grandfather Angelo, O my uncle Zaverio, where are you? What has brought this honor upon you? Continue to pray for me."

During the first few months of his pontificate the contrast between John and his predecessor became apparent: John was more loving grandfather than stern uncle. And he better understood how to engage the world outside the Vatican walls. During his first Christmas as pope, John visited the Bambino Gesù children's hospital and also revived the custom of visiting prisoners at the nearby Regina Coeli prison. While there, the pope embraced a prisoner who had asked, "Can there be forgiveness for me?" His visit was much noted in a world accustomed to his seemingly otherworldly predecessor. But for Angelo Roncalli, this was simply what needed to be done as *Pastor et Pater*.

Besides, as he explained to the prisoners, his uncle was once thrown into this same jail for poaching. (The comment was not repeated by the official Vatican news account at the time.)

John Long, a Jesuit studying in Rome at the time, once told me of a visit John XXIII made to the Pontifical Oriental Institute. The pope, seated on a thronelike chair in the middle of a large hall, read out his prepared remarks to a group of 120 students gathered in one of the Church's most prestigious schools. (Fr. Long remembers the pope's feet not even touching the floor.) After he had finished delivering a dry, formal address, the pope handed the text to an aide and settled comfortably into his chair. "That was the official part," he said. "Now let's *talk!*"

In 1959, only three months after his election, following a Mass with a handful of cardinals, he astonished his listeners by announcing his intention for an ecumenical council. His reason, to "let some fresh air" into the Church, to encourage a kind of *aggiornamento*, or updating, caught almost everyone off guard. Including, it would seem, himself. "The Council did not ripen in me as the fruit of long meditation," he said, "but came forth like the flower of an unexpected spring." He envisioned not a "doctrinal" council that would propose theological dogmas and issue condemnations, but rather a "pastoral" council that would address the relationship of the Church to the modern world.

Many observers, and a few cardinals, had predicted that Pope John XXIII would be a "transitional pope," who would continue the policies of his predecessor until a younger man could be elected. As Robert Ellsberg notes in his book *All Saints*, John would indeed be a transitional pope—by bridging two eras of the Church. John saw the Church move from being largely suspicious of the modern world to seeking to engage that same world with a spirit of openness and optimism.

Privately, some bishops expressed anger at what they saw as his presumption. What was wrong with the Church that it needed to be changed? Francis Cardinal Spellman, the powerful archbishop of New York, wrote to a friend, "How dare he summon a council after one hundred years, and only three months after his election? Pope John is rash and impulsive."

While John never learned of Spellman's comments, he heard similar things from other fearful cardinals, suspicious bishops, and threatened members of the Roman Curia. In his opening address to the Second Vatican Council, on October 11, 1962, he responded to this kind of pessimistic thinking, as well as to those in the Church who were fearful of the contemporary world.

"In the daily exercise of our public office," he told twenty-five hundred bishops gathered from around the world in St. Peter's Basilica,

> we sometimes have to listen—much to our regret—to voices of persons who, though burning with religious zeal, are not endowed with too much sense of discretion of measure. In these modern times they can see nothing but prevarication and ruin. . . . We feel we must disagree with these prophets of gloom. In the present order of things, divine providence is leading us to a new order of human relations which, by human effort, and even beyond human expectation, are directed toward the fulfillment of God's higher and inscrutable designs; and everything, even human differences, leads to the greater good of the church.

The Second Vatican Council would be called the most important religious event of the twentieth century. The assembled cardinals, archbishops, and bishops were joined by Catholic laypersons, women religious, and—another innovation—representatives of other religious denominations. Over the next three years the council would address an astonishing array of topics: relations with other Christian denominations, religious liberty, relations with the Jewish people, the Church in the modern world, and the liturgy.

Throughout his short pontificate, John emphasized similar themes. He was a tireless advocate of the cause of Christian unity, of social justice, of human rights, and of world peace. His 1963 encyclical, *Pacem in Terris* ("Peace on Earth"), was conceived during the Cuban missile crisis (an event in which John played an important behind-the-scenes role). In this document, the first encyclical to be addressed not simply to Catholics but to "all men of good will," he emphasized the dignity of the human person as the foundation for any moral system.

Seeking to read the "signs of the times," in *Pacem in Terris* John contemplated the world and saw many positive developments: among them the desire of workers for a just wage, the desire of women to be treated with dignity and respect, and the growing belief that imperialism was rapidly becoming an anachronism. All of these observations, as Peter Hebblethwaite pointed out, "were instances of emancipation or liberation."

To protect and promote these and other fundamental human rights that flow from the "astonishing order" in the universe created by God, John identified in *Pacem in Terris* the need for bills of rights, written constitutions, and the "rule of law." He spoke of the "universal common good" with its support of the work of the United Nations system. And—something new for a Church that had previously argued the opposite—he affirmed the right of every person "to worship God in accordance with the rights of his own conscience."

In particular, John called for peace in the midst of a dangerous nuclear age: "In this age which boasts of its atomic power, it no longer makes sense to maintain that war is a fit instrument with which to repair the violation of justice." The only options in an increasingly complex political world were dialogue and reconciliation, also themes from his council.

In his encyclical, John echoed the work of the council fathers; like them, he saw the Holy Spirit at work in the modern world, and he called on the Catholic community to respond.

John's colleagues described him as particularly determined to publish *Pacem in Terris* as a means of influencing the later progress of the council. For Angelo Roncalli now knew that he would not live to see the conclusion of the ecumenical council he had called. In September 1962, he was diagnosed with stomach cancer.

His last few months were painful ones; he grew increasingly feeble and was eventually bedridden. During his illness he confided this to a friend visiting him: "The secret of my ministry is in that crucifix you see opposite my bed. It's there so I can see it in my first waking moment and before going to sleep. It's there, also, so that I can talk to it during the long evening hours. Look at it, see it as I see it. Those open arms have been the program for my pontificate: they say that Christ died for all, for all. No one is excluded from his love, his forgiveness."

When Angelo Roncalli died on June 3, 1963, he was universally mourned. A Jesuit friend of mine, living in Rome in 1963, found himself in a taxi when the news of John's death was reported over the radio. "I'm not a Catholic," said the tearful cabdriver to my friend, "but he was our pope, too."

❧

Soon after finishing the long retreat, I decided that I wanted to know more about Angelo Roncalli than just the few funny stories I had read in the retreat house library. So I slowly made my way through *Journal of a Soul* and Peter Hebblethwaite's biography *John XXIII: Pope of the Century* as a way of getting to know him better.

In time, I realized that I was drawn to John XXIII not as much for his wit, or his writings, or his love of the Church, or even his accomplishments as for something more basic: his love for God and for other people. The gentle old man seemed to be one of the most loving of all the saints: always a loving son, a loving brother, a loving priest, a loving bishop, and a loving pope. John radiated Christian love. Was it any wonder that so many people were drawn to him?

These stories from *Wit and Wisdom of Good Pope John*, collected by Henri Fesquet and published in 1964, are some of those that first attracted me to the person of John XXIII. They are slightly adapted from his book:

> As the papal nuncio in France, Angelo Cardinal Roncalli, already a heavyset man, once attended a meeting of the august French Academy. At the end of the meeting the nuncio commented, "It is a beautiful, most impressive place. One hears beautiful things there. Unfortunately, the seats are only large enough for a demi-nuncio."

⸙

> Walking through the streets of Rome one day, Pope John overheard a woman commenting about his obesity to her companion. "God, but he's fat," she said. The pope turned to her and said benignly, "But Madame, surely you know the conclave is not a beauty contest!"

⸙

> On the night after he announced his plans to convene the Second Vatican Council, John had trouble falling asleep. He later admitted that he talked to himself as follows that night: "Giovanni, why don't you sleep? Is it the pope or the Holy

Spirit who governs the church? It's the Holy Spirit, no? Well, then, go to sleep, Giovanni!"

※

After reading a preparatory schema for the Second Vatican Council that was exceptionally hostile in its treatment of modern theologians and biblical scholars, Pope John grabbed a ruler, measured the page, and exclaimed to one of his colleagues, "Look, there are thirty centimeters of condemnations in the schema!"

※

Early in John's pontificate, a young boy named Bruno wrote the pontiff to ask for some career advice. "My dear pope," he wrote. "I am undecided. I want to be a policeman or a pope. What do you think?"

"My little Bruno," responded the pope, "if you want my opinion, learn how to be a policeman, because that cannot be improvised. As regards being pope, you will see later. Anybody can be pope; the proof of this is that I have become one. If you should ever be in Rome, come to see me. I would be glad to talk all this over with you."

I realized that John could teach me a great deal about love and about something else as well: chastity.

Chastity may be the most difficult thing to explain about life in a religious order. For most people, it conjures up the stereotype of the hateful, cold priest or the repressed, bitter nun—both of them out of touch with their own sexuality, closed off to the world of love and human relationships, as well as rigid, spiteful, and even a little cruel. And crazy, too. Definitely crazy.

Before continuing, I should explain that, even though they are used interchangeably, there is a difference between chastity and celibacy. Chastity refers to the proper and loving use of one's sexuality, and this is something everyone is called to. In his book on human sexuality, *In Pursuit of Love*, Vincent J. Genovesi, SJ, offers this helpful reflection on chastity:

> Living as a chaste person requires that the physical and external expressions of our sexuality be "under the control of love, with tenderness and full awareness of the other." John A. T. Robinson has made the suggestion that chastity is honesty in sex, that is, chastity implies that we have "physical relationships that *truly express* the degree of personal commitment" that is shared with the other. . . .
>
> Chastity, then, is for all people and not just for those who are single. . . .
>
> Far from being in any way opposed to sexuality, chastity accepts a person's striving for pleasure and "attempts to put that striving at the service of other human and Christian values."

Simply put, chastity, as another author states, is the "ability to receive and give love."

Celibacy is a little different. Technically, it is the restriction against marriage for the Catholic clergy. Another way of seeing it is that celibacy as a requirement could be lifted by the Church at any time. During the first three centuries of the Church, in fact, no restrictions at all existed against marriage, and many priests were married. (We know that St. Peter himself was married, since the Gospels speak of his mother-in-law.)

Chastity, on the other hand, is a freely chosen way of life for members of religious orders. Even among Catholics, and especially when referring to priests, brothers, and sisters, the two terms are often taken to mean the same thing—choosing not to marry out of a religious commitment—and the spirituality surrounding both celibacy and chastity is similar.

But back to the stereotype of the rigid, bitter celibate that is so popular in jokes, in movies, and on television. The great irony is that some of history's most loving people—those whom even nonbelievers would point to as role models—were celibate men and women. Think of Francis of Assisi and Mother Teresa and John XXIII, to name a few examples. Would anyone say that they were not loving people?

More to the point, think of Jesus of Nazareth, who, Scripture scholars agree, never married. Is there anyone who doubts that Jesus the celibate man was loving?

Jesus demonstrated that the underlying goal of celibacy is to love as many people as possible as deeply as possible. That may seem strange to people used to defining celibacy *negatively*—that is, as not having sex—but it's true. The central aim of chastity and celibacy is an increased capacity to love.

The life of celibacy is obviously not for everyone. Most people are called to marriage and sexual intimacy and children and family life. For them, the primary way of living chastely is by loving their spouses and their children with their whole hearts. It is a more focused, exclusive kind of loving. That is not to imply that married couples and parents do not love others outside their families, and love them well. Rather, the focus of their love is necessarily centered on their family.

For the vowed religious the situation is the opposite. You vow chastity so that you give yourself to God as totally as possible and make yourself available to love as many other people as possible. You take this vow for a more practical reason, too: to give yourself as fully as possible to your ministry. Vowed chastity is also a way of imitating the life and ministry of Jesus. This is not a "better" or "worse" way of loving than a sexual or committed relationship; it's simply different. Nor does it diminish the witness of married clergy in other denominations, who find that they can also give themselves fully to their ministries. It is simply a different way to live out one's call.

Chastity is the best way for me and others in religious orders to love. While many may love most fully in a committed relationship, for me this way works best. My experience says that this is the path to which I'm best suited, because this is the way that brings me the most joy. It seems that this is how God designed me to function best.

Practically speaking, celibacy is an art, something you have to practice. You don't learn how to be a good husband or wife on the day of your wedding. And I didn't learn how to be a good celibate on my ordination day; nor did I fully understand my chastity the moment I made my first vows. It takes time to grow into those vows in a healthy and integrated way. That's one reason for novitiates and seminaries—they function almost like an engagement, allowing people to see if this way of life is a good fit.

Part of that growth process is discovering what works for you and what doesn't, understanding the way sexuality works in your life, and, along the way, finding out how to support a life of celibacy. For me it's pretty straightforward: I experience God's love primarily through my friends, with those I minister to, and in my family. Even so, to do this well, I must have an active prayer life. I've discovered that it's easier to experience intimacy with others if I experience intimacy with God in prayer.

Sometimes I am overwhelmed by the love that I encounter: from parishioners, Jesuits, other friends, family members, professional colleagues, and those who come to me for spiritual direction, counseling, and even confession. There are days when all I can think is how lucky I am. And the love comes in a variety of ways. I spend time with Jesuit friends over dinner and we share our common struggles and joys, and I feel what it means to be what St. Ignatius called "friends in the Lord." Or I listen to someone during spiritual direction and I am able to see the amazing ways that God is active in that person's life. Or I meet someone I could have met only as a Jesuit and who shares with me an intimate part of his life. Or I spend time with my six-year-old nephew and laugh and laugh at his jokes, and I marvel at his goodness and hopefulness.

Recently, at a Jesuit church in New York City, I celebrated Mass during a Sunday in Advent. Toward the middle of the liturgy, during the distribution of communion, I stood in the main aisle of the gorgeous baroque church while the colossal organ breathed its voice over the congregation, and I offered the consecrated Host to parishioners, many of whom I knew well. As they came one by one to receive the Host, many smiling in recognition, I was filled with a sense of belonging. I belonged to them. And I thought, *What a wonderful life this is!*

For me, all of those things make up chastity and celibacy.

My chastity also helps other people feel safe. People know that I've made a commitment to love them in a way that precludes using them, or manipulating them, or spending time with them simply as a means to an end. It gives people a space to relax. Just recently, I spent a few months working with an acting company in New York City that was developing a play about the relationship between Jesus and Judas. Initially, I was asked by the playwright to help him with the research for his script, and then I began working closely with the actor who would play Judas. In time, I was invited to talk with the director and the entire cast. During the midwinter months, we spent long hours sitting around a huge table in an Off-Broadway theater discussing the Gospels, Jesus, Judas, and concepts such as sin and grace and despair and hope. These were wonderful conversations, too, so different from those that I have with Catholics, who sometimes feel (myself included) that we already have all the answers.

Here was a group of people who inhabited a world far different from my own: the world of the theater. When we began, they didn't know me at all (and only a few of them were Catholic). I wondered, "How will they react to a priest in their midst?" But slowly I realized that since they knew I was a priest, they also knew I was celibate, and therefore they knew I wasn't there for any other reason than to help them and to love them. As a result, some of them felt comfortable sharing some intimate details of their lives with me, opening up at times of stress or difficulty or sadness.

Their trust was a great gift to me, and it helped me not simply become friends with them, but, in a real sense, love all of them. Whenever I entered the dressing room, I was usually greeted with plenty of hugs and kisses, from both the men and the women. (Actors, or at least these actors, I discovered, are very affectionate!) And on opening night, though I had seen the play a dozen times already, I found myself filled with gratitude as I watched how each of my friends had used his or her talents to create something new and exciting for the audience. I rejoiced with them in their vocations.

As in other situations, I also realized that I was there not only to love but to be loved. As the show drew to a close, I saw once again that I was called not to hold onto their love, not to cling to it. While I hoped that some of us would remain friends long after the show closed, I knew that I couldn't *expect* anyone's love. It had to be freely given and freely received. That's a bittersweet but important lesson I learn over and over as I live out my vocation. One Jesuit friend who had spent many years teaching told me that it was similar in schools. When I mentioned to him how sad I was that the show was ending, he said, "It's the same for me when a school year ends. You have to freely accept love from the students, but you have to remember that you can't hold onto it." It reminded me of the experience of the apostles after the Resurrection, who wanted nothing more than for Jesus to stay around. His response: "Do not cling to me."

But that free kind of love can be a magnificent blessing. Just a few days before opening night, after a round of hugs and kisses and smiles in the dressing room, I looked around at all these former strangers who had become my friends and thought, *This is chastity.*

Some days I think of my relationship with God as one of those gorgeous Byzantine mosaics of the face of Christ. Each of the people I love and who loves me is a brightly colored tile in this intricate design, and the image of the face of Christ becomes clear only when I am able to stand back in contemplation and take in the whole picture.

❦

The celibate person also has to accept the possibility that he will fall in love from time to time. This is an integral part of the human condition and it affects everyone, celibate or not. If you hope to be a loving man or woman, you will inevitably run the "risk" of falling in love. Jesus, as a fully human person, also ran that risk, when he offered his heart to others and opened himself to receiving their love. In his essential humanity, Jesus was as prone as anyone to falling in love and having others fall in love with him. His response was to love others chastely and well.

A few months into my novitiate, my novice director said that as a Jesuit I would almost certainly fall in love and that others would fall in love with me. I was horrified!

His response was memorable. "If you don't fall in love as a Jesuit, then there's something wrong with you," he said. "It's human and it's natural. Loving is the most important part of being a Christian. The question is what do you *do* when you fall in love?"

In other words, if you find yourself falling in love as a vowed religious, what choices do you make and how do you respond? Either you find that you cannot live the vow of chastity and you must leave your religious order (and I've had friends who have made this decision), or you reaffirm your commitment to your vows and move away in a healthy way from the object of your affection.

My novice director was right. It happened once in my Jesuit life: I fell head over heels in love despite my determination to avoid that situation. A few years after the novitiate, I found myself in love for the very first time. And the depth of my love and the passion I felt were completely unexpected and totally overwhelming. As anyone who has been in love will understand, it was a turbulent time. For some weeks, I believed that this was the person for me, the one I could spend the rest of my life with. I understood what it meant to be "lovesick" and could barely eat or sleep. Compounded with these feelings was the fear that all this might be a sign that I should leave the Jesuits.

In the midst of this turmoil, I met with my spiritual director, a wise and elderly Jesuit. I told him what was happening. He calmly listened to my story, which came out only with many tears. In response, he said just what my novice director had told me: "Falling in love is a wonderful part of being human, perhaps the most human thing you could do. It shows that you are a loving person. And that's a wonderful thing for a Jesuit and for a priest." He paused. "But you know that you have to decide what you want to do. You are free to leave the Jesuits and pursue this relationship, or you are free to stay and end the relationship."

After more prayer and spiritual direction and conversations with friends (Jesuits and otherwise), I started to see that though I had fallen in love, I was still committed to being a Jesuit and keeping my vows. At the time, leaving the Jesuits was a tempting idea, but when I looked back over the years I realized how very happy I had been precisely because of my life as a Jesuit.

In the end, that turbulent experience enabled me to grow in wisdom about the way my heart and head work. It also furnished me with some good insights into the human condition that I've been able to put to use when counseling others. In a sense, it helped me become more fully human.

Celibacy is not easy. The more loving you are, the more likely it is that you will fall in love, and the more likely it is that others will fall in love with you. And celibate men and women are prone to the same things that other human beings are: becoming infatuated, getting crushes, falling in love, and so on.

What's more, for all the talk about colorful mosaics and all that, the life of the celibate priest or the chaste religious can at times be a lonely one. No matter how many friends you have, no matter how close you are to your family, no matter how supportive your community is, and no matter how satisfying your ministry is, you still have to face an empty bed at night. There is no one person with whom you share good news, on whose shoulder you can cry, or upon whom you can always count for a hug after a hard day. And that's rough.

There are also few cultural supports for a solitary, sexless life. While American society smiles on engagements and weddings and births, when it comes to celibacy, that same culture—perhaps perceiving it as a threat to either married life or the easy commodification of sexuality—offers instead jokes and sidelong glances and outright hostility. During the sexual abuse crisis in 2002, for example, the most common explanation for clerical abuse was "Well, celibacy, of course; it's *unnatural*." People believe that not having sex is weird and unhealthy and sick, so people who are celibate are weird and unhealthy and sick. It is an almost insurmountable stereotype.

The lack of societal support means that it's crucial for celibates to nourish our life with close friendships, with a healthy attitude toward work, with frequent spiritual direction, and with prayer. Like any state of life—married, single, divorced, vowed, ordained—it requires attention and work.

For me, the loneliness is the toughest part; just as difficult as the lack of sexual intimacy and sexual relationships is the lack of an exclusive emotional relationship. Sacrifice, though, is at the heart of celibacy, as it is at the heart of any committed relationship. And here I like to think of what one theologian calls the "God-shaped hole," the space in your heart that only God can fill. That's why an absolutely essential element of celibacy is an attentiveness to an intimate relationship with God, who provides the celibate person with a different kind of love, which he reveals in ministry, relationships, and prayer.

❦

This is one reason I think that Angelo Roncalli, who was canonized in 2014, was able to exemplify the ideal of chastity so well—because he himself experienced the love of God. He also understood the absolute need for a vibrant life of prayer and the way that a close relationship with God helped him love so well. In 1959, after his election as pope, he wrote these words in his journal during an annual retreat: "This vision, this feeling of belonging to the whole world, will give a new impulse to my constant and continual daily prayer: the Breviary, Holy Mass, the whole rosary and my faithful visits to Jesus in the tabernacle, all varied and ritual forms of close and trustful union with Jesus." John's relationship with Jesus enabled him to be a most charitable and kind man. He was friendly and approachable, human and funny, warm and caring, and always loving.

John's model of chastity was Jesus, because John's model of loving was Jesus. "But above all and in all things," he wrote in his journal in 1931, "I must endeavor to express in my inner life and outward behavior the image of Jesus, 'gentle and lowly of heart.'"

"May God help me," he concluded.

So when I look back on the life of Angelo Roncalli, I see a man who led a life vastly different from my own. He was born many years before me, on another continent, in an entirely different world, with far more important responsibilities, cares, and concerns. I know that it is highly unlikely—probably impossible—that my daily life will ever mirror that of Angelo Roncalli. He and I are very different and are called to be holy in different ways.

But there is one thing I do share with John: the desire to become a good priest, a good Christian, and, especially, a loving person. I hope that I can freely love and freely be loved. I hope that I can always live freely in the God-given world of friendship, love, sexuality, and intimacy and be true to my vows. I hope that I can always accept and appreciate the love I receive from others without trying to possess it or hold onto it.

Like anyone else, I hope to be a loving person.

May God help me, too.

10

Living in Her World

Dorothy Day

We have all known the long loneliness and we have
learned that the only solution is love and that love comes
with community.
—DOROTHY DAY, *THE LONG LONELINESS*

When I first saw the photo on the cover of her autobiography, I knew I had to know more about her. A gaunt woman strides through the woods. Pulled down over her pure white hair is a dark woolen cap, the cheap kind we used to wear in high school, the kind you could buy at a flea market or in an Army-Navy store. It is either late fall or early winter, for the sky is gray and the trees are bare, and the muddy ground is blanketed with dried leaves. Her hands are thrust into the pockets of an old tweed overcoat. The coat is blown open—it looks as if it's missing a button—and reveals a drab dark dress underneath.

And on her face is the oddest expression: lips pursed, head down, eyes closed. She appears to be thinking about something very important.

It seems crazy to say, but when I saw that book jacket photo I felt that I wanted to follow this woman, to know her story, to be like her—a person about whom I knew nothing! The image seemed to indicate an attractive way of life. I wanted not to care about what I looked like or what I wore, and to live a simple lifestyle. I wanted not to worry about how my actions appeared to others. I wanted a sense of resolve about my direction in life. I wanted to marry the active (it seemed that she knew exactly where she was going) with the contemplative (I knew somehow that she came to the woods to pray). I wanted to be like Dorothy Day, and I had merely seen her picture.

My first introduction to a saint is often through an image: a photo, a mosaic, a fresco. Sometimes these images, pregnant with meaning and symbolism, transcend anything I later read about the saint. I find this to be true especially with photographs. Something of the saint's situation is communicated by what she wears. Something of her soul is communicated in her face. And something of her message is communicated in her gaze.

Kathryn Harrison, in her incisive biography *Saint Thérèse of Lisieux*, discusses an arresting photograph of Thérèse taken toward the end of the saint's short life. "She looks amused, almost," writes her biographer. "Her small, prim mouth resists an actual smile, and her eyes express merriment: she is party to a wonderful secret."

About another photo Harrison says, "The manner in which she returns our stares without wavering from the shining path she sees before her, bright as sunlight on water—all these announce Thérèse as one of the elect."

This is what those images of Thérèse said to Kathryn Harrison. To another person they would be unremarkable photos of an unknown nun. But to the believer, or the admirer, such representations distill the essence of the person so effectively that the saint's message is received in the seeing of the image. The image becomes an icon.

On the frontispiece of a book called *Hearts on Fire*, a history of the Maryknoll sisters, is a photo of their foundress, Mother Mary

Joseph Rogers. She is a large woman swathed in a voluminous black habit and a billowing cape. Exiting a church, caught in midstride, she turns toward the viewer with a book gripped firmly in her right hand. Her left hand is blurred; it makes an expansive, outward gesture. On her face is a hearty smile: Mother Mary Joseph seems in the middle of a booming laugh. A distinctive spirituality is communicated—expansive, welcoming, confident. Having met many Maryknoll sisters in the years since I first saw that picture, I know that the photo is surprisingly accurate. Each of the Maryknoll sisters I met was in fact expansive, welcoming, and confident.

Often, no matter how much I read or learn about a saint, that initial image remains imprinted on my soul as the truest portrait of the person.

Here is how Dorothy Day seemed to me in the picture on that book: intelligent, resourceful, dedicated, straightforward, kind, hardworking, holy. Everything I have read about her since I first saw that photo has only confirmed those initial impressions.

⚜

Dorothy was born in Brooklyn to a nominally Episcopalian family in 1897, and at a young age she moved to Chicago with her family. (Her father was a newspaperman always on the lookout for a good job.) As a student at the University of Illinois, she became interested in a career in writing, as well as in the pressing political issues of the day: poverty, radical social change, and organized labor. But she was not interested, significantly, in religion. With the clear-eyed reasoning that would come to characterize her writing (and her thinking), she described this period in her autobiography, *The Long Loneliness*. "I felt at the time religion would only impede my work," she wrote. "I felt it indeed to be an opiate of the people, and not a very attractive one, so I hardened my heart. It was a conscious and deliberate process."

Eventually Dorothy dropped out of college to make her way as a journalist in New York City. She plunged into the bohemian world of Greenwich Village and took assignments with radical papers like *The Call* and *The Masses*, covering socialist movements, syndicalism, the International Workers of the World, "bread riots," unemployment, protest marches on city hall, and child labor laws. "I met Trotsky in New York," she wrote in passing, "before he returned to Russia." During a suffragist march in Washington, DC, she was arrested and thrown into jail alongside many other women protesters.

Her sojourn in jail left a lasting impression. During their incarceration, she and her companions began a hunger strike to protest the treatment of those imprisoned, and Dorothy deepened her identification with an even larger group: the poor and abused in society. *The Long Loneliness* recounts how jail prompted her to meditate on how her own sinfulness contributed to suffering and evil in the larger world. In the language of Ignatian spirituality, Dorothy was engaging in the meditation on sin of the First Week of the Spiritual Exercises.

> That I would be free after thirty days meant nothing to me. I would never be free again, never free when I knew that behind bars all over the world there were women and men, young girls and boys, suffering constraint, punishment, isolation, and hardship for crimes of which all of us were guilty. . . .
>
> Is this exaggeration? There are not so many of us who have lain for six days and nights in darkness, cold, and hunger, pondering in our heart the world and our part in it.

Dorothy's intellect and growing concern for social justice brought her in contact with a host of prominent New York intellectuals and activists, among them Emma Goldman, John Dos Passos, Max Eastman, John Reed, and Eugene O'Neill. Around this time she fell in love with a man named Forster Batterham, with whom she lived as a common-law wife in a ramshackle house on Staten Island. (Only a few years ago the house was torn down to make room for new construction, to the dismay of Dorothy's latter-day admirers.) In 1926, Dorothy became pregnant, an event that gave rise to a kind of natural religious conversion.

Her pregnancy awakened something new in Dorothy: an appreciation of creation and a desire to be in relationship with God. These feelings arose in the midst of a life filled in many ways with sadness. Just a few years before she had had an affair with a man she had met while working in a local hospital. Dorothy became pregnant and had the child aborted. She never directly spoke of this episode, except to close friends (though in her book *The Eleventh Virgin*, a novel loosely based on her life, the main character has an abortion). After the affairs, hard-drinking days, and other excesses (staying in a flophouse one night, she was mistakenly arrested as a prostitute), Dorothy came to see herself as one person in a long line of forgiven sinners. Her pregnancy helped her feel washed clean by God and able to start life anew. And in the soil of her gratitude grew the seed of faith.

"I was surprised that I found myself beginning to pray daily," she wrote. During her pregnancy Dorothy began reading *The Imitation of Christ*, a fifteenth-century devotional manual she had picked up many years before. As one biographer notes, from her youth Dorothy sought out books that might provide a pattern for life: the Psalms, Dostoyevsky, Tolstoy, Dickens, James. Now she was ready to resume the path of her youth in earnest. "*The Imitation of Christ* simply made the process explicit," writes Paul Elie in his book *The Life You Save*

May Be Your Own. "It identified her approach to life as religious." In the process, she decided to have her child baptized.

Living near Dorothy on Staten Island was a Sister of Charity named Sr. Aloysia, who worked in a house for unmarried mothers and their children. The sister's simple life fascinated Dorothy. One day Sr. Aloysia asked Dorothy bluntly, "How can your daughter be brought up Catholic if you don't become one yourself?" Dorothy took her point, and so, after her daughter Tamar Teresa was baptized, Dorothy was received into the Catholic Church.

Dorothy Day had had little contact with the Church—any church—since her childhood. But her background and interests would make the Catholic Church a natural home for her. Not surprising for someone committed to so many "causes," she had been searching for an ethical code that called for a demanding, even heroic response to the world's needs. And while she found among her radical friends a love of community and the "brotherhood of man," their philosophies lacked the coherent moral worldview she saw in Catholicism.

Also leading her to the door of the Catholic Church was a heartfelt identification with the poor and immigrants. During her days in Greenwich Village, she would often drop by St. Joseph's Church, where she found not only her beloved poor but also an atmosphere of prayer. Finally, Dorothy sought a path of humility and obedience to God that was expressed most fully for her in traditional Catholic spirituality—for example, in the devotion to the saints. The Catholic Church bound together Dorothy's love for the poor, her desire to be in communion with God, her search for moral clarity, and her hope for a life of humility and obedience.

So for Dorothy Day, as for Thomas Merton, it was this large and mysterious church, sure of itself and its place in the world, that satisfied her idealism and her desire for a new life with God.

Forster, on the other hand, was an anarchist with absolutely no interest in organized religion, or organized anything, for that matter. "It was impossible to talk with him about religion," wrote Dorothy sadly. "A wall immediately separated us." Dorothy described the day of Tamar's baptism as tense. After the brief ceremony Forster left the celebration to set lobster traps for the evening meal. He returned to dinner, only to quarrel with Dorothy. A year later the two finally parted, a painful experience for Dorothy, who feared being left alone with her child. It was a stiff price to pay for her conversion.

But even as she embraced Catholicism, Dorothy was troubled that the Church, though often a haven for the poor, nonetheless seemed blind to the systemic causes of poverty. Why, she wondered, did the Communists seem to be the only ones helping the poor? On a more personal level, she began to wonder whether there was a way for her to marry her concern for social justice with her new Catholicism.

An answer came in 1932, with her meeting of Peter Maurin, a self-described French peasant who had been educated by the Christian Brothers. Maurin was a lively man about whom Dorothy wrote affectionately, "He was one of those people who could talk you deaf, dumb, and blind." In *The Long Loneliness* she describes his ideas for a world where, rather than seeing themselves as slaves to an industrial machine, men and women would take part in the production of a good life.

> Peter rejoiced to see men do great things and dream great dreams. He wanted them to stretch out their arms to their brothers, because he knew the surest way to find God, to find the good, was through one's brothers. Peter wanted this striving to result in a better physical life in which all men would be able to fulfill themselves,

develop their capacities for love and worship, expressed in all the arts.

The basis for this utopian vision was the gospel. And Peter's understanding of it captivated Dorothy Day.

Peter Maurin, whom Dorothy would always call her mentor, encouraged his new friend to use her journalistic talents to found a newspaper. The paper would offer solidarity with the workers and a critique of the status quo from the perspective of the Gospels. The first issue of the *Catholic Worker* was distributed, fittingly, on May 1, 1933: May Day and later the Feast of St. Joseph the Worker. It sold for a penny (and still does). That issue sold twenty-five hundred copies. By the end of the year, circulation was up to one hundred thousand.

Along with publishing the paper, Dorothy Day and Peter Maurin opened "houses of hospitality" for the poor in New York City. These centers offered food and shelter during the Depression for hundreds of men and women. Dorothy and Peter also began communal farms for the poor as another way of building community. "It is strange to live in a world of so many strangers," she wrote in *The Long Loneliness*. While the communal farms proved difficult to replicate elsewhere, the houses of hospitality and what became known as the Catholic Worker movement gradually began to spread throughout the United States.

Dorothy's life at the Catholic Worker house and on the farm in upstate New York was varied and exciting. For the next several decades, she worked in her own house alongside other volunteers and traveled extensively, visiting Catholic Worker houses around the country. She also spent much of her time as a journalist, writing articles and editorials for the paper, while serving as a model for her followers through her presence and prayer.

Days were busy for everyone living in a Catholic Worker house. Early in the morning someone would rise to begin boiling water for the soup that would soon serve the many visitors at lunchtime. For a few hours the poor men and women would drop by to eat and relax, all the while talking to the volunteers. Afterward some of the volunteers, many of them young college graduates, would wash the pots and pans, while others might run to the post office, venture out for food, spend time paying bills and keeping the books, or tidy the house. In the evening came dinner, a Vespers service, and again more people to be met at the door, before the house was finally locked up for the evening. Friday nights were given over to public meetings and discussions, open to whoever wished to come. At some point in the day came Mass, perhaps at a local church or celebrated by a priest in the house.

One of the many volunteers to work with Dorothy Day was Robert Ellsberg, author of the book *All Saints*. In the 1970s, Ellsberg took a five-year leave from his undergraduate studies at Harvard College to spend time at the Catholic Worker house in New York City. During that time he got to know Dorothy well. I asked him to describe what it was like working with her. Although I had read a good deal about her, I found it difficult to get a sense of her personality. I knew that she was prayerful, generous, and hardworking, but in her autobiography she can come across as dour. The grim-faced photo on the cover of my copy of *The Long Loneliness* underscored this impression for me. So when Ellsberg described her as "fun to be around," I was surprised.

"Dorothy could be funny," he said, "and a good storyteller who told funny stories about herself." I thought of the French novelist Léon Bloy's comment about joy being the surest sign of the Holy Spirit. She enjoyed company of all sorts, said Ellsberg, from the college-age Catholic Workers to the elderly homeless people from the neighborhood, who held her in great respect, calling her "Miss Day." She took a genuine interest in people, he continued, and appreciated individuals for their own gifts. Yet she was a real person who could occasionally grow discouraged and exasperated at life's problems. Finally, he said, she disliked "being venerated" and had little time for people who treated her as The Legendary Dorothy Day.

Overall she was warm and accessible. "And she took a real interest in me," Ellsberg remembered fondly.

I asked him what she liked to do. "Oh, Dorothy loved to read," he said. "She enjoyed everything from classic novels to detective stories. And from time to time she liked to watch TV."

What did she watch?

"*Masterpiece Theatre*," he said. I laughed when I heard this. It was the first time I had learned what TV show a saint liked to watch.

Throughout her long life, Dorothy Day adhered to a practice of voluntary poverty, living simply, wearing clothes that had been donated to Catholic Worker houses, traveling by bus, and striving to have as few possessions as possible. But she was careful to distinguish between the dignity and freedom of such a choice and the bondage of destitution that enslaves so many of the poor. The latter type of poverty was not a way to freedom but a form of injustice and oppression, a sign of institutional sin to be combated.

In keeping with her understanding of the Gospels, Dorothy also became a tireless advocate for peace. For her, the message of the Sermon on the Mount led to an unshakable commitment to nonviolence. Her stance on nonviolence and her willingness to engage in campaigns of civil disobedience began shortly after World War II (protesting the civil defense drills of the 1950s) and continued through the Cold War and Vietnam.

As a result of this work she was shot at, imprisoned, and was investigated by the FBI. This did not deter her. "The servant is not greater than his master," she would say. She received criticism even from some of her staunchest Catholic supporters, who admired her work with the poor but found her pacifism a bitter pill to swallow, especially during times of war. Neither did this deter her. And in the 1960s, when public social protest became more commonplace, the witness of Dorothy Day was a potent symbol to a new generation of advocates for social justice.

In 1973, at the age of seventy-six, she was arrested and jailed for her participation in a United Farm Workers rally supporting Cesar Chavez and the rights of migrant workers. A striking black-and-white photograph taken that day shows the birdlike, gray-haired woman wearing a secondhand dress and sitting on a folding chair. Dorothy gazes up calmly at two burly police officers, armed, who tower over her. It is a portrait of a lifetime of commitment, the dignity of discipleship, and the absolute rightness of the gospel.

In *The Long Loneliness*, first published in 1952, the famous pacifist responds with an earthy example to an oft-cited objection to pacifism. It is typical Dorothy Day: blunt, honest, grounded in experience, and, above all, Christian:

What would you do if an armed maniac were to attack you, your child, your mother? How many times have we heard this. Restrain him, of course, but not kill him. Confine him if necessary. But perfect love casts out fear and love overcomes hatred. All this sounds trite but experience is not trite.

On one occasion an armed maniac did try to kill Arthur Sheehan, one of our editors during the war. A victim of World War I, who had already assaulted several other men in the house and almost broken my wrist one day when I tried to turn off the radio in the kitchen, took a large breadknife and a crucifix and announced he was going to kill Arthur. Another woman and I seized him, forcing him to drop the knife. We could not hold him, however, and after he had hurled a gallon can of vegetables at Arthur and smashed a hole in the wall, we restrained him long enough to allow Arthur to escape. We called the police and asked that Harry be confined to Bellevue for observation, but since we would not bring charges against him, the hospital released him the next day. Later we persuaded them to keep him for a month in the psychiatric ward. He was returned to the hospital, but at the end of thirty days he was out again, and continued to eat on our breadline during the war. Some time later we heard that he had shipped out on an oil tanker.

There were many other incidents that would have resulted in violence if moral force had not been substituted for coercion, which would have resulted in greater trouble.

For all of her radical causes, Dorothy Day boasted a surprisingly traditional piety. In 1960, she authored a slim book about one of her favorite saints, Thérèse of Lisieux, whose Little Way of doing small things out of love for God gave Dorothy's work with the poor an added dimension. And while she remained faithful to the Catholic Church, as a journalist and an intellectual she also remained critical of its failings and limitations, particularly concerning issues of social justice. This devout Catholic liked to quote the twentieth-century theologian Romano Guardini's dictum: "The church is the cross on which Christ is crucified today."

. With her good friend Thomas Merton (with whom she disagreed from time to time), Dorothy enjoyed a deep prayer life, seeing mysticism as something available to all believers.

And like Merton, she had an expansive view of prayer. "Does God have a set way of prayer, a way that he expects each of us to follow?" she asked. She answered her own question bluntly: "I doubt it." She maintained that people can pray through the witness of their lives, the friendships they enjoy, and the love they offer and receive from others. As sickness and age began to wear on her, and Dorothy could no longer maintain as active a schedule, she was increasingly confined to her room. During those difficult times she would say, "My job is prayer." She died on November 29, 1980.

Dorothy Day stands for many values: the importance of solidarity with the poor in living out the gospel, the value of nonviolence as a way of promoting peace, the importance of community in the life of the Church. She also stands for those who think themselves too damaged or sinful to do anything meaningful for God. Her frustrating experiences with casual sexual affairs, her abortion, and her tumultuous relationship with Forster prompted her to search even more earnestly for meaning. They also seem to have enabled her to receive the blessings of a child and her vocation with increased gratitude. In this way, she also mirrors Thomas Merton, whose own past—he had fathered a child while still a young man—moved him to find his place in the world of grace. Sometimes the most grateful pilgrim is the one whose road has been the rockiest.

This side of Dorothy's life was illuminated for me while I was helping run a parish retreat some years ago. The theme of the retreat, held at a ramshackle Jesuit retreat house north of New York City, was "Praying with the Saints."

During a talk on her favorite saints, the other retreat director—a laywoman and mother—movingly recounted the life of her great hero, Dorothy Day.

At the end of her presentation she spoke about Dorothy's past. "Imagine," she said, "if Dorothy Day had thought to herself: *I had an abortion. What could God do with me?* Imagine all the wonderful things that would never have gotten done."

My first year as Jesuit novice was one of exhilarating new experiences: discovering prayer and Christian spirituality; working with the poor and living in a religious community; encountering the joys of the liturgical year; and, not incidentally, learning about the saints.

It seemed that each novice entered the novitiate with a favorite saint or holy person. For the most part, it was easy to tell who the favorite saint was. Occasionally you were told outright. But usually the means of discovery was subtler: sometimes you could tell by the way a particular saint kept popping up in conversation, or by the way a person seemed almost imperceptibly happier on his saint's feast day, or by spying a holy card falling silently from his Bible as he turned a page while in chapel.

Within a few weeks of entering the novitiate, I was introduced to Dorothy Day by a second-year novice named George. George was something of a Dorothy Day nut, drawing inspiration from her work with the poor, her advocacy for social justice, and her simple lifestyle. One September evening I accompanied him to a Catholic Worker house in downtown Boston for one of their Friday night lectures. These were called "clarification of thought" meetings, a phrase that sounded suspiciously Maoist (or at least Marxist) as well as vaguely threatening. But the Catholic Worker volunteers couldn't have been more inviting. Moreover, their work with the homeless in Boston, their efforts on behalf of social justice (in the States and abroad), and their exceedingly simple style of life were inspiring to a young novice. The talk that night was on the need for nonviolence in the conflicts then raging in Central America.

When we returned home that night, George gave me his copy of *The Long Loneliness*. "If you lose this," he said, "I'll kill you."

"So much for nonviolence," I said.

I didn't begin reading the book for some time. There were so many other things we were supposed to read that year—all those biographies of St. Ignatius. So George's book sat on my desk for many months. Every once in a while, I would pick it up and stare at the cover photo of the old woman in the woods. Her expression seemed to grow more reproachful each time I looked at her: *When are you going to read my book?*

It wasn't until the following year that I read her autobiography and came to know Dorothy and her world. In January, we second-year novices were sent away on the "long experiment," a four-month period where we would work in a Jesuit ministry away from the novitiate. This was one of a variety of "experiments" that novices undertook: in hospitals, in homeless shelters, in the developing world, and so on.

At the time, I had been hearing a good deal about a Jesuit middle school in New York City for boys living in the poor neighborhoods on the Lower East Side. The Nativity Mission School, housed in a former tenement building, seemed an exciting place for a young Jesuit. My novice director agreed and sent me to work there.

I was astonished by the dedication of the teachers, many of whom were recent college graduates and members of the Jesuit Volunteer Corps. Classes began at 8:00 a.m. and continued until 3:00 p.m., with a short break for lunch and recess. After classes students stayed for the tutoring that many desperately needed as well as something simpler: a place to study. Many of their families' small tenement apartments were crowded and noisy, making it difficult for the students to concentrate on homework. The kids went home for dinner and returned again to school for still more tutoring. The day finally ended at 10:00 p.m. The now-exhausted teachers loaded up the battered school van with children who lived in especially dangerous neighborhoods and drove them home. For both teachers and students it was a long day.

The combination of teaching, tutoring, and the overall attention that Jesuit educators call *cura personalis* (care for the person) meant that the Nativity School students received an extraordinary education. Not surprisingly, their parents—many of them recent immigrants from the Dominican Republic, Mexico, Ecuador, and Vietnam—were exceedingly grateful. Most graduates continued on to high school. Some went to college, and quite a few went to the best schools in the country.

One freezing February evening, I crawled into bed and finally started the book that George had lent me a few months before. To my complete surprise, after only a few chapters it dawned on me that Dorothy Day had begun her work of running houses of hospitality in this very neighborhood, just a few blocks from where I was now living.

The next morning, when I mentioned this to a Jesuit in the community, he laughed.

"Of course," he said. "You didn't know that? She worked right around the corner! You're living in her world!"

That day I wandered over to the Catholic Worker houses, just two blocks away, and stood in the cold, staring. In the mid-1960s, St. Joseph's House was founded for men, and Maryhouse in the 1970s for women. Both were unremarkable brownstones. Neither sported any indication of their historical significance. I suppose I expected a little brass plaque saying something like "Dorothy Day, Founder of the Catholic Worker Movement, Lived Here." But in a sense there was no need: the buildings were still operating as houses of hospitality and serving the homeless on the Lower East Side. The only sign needed was the sign of the poor men and women who gathered on the icy sidewalks outside.

Soon afterward, I began hearing stories from the local Jesuits about Dorothy. As it turned out, she had attended the daily 5:15 p.m. Mass at the Nativity Parish on a regular basis. "Dorothy was a tough old bird," said one Jesuit. "No nonsense." Another Jesuit told me that during a time of painful anxiety in his life as a priest, he confessed his concerns to Dorothy. In response, she took his hands in hers and said, "You are meant to be a priest." I remember thinking, if Dorothy Day were to say that to me, any vocational doubts would evaporate instantaneously.

But it wasn't simply the physical surroundings that reminded me of Dorothy Day; it was the work of the teachers—long hours in spartan conditions, dedicated service in the name of the Church, largely unrecognized labor with little pay, all on behalf of the poor.

Most of all, I was reminded of Dorothy in the Mass.

At the end of the day (or, for the teachers, in the middle), Mass was celebrated in our small house chapel. Ancient wooden pews, nicked and scraped, surrounded a simple wooden altar covered by a plain white cloth. Affixed to the wall were tall, slender wooden carvings of Mary and Joseph. Joining the schoolteachers at 5:15 was an assortment of people from the neighborhood, some elderly, some poor. Usually there came two ancient women, including one who prayed each day for "my son, Alexander, the priest"; a few parishioners; and the odd passerby or homeless person. For some reason (grace, probably) I found Masses in that warm chapel on cold days intensely moving. I felt bound together as much with the teachers with whom I had grown close as with the homeless man I knew not at all.

Near the close of my time at Nativity, I reached the end of Dorothy's autobiography, where she talks about the antidote for the "long loneliness," the feeling of longing and desire that dwells within all of us. It's pretty simple, she says: community. I thought about the teachers, students, and parents at the Nativity School, of the Jesuits with whom I lived, of Maryhouse and St. Joseph's House and the homeless men and women, of the Catholic Worker volunteers in Boston, and of the novitiate, and I thought: *Yes, she's right, of course.*

After her death in 1980, Dorothy Day was lionized by both secular and religious commentators. Writing in *Commonweal* magazine, the Catholic historian David O'Brien called her "the most influential, interesting, and significant figure" in the history of American Catholicism. But, as Robert Ellsberg noted, she was always uncomfortable with her legendary status. "Don't call me a saint," she said. "I don't want to be dismissed that easily."

Perhaps, then, she might be annoyed that she is already being considered for canonization by the Vatican. On the one hand, Dorothy Day is a traditional brand of saint. She was someone who espoused voluntary poverty and proclaimed the necessity for peacemaking, as was Francis of Assisi. She was a person whose vocation was to work directly with the poor and alleviate their suffering, as was Mother Teresa. She was a woman whose life of prayer animated her good works, as was Thérèse of Lisieux. And, like the apostle Peter, she didn't let her sinfulness stand in the way of her responding to the call of God. So she seems a very traditional saint.

But she is more likely a nontraditional one. Unlike many canonized saints, she combined her service to the poor with a slashing critique of the political and economic systems that give rise to contemporary poverty. In retrospect, it's clear that this was a natural outgrowth of her career as a journalist: she understood where money came from and where it went. (Unlike Mother Teresa, she was vigorously opposed to accepting money from those she felt had earned it off the backs of the poor.) She not only stood *with* the marginalized, but she stood *against* the systems that would keep them in the margins. She was the bearer of what Robert Ellsberg has called a political kind of holiness, which makes even some devout Christians uncomfortable.

It doesn't make me uncomfortable at all. In her writing I find a realistic look at the world, and her comments on the plight of the poor are, sadly, all too relevant today. Still, I am less interested in Dorothy Day's astute political analyses than in her personal witness of poverty. Since I first read *The Long Loneliness*, the most prosaic aspect of her life has become the most meaningful to me. She never professed a vow of poverty, yet she lived more simply than I ever have. Her witness is both goal and goad for me as a Jesuit. She says to me, "Do you really need to buy this? Do you really need one more possession in your life? Wouldn't this money better serve the poor?" And "How is your work benefiting the poor? How are they in your prayers? How much do you love them?"

For me, Dorothy Day represents a sort of telos, an earthly endpoint in my desire to live simply and work among the poor, as Jesus of Nazareth did.

Once again I return to the photo on my old copy of *The Long Loneliness*. In a world that tells us that we are what we buy, what we wear, where we live, what we eat, what we drive, and where we vacation, Dorothy Day puts her head down, thrusts her hands into that used overcoat, pulls the knit cap over her white hair, shakes her head to all that nonsense, and goes about her business. For this reason alone, I think, she is already a saint.

I am far from alone in my estimation. Her "cause" for canonization, as of this writing, has begun. And recently I was talking to a Jesuit priest who had worked at the Nativity School during the time when Dorothy was a fixture in the parish. He astonished me by telling me that Dorothy Day's funeral Mass was, in fact, held at Nativity Parish. And there were, apparently, several odd happenings on that day. A light fixture high in the ceiling exploded dramatically during the Mass. After the Mass, as her coffin was carried out onto Second

Avenue, a homeless man ran down the street, burst through the large crowd, and threw himself on the coffin, weeping.

That day my friend gave his class at Nativity the morning off, telling his students something Dorothy Day may not have wanted to hear.

"Go to church today," he said, "and see the funeral of a saint."

11

For I Am a Sinful Man

Peter

> On the personal level, which is where it all starts, Peter is
> a grand and honest statement about how we all come to
> God. The pattern is a great surprise, and for many a great
> shock and even a disappointment. We clearly come to
> God not by doing it right but ironically by doing
> it wrong.
> —RICHARD ROHR, *SOUL BROTHERS*

After two years in the novitiate a Jesuit pronounces vows of poverty, chastity, and obedience. During a special Mass, the Jesuit novice kneels in front of his religious superior, who holds before him the consecrated Host. Reading from a formula that dates back to the time of St. Ignatius, the Jesuit makes his vows to God.

"Vow day" is a significant milestone in the life of a Jesuit. For not only does the Jesuit commit himself to a lifelong promise to God, but he does so publicly, before his brother Jesuits, his family, and his friends. After vows he is no longer a novice: he may write *SJ* after his name, and he begins his philosophy and theology studies.

As with many aspects of religious life, there are a number of long-standing traditions that accompany vow day. In my own novitiate, the primi (or first-year novices) were responsible for arranging the particulars of the vow Mass. In this way we were supposed to lessen any worries for the vovendi (those taking vows). In August of my first year, the novice director asked me to prepare the necessary items for the vow Mass: a paten, a chalice, a corporal, and two purificators.

Owing to my lukewarm Catholic upbringing, I was less familiar than I should have been with these terms. I stared at him, dumbfounded.

Remembering my lack of religious training he said, "In other words, a saucer, a cup, a place mat, and two napkins."

Another tradition is taking a "vow name." Some American Jesuits, when pronouncing their vows, use a special name, following their first name, as a sign of reverence to a particular saint. Similar to the name that Catholics take at confirmation, a vow name is taken to remind the person of a particular trait of the saint he wishes to emulate, to ask the saint's help in his vocation, or to remind him of a particular aspect of the saint's life. Another tradition: in the Maryland Province some novices take the name of Mary, patroness of their province.

My friend George, in the novitiate class one year ahead of mine, decided to take "Dorothy Day" as his vow name. He figured that if the Maryland novices could take "Mary," why not take the name of his favorite saint-to-be? This was nixed by the novice director. She's not a saint yet, he said. George protested that she was a holy woman who had influenced his vocation. But the novice director was intransigent.

Years later, during his theology studies, George was given a pet ferret, which he kept in a cage in his room in the Jesuit community. He called it Dorothy Day, the name he had hoped to take on vow day. "At least *someone* gets to have her name," he explained.

Though some Jesuits eschew the taking of a vow name, thinking it overly pious or antiquated or unnecessary, my reaction was the opposite. As soon as I learned about the tradition, I knew I would take a vow name: how could I pass up the opportunity to have another saint praying for me? Besides, the last time I had gotten to choose a name was twenty years ago at confirmation. And at nine years old I didn't have much of a say: my parents chose "Thomas" out of remembrance of my maternal grandfather. (In later years, though, I've been happy to have St. Thomas praying for me.)

The more I thought about it, the more I wanted to adopt a vow name. But it wasn't clear which one I should choose.

⚜

A few months before my vow day, my classmate and I made an eight-day retreat at the Jesuit house in Gloucester, Massachusetts. After a busy two years as novices, Bill and I were looking forward to a relaxing eight days by the Atlantic.

God, however, had other things in mind.

On the first day, after just an hour in prayer, I was overwhelmed with doubts about taking vows. While the past two years had been wonderfully satisfying, I began to wonder if I were cut out to be a Jesuit. And though the novitiate had provided ample opportunity for reflection on Jesuit life, it seemed that at Gloucester all my worries were unleashed—as if I had opened a spiritual Pandora's box.

Questions I had kept locked away came spilling out: How could I live celibately when I seemed prone to falling in love? How could I accept assignments in far-flung locales when I was so intent on security and stability? How could I help others when I was so selfish, so focused on my own physical and emotional well-being? How could I be a humble Jesuit when I still craved attention and admiration? How could I hope to envision myself as a good priest with so many sinful attitudes still ruling my life: pride, ambition, selfishness?

The next day I confessed these struggles to my retreat director, a young and patient Jesuit priest. I fully expected him to say, "You should seriously consider whether you're fit to be a Jesuit."

Instead he was unfazed. He asked me to meditate on a passage from the Gospel of John, when Jesus appears by the seashore to Peter after the Resurrection. "Do you love me?" Jesus asks Peter—who denied him just a few days before.

The passage seemed an odd one. I wondered, *Doesn't my director think I love Jesus?* But by now I knew better than to question the way that the Holy Spirit works during a retreat. No matter how odd the "assignment" may appear, typically it turns out to be exactly what one needs to pray about.

That evening in the chapel, I envisioned myself as Peter, standing by the shore with Jesus. I could easily imagine the sun beating down on the battered wooden fishing boats, the loud talk of the fishermen mending their nets by the shore, the rhythmic lapping of the waves on the sandy beach. I could almost smell the salty air and feel the breeze on my face. Being at Gloucester, hard by the Atlantic, helped with the meditation.

I had little trouble sharing my struggles with Jesus. In my retreat journal I wrote: "I can clearly picture myself asking Jesus at the shore of Lake Tiberias: *Do you want me to be a Jesuit?* and *How can I be a Jesuit with all of my faults?* Still, I find no answer from him at all. It's very frustrating!"

On that cool evening I went to bed confused and discouraged. I wondered how God would ever answer these questions. After all, I had only eight days on retreat and a few weeks until vow day. How could he take away all of my limitations by then?

During prayer the next morning, I stopped asking so many questions and tried to listen to God. As soon as I did so I felt a noticeable calm settle over me. The more I prayed about my vocation and the more I imagined myself with Jesus by the seashore, the more it seemed that I was being called to be a Jesuit not despite my faults, my limitations, and my neuroses, but *with* them, maybe even *because* of them. God was calling all of me—even the parts I didn't especially like—to be with him.

In this light I began to think about St. Peter. Over the course of the year, I had gotten to know him better as we followed the progress of the disciples through the readings at our daily Masses. And what I discovered surprised me. While it wasn't an especially novel theological insight, it was news to me: far from being the perfect disciple, Peter, like the other apostles, was thoroughly human.

§

When he called his first disciples on the shores of the Sea of Galilee, Jesus of Nazareth probably had a good idea of what he was getting. In his commentary on the Gospel of Matthew, the Scripture scholar William Barclay says of the apostles: "They were not men of great scholarship, or influence, or wealth, or social background. They were not poor, they were simply ordinary working people with no great background, and certainly, anyone would have said, with no great future. It was these ordinary men whom Jesus called."

Moreover, observes Barclay, in choosing fishermen for his first disciples Jesus knew that he was choosing men whose qualities would make them good "fishers of people." First, a wise fisherman must have patience to wait until the fish takes the bait. A good preacher must also learn to wait for results, if indeed they ever come. A good fisherman must have perseverance, continuing to push on even when the odds for success seem low, just as teachers or preachers of the gospel must always be ready to try again. The fisherman must have courage—after all, he might face sudden storms at sea and even shipwreck or drowning. Likewise, as Barclay points out, a preacher must have courage, for there is always danger in telling others the truth.

A fisherman must also have an eye for the right moment, knowing when to cast a line or drop a net, just as "the wise preacher knows that there is a time to speak and a time to be silent." The fisherman must fit the bait to the fish, knowing that the same lure will not work for all circumstances, much as the same approach will not work with all people in spreading the gospel. Finally, the wise fisherman must keep out of sight, much like the wise Christian, who seeks to present others with Christ while remaining in the background.

Jesus understood that these were some of the strengths he could expect from the first disciples.

But in choosing these men, Jesus was also aware that he was selecting men prone to the faults that many of his latter-day disciples are: anger, confusion, pride, selfishness, and, especially, doubt. And they carried with them a host of physical, emotional, and spiritual limitations. They were human.

For one thing, the Gospels show Peter and his fellow disciples as embarrassingly dense, particularly when one remembers that they had the benefit of constantly being in the presence of Jesus. Over and over, the apostles, having just seen some miracle or another—someone raised from the dead, a crowd fed, a sick woman cured, a paralytic restored, a blind man healed, a sin forgiven, a storm stilled—demonstrate their fundamental misunderstanding of Christ and his mission.

Reading the Gospels as a novice, I found it easy to imagine Simon Peter—companion of Jesus, prince of the apostles, leader of the early church, and, traditionally, the "first" pope—saying to himself on a fairly regular basis, "What a loser I am!"

Much later, during theology studies, my New Testament professor drew on the blackboard a handy chart entitled "Distinctive Theological Perspectives." Along the top of the chart, from left to right, he wrote the names of the synoptic Gospels: *Matthew, Mark,* and *Luke.* Along the side of the chart, from top to bottom, were the terms *Jesus, Disciples,* and *Christian Life.* In each box the professor wrote a short description of how these subjects were presented in each Gospel.

In the box for disciples under the Gospel of Mark, our professor wrote: "Fools and cowards." In the box for disciples under Matthew, he wrote: "Those of little faith."

In all these situations Peter was *primus inter pares,* first among equals. He was always getting things wrong after getting things right. In the Gospel of Mark, Jesus asks his disciples, "Who do you say that I am?"

No one answers satisfactorily. "Elijah?" they say. "John the Baptist?" Finally, Peter opens his mouth and blurts out, "You are the Christ!"

Not a bad answer, the reader thinks. But later, when Jesus tells them that he will have to face suffering, Peter misunderstands and *rebukes* Jesus—the one whom he has just declared to be the Messiah. Jesus will have none of this; he knows that he must suffer and utters his famous condemnation: "Get behind me, Satan!" Jesus is not saying that Peter is Satan. He's voicing what he knows from experience—that the temptation that leads us away from accepting the reality of suffering does not come from God. Still, it's hard not to feel sorry for Peter. You can imagine him cringing at Jesus' words.

Eventually chosen by Jesus to lead the Christian community, Peter stands beside his Lord throughout the entire ministry in Palestine. Yet at the crucial moment, when asked if he knows his teacher, Peter famously denies it—three times, just as Jesus predicted. How it must have added coal to the fire of Peter's humiliation to recall that Jesus had known all along that Peter would fail him.

Peter, whom Jesus later called to "feed my sheep," to shepherd the fledgling Christian community, was a flawed human being. (Even the nickname apparently bestowed on him by Jesus—Cephas, or Peter, meaning "rocky"—affirms the angularity of Peter's character.) From the beginning, Peter was acutely aware of his own sinfulness and weakness. Near the opening of the Gospel of Luke, when Jesus first meets Peter and performs a miracle in his presence, Peter cowers in shame and says, "Go away from me, Lord, for I am a sinful man."

This is not false humility. These are the words of someone who, in the face of the divine mystery, manifests a clear understanding of his own sinfulness and personal limitations. And it is a natural response to the transcendent. Such awareness is also central to the development of the Christian life: it is the sign of humility that marks the beginning of a true relationship with God. This is the reason that early in his *Spiritual Exercises*, St. Ignatius of Loyola asks the one making the retreat to pray for "an interior knowledge of my sins . . . and the disorder of my actions."

Anyone who reads even a few Gospel stories will encounter what could be called the "historical Peter." He is headstrong, doubtful, confused, and impulsive. The reader will also discover that Jesus loves Peter and loves him with abandon. Jesus is constantly offering him forgiveness, even for his craven behavior at the Crucifixion, and is consistently placing his trust in him. (Scripture scholars surmise that when Jesus asks Peter, "Do you love me?" three times by the seashore, it is meant to counterbalance Peter's triple denial of Jesus.)

Peter is among the greatest of the saints because of his humanity, his shortcomings, his doubt, and, moreover, his deeply felt understanding of all these things. Only someone like Peter, who understood his own sinfulness and the redeeming love of Christ, would be able to lead the infant church and lead others to Jesus. Only someone as *weak* as Peter could do what he did.

Here is the passage from the Gospel of Luke that, for me, shows the place of humility in St. Peter's life:

> Once while Jesus was standing beside the lake of Gennesaret, and the crowd was pressing in on him to hear the word of God, he saw two boats there at the shore of the lake; the fishermen had gone out of them and were washing their nets. He got into one of the boats, the one belonging to Simon, and asked him to put out a little way from the shore. Then he sat down and taught the crowds from the boat. When he had finished speaking, he said to Simon, "Put out into the deep water and let down your nets for a catch." Simon answered, "Master, we have worked all night long but have caught nothing. Yet if you say so, I will let down the nets." When they had done this, they caught so many fish that their nets were beginning to break. So they signaled their partners in the other boat to come and help them. And they came and filled both boats, so that they began to sink. But when Simon Peter saw it, he fell down at Jesus' knees, saying, "Go away from me, Lord, for I am a sinful man!" For he and all who were with him were amazed at the catch of fish that they had taken; and so also were James and John, sons of Zebedee, who were partners with Simon. Then Jesus said to Simon, "Do not be afraid; from now on you will be catching people." When they had brought their boats to shore, they left everything and followed him.

Understanding Peter's humanity was a liberating insight for me. For if God calls each of us individually, he calls us with both our gifts and our failings. And it is in our failings, and in the parts of our lives that embarrass us, that we are often drawn closest to God.

For all of these reasons, I ended up choosing Peter as my vow name. I wanted to remind myself of the way God loves us.

Everyone needs to be reminded of this: it is difficult to accept that God loves us as we are, with our limitations, as well as our tendencies to sin. Certainly God is constantly calling us to conversion, to turn from any sinful behavior. And certainly God asks us to cast off anything that keeps us from following him more closely. At the same time, God is always inviting us to follow him, with a full and forgiving knowledge of our human nature.

In a passage written by one of the General Congregations of the Society of Jesus, there is a surprising definition of a Jesuit. "What is it to be a Jesuit? It is to know that one is a sinner, yet called to be a companion of Jesus." This is also what it means to be a Christian. Being a Christian means being a "loved sinner."

But it can be difficult to believe that God loves us so generously. For one thing, we can wrongly imagine God as too closely mirroring us, and therefore loving in the way we do—conditionally. But God's love is richer and deeper than any love we can know. His willingness to become human and die a human death is one sign of this. It is also difficult for us to believe in God's generous love because it is hard to accept *any* limitations that we see in ourselves. We wish we were something other than who we are. If only I were *holier*, people think, maybe then I would be worthy of God's love.

Yet all God wants us to be is ourselves, or, in Thomas Merton's phrase, our "true selves." The road to holiness is in many ways the road to being oneself.

Not long ago, a young father admitted to me in spiritual direction that he was consumed with an awareness of his sinfulness—what he felt was his self-regard, his desire for financial success, his pride. It was a painful experience of what the church fathers called "compunction." He wondered how God could love him with his faults.

I knew him well, so I asked if he loved his young son—a rambunctious, impetuous three-year-old. He nodded vigorously.

Did he love his son with all of his son's imperfections?

"I love him *more* because of his imperfections," he said through sudden tears. I could tell that he had surprised himself.

This is the way God loves us, I wanted to say. But I didn't have to say anything; this young father's face told me that he understood.

In a sly way, our disbelief in God's unconditional love can also encourage laziness. We ignore the call for true discipleship by protesting that we are too imperfect or too untalented or too ordinary or too whatever to be a true disciple: "I'm no Mother Teresa, or Dorothy Day, or John XXIII. I'm too human to be of any use to God." Since I'm so flawed, there's nothing I can do for God, and therefore nothing I *have* to do. Using our humanity as an excuse for not following God allows us to avoid our individual calls and our responsibility to one another.

What's more, often it's *precisely* our limitations, and even our tendency to sin, that draw us nearer to God and make us better disciples. I learned this during my theology studies, but not in the way you might suspect.

⚜

Almost ten years after the novitiate, I began theology studies, the final part of preparation for ordination, at the Weston Jesuit School of Theology, in Cambridge, Massachusetts. After so many years of training, I was looking forward to studies and imagined myself happily immersed in Scripture, moral theology, systematic theology, and church history.

The first few months in school were just what I had hoped for: talented professors teaching fascinating courses to classes full of energetic students. Since I was enjoying studies so much, I began considering the possibility of continuing on for a PhD, possibly in Scripture. I envisioned myself sitting comfortably at a desk, a cup of coffee beside me and classical music playing on the radio, surrounded by stacks of books in Hebrew and Greek, Bible commentaries, and writings from the church fathers—totally immersed in the word of God. How life-giving that prospect seemed!

But after a few months, I began to experience pain in my hands and wrists. I ascribed it to typing too much and cut back on my time on the computer. Still, the pain continued.

My friends offered well-meaning advice: stop typing so much, stop working so hard, start stretching, get more exercise, rest more. Though I tried to follow their advice, the pain grew worse: it woke me at night, made simple tasks difficult, and finally prevented me from typing or writing at all.

Since all this came at the beginning of what was supposed to be an extended time in studies, I grew worried. How could I be a student if I couldn't type or take notes?

My regular doctor sent me to a variety of specialists. Between theology classes, I visited a dozen physicians in Boston: neurologists, rheumatologists, orthopedists, even hand specialists (I hadn't even known there was such a thing). I underwent a number of medical tests: MRIs, X-rays, and an electromagnetic test—a miserable procedure in which a machine shot electrical currents through my wrists. In the end, the tests only increased the pain. ("Who's your doctor, Doctor Mengele?" asked one of my housemates.) I visited chiropractors (It's your neck, said one doctor), massage therapists (You're too tense, said another), and even acupuncturists (Try it, said another; it couldn't hurt). No one seemed able to provide a clear diagnosis.

Over the next few months, the situation grew worse. In our New Testament class one day, we read the story of the woman with the hemorrhage who sought healing from Jesus: After twelve years of "enduring much under many physicians," and spending all of her money, she "was no better, but rather grew worse." I wondered if I'd have to wait that long for healing.

It wasn't a life-threatening illness, but it was a trying experience that stopped me from doing what I was supposed to be doing. The discomfort also made it hard to relax and increased my fear about the future. On top of this, I was embarrassed: I prided myself on being a good student. Though I prayed about it constantly, I had no idea what it all meant. Where was God in all of this?

More to the point, what was I supposed to *do?* Accept my limitations, quit studies, and forget about ordination? Or accept my limitations and just soldier on? My struggle involved not only the pain and the frustration of not being able to complete my work, but also the confusion about not knowing how to respond.

Eventually I decided to push on with studies. Fortunately, my professors were understanding; all of them offered to let me take my exams orally. And my friends got into the habit of loaning me their notes. But I continued to struggle with understanding the meaning of the roadblocks that this mysterious illness presented.

During my second year of studies I took a class called "Suffering and Salvation." ("You should get extra credit!" said a friend.) In the course, we discussed the various explanations in Scripture of the question, "Why do we suffer?" We read in the Old Testament the psalms of lament, the book of Job, and passages in the book of Isaiah about the "suffering servant," and we read excerpts in the New Testament about the suffering and passion of Jesus and meditated on the meaning of the "cross" in St. Paul's writings. We also studied the history of explanations for suffering found in Scripture: suffering is a punishment for one's sins, suffering is a sort of purification, suffering enables us to participate in the life of Christ, suffering is part of the human condition in an imperfect world, suffering enables us to "fill up" what was lacking in Christ's suffering, and so on.

But none of these explanations rang true for me, or they rang true only in part.

We also read the writings of numerous theologians. The most helpful of these was Dorothee Soelle. In her book *Suffering*, she describes a Christian approach that moves through three stages. First, one accepts the "reality" of suffering. Second, one "dies to self," letting go of the part of oneself that wants to control the future or deny the suffering. Finally, one experiences a new receptiveness to God that replaces the former "love of self."

Using the insights of the German mystic Meister Eckhart, Soelle offers an approach that concentrates more on the love of God than on the affliction, while not denying the reality of the suffering. "The strength of this position," she writes, "is its relationship to reality, even to wretched conditions." Her way is not one of stoicism or mere toleration, but of affirming that suffering is part of the great *yes* to life as a whole.

In other words, an acceptance of suffering (not welcoming it, but accepting its reality) can open us up to experiencing God in a new way.

But while Dorothee Soelle's idea made sense intellectually, it made little sense experientially. How was my experience of suffering, limited as it was, enabling me to encounter God in a new way? It certainly didn't feel as if I was experiencing any great "receptiveness." When I thought about the physical pain, all I felt was anger.

"I don't want this cross!" I told my spiritual director at the time, who reminded me that a cross would hardly be a cross if I *wanted* it.

Though the pain never completely subsided, it lessened, and I was able to complete my studies. A combination of physical therapy, massage, and exercise helped me manage the pain and enabled me to type for a half hour a day. Still, I had to abandon my desire to do further studies, as well as my hope of studying Scripture and getting a PhD. Even as I resisted this reality, I knew that it was somehow part of the "dying to self" that Dorothee Soelle spoke of. But at the graduation Mass, as I sat with my friends and celebrated the end of three years of theology, I wondered what the purpose of all of that heartache was.

Only later would I begin to understand the meaning of this part of my life and how it fit into my life as a Christian.

⚜

After ordination I was sent to *America* magazine to work as an associate editor. As it had during my theology studies, the pain in my hands would flare up every few months and I would be plunged into a temporary slough of despond. During a week when I felt particularly low and the discomfort was especially noticeable, I met with my spiritual director, named Jeff, a Jesuit priest who lived in the Nativity Parish on the Lower East Side, where I had worked as a novice.

Before we even sat down in the cluttered parlor of the rectory, I told Jeff how angry I was over having spent the past six years dealing with this situation: the attention it required (daily stretching, swimming, exercise) and the way it sapped my emotional energy and made me overly focused on self; how frustrated I was at being unable to write as much as I wanted to, how others had it easier than I did, how unfair it was. And so on.

My own psalm of lament lasted for a long while, and rather than feeling unburdened I felt myself moving into despair.

Jeff listened to my complaining and fell silent for a few seconds.

Finally he asked, "Is God anywhere in this?"

"No!" I snapped. "Not at all."

How I hated that question! Over the past few years I had failed to see how God could be in any of this.

Then, almost despite myself, I began to talk about not so much where I had found God as what the experience had meant in my life.

"Well, I guess," I said, "the pain makes me more grateful for what I write. I know that anything I write is thanks to God's grace and the gift of health, even if it's temporary. And the pain makes me more careful about what I write, since I'm limited in my ability to write."

Jeff nodded.

"Maybe I'm more patient, too. I can't do everything at once. I have to take things one day at a time. I'm also less likely to get a swelled head about my writing, since I can't plan any great projects or tell anyone about all the wonderful things I'm going to write—since I don't know if I'll even be able to type the next day. And I'm probably more aware of other people's physical limitations—like people in wheelchairs and people on crutches and those with disabilities—than I was before."

"Anything else?" said Jeff.

"I'm more conscious of my reliance on God, too," I said, "since I know I can't do anything on my own. I guess I'm less likely to forget that everything depends on God. I guess the pain makes me a more compassionate person."

Though it was all true, I could hardly believe what I had said.

Jeff smiled. "But God isn't *anywhere* in this?"

I laughed. Suddenly, it was so obvious! God was in the midst of the suffering. I suppose I had "died to self" more than I had realized. While I knew that God hadn't *caused* the suffering to make me receptive to those things, my openness seemed an outgrowth of my experience during the past few years. Dorothee Soelle's insights finally made sense. Was it possible that the suffering was helping make me a better Christian, a better disciple?

"By the way," Jeff said, "didn't you pray for humility as a novice, during your long retreat?"

"Sure," I said. Asking for that grace is an essential part of the Spiritual Exercises.

"Well, this is a kind of humility," he said, "the humility that comes with knowing that you're powerless to change things, and discovering your reliance on God nonetheless."

"It's not the kind of humility I wanted," I said.

"What do you mean?"

"I wanted the kind of humility that when others saw me they would say, 'Wow, he's so humble! What a great guy!'"

Jeff laughed.

"I wanted a humility I could be proud of!" I said.

⚜

Jeff's insight helped me find God in the midst of that small but lengthy trial. For one thing, I wouldn't have encountered God in this way were I not forced to face those difficulties. When things are going smoothly, we tend to forget our essential dependence on God. At least I do. It's a subtle form of pride: I can take care of everything, things are humming along, life is sweet—why do I need God? It's usually when our defenses are lowered (usually against our will) and we find ourselves more vulnerable that we appreciate our reliance on God. In the face of life's problems, we remember that we are "contingent" beings, to use a philosophical term. We are dependent on God's mercy for our very life.

That's why humility is central to the spiritual life. For it is when we are where we don't want to be that we often meet God.

Most of us are so accustomed to going it on our own that we overlook our ultimate dependence on God. This is a key weakness of our affluent culture. We feel so self-sufficient that we are rarely reminded of our reliance on God, except during times of suffering—in the face of illness or death, for example. In his wonderful little book called *Poverty of Spirit*, Johannes Baptist Metz, the German theologian, writes: "All too easily we live alienated from the truth of our being. The threatening nothingness of our poor infinity and infinite poverty drives us here and there among the distractions of everyday cares." Not only are we distracted from our innate spiritual poverty by our wealth and self-sufficiency, but we also actively ignore it, because to admit it would upend our world and force upon us a radical reorientation.

The materially poor, on the other hand, are more likely to be reminded of their inherent reliance on God because of the tenuousness of their lives. A few years after the novitiate, while working with the Jesuit Refugee Service in Nairobi, I noticed how often the refugees spoke about God in their daily conversations. "Thank God!" they would say, in the face of both large and small events. One poor Rwandese woman who ran a small business sponsored by the Jesuits spoke about her troubles one day. Despite a run of hard luck, she kept exclaiming, "God is good!"

"Why is God so good?" I finally asked.

She laughed and recounted in great detail all the small events that had happened to her that day, until I agreed that God was indeed good. Many people who are poor have a greater appreciation of God's presence because they have a greater appreciation of their reliance on God. God is close to the poor because the poor are close to God.

I have also found that God meets us especially in those parts of ourselves that we would rather have go away. And here I'm not talking about the parts of our personalities that are drawn to sin, but the parts of ourselves that embarrass us, frustrate us, or even shame us—the parts that we wish to conceal from the world and that we spend so much time trying to hide. But it is here that we find ourselves most vulnerable and therefore most open to God. Many of my friends who are gay men and women, for example, say that one of the primary ways they have discovered God is by accepting that God loves them as they are. "For I am fearfully and wonderfully made," as the psalmist says. And the very place that they had formerly rejected as unlovable becomes the locus for God's saving activity in their lives. "The stone that the builders rejected," as Psalm 118 says, "has become the cornerstone."

❀

Something like a serious illness, a family crisis, or a crushing disappointment also can help us recognize our dependence on God. Around Thanksgiving a few years ago, my father was diagnosed with the lung cancer that would take his life in nine short months. Though raised a Catholic and educated by priests, brothers, and sisters during grammar school and high school, my father was never very religious. When my sister and I were small, he occasionally drove us to our parish church on Sundays and sat in the car reading the newspaper. It became a running joke in our family. "I've been to Mass plenty of times," he would say. "When you're old enough, you can skip Mass, too."

Over the next few months after his diagnosis, however, as his physical condition deteriorated and he moved from chemotherapy to radiation to being bedridden at home to hospice care to a nursing home and finally to death, he grew more interested in talking about God—even with me, with whom he had never discussed religion. My father sought out those with whom he felt he needed to reconcile; he thought and talked about the people he hoped to meet in heaven; he treasured holy cards that friends sent him; and he asked for the sacraments of reconciliation and anointing of the sick before his death.

He grew especially close to a former theology teacher of mine, a woman religious named Janice. She had met my parents at my diaconate ordination in Boston four years before my father's illness, and they became fast friends. Sr. Janice was a generous and loving woman as well as the first sister my parents had ever known well. My father, in particular, seemed remarkably at ease with her, and whenever her name came up in conversation, he would always say, "She's a great lady." Occasionally I would first hear family news not from my sister or brother-in-law or cousins, but from Janice.

When my father got sick, Janice telephoned and wrote him frequently and, a few weeks before his death, made the long trip from Boston to Philadelphia to see him in his hospital room. They spent an hour together talking, and after I thanked her I told her that it seemed that my father was getting more religious.

"Yes," Janice said, "dying is about becoming more human."

I knew what she meant. When I told some people that my father was becoming more religious, they smiled politely, as if to say, "Well, it's all just a crutch isn't it? A last resort?" But I knew that he was becoming more himself, more aware of his dependence on God, more *naturally* religious, more human. And I like to think that when he died, he became fully united with God, fully himself, the person he was meant to be.

In *Poverty of Spirit*, Metz writes, "When the mask falls and the core of our being is revealed, it soon becomes obvious that we are religious by nature, that religion is the secret dowry of our being." This is what happened with my father as he moved toward the end of his life. And if we are open to it, this is what happens to us as we move through our own lives.

St. Peter's limitations were precisely what led him to be closer to Jesus. Certainly Peter had many talents that enabled him to be a good disciple. He seems to have been forthright, confident, hardworking, and, in the end, a friend to Jesus.

But Peter was not perfect, and a perfect man might never have been willing to set down his nets and follow Jesus. ("Hey, I have my fishing business, things are going great for me, I have everything I need, so why should I follow you?") A perfect man would never have denied Jesus and therefore would never have understood the human desire for forgiveness. A perfect man would never have argued with the other disciples and therefore would never have understood the need for reconciliation. A perfect man would never have realized how desperately he really needed Jesus, and would never have understood how this truth is the basis of all discipleship.

Peter was as imperfect as the rest of the disciples, but in his humility he recognized his ultimate dependence on God. For this reason he is, at least for me, the most human of the saints and one of the most lovable.

Sometimes I wonder if Jesus chose Peter not despite his imperfections but *because* of them. Peter's knowledge of his own limits led him to understand his reliance on God. It also enabled him to appreciate the love that Jesus had for him, as well as to celebrate the fact that God can work through anyone, no matter how human. And that's not such a bad message to carry to the ends of the earth.

I still have trouble with my hands, and I'm still unable to type more than a half hour a day. But now when the pain flares up, I remember what I learned during theology studies and my meeting with Jeff. And I think of St. Peter, too—how his own poverty of spirit led him to follow Christ. How he serves as a model for everyone who struggles with human frailties and limitations. How courageous he was in his discipleship, and how much Jesus loved, trusted, and forgave him. How even his severest limitations were ultimately put to good use by God. And, most of all, how glad I am that I took his name on vow day.

12

Fides Quaerens Intellectum

Thomas Aquinas

> To place our purpose within definite limits, we must first
> investigate the nature and domain of sacred doctrine.
> —St. Thomas Aquinas, *Summa Theologica*

Pious legend has it that Friar Tommaso, of the town of Aquino, was an enormous man, so large that his Dominican brothers found it necessary to cut away a section of the refectory table so that he could reach his food. Most physical representations of Thomas, while striving to be polite, show him to be, at the very least, overweight.

In his touching biography *Saint Thomas Aquinas*, the English writer G. K. Chesterton compares Thomas and another beloved saint, Francis of Assisi. Were we to see the two of them coming over the hill in their friars' habits, the contrast between them would seem almost comic. (But what a wonderful conversation they would surely have!) Francis, writes Chesterton, was a "lean and lively little man; thin as a thread and vibrant as a bowstring; and in his motions like an arrow from a bow." Thomas, on the other hand, he describes as a "huge, heavy bull of a man, fat and slow and quiet; very mild and magnanimous but not very sociable; shy, even apart from the humility of holiness."

Yet this caricature of Thomas Aquinas may be apocryphal. As my professor of moral theology liked to point out, Thomas was an inveterate traveler, crisscrossing Europe—moving between Rome, Naples, Paris, and a number of other cities. And in his day, traveling required one to walk—which would have been a difficult task for someone with an excessively large frame. Moreover, members of the Dominican Order, of which Thomas was a member, were asked to walk rather than, say, ride a horse as part of their spiritual asceticism.

Thomas Aquinas was always on the move, physically, mentally, and spiritually. He is arguably the greatest Catholic philosopher and theologian in history, as well as the greatest of those called the "Scholastic" thinkers and the father of Thomistic theology, an attempt to understand God's universe through human reason, which advanced the fundamental insight that "grace perfects nature." Thomas's life offers a good example of just how that grace works.

❧

Butler's Lives of the Saints states that the counts of Aquino, in southern Italy, came from a family of "noble lineage." Thomas's father, named Landulf, was a knight, and his mother, Theodora, was of Norman descent.

The exact date of Thomas's birth is uncertain, but most scholars agree that it occurred sometime in 1225, in the castle of Roccasecca, near the small town of Aquino. The youngest of four sons, Thomas also had several sisters. (Butler is certain about the number of sons but seems less interested in the precise number of daughters.) One night in the castle, while Thomas slept in the same room, one of his sisters was killed by lightning. Not surprisingly, Thomas was terrified of thunderstorms for the rest of his life and would duck into a church whenever one approached. (As a result, he is the patron saint for those in danger of thunderstorms and those facing a sudden death.)

When Thomas was five, his mother and father sent him to the famous Abbey of Monte Cassino to live as an oblate, or associate member. His parents maintained great hopes for a monastic career for their young son. Perhaps they thought he might one day be named abbot of the renowned Benedictine monastery, advancing the family's fortunes and honor. The boy was educated at Monte Cassino until the age of thirteen, when he was sent to the University of Naples. There Thomas first became interested in the writings of Aristotle and of one of his commentators, the great Islamic philosopher Averroës of Córdoba. It was also in Naples that he was first attracted to the Dominicans, in whose church he liked to pray.

In time, Thomas decided to join the order. The Dominicans, probably anticipating his parents' opposition, advised Thomas to wait for a time before entering. At nineteen, he received the Dominican habit.

News of his decision reached the castle of Roccasecca to the dismay of his parents, who were still pinning their hopes on a career for their son with the Benedictines at Monte Cassino. Horrified parents, though, were the lot of many saints. When Aloysius Gonzaga announced his desire to enter the Jesuits, his father, the marquis of Castiglione, threatened to whip him. Pietro di Bernardone, the wealthy cloth merchant of Assisi, was deeply offended by his son Francis's rejection of his patrimony. (It didn't help matters that as a symbol of his renunciation of his father's wealth and of his own reliance on God, Francis stripped himself naked before Pietro in the town square and returned his clothing to his father.)

In Thomas's case, his mother, Theodora, set out to Naples to persuade him to return home. But before she arrived, the Dominicans spirited him away to a convent in Rome. Theodora gave chase, but her son was already on his way to Bologna, traveling with the master general of the Dominicans.

Thus began one of the strangest episodes in the lives of the saints (which, if you think about it, is really saying something). Infuriated by her son's recalcitrance, and no doubt worn out from her long journeys, Theodora sent word to Thomas's brothers, then in the service of the emperor's army in nearby Tuscany. Their mission was simple: capture their younger brother.

So one day, as Thomas rested near Siena, his brothers waylaid him. First they attempted to strip him of his habit. When this failed, they took him by force back to the castle at Roccasecca and then to the castle of Monte San Giovanni, two miles away, where he was, in essence, jailed. His only visits would be from his sister Marotta, or, as *Butler's* has it, his "worldly minded sister Marotta." That is, his not very religious sister, who would presumably be less likely to do things like pray with her brother. Thomas passed the time by reading the Bible and studying the theologian Peter Lombard's anthologies of the early church fathers.

Later, the brothers sent a courtesan (*Butler's* calls her "a woman of bad character") to seduce Thomas. By this point, they had apparently given up on even the possibility that he would become a Benedictine monk. In any event, upon seeing the woman Thomas seized a burning poker from the fire and chased her from his chamber.

In 1245, after Thomas had been imprisoned for two years, his family, worn down by his patience, finally gave up and released him. Thomas immediately returned to the Dominicans, who sent him to study first for a year in Paris and then in Cologne.

Among the other students in Cologne, Thomas Aquinas stood out: he was quiet, humble, and heavy. So "stolid," to borrow Chesterton's description, that his professors thought him a dunce. His behavior earned him the unfortunate nickname "the Dumb Sicilian Ox." One day a friendly classmate took pity on the poor young man and offered to explain some classwork. But when they arrived at a difficult passage, Thomas, to the classmate's surprise, explained it in elegant detail.

Soon afterward, another student came upon a stray page of Thomas's notes and passed it along to their teacher Albertus Magnus (later St. Albert the Great). At the close of the next day's lecture, the esteemed professor said, "We call Brother Thomas the dumb ox, but I tell you that he will make his bellowing heard to the furthest places of the earth." During his studies, sometime before 1252, Thomas was ordained a priest.

Thomas later returned to the University of Paris to begin his teaching career. While in Paris, he published his first works on philosophy and theology—mostly commentaries on Scripture and on Peter Lombard. Four years later, Thomas received the equivalent of a doctorate and began his professional career in earnest. From 1259 to 1268, he worked in the Italian cities of Naples, Orvieto, Viterbo, and Rome, teaching his fellow Dominicans. At the same time, he was busy writing his *Summa contra Gentiles*, his vigorous defense of Christianity.

Even at the time, he was recognized for his brilliance, and his scholarship and teaching were in wide demand. As did many other philosophers in the Scholastic movement, Thomas realized that the work of any number of scholars—Christian, Jewish, or pagan—could lead him to greater understanding of the world around him and the transcendent mystery of God. The novelty of Thomas's work was his insight that Aristotle's writings, which had been suspect in the Church, could be useful for Christian theology. This gave rise to the common expression—at least common in my own philosophy classes—that Thomas "baptized Aristotle."

Not long ago, I asked Joseph Koterski, SJ, chair of the department of philosophy of Fordham University, in New York, about what made Thomas Aquinas so important in the history of philosophy. After all, many of his insights, so revolutionary at the time, have become commonplace.

Fr. Koterski explained that, like the other Scholastic philosophers, Thomas understood that faith and reason were not simply two ways of knowing but were deeply complementary. Sometimes they reinforced each other by providing alternate routes to the same knowledge; sometimes one provided what the other did not; and in no way did they contradict each other. And when faith and reason did seem to contradict each other, the Scholastics would wrestle with the texts until they thought they found a way to show that they were not truly contradictory, but only apparently so.

In this regard, explained Fr. Koterski, Thomas Aquinas was part of the mainstream. St. Anselm, the eleventh-century theologian, had summarized the long tradition of medieval thought as *fides quaerens intellectum*: faith seeking understanding. "What distinguishes Thomas," Fr. Koterski said, "is not the project of reconciling faith and reason, but his particular way of doing so, and his use of Aristotle in this effort."

Rather than appealing to authority (as most theologians did at the time), Thomas set forth a more rigorous, almost scientific, approach to theology, offering questions and answers, anticipating objections, carefully sifting the evidence, and finally offering a response.

This was the facet of Thomas's work that most appealed to me when I was in philosophy studies, and that still does. He helped make the study of God and the consideration of religious topics straightforward. Too much writing about religion and spirituality is cloaked in obscure language and proffered only guardedly, as if the writer has a secret too precious to share without first disguising it. I remember reading somewhere that a few theologians and philosophers use language that is so confusing that the reader has to wonder if they don't have an underlying fear that if they used simpler language, their ideas would be revealed as not especially innovative or even sensible.

Jesus of Nazareth certainly didn't speak that way: he made himself plain to his disciples, he said what he meant, and while his hearers may not have always understood, he used simple parables and stories to explain the kingdom of God. Thomas Aquinas also cut through a lot of the cant and offered his readers the gift of clarity.

In 1266, while in Rome, Thomas began his most influential work, the *Summa Theologica*, or theological synthesis, whose grand aim was to examine systematically a vast range of theological questions. In this case, "systematic" means that everything is tied together in a sort of system, in which what one says about, say, Scripture has an effect on questions of morals, and so on.

The *Summa*'s presentation of difficult theological topics was revolutionary. Thomas's simple method was to first pose a straightforward question ("Whether God exists"), then raise the inevitable reasonable objections ("It seems that God does not exist, because . . ."), and finally answer both the original question and the objections in a lucid fashion beginning with his usual *Respondeo*, or "I answer" ("I answer that God's existence can be proven in five ways . . .").

From 1268 to 1272, Thomas taught in Paris, continuing to work on his Scripture commentaries and on the *Summa Theologica*. He also spent much of his time preparing for the *quodlibetales*, a popular question-and-answer period during which the university students gathered in a large lecture hall to pose to their teachers any theological or philosophical questions of their choosing. Thomas, it was said, employed three busy scribes, who worked simultaneously, furiously writing down his wide-ranging thoughts, which he dictated while pacing back and forth. He was a thirteenth-century multitasker.

But this most intellectual of men was also deeply devout and frequently enjoyed intense experiences of mystical prayer. He was admired for his humility and piety. One of his friends said of him: "His marvelous science was far less due to his genius than to the efficacy of his prayers." Richard McBrien writes in his *Lives of the Saints*, "His entire ministry as teacher and preacher was a matter of giving to others what he had himself contemplated, which was for him the highest of all activities when done out of charity."

Besides his theological treatises, Thomas is also responsible for some of the most beautiful poetry in the Catholic tradition. Thomas, in G. K. Chesterton's delightful phrase, "occasionally wrote a hymn like a man taking a holiday." Some of these, like "Pange lingua" and "Tantum ergo," are among the most popular in the Latin hymnbook and give the lie to the stereotype of the cold, ascetic scholar.

During philosophy studies, I was excited to come across Aquinas's famous proofs for the existence of God in the *Summa Theologica*, thinking that I would somehow be able to use them to "convince" my atheist or agnostic friends. But while the five proofs do not definitively "prove" God's existence to the nonbeliever (perhaps only experience can do this), they remain elegant ways of considering how God lies at the center of everything. I found most persuasive the proof, or argument, "from motion" (that is, there must be a kind of initial mover to set everything in motion), but most beautiful the argument "from design," which follows:

> The fifth way is taken from the governance of the world. We see that things which lack knowledge, such as natural bodies, act for an end, and this is evident from their acting always, or nearly always, in the same way, so as to obtain the best result. Hence it is plain that they achieve their end, not fortuitously, but designedly. Now whatever lacks knowledge cannot move toward an end, unless it be directed

by some being endowed with knowledge and intelligence; as the arrow is directed by the archer. Therefore some intelligent being exists by whom all natural things are directed to their end; and this being we call God.

Despite his renown (King Louis IX consulted him on important matters of state), Thomas drew a certain amount of criticism for his writings. In 1270, the bishop of Paris, who was also chancellor of the university, established a commission to examine the works of many commentators on Aristotle, including Thomas. The commission drew up a list of condemnable errors and propositions from his writings, a list that was revised and expanded in 1277, three years after his death.

Thomas had returned to Italy in 1272 and stayed two years, teaching Scripture at the University of Naples and beginning the third part of his *Summa*. But the ambitious *Summa* would have to be completed by one of his disciples, for by this time Aquinas was growing increasingly worn out from his many arduous tasks. He was already ill when Pope Gregory X asked him to attend the Second Council of Lyons.

On his way to the council, Thomas was apparently riding a donkey (unusual for a Dominican, but he was granted that assistance because of his weariness), and in his weakened condition, or perhaps lost in thought, he struck his head on a low-hanging branch. Initially, he was taken to a public inn, but he pleaded to be taken to a religious community.

His condition worsened on the way to a Cistercian abbey of Fossanova, where he lodged in the room of the abbot. He rallied for a while, and the admiring monks asked him to lecture them. Thomas initially put them off, but when pressed, he spoke to them about the Song of Songs, a text that had been dear to the great Cistercian, Bernard of Clairvaux. But before long Thomas relapsed.

After confessing his sins and receiving the last rites from the abbot, he died, around the age of fifty. That same day, so goes the legend, his great friend Albertus Magnus burst into tears in the presence of his community and told them that he felt in prayer that Thomas had died.

St. Thomas Aquinas was canonized in 1323, and in 1567 he was declared a doctor of the church, that is, an eminent teacher of the faith. He is popularly known as the Angelic Doctor because of his long and typically detailed accounts of the angels as purely spiritual substances. In 1879, the papal encyclical *Aeterni Patris* commended the theology of St. Thomas to theology students and thus heralded a revival of interest in Thomistic theology.

But it was not the philosophy or the theology of Thomas that drew me to the saint—that is to say, it was less his elegant argumentation and more the person of Thomas, and his life. I liked him more for who he was than for what he wrote. Specifically, it was the person I met in G. K. Chesterton's biography *Saint Thomas Aquinas* whom I found so compelling and attractive. The immensely learned man given to deep humility. The theologian whose lifelong study of God drew him ever closer to God. The famously busy scholar who was not too busy to write a poem or a hymn. The active person whose life was rooted in prayer.

Since entering the Jesuits, I have met many men and women who also have these qualities, and I am drawn not only to the seriousness with which they take their scholarship, but also the ways in which they combine it with charity and love. Many of them were my teachers, and they taught me as much about the Christian message in their own lives as they did in their classes. Perhaps not surprisingly, many of these men and women express a fondness for Aquinas.

One such person was a remarkable woman I met shortly after entering the Jesuits. Were it not for her, I would know nothing about St. Thomas Aquinas, the *Summa Theologica*, or, for that matter, philosophy.

❧

Immediately after the novitiate all Jesuits study philosophy—in my case, at Loyola University Chicago. Since my novitiate class was so small (just two of us), I was eagerly anticipating meeting other young Jesuits. I was also looking forward to living in Chicago, a city I had never visited.

What I was *not* looking forward to was studying philosophy. During college I had concentrated on business courses, to the exclusion of almost all other subjects. Even my faculty adviser at Wharton—who supposedly had a broader understanding of the intellectual life—counseled that taking courses in the liberal arts was a waste of time for a business major. "What company will care if you studied art history or philosophy?" Worse advice I have never received.

So while my supposedly liberal education left me at ease reading the financial section of the newspaper, it made the prospect of laboring over abstruse philosophical manuscripts worrisome at best.

Many of the other young Jesuits in Chicago had similar fears. Fortunately, our worries were assuaged by the second-year men, all of whom responded to such concerns in precisely the same manner. There was, they explained, a legendary member of the faculty who did an excellent job of navigating Jesuits through the rocky shoals of philosophy. If we knew what was good for us, we would sign up for all of her classes, no matter how inconvenient they might prove for our schedules.

The week after I arrived, another Jesuit made this point more succinctly.

"I have two words for you to remember during philosophy," he said dramatically. Then he paused. I thought he would say "Study hard" or, perhaps, "Pray always."

Instead he said, "Those two words are *Sister French.*"

Sr. Louise French was a member of the religious order called the Sisters of Charity of the Blessed Virgin Mary and a longtime member of the philosophy faculty at Loyola. In a sense, for generations of Jesuit "philosophers" (as we were then called) she was the philosophy faculty. Sr. French taught, among other courses, "Ancient" (an introduction to philosophy beginning with Plato and Aristotle), "Classical Modern" (continuing on with Descartes, Berkeley, Hume, Kant, and the like), and a course on Aquinas (more about that later).

The redoubtable Sr. French stood about five feet in her stocking feet. I should point out, however, that she was never seen in her stocking feet: Sister always appeared in class perfectly turned out, wearing simple but elegant dresses usually adorned with brightly patterned silk scarves. (She would receive more than a few of these scarves from legions of grateful Jesuit graduates.) Her hair was always done in a soft, upswept white coif, and her eyes, believe it or not, twinkled.

At this point in my life I had little experience with any real-life nuns, or, to use a more contemporary term, women religious. As a boy, I had run into a few at our local parish during CCD classes (a sort of Catholic Sunday school). But apart from seeing *The Sound of Music* and *The Flying Nun* and bumping into a few nuns during my novitiate years, I remained ignorant about religious life for women. As a result, I arrived in Chicago carrying the same Hollywood stereotypes about women religious that many Americans hold: sisters are compassionate, of course, but they are also a little clueless, rather uneducated, somewhat naive, and perhaps even silly.

None of those adjectives described Sr. French—except *compassionate*. She had completed her PhD in philosophy at Saint Louis

University, and by the time I met her she had enjoyed a long and distinguished teaching career. (No one was sure exactly how long, but we used to joke that the statement "Sr. French taught Aristotle" could be taken in two ways.) Her intellect, memory, and grasp of even the most mind-bending philosophical proofs were nothing short of astonishing. As all great teachers do, Sr. French could make difficult concepts seem easy: this was one reason she was so valued by the Jesuit seminarians. After completing one of her courses, you understood the material: to use a term from her beloved Aristotle, you *apprehended* it.

Her approach was very much like that of Thomas Aquinas. She spoke about philosophy in straightforward terms, using homey examples. A few Jesuits found her teaching style too elementary, but never having studied philosophy before, I was delighted with her lucid presentations. Some of her examples became legendary. To illustrate Aristotle's idea of the "first cause," the action or being that initially set the universe in motion, she asked us to imagine the entire class standing in a circle. "Now," she would say, "what if I asked you to tap the person ahead of you on the shoulder, but only after someone had tapped you?" We paused to think about this. "We would all be waiting around until one person started the tapping. There has to be an untapped tapper." Thus the first cause, or the prime mover.

The other reason we valued Sr. French was Sr. French herself: she was a patient, gentle, and caring woman. If you were having a tough time grasping a thorny philosophical idea, she'd invariably say, "Oh, you know this *already!*" by way of grandmotherly encouragement. It was a testimony to how much she was trusted that no matter how utterly lost you were in Aristotle or Plato or Kant, you believed her: all would be well. When she was preparing many of us for our final comprehensive exams, at the end of two years of study, her refrain was "You're doing fine! You could take this test tomorrow!"

And during those comprehensive exams, when one professor of the three examiners asked me to explain Aristotle's notion of the first cause, I blurted out, "The untapped tapper!" Sr. French said, "Excellent answer," and we moved on to the next question as the other two examiners looked on dumbfounded.

My time at Loyola turned out to be one of the happiest in my life. Much of this had to do with the good friends I made there—so many young Jesuits from all over the country. But thanks to teachers like Sr. French, I found the studies themselves to be engrossing. This was a pleasant surprise. I could almost feel my mind expanding as we tackled questions I had never even thought to consider. (Certainly I hadn't done so in college during any of my business courses.) Can we prove there is a God? How does one live ethically? How do we know what is real? Why do we have free will? How do we come to "know" something? And my favorite cosmological question: Why is there something rather than nothing at all? That is, where did the untapped tapper come from? (Try that on your favorite atheist.)

And we read and read and read. Sometimes, in fact, it seemed that all we did during those two years was read. I liked what I read, too: Plato's *Republic*, Aristotle's *Nicomachean Ethics*, Augustine's *Confessions*, Descartes's *Meditations*, Kant's *Critique of Pure Reason*, Nietzsche's *On the Genealogy of Morals*, Heidegger's *Being and Time*. And while I could have done without Kant, it was astonishing how much more interesting I found philosophy than accounting or finance.

During that first year, I also decided to take Ancient Greek as an elective course and quickly found myself reading the Gospel of John—in the language in which St. John had written it. How marvelous it was to be able to identify the Greek letters, to sound them out—hearing the Gospel almost the way it was heard two thousand years ago—and to understand what I was reading! I couldn't imagine education being more satisfying.

Despite some initial misgivings, most of my brother Jesuits also found themselves enjoying studies. In time, we even began incorporating what we had learned into our daily routines. Humorously, that is: you didn't want to incorporate *too much* philosophy into your daily life, lest you, like Descartes, be prompted to doubt your own existence. My friend Dave spent so much time laboring over the *Summa Theologica* that he occasionally took to imitating Thomas's trademark method of answering questions.

"Hey, Dave," we would say, "what time is the movie tonight?"

"*Respondeo* . . . 7:00, 9:30, and 10:45."

During our first summer break at Loyola, two Jesuit friends and I decided to get a head start on the next year's work by taking a reading course with Sr. French. When we asked her to suggest a topic, she said without hesitation, "Aquinas, of course." So during that sultry Chicago summer, Peter, Ross, and I spent the days poring over the *Summa,* concentrating on the sections on God: outlining the relevant passages on long sheets of yellow paper; turning over in our minds Thomas's questions, objections, and responses; and discussing his work in lively meetings, all under the careful tutelage of Sr. French. For good measure, we read Chesterton's biography as well.

During one meeting in Sr. French's tidy office, it dawned on me that our teacher—this Catholic, this woman religious, this good and kind person—embodied what St. Anselm meant when he talked of theology as *fides quaerens intellectum*: how God can draw us to understand the transcendent through reason, and how learning and erudition can coexist with humility and love. I began to see for the first time how the life of the mind is not divorced from the life of faith. Most of all, thanks to Sr. French, I began to understand what

Thomas Aquinas meant in his *Summa* when he wrote, "We can testify to something only in the measure that we have shared in it." And in realizing these things, it seemed that I had received a beautiful gift.

❧

Today Thomas might be taken as a model for our rational age, with his reasoned approach to difficult theological questions. He thought that all theology flowed naturally from God and God's purposes. And since God has given us the gift of reason, we should use reason in service to God, by trying to understand his world better.

Yet this rational man was also a mystic. Near the end of his fruitful life, Thomas was living at the Dominican house of studies in Naples. His order had sent him there as a way for him to escape some of the controversy that his writings had stirred up in Paris. During a Mass on the Feast of St. Nicholas, Thomas received a mystical vision that put into perspective all his theological initiatives—the *Summas*, the logic, the lectures, the argumentation, the proofs, the words. Afterward he put down his pen and ceased his writing.

"All I have written," he said, "seems to me like straw compared with what I have seen and what has been revealed to me."

13

Fools for Christ

Francis of Assisi

Preach the gospel. Use words if necessary.
—St. Francis of Assisi

I spent a good deal of my time during philosophy studies hanging out with street gangs.

In our Jesuit philosophy program in Chicago, this was not as uncommon as it might sound. Along with our studies, we scholastics (that's what Jesuit seminarians are called) were required to work from ten to fifteen hours a week in a ministry of our choosing. Though we were unceasingly reminded that our primary objective was studying philosophy, our weekly ministries reminded us of the ultimate goal of all our training: service to God and to the larger community. We were to become, in Pedro Arrupe's phrase, "men for others." Ministry was also a way to keep in touch with the world outside our books, a world that, when we were reading Kant or Heidegger, could seem far away indeed. And for those Jesuits who loathed philosophy, the work outside of school helped keep them saner.

Fortunately, in a big city there were plenty of opportunities to choose from. During my first few weeks at Loyola University, the Jesuits in the year ahead offered advice on the most popular ministries.

261

My friend Ross, for example, ended up working in a hospital ward caring for babies born to crack-addicted mothers who were being processed by the city's penal system. The next year he worked at Misericordia, a large community set on several acres in Chicago that cared for the mentally and physically disabled. Others worked as dorm chaplains counseling college students, as tutors for undergraduates, or with the school's campus ministry helping prepare Sunday liturgies. Still others served at homeless shelters, employment centers, and soup kitchens.

Right away I knew what I wanted to do. One ministry sounded like the most exciting, the most intriguing, and without a doubt the coolest work I could imagine. Over the years, a few scholastics had worked with a quasi-legendary man named Brother Bill, who ministered to street gang members in the housing projects of Chicago. Brother Bill worked with one or two scholastics every year—not for reasons of selectivity, but rather because only a few were willing to work in such dangerous conditions. Stories circulated among the scholastics about the ministry: being caught in the middle of gang "rumbles," seeing the inside of Chicago's worst housing projects, even hearing the apparently dramatic story of Brother Bill's religious conversion, which led to his work of peacemaking in the inner city.

But the tale that grabbed my attention was that of the young Jesuit who had barely missed being killed by a bullet, which tore a hole in his cassock. Brother Bill asked the scholastics with whom he worked to wear a traditional Jesuit cassock when visiting the inner-city housing projects. For protection the Jesuits needed recognizable garb in the housing projects, and only the habit would do. Bill himself wore a sort of modified Franciscan habit. One day a Jesuit proudly pointed out a small bullet hole in the sleeve of the cassock in question. He said that the Jesuit wearing it had found himself in the middle of a gang war and had ducked out of the way just in time.

Whether or not this was true was debatable. "Oh, give me a *break!*" said another scholastic in my community. "It's probably a cigarette burn." Still, this was not a typical ministry.

While I wasn't sure I wanted to get shot at, I was certain that I wanted to work in a job that helped so many "at risk" young people. So after checking with my Jesuit superior, I gave Bill a call.

"Okay, buddy," he said, after a brief interview over the phone. (He called everyone "buddy.") "I'll see you next week. Don't forget the cassock."

Though I didn't tell anyone at the time, secretly I was glad for an excuse to wear a Jesuit habit. Certainly there was the novelty that came with wearing any kind of uniform for the first time, but there was more to my affinity for the Jesuit cassock than that. Worn almost from the time of St. Ignatius until it was discarded sometime in the late 1960s, the cassock represented a tangible link to the past and was a distinctly Jesuit symbol. Unlike the black cassocks still worn by some diocesan priests, with the long row of buttons running down the front, the Jesuit habit was tied together with a black cincture at the waist. It had even given rise to an old nickname for the Jesuits: the "long black line."

Ironically, this traditional Jesuit symbol was nearly the opposite of what St. Ignatius intended for his men. The Jesuit *Constitutions* indicated that there was to be no specific habit for the Jesuits: they were to wear the garb of other priests and brothers in the region. Still, since entering the Jesuits, I had begun to lament that we had given up the cassock, for a few reasons. First, wearing a simple item of clothing everyday makes the question of what clothes to wear and to buy much easier.

Second is what theologians call the "sign" value. The habit is a visible symbol of one's commitment and mission—something like a police officer's uniform or a doctor's white lab coat. It is a potent reminder to those who see it that there are still, in our daily lives—on the street, in subways, on buses—men and women who choose lives of poverty, chastity, and obedience.

The habit also connects the wearer (and those who see him or her) to history and tradition. The first time I visited a Trappist monastery and saw the monks process into the chapel in their black and white habits, the sight nearly knocked me out. There was no need for them to say, "We're Trappists and we take a vow of stability and pray constantly, and you might recognize the habit as the same one that your hero Thomas Merton wore, and we still wear it as a sign of our commitment." They didn't have to say any of that. Their habit said it all.

Another reason I wanted to wear a cassock was that I thought it looked really cool.

But cool or not, Jesuits no longer wear cassocks. Still, finding a cassock for my work with Brother Bill was easy. Crammed into a musty closet at the main Jesuit residence at Loyola University were a few leftover cassocks from the 1960s, which the scholastics borrowed for their work with Bill.

On the first afternoon of my work with Brother Bill, on a breezy September day, I put on the cassock over a polo shirt and black pants and tied the cincture as I had been taught by one of the older fathers in my community.

Standing before the mirror in my room, I adjusted the unfamiliar robe and was taken aback. What I saw in the mirror reminded me immediately of Isaac Jogues, one of my favorite saints and one of the North American martyrs, the heroic Jesuits who journeyed from France in the seventeenth century to work with Native Americans in North America, mostly in New York and Canada, before their eventual martyrdom. (The movie *Black Robe* is loosely based on the life of Isaac Jogues and his companions.) High on the outside walls of the university chapel, which I passed every day, were the names of the North American martyrs, incised deep into the granite. Letters almost a foot high spelled out JOGUES, BRÉBEUF, LALEMANT, CHABANEL, GOUPIL, DE LA LANDE, DANIEL, GARNIER. Inside the chapel, at a side altar where I liked to pray, was a vividly colored mosaic of the eight martyrs, almost life-sized, standing side by side. Halos of gold tiles encircled each of their heads. Some were dressed in the Native American garb that they had adopted in their work among the Hurons, but most were wearing the very same habit that I wore now.

Outside our house, Brother Bill was waiting for me in his beat-up car. "Hey, buddy," he said. In the front seat was another scholastic, an African American Jesuit named Dave, who had also decided to join Bill for the semester.

The first thing you noticed about Bill was not his oversized glasses, or his thinning gray hair, or even his stocky build; the first thing you noticed was his habit. Whenever he was working with the gangs, Brother Bill sported a long robe and cowl, in the Franciscan style, made up entirely of faded blue denim patches. "It looks like a Levi's factory exploded on him," said a Jesuit friend.

On the way to the projects that first day Bill described the outline of his life. A graduate of Loyola Academy, a Jesuit high school outside Chicago, Bill studied English and philosophy as an undergraduate at Notre Dame and later earned a master's degree in counseling, also at Notre Dame. For the next fifteen years he worked as a counselor with Catholic Charities in Chicago. Bill described what sounded like an ordinary life—enjoying his job, trying to make ends meet, drinking with his pals, and dating women. In 1980, he was offered two lucrative jobs, one as a hospital therapist and one as an executive trainer with a major airline.

Around this time, Bill passed a church and went inside, thinking it would be a good place to pray about his decision. As he entered the church, he described everything as going fuzzy except for the face of Christ, which he noticed on a painting. "Love," said Jesus, in what Bill described to us as a vision. "You are forbidden from doing anything else." Then Bill said that he heard, "I'll lead; you follow" repeated three times, and "Never be afraid. All your trust." He told Dave and me that, at the time, he didn't know what to be afraid of.

A few months later, he opened a Bible at random and came upon the words "Take nothing with you for your journey." Two hours later, he opened to the same words, but in a different section of the Bible. The next day, he was careful to open the Bible to the letters of Paul, where he was certain he wouldn't find those words, but he found them again. A priest with whom Bill spoke said, "It means you are to give up your possessions."

Not surprisingly, Bill considered all this, in his words, "a lot of baloney." But at his parents' home that night he opened an art book and saw a picture of a book of the Gospels with the caption "Take nothing with you for your journey."

After this kind of thing happened a few more times, Bill knelt down to pray. "Seven is supposed to be a lucky number, so if you show this to me for the seventh time, I will give away all my possessions." For the seventh time, he opened the Bible to another page and came upon the same sentence. Seeing in this an invitation from God, Bill decided to give away all of his possessions, moved into the basement of a friend's house, and slept on a cardboard mat.

Bill returned to his job with Catholic Charities and volunteered one day a week at St. Malachy Church, near the Henry Horner Homes and Rockwell Gardens, two Chicago Housing Authority projects in some of the poorest and most violent areas in the city. After a few months, the pastor asked if Bill would like to become youth minister for the parish, saying, "Here that means working with gangs." In this way Bill found his ministry.

On June 1, 1983, the man with the crazy outfit began walking among the members of two gangs at the Henry Horner Homes, the Gangster Disciples and the Vice Lords. The following day the Gangster Disciples held a council meeting to decide whether or not Bill should be killed. In the end, they decided that he was a good guy, that he should be allowed to do what he wanted to do, and, further, that they would protect him. The Disciples told Bill that this meant killing anyone who hurt him. Bill countered that even his murderer would be his brother and should be loved more than anyone.

So Brother Bill's work began in earnest. When gunfights erupted, Bill simply walked in the middle of the shooting until it stopped. If he was at home in Evanston, a few miles north, and heard about a gunfight, he would pull on his robe, begin praying, and jump in his car. Sometimes angry gang members would shout out, "Brother Bill, get out of the way!" He would visit gang members recovering from wounds in the hospital, attend dozens of funerals of his "buddies," counsel their families, give the younger gang members rides in his beat-up car, take large groups of them to Notre Dame to football and basketball games, and generally just spend time with them. And eventually he began to take along Jesuit scholastics.

When I asked him in the car that afternoon what our work would be, he said, "Love them."

That night I told the story at dinner, and one of the scholastics voiced one of my fears, "He sounds like a *nut*!" Ever since our car ride, I had wondered: Was my ministry this year going to be working with a lunatic?

An older priest at the table laughed. "Be careful who you're calling nuts." He reminded us that Bill's experiences, while seemingly outlandish, were similar to stories from the lives of the saints. Just that semester, in my Medieval Philosophy class, we would read the *Confessions* by St. Augustine. For all of his love of reason and philosophy, even Augustine relied on the method of opening a book to a random page to receive some divine guidance. (What Augustine read was a line from St. Paul that spoke to the libertine youth: "Arm yourself with the Lord Jesus Christ. Spend no more time on nature and nature's appetites.")

Likewise, said the priest, the experience of imagining Christ speaking from a painting had an equally impressive provenance: St. Francis of Assisi, who had heard the voice of Christ speaking to him from a crucifix in the church at San Damiano, telling him, "Repair my church."

"If Bill's crazy," said the Jesuit, "then so were Augustine and Francis. And maybe they were!"

The more I thought about it, the clearer it became who Bill reminded me of, with his goofy habit and crazy attitude, his penchant for peacemaking, his talk of visions, and his deceptively simple "Love them." He reminded me of Francis of Assisi. I found myself agreeing with the older Jesuit. If Bill is crazy, then he's crazy like St. Francis, and that's a kind of crazy I'd like to be around.

I reached this conclusion knowing very little about the life of St. Francis. At the time, if pressed, I would have been able to say only the following about him: he renounced his father's wealth, founded the Franciscans, loved nature, sang songs, wrote some poems, and undoubtedly died a happy death. (Oh, and he lived in Assisi.)

But as much as I found him a charming figure, my understanding of the world's most popular saint was the rather sentimental one that is common today: as a sort of dopey but well-meaning hippie who talked to birds. As Lawrence S. Cunningham notes in *Francis of Assisi*, such a view is "most completely summed up by the ubiquity of those concrete garden statues with a bird perched on the saint's shoulder found in everyone's garden center." In this conception, Francis was cheerful no doubt, but also a little bland. "Such an understanding is coterminous with what I would call *spirituality lite*."

Francis of Assisi is a good example of why the legends should never overshadow the actual life. For within his life, many surprises await those willing to meet Francis on his own terms. As Cunningham emphasizes, unlike the figure many wish to claim for all religions, or for no religion, Francis was deeply and thoroughly Catholic. At the same time, he did not hesitate to travel to the Middle East during the Crusades to make peace with the sultan. Toward the end of his life, suffering from great physical torment—including horrible problems with his eyes—he was rejected by some of his brother Franciscans who found his way of poverty too difficult to live. When riled, he was far less pacific than his garden-variety likeness, once climbing upon a roof in order to tear down a modest building that housed his Franciscan brothers, which he found inconsistent with their vow of poverty.

Throughout his short life, his actions confused, angered, and annoyed both supporters and detractors. His real life, which we know a good deal about, prevents him from ever being completely tamed by the legends.

❁

His father, Pietro di Bernardone, was wealthy. This is at the heart of understanding Francis. Though baptized as Giovanni, he was called Francesco by his father, a cloth merchant who loved all things French.

(Pietro was on a business trip in France during his son's baptism and gave him the nickname upon his return.) As a youth, Francis was spoiled and dissolute, spending his early years running with, as Thomas Merton called his own friends, a "pack of hearties." At the same time, he was a charming and generous young man, according to his chroniclers, and well liked in Assisi despite his penchant for pranks and love of the high life. In his superb biography of Francis, Julien Green writes, "With his seductive charm, Francesco was the king of all youth, and all was forgiven him."

At the age of twenty, Francis was taken prisoner during a war between Assisi and Perugia, a neighboring town. Though he bore the ordeal cheerfully, his time in jail left him sick and weakened. On his release a year later he decided to become a knight. In preparation for his new state of life, he promptly purchased an expensive suit of armor, complete with a lavish cloak embroidered with gold. His father paid for this, of course, as he paid for all of Francis's early interests. According to tradition, the day after purchasing the armor, Francis came across a nobleman reduced to poverty and spontaneously gave him his new cloak. In the thirteenth century, this would have been an especially charitable action. It was considered nobler to come to the aid of the poor nobility, since they were not only poor but also shamed.

One night, in Spoleto, en route to his military service, Francis had a dream in which a heavenly voice urged him to "serve the master, not the man" and return to Assisi. He did so, and began to find his old life of partying less and less attractive. Over time, he started living more simply, praying more, and giving alms.

Riding his horse one day in the plain of Assisi, Francis chanced upon a "leper," that is, a person suffering from one of the skin diseases so common in those days. From childhood, the delicate Francis had had a horror of lepers, and his whole being was revolted by the sight of this man. Yet somehow his dream had led him to understand that his life was being changed. Grasping the demands of his new call, Francis dismounted and prepared to embrace the man.

The Little Flowers of St. Francis of Assisi is a compendium of charming stories about the saint. While a number of them are clearly legendary, they effectively convey many of the saint's most important qualities: his gentle spirit, his love of nature, his desire for peace. Included, for example, is the tale of Francis preaching to the swallows (who are rudely disturbing the Masses with their loud chirping). My favorite is the story of the wolf of Gubbio, a fearsome animal who has so terrorized the town that both men and women are afraid to venture beyond its walls. Taking pity on Gubbio, Francis decides to speak with "friar wolf." *The Little Flowers* recounts what happens after Francis asks the wolf if there can be peace between him and the town.

> At these words, the wolf, by movements of his body and tail and eyes, and by bowing his head, showed that he accepted what St. Francis said and was determined to observe it. Thereupon St. Francis spoke to him again, saying, "Friar wolf, because it seems good to you to make and keep this peace, I promise you that, so long as you shall live, I will cause you to be fed regularly by the men of this city, so that you shall no more suffer hunger. For I know full well that whatever evil you have done, you have done out of hunger. But seeing that I beg for you this grace, I desire, friar wolf, that you should promise me that never from now on will you injure any human being or any animal. Do you promise me this?" And the wolf, by bowing his head, gave evidence that he promised it. . . . Then St. Francis held forth his hand to receive his fealty, and the wolf lifted up his right forepaw and put it with friendly confidence in the hand of St. Francis, giving thereby such token of fealty as he was able. Then St. Francis said, "Friar wolf, I command you in the name of Jesus Christ to come now with me, in confidence, and let us

go and establish this peace in the name of God." And the wolf went with him obediently, like a gentle lamb, at which the citizens marveled greatly.

The wolf, by the way, holds to his promise. He becomes a welcome visitor to Gubbio who "entered familiarly into its houses" and was "courteously nourished" by the inhabitants. And when he died, friar wolf was lamented, for he reminded the citizens of the "virtue and sanctity of St. Francis."

In her moving book *Salvation*, Valerie Martin traces the story of St. Francis backward in time, beginning with his death and ending with his meeting the leper on the road, an encounter that she describes in mystical terms. The embrace therefore becomes the poetic climax of her narrative, just as it was a pivotal event in the conversion of the rich young man. Her retelling deserves to be quoted at length:

Carefully, Francesco places his coin in the open palm, where it glitters, hot and white. For a moment he tries to form some simple speech, some pleasantry that will restore him to the ordinary world, but even as he struggles, he understands that this world is gone from him now, that there is no turning back; it was only so much smoke, blinding and confusing him, but he has come through it somehow, he has found the source of it, and now, at last, he is standing in the fire. Tenderly he takes the leper's hand, tenderly he brings it to his lips. At once his mouth is flooded with an unearthly sweetness, which pours over his tongue, sweet and hot, burning his throat and bringing sudden tears to his eyes. These tears moisten the corrupted hand he presses to his mouth.

His ears are filled with the sound of wind, and he can feel the wind chilling his face, a cold, harsh wind blowing toward him from the future, blowing away everything that has come before this moment, which he has longed for and dreaded, as if he thought he might not live through it.

From this time forward, Francis began visiting hospitals and giving even more of his money to the poor, and sometimes even his clothes. Walking outside the walls of Assisi one afternoon, Francis, still wondering what path his life would take, stumbled onto an old church that had fallen into disrepair, called San Damiano.

As he stared at the large crucifix hanging in the church, he began to meditate on the passion and death of Jesus, and he wept for his own sinfulness. In the midst of this meditation, Francis heard Christ speaking to him from the cross. "Francesco," the voice said to him three times. "Go and repair my house, which you see is falling down."

Like Brother Bill centuries later in Chicago, Francis was thunderstruck. But unlike Brother Bill, Francis was certain about what he needed to do. God had asked him to repair the church at San Damiano. So he confidently went to his father's warehouse, stole a bolt of scarlet cloth, sold it, brought the proceeds to the parish priest, and asked to stay there in order that he might help rebuild the church.

But the saint was mistaken. God was asking him to repair *the* Church, not *a* church.

By now Francis's appearance appalled the people of Assisi. Dressed in rags and begging for his meals, he brought shame to his family. His father, furious over the loss of his money and probably equally upset about his son's ignominious behavior, carried Francis home, shackled his feet, and locked him up, until his mother set him free. He promptly returned to San Damiano to begin his repairs. Further enraged, Bernardone brought public charges against Francis. He insisted that his son either return the money he had stolen or renounce his patrimony and return home.

On April 10, 1206, after being summoned by the bishop to account for his actions, Francis stood before a crowd of townspeople in the square of Assisi, not far from his father's house. The bishop told Francis to return his father's money and place his trust in God. Francis did what he was told, and "with his usual literalness," as *Butler's* says, Francis added this: "The clothes I wear are also his. I'll give them back."

With that, he stripped off his clothes and laid them at his father's feet, and stood naked in the square.

The gesture would be just as shocking today. The bishop wept, stunned by the force of Francis's actions, and wrapped the young man in his cope. The symbolism was thus complete: Francis had stripped himself of his allegiance to his father (and, incidentally, to his father's business as a cloth merchant) and was wrapped in the protection of the Church. He had thrown himself entirely on God's providence. He had abandoned the pride of his youth. He had embraced a life of radical poverty, in imitation of Christ. "Sister Poverty" would be "the fairest bride in the whole world, in imitation of Christ." And he had engaged in what would have been seen at the time as an act of public penance.

But there was more to it than even that. As Julien Green notes in his biography, "The renunciation in the presence of the crowd was in itself, according to medieval mentality, a juridical act. From now on, Francis, with nothing to his name, was taking sides with the outcast and the disinherited."

❦

Brother Bill's ministry was devoted to the same people. In the car on that first afternoon, he began to tell us about each of the members of the Vice Lords and the Gangster Disciples who was in trouble. This one in jail. This one having problems with his girlfriend. This one doing drugs. This one shot last night.

In the backseat of his big Buick, with Lake Michigan on our left and the variegated skyline of Chicago on our right, I listened as we barreled down Lake Shore Drive en route to the housing projects. And I started to grow disquieted about the ministry. Suddenly I felt idiotic in my getup—I was wearing a cassock to do ministry with gang members—and frightened about what I was hearing.

The neighborhoods grew less and less appealing, and in a few minutes we pulled into a small trash-filled parking lot in front of the Cabrini-Green Homes, one of the worst housing projects in the city. Before we emerged from the car, some young men spotted us. "Hey, Brother Bill!" one shouted. "What up?"

"Hey," he said back. "These are my friends, Jim and Dave." We shook hands with a gathering group of tough-looking young men and listened to them speak with Brother Bill. The conversation was by turns friendly (asking about each other's families), polite (asking about us), lighthearted (teasing about his habit and ours), and serious (talking about who had been shot recently, who was in the hospital, whose mother was ill, who had lost a job, and who was looking for one).

After our brief chat, the young men dispersed, and Bill, Dave, and I visited one of the gang members in his apartment in Cabrini-Green. Though by now I had worked with the poor in a variety of settings, I was still shocked by the condition of the apartment buildings in the project. The sticky-floored elevator smelled like urine, the filthy cinder-block hallways were open on one side to the courtyard below (but fenced in with wire), and the walls echoed with harsh noises. Televisions blared and people shouted and argued; trash cans banged and babies cried. I thought of how hard it must be to live there and raise children.

Inside the young man's apartment (his mother's, really) we were invited to sit down on a faded but clean couch and were given cups of coffee as we listened to his problems. He was unable to find work because of his poor educational background. His mother and sister were struggling to make ends meet, even though his mother worked two jobs. His father was nowhere to be found. Over the next few months, we would hear similar stories, nearly all of them ending with Brother Bill promising to do what he could.

In truth, there was little Bill could do other than be their friend and, as he said, "love them." This love took many forms. Some days, particularly during the frigid Chicago winters, we took the younger members of the gangs for rides in Bill's big car, which they enjoyed. One bright December day, we drove through the city to Lake Michigan, and one young adolescent who had lived in Chicago his entire life said, unexpectedly, "I never seen the lake before."

The gang members gradually became more comfortable having Dave and me around. (In an interesting historical twist, they called us "Blackrobes," the same term used by the Native Americans for Isaac Jogues and his companions in the seventeenth century.) They asked about our lives, where we were from, and how school was going for us. They also asked us, frequently, one question that seemed a sort of test: "Are you scared of coming here?" Toward the close of the semester I arranged for my Jesuit community to host some of the young men for dinner. One afternoon, we drove three of them up Lake Shore Drive onto the campus of Loyola University. The men, in their early twenties, had seen much of Chicago and so appeared unfazed by the journey.

Inside Arrupe House, my Jesuit community, it was another story. The gang members asked questions about the way we lived, fell quiet when we escorted them into the house chapel, and laughed when they saw all the food we had. I explained that thirty people lived there, but they thought it was a lot of food anyway. In the dining room my Jesuit brothers were unfailingly courteous and tried their best to make the young men feel at home. Still, the young men seemed nervous, so we reserved a table for ourselves: Brother Bill, Dave, me, and our guests.

One visitor to Arrupe House that night was a Ugandan man from a religious congregation called the Brothers of Charles Lwanga, named after one of the Ugandan martyrs killed in the late nineteenth century. Brother Bill's friends were shocked to run into someone from Africa. When he greeted them with an elegant East African accent, the young men burst into laughter. They couldn't understand him. He couldn't understand them either. So I ended up translating for both sides.

They peppered him with questions. "Do you hunt lions? Do you live in a hut?"

"I live in Kampala, one of the largest cities in Africa," he explained. "Very far from the lions."

They laughed in disbelief.

Eventually Dave and I grew more relaxed working with Brother Bill and the gang members. Normally, I would join Bill twice a week. Each time he would be waiting for me outside Arrupe House, his hulking car idling noisily on the street. If it was raining or snowing, there would typically be few kids around the housing projects, and Bill and I would wait in the car and talk about what he had seen or experienced the day or night before. Sometimes it seemed that I did more talking with Bill than with the gang members. But that was okay. I was happy to hear his stories, and he seemed to enjoy the companionship. "Part of your ministry," explained my Jesuit superior, "is ministry to Bill."

But there were always surprises in store. One sunny afternoon in November, when I was in the middle of a conversation at the

Henry Horner Homes with an affable gang member, Bill abruptly announced that it was time to leave. Someone had just told him that a gang war was starting up nearby. We jumped into the car and sped to a neighborhood just a few minutes away. Along the route, Brother Bill peered intently out the window, as if scanning for trouble.

When we arrived at the designated street corner, Bill seemed to know instinctively where to go. He walked quickly toward a small group of men clustered under an El stop. As we approached I noticed that some were carrying chains and pieces of lumber. Bill spoke with them quickly and told me that we were going to stand between the two groups. Only then did I notice that on an opposite corner stood another group—of Asian American young men, similarly armed with clubs and chains. And guns? I couldn't be sure.

Oh brother, I thought, *what are we doing here?*

What we were doing was what Francis of Assisi did when he visited the sultan during the Crusades. And what Dorothy Day did when she protested against the First and Second World Wars. And, for that matter, what Jesus did when he interposed himself between the crowds and the woman caught in adultery. That is, using our bodies as a sign of peace, trying to embody Christ's message of reconciliation.

So though I was scared, and crazy as it might have looked to see a heavyset guy in a patchwork denim getup and a skinny guy in an old black cassock standing in the middle of a Chicago street, I knew we were doing the right thing. "Now we pray," said Bill.

We stood for a few uncomfortable minutes under the sunny sky, until the two groups drew closer to each other and began shouting epithets. Without warning, an empty soda bottle flew silently over our heads and shattered in the street. Another bottle answered from the other side, with another crash, and the shouting grew louder.

But gradually the shouting died down, and the two groups simply left. Bill and I were left standing in the middle of the street. It was strangely quiet, with no traffic even though it was the middle of the day. Brother Bill just smiled. "We gave them an excuse not to fight," he explained. "With us here they don't lose face leaving the fight."

That night I told the story at dinner. "He's insane," said one of the scholastics.

Perhaps. But Bill knew just what he was doing. After all, he had walked into such situations dozens of times before, and, as he consistently explained, his nonviolent presence gave the men the loophole they needed to avoid bloodshed. His insane approach seemed to make more sense than the usual response of Americans to the struggles of the urban poor, which is either blame and indifference or resignation to the situation. More to the point, his insanity probably saved many lives, the lives of his "buddies."

⁂

Since entering the Jesuits, I've met a few such memorable "fools for Christ," as St. Paul says—people with the same brand of charisma and foolhardiness that Francis of Assisi had. But only a few. In Kenya, for instance, just a few years after Chicago, I worked closely with a Dominican sister from Germany named Sr. Luise.

She was in charge of the Jesuit Refugee Service's scholarship program in Nairobi. At least that was her official job description. On the side, however, Sr. Luise had founded a settlement house for Sudanese refugees, which she funded through a complicated network of personal donations and support from a host of international agencies. At the time, Sudan was in the midst of a bloody civil war, with southern Sudanese streaming into refugee camps in Kenya and into the capital. Sr. Luise tried to find homes, jobs, and food for as many of these people as she could. And in the Jesuit Refugee Service office where she worked, Sr. Luise had finagled jobs for five refugees (when there was really only work for one or two). A group of Sudanese refugees once told me that the only name they were told when they left their village in Sudan was "Sr. Luise."

I accompanied her one warm day to the small town where she lived, called Juja, a few kilometers north of Nairobi. In the middle of the town stood an apartment complex entirely filled with Sudanese refugees whom Sr. Luise had sponsored or had helped get jobs or was planning to help resettle abroad. When she parked her little car in front of the building, dozens of Sudanese children ran out to greet her. Just as Brother Bill's beat-up car and distinctive dress were familiar to the residents of Chicago's housing projects, so both Sr. Luise's car and her simple habit (a blue skirt and blue veil) were instantly recognizable. The children eagerly grabbed her hands and led her to the building, where in the open-air courtyard mothers washed clothes and cooked food in small pots and nursed children. When we entered the courtyard, everyone stood and waved.

"How did they ever find me?" she asked with a laugh.

Sr. Luise was deemed crazy for agreeing to take on the care of so many people. She was deemed crazy for running what was, in essence, a small Sudanese town. She was deemed crazy when, a few years after I left Nairobi, her home was broken into and she was severely beaten by robbers, but she decided to stay anyway—by then in her late seventies—with a broken arm. But like Brother Bill, she saved lives with her craziness, and like Francis of Assisi, she had a brand of craziness that came straight out of the Gospels.

❧

After his conversion, St. Francis of Assisi conformed his life to the example of Jesus and, as Lawrence S. Cunningham notes, offered his life "as a gift to others."

In the spring of 1208, during a Mass in Assisi, Francis heard the Gospel story in which Jesus asks his followers to "take nothing with you for the journey." Taking this as a personal call, he threw away his shoes, tunic, and staff and put on the simple garb of a shepherd—what would become the familiar Franciscan tunic and hood, tied with a cord around his waist. The poor man's preaching was so compelling that he began attracting adherents immediately. Within a year there were twelve followers, who became known as the Fratres Minores (Latin for "Lesser Brothers"), better known as the Franciscans.

In 1210, Francis presented to Pope Innocent III a formal petition to found a religious order. Some of the papal advisers scoffed at Francis's simple plans for his Rule, finding its emphasis on radical poverty overly idealistic and almost willfully impractical. But the Pope was so impressed with the man who stood before him that he swiftly granted approval.

Francis returned to Assisi to reside with his brothers in a small rural chapel in the countryside. From there, they fanned out through central Italy, preaching, begging for alms, and performing manual labor. In 1212, a women's division of the order was founded under the leadership of Francis's close friend Clare, a young woman of Assisi. Francis himself cut off her hair, marking her for a life of poverty. The group became known as the Poor Ladies of San Damiano, called today the Poor Clares.

In 1219, during the middle of the Crusades, Francis journeyed to Egypt and was received by the sultan Malik al-Kamil. This visit was an expression of Francis's desire for nonviolence, peacemaking, and reconciliation during an era in which "sacred violence" was embraced even by religious leaders. As Brother Bill would do in the housing projects, Francis placed himself in a dangerous place and employed his body as an instrument for peace. His hopes to convert the sultan were unrealized, but al-Kamil listened to Francis with goodwill. At the end of their lengthy discussion, the sultan is supposed to have said, "I would convert to your religion, which is a beautiful one, but I cannot: both of us would be massacred."

After Francis's return to Italy, the number of friars grew, as did tensions among the new Franciscans, who had competing ideas about what it meant to lead a religious life. Sensing that he was not up to the challenges of running a rapidly growing religious order, Francis resigned, turning over the management of his group to another brother.

With his health failing (he suffered from virulent eye infections as well as tuberculosis during much of his later life), he spent increasing lengths of time in prayer. During one retreat, at Mount La Verna, Francis had a deep mystical experience in prayer and felt an intense identification with the sufferings of Christ. During this retreat, he became the first person to receive the stigmata; the wounds of Christ's passion were mysteriously imprinted in his hands, feet, and sides. Greatly embarrassed by this, he concealed them for the rest of his life by covering his hands with his habit and wearing shoes and stockings on his feet. Much of his time was now spent in prayer.

Francis's last few years were filled with pain and discomfort, from both his eyes and the stigmata. Still, he composed during this time his joyful "Canticle of Brother Sun," which he wrote on his last visit to San Damiano. It was a final expression of his lifelong love of creation and his innate sense of the sacramentality, or holiness, of all things, animate or inanimate.

As he was dying, Francis asked to be laid on the bare earth near a favorite chapel in the woods and to be dressed in an old gray habit. On October 3, 1226, he welcomed "Brother Death." Though he requested burial in the criminals' cemetery, the next day his brothers, who loved him so much, went against his wishes and took his body in solemn procession to the church in Assisi. There it remained until 1230, two years after his canonization, when it was removed to the basilica that still holds it today.

⚬◈⚬

I knew very little about Francis when I first met Brother Bill, and even when I met Sr. Luise. But on my way back from East Africa, while stopping in Rome, I was urged by the Jesuits to visit Assisi.

I had only one day in Assisi, which was reached easily by bus from Rome. But there, in that little town in the Umbrian countryside, surrounded by pilgrims, threading my way through the narrow streets, standing in the very places in which Francis had stood, I was overwhelmed with the holiness of the place. All of Assisi felt to me like a church: the very paving stones seemed holy. Though I was there for only a few hours, I spent most of the time wandering around inside the great basilica, staring at the gorgeous cycle of frescos of Francis's life, painted by Giotto, and, most of all, praying near his tomb. A separate portrait of Francis by Cimabue is almost life-sized, with Francis's feet painted very near the floor. Staring into the flecked eyes of the fresco, I wondered what it must have been like to meet him here in Assisi.

Francis is buried in the lower church, and the area surrounding his earthen tomb has been opened up and turned into a little chapel, with wooden pews for the pilgrims. You can even touch the cool, wet stones that surround his remains.

After I returned from Rome I began a long reading tour, which has never really ended, of the many biographies of St. Francis, each of which shades his portrait with different colors: Adrian House's factual account, Nikos Kazantzakis's lively portrait of a vibrant man, G. K. Chesterton's affectionate one, Valerie Martin's poetic narrative, and Lawrence S. Cunningham's more theological consideration of the world's most popular saint. Along with these I read through the collection of popular stories about Francis, some true, some probably legendary, called *The Little Flowers of St. Francis of Assisi*. One of my favorite biographies is by Julien Green and combines fact, legend, theology, and personal experience. It was originally published in French under the name *Frère François*. But I like the English name much better: *God's Fool*.

⚜

Since leaving Chicago, I've never had the chance to meet up again with Brother Bill. Just recently, however, Sr. Luise visited the United States for the first time. I hadn't seen her for ten years. Of course she had changed: a little heavier (though wearing the exact habit she always wore) and a little slower (thanks to her bad knees), but still full of life.

She was accompanying a group of Sudanese refugees who were being resettled in America. "They didn't know how to use the toilets on the airplane," she said, "so I had to come along with them." Many of her former Sudanese students from Nairobi, who had long ago settled in the States, helped pay her way. Her long journey in the States took her from New York to Syracuse to Kansas City to Denver to Dallas and back to New York, where she was staying at a Dominican friary. She laughed when she told me about her experiences on the trip. Elderly, with bad knees, far from home, suffering from a cold, at the tail end of a grueling trip, Sr. Luise was nonetheless in high spirits.

At the end of our conversation I asked something that I had wanted to ask in Nairobi but never had: How do you find the energy to do all these things?

"Oh," she said instantly, "the prayers of the people."

As I said good-bye, she gave me a big hug and startled me with a question. "Will I ever see you again?"

I was too shocked to answer, but I knew what she meant. Nearing eighty now, she would probably never visit the States again, and who knew if I would ever return to Kenya? "Of course," I said, not wanting to admit the truth.

She smiled and hugged me again. The door of the friary closed, and I was reminded once again of the saints that God raises up in every age, and how lucky I have been to meet some of them.

14

Hidden Lives

Joseph

Is not this the carpenter's son?
—MATTHEW 13:55

After completing philosophy studies, Jesuit scholastics spend two or three years working full-time in ministry. When the time came for me to "discern" with my superiors where to go, two possibilities came to my mind. The first was the Nativity Mission Center, a middle school for underprivileged boys in New York, where I had worked as a novice. The second option, undeniably more glamorous, was a job with the Jesuit Refugee Service.

At the time, I had been reading a good deal about the Jesuit Refugee Service, an organization founded in 1980 by Pedro Arrupe, who was at the time superior general of the Society of Jesus. Everything I heard about JRS inspired me: their work with refugees in the most desperate of situations, their model of Jesuits living and working with diocesan priests and laypersons and members of other religious orders, their commitment to a simple lifestyle, and their desire to be mobile enough to go wherever the refugee situation demanded. It seemed exactly like the kind of work that a Jesuit should be doing.

After a few weeks of prayer and reflection, I found myself equally at home with either choice: staying in the States to work in a middle school or going overseas with the Jesuit Refugee Service. As Jesuits like to say, I was "indifferent" to the two choices. In common parlance, that word carries a negative tone, but it is a cherished phrase in Ignatian spirituality. Indifference in the Jesuit perspective connotes having the interior freedom to go wherever one is most needed and to do whatever seems best: one is open to following the will of God, wherever it may lead. Indifference, like availability, is a kind of goal in the Jesuit life. Sometimes, though, indifference can seem a distant goal. When I was going through the discernment process, a Jesuit friend joked: "You're indifferent? Enjoy it while it lasts!"

A few months before the end of philosophy studies, I met with my superior and told him that I would be willing to accept either assignment.

"You're indifferent?" he asked, staring at me intently.

I nodded more tentatively now as I began to grasp the importance of the word.

"In that case," he said, "You're going to JRS."

"I am?" I was astonished at the speed of what was typically a lengthy decision-making process.

"Sure," he continued. "If you're really indifferent, it would be a fine thing to work with JRS and get some experience working in another country. The greater need is clearly the work with the refugees, and the time overseas will be invaluable for your training as a Jesuit." (My superior, I now recalled, had worked for a number of years in Brazil and counted his time there among his happiest days.)

I gulped, thinking of two years away from home. I didn't feel so indifferent now.

"So," he said, wrapping up, "why don't you find out where JRS needs you the most, and get back to me?"

Once the shock of being taken at my word wore off, I warmed to the prospect of working with the Jesuit Refugee Service. And when I heard that they needed me most in East Africa, I grew even more excited. In a few days I had booked my flight (it would be a twenty-six-hour journey with no layovers), packed my bags with lots of mosquito repellent (which would prove laughably useless, seeming to attract rather than repel mosquitoes), and said good-bye to my parents (who were not as indifferent as I was about my leaving). I would be living in Nairobi, Kenya, where I would help refugees in the city start "income-generating activities," that is, small businesses to help them earn a living.

❧

A few months into my stay, an Ethiopian Jesuit visited our community in Nairobi. At the time, Groum was serving as assistant novice director at the novitiate in Arusha, Tanzania, a few hours from Nairobi. He was a friendly and talkative man who cemented our incipient friendship by taking me to a local Ethiopian restaurant (and patiently explaining the menu) at a time when my spirits were in low ebb.

Near the end of his visit, Groum asked if I might do him a small favor. A few hundred meters from our house lived a group of Catholic sisters called the Little Sisters of Jesus, whose community included two Ethiopian women. Groum had brought along an Amharic-language Bible for the two sisters but hadn't found the chance to drop it off. Would I mind taking it to them? Not at all, I said.

Before leaving for Tanzania, he pointed out their house—as it turned out, directly across the street from the Ethiopian restaurant, and well hidden behind a tall black metal gate.

The Bible, whose black cover was decorated with golden filigreed Amharic letters, sat reproachfully on my desk for a few days. After a week had passed, I thought about those two Scriptureless sisters and decided it was time to do my favor. One sunny morning (actually, nearly every morning in Nairobi was a sunny one) I ambled over a dusty path to the Little Sisters of Jesus.

I rapped on the high gate that surrounded their house and soon heard a light crunching of gravel. The gate swung open to reveal an African woman clad in what one could call Marian colors: a powder blue blouse, a dark blue skirt, and a royal blue kerchief. Pale green flip-flops were the only non-blue items in her outfit.

"Oh, Brother," she said, smiling. "You are most welcome! We are so *glad* you have come! Come in! Come in!"

Her greeting surprised and delighted me, for I knew that she had no idea who I was. Groum mentioned that the sisters did not have a phone in their house, so there was no way they could know I was coming to see them. Though they were not Benedictine sisters, their hospitality reminded me of a line from the monastic *Rule of St. Benedict*: "All guests to the monastery should be welcomed as Christ."

As I followed the Little Sister of Jesus up the gravel path, I noticed that their tiny green and white bungalow was surrounded by a flourishing garden: pale irises, mounds of magenta bougainvillea bushes, wild sisal plants, towering green Norfolk pines, hibiscus bushes with lurid red flowers, sweet-smelling gardenia bushes, and orange daylilies whose heads nodded drowsily under the hot sun.

The sister led me onto a cool, shady porch, and before she could open the door, the community of nine sisters—from Malta, Tanzania, Kenya, Nigeria, and Ethiopia—spilled out of the house to greet me. Their superior was Sr. Monique, a grinning French nun who pumped my hand and pulled me inside. When I held out Groum's Bible, I was lavished with praise for my great act of charity (which had consisted of walking a few hundred meters).

Sr. Askalemariam, one of the Ethiopian sisters (her name, she told me, meant "gift of Mary"), led me on a tour of their one-story bungalow. It was a short tour. A few items of locally made wooden furniture were crammed into a tiny living room. Behind this room lay a small pantry that doubled as a kitchen. Pots hung from a Peg-Board on the walls, and a small kerosene stove hissed in the middle of the space. The remainder of the house, however, was off-limits, consisting of the sleeping quarters, where the sisters shared rooms with one another. I was astonished that nine people lived here, without electricity and with only very little water.

Behind the house, in the middle of a small yard, sat a tiny chapel—a low wooden structure topped with a corrugated iron roof. Arching over the chapel was a tall tree, whose berries, falling from a great height, hit the roof with a sound like gunshots. Inside, low wooden benches surrounded a plain wooden altar, before which lay an unpainted terra-cotta statue of the child Jesus curled in sleep. Sr. Askalemariam bowed reverently before the altar and explained that their community in Rome made these statues to raise funds for their order.

Inside again, the sisters begged me to stay and "visit," as they said. By way of convincing me, a pot of tea and a plate of cookies materialized before me. The entire community, setting aside their tasks, sat down and began to chat away, asking questions about my work with the refugees, my Jesuit community, my parents, my health, and on and on for a good hour. Their interest and care for me, a stranger, were both surprising and touching.

More surprising was their joy. I had never before met people who were so joyful. The Little Sisters laughed constantly—or so it seemed to me—and laughed about everything, making jokes about their community, their studies (most of the sisters were studying at a nearby Jesuit theology school), their foibles, their clothes, even their superior. Sr. Monique laughed longest and loudest when they teased her playfully about her French cooking (which, I gathered, some of the East African sisters found mystifying). Theirs was an infectious joy, and I found my spirits growing lighter by the moment.

At the close of my visit, Sr. Monique shook my hand and cheerfully announced, "Brother, you will be visiting us often." Drawn to their joy, I accepted Sr. Monique's invitation and visited often—perhaps once a month—for a quick hello, a cup of tea, or a long, laughter-filled dinner.

❦

This was my first introduction to the Little Sisters of Jesus, an extraordinary religious order founded in 1939 by Magdeleine Hutin, in Algeria. The original members of this order set out to live a simple life of contemplation and service among the nomadic tribes of the Sahara. They took their inspiration from the life of a remarkable man named Charles de Foucauld, a French nobleman and soldier who left his luxe life in 1886 to spend his days living in extreme poverty.

The deceptively simple insight of Charles de Foucauld lay in the idea that Jesus of Nazareth—before he was baptized in the Jordan River, before he gathered together his disciples, before he performed his miracles, and before he suffered his passion, death, and resurrection—was a poor man who worked as a carpenter in his hometown. Indeed, this period in the life of Jesus, traditionally called his "hidden life," lasted far longer than his three years of active ministry. For Charles de Foucauld, the invitation to holiness came through the desire to emulate the hidden life of Jesus, in Foucauld's case in the desert among the Tuareg people of Algeria.

Charles hoped to found a new religious order whose members would work and live among the poor, emulating the carpenter of Nazareth. He also hoped to bring Christianity to the nomadic peoples of the desert. Both goals were to be accomplished not so much by preaching as through the example of his life. In this, Charles de Foucauld embodied the spirit of St. Francis of Assisi, who said, "Preach the gospel. Use words when necessary."

Though greatly respected by the local peoples, Charles was killed in 1916 by a fanatic band of Senussi rebels. And so the followers Charles had hoped for failed to appear in his lifetime. Eventually, however, his writings and his example—made even more powerful by his death—led to the founding in 1933 of the Little Brothers of Jesus by René Voillaume and, a few years later, of the Little Sisters by Magdeleine Hutin.

For these two groups, then, fulfilling the call of Charles de Foucauld means living the life of Jesus of Nazareth alongside the working people of the world.

This sounds sensible enough. But I was shocked when Sr. Monique explained that their vocation means that the Little Sisters typically engage in menial labor—working in factories, in hospitals, and on farms—choosing to insert themselves into places overlooked and neglected by many in the Church, and to do so joyfully. The Little Sisters who were studying diligently in Nairobi might one day find themselves factory workers, housemaids, farmworkers, or hospital orderlies.

Initially I recoiled from this concept of religious life, so far did it seem from the Jesuit way. But as I grew closer to the Little Sisters I began to find the notion of living the hidden life attractive. After all, why not live the way that Jesus lived for most of his adult life? Why not experience God in the type of labor shared by so many people around the world? Perhaps the Little Sisters' vocation wasn't so far from St. Ignatius of Loyola's ideal of "finding God in all things." Their emphasis on poverty was also not far from St. Ignatius's counsel in the *Spiritual Exercises* that one should wish to follow the poor Christ not simply because poverty is itself a good, but because this was the way that Jesus chose to live while on earth.

In many of his journal entries, Charles de Foucauld imagines what Jesus of Nazareth might say to him, by way of advice and inspiration. Here is a beautiful passage, written in the voice of Jesus, from Robert Ellsberg's collection *Charles de Foucauld*:

After my presentation and my flight into Egypt, I withdrew to Nazareth. There I spent the years of my childhood and youth, till I was thirty years of age. Once again, it was for your sake I went there, for love of you. What was the meaning of that part of my life? I led it for your instruction. I instructed you continually for thirty years, not in words, but by my silence and example. What was it I was teaching you? I was teaching you primarily that it is possible to do good to men—great good, infinite good, divine good—without using words, without preaching, without fuss, but by silence and by giving them a good example. What kind of example? The example of devotion of duty toward God lovingly fulfilled, and goodness toward all men, loving kindness to those about one, and domestic duties fulfilled in holiness. The example of poverty, lowliness, recollection, withdrawal: the obscurity of a life hidden in God, a life of prayer, penance, and withdrawal, completely lost in God, buried deep in him. I was teaching you to live by the labor of your own hands, so as to be a burden on no one and to have something to give to the poor. And I was giving this way of life an incomparable beauty—the beauty of being a copy of mine.

After spending more time with the sisters and reading about Charles de Foucauld, I found myself wondering more about this hidden life of Jesus. I also began to read as much as I could about the "historical Jesus," that is, the Jesus who lived in first-century Palestine, to understand more about his formative years. In the house library in Nairobi was a short book called *Jesus before Christianity*, by Albert Nolan, that sketched the historical context into which Jesus was born, in which he worked, and in which he would preach.

Soon the hidden life invaded my prayer. And perhaps the most appealing part of meditating on those years in the life of Christ is that there are few limits to what a person can imagine. The Gospel writers, in their omission of any information about the early adulthood of Jesus, have given our imaginations a blank slate.

The hidden life seemed to me an irresistible idea. And so mysterious! There were so many new questions to ponder: What was Jesus like as a young adult? What was the pattern of his daily life in Nazareth? Who were his friends? Did he ever fall in love? What made him laugh? How did he come to realize that he was called to do his particular ministry? Thinking about the hidden life helped me realize that though I had spent many hours in prayer pondering the active ministry of Jesus, I knew little about the greatest portion of his life, which he spent as a carpenter in Nazareth.

Gradually, all this wondering led me to one of the most important influences on Jesus of Nazareth: Joseph.

Like many saints whose lineage is traced back to the earliest days of the Church, very little is known about St. Joseph, other than the few lines written about him in the Gospels. He was of King David's line and was to be engaged to a young woman from Nazareth. Mary was found, quite unexpectedly, to be pregnant. But Joseph, "being a righteous man and unwilling to expose her to public disgrace," as the Gospel of Matthew tells it, planned to dissolve his betrothal quietly. And so, even before Jesus was born, Joseph's tender compassion and forgiving heart were on full display.

But God had other plans. As he had done for another troubled Joseph—a patriarch of the book of Genesis—God used a dream to reveal his saving plans for the carpenter from Nazareth. In the dream, an angel let Joseph in on Mary's secret: "Joseph, son of David, do not be afraid to take Mary as your wife, for the child conceived in her is from the Holy Spirit." That same angel, after the birth of Mary's son, advised Joseph to take the child and his mother to Egypt to flee the murderous Herod. And Joseph listened.

A few more stories about the boy Jesus—he is lost on a journey and found teaching in the temple—and we are into his hidden life. All the Gospel of Luke says about those eighteen years is this: "And Jesus increased in wisdom and in years, and in divine and human favor."

This is Joseph's time. A time spent caring for his son—or, to put it more precisely, his foster son—and teaching him the trade of carpentry. (The Greek word used in the Gospels of Mark and Matthew is *tekton*, which can be variously translated as "craftsman" or "woodworker" but is traditionally rendered as "carpenter.") In Joseph's workshop in Nazareth, Jesus would have learned about the raw materials of his craft: which wood was best suited for chairs and tables, which worked best for yokes and plows. An experienced Joseph would have taught his apprentice the right way to drive a nail with a hammer, to drill a clean and deep hole in a plank, and to level a ledge or lintel.

Undoubtedly, Joseph would have passed on to Jesus the values required to become a good carpenter. You need patience (for waiting until the wood is dry and ready), judgment (for ensuring that your plumb line is straight), honesty (for charging people a fair price), and persistence (for sanding until the tabletop is smooth). Alongside his teacher, a young Jesus labored and built, contributing all the while to the common good of Nazareth and the surrounding towns. It is not difficult to imagine that the skills Jesus learned from his teacher—patience, judgment, honesty, and persistence—served him well in his later ministry. Joseph helped fashion Jesus into what the theologian John Haughey, SJ, called "the instrument most needed for the salvation of the world."

As a father, Joseph would have been one of his son's primary teachers in his religious faith as well: introducing him to the great men and women of the Scriptures, teaching him the Hebrew prayers, preparing him for his bar mitzvah, and encouraging him to listen to the rabbis and religious leaders of the town. And talking to him about God. Children and adolescents are usually bursting with questions about God. Joseph was probably the first one Jesus went to with his questions. So Jesus' understanding of God his Father may have been shaped not only by Joseph's life but by also Joseph's answers to his questions. Joseph's faith was one of the foundations of Jesus' faith.

But almost as soon as Jesus started his ministry, Joseph disappeared, at least in the Gospel narratives. What happened to the guardian of Jesus? Tradition holds that by the time Jesus began his preaching, Joseph had already died. Significantly, Joseph is not listed among the guests at the wedding feast at Cana, which marked the beginning of the public ministry of Jesus. But did he die before his son had reached adulthood? How would Jesus have mourned his father's death?

At an art exhibit at the Cathedral of St. John the Divine in New York City a few years ago, I came upon a portrait entitled *The Death of Joseph*, a subject rarely tackled by artists. In the huge portrait by the Spanish artist Francisco Goya, an ailing Joseph lies in bed. Standing beside his bed is a youthful-looking Jesus, perhaps sixteen or seventeen years old, beardless, wearing a long red tunic, staring intently at Joseph. Sitting by the bed is Mary. It is an unusual picture of the holy family, and one that captures the sadness of the early death of Joseph.

Joseph is traditionally invoked by Catholics as the patron of a "happy death." In his book *Soul Brothers*, Richard Rohr asks, "How could it not have been happy? He knew that he had listened to the dreams that God had given him. He let those dreams take him to far-off Egypt, just like the first Joseph, and he let them bring him to a new hometown, where he surely had to start all over for a third time." Fair enough. But it could not have been a happy death for Jesus or Mary. How they must have wished Joseph could have seen and heard about his son's work among the people of Israel. How they must have wished for the counsel of Joseph during the confusing and painful times in Jesus' public ministry. And how Mary must have longed for Joseph to support her during her son's passion and death.

Whenever the death of Joseph occurred, he is not mentioned beyond those few early passages in Scripture. After that, it is Joseph's life that becomes hidden.

It is this hiddenness of Joseph's life that speaks to me. Appearing only briefly in the Gospels, given no words to speak, Joseph leads a life of quiet service to God, a life that remains almost totally unknown to us. It was, necessarily, a life of humility, and a life I saw mirrored in many in Nairobi: in local Kenyans and in the Little Sisters of Jesus.

Joseph's life was also mirrored in the refugees with whom I worked. While working with the Jesuit Refugee Service, I frequently visited many of the refugees in their small homes—hovels, really—in the slums of Nairobi. One day I visited a woman to whom we had given a small sewing machine to help with her business of mending her neighbors' clothes. She lived in a single dark room crammed with her few possessions: an old mattress where her four children slept, a small hissing kerosene stove, a plastic pail of water, and a cardboard box of clothes. Who is more hidden than the refugee, secreted away in her small hovel in a sprawling slum, huddled over her little sewing machine, trying to earn a living for her family? It sometimes seemed that the refugees, shorn of their connection to their country, bereft of friends, lacking money, and facing the bleakest economic prospects, were utterly submerged in a sea of misery, hidden from the sight of the world.

The hidden life is shared by many people, even in the more affluent parts of the world. The middle-aged unmarried woman who looks after her aged mother but whose sacrifices remain largely hidden from her neighbors. The loving parents of the autistic boy who will care for him for his entire life and whose heartaches remain unknown to their friends. The single mother in the inner city who works two jobs to provide an education for her children and whose tiring night shifts are still, after many years, a secret to her daytime coworkers. Countless hidden lives of love and service of others. The day-to-day pouring out of oneself for God.

It astonishes me how many of these people embrace their hidden lives of service with joy. During the first few months of my novitiate, I worked at Youville Hospital, in Cambridge, Massachusetts, run by the Grey Nuns, a small Catholic order that tends to the seriously ill. Those who lived there suffered from a variety of illnesses: cancer, dementia, degenerative muscular diseases. Many were surprisingly young—for example, young men who had suffered brain injuries resulting from car or motorcycle accidents. One mother used to come daily to visit her twenty-year-old son, to feed him, read to him, and sit by his bed. Here was a life entirely hidden from the world, in a lonely hospital that few knew about, even those in the immediate vicinity. ("Youville? Where's that?" I was asked by longtime Bostonians.) One winter afternoon I came in to find the mother carefully combing her son's hair. "Doesn't he look handsome today?" she said with a radiant smile.

This kind of hiddenness is attractive to me because it is so far from the goals of my own selfish desires. In a culture that prizes the bold gesture, the public proclamation, the newsworthy article, I find myself consistently drawn to achieving things so that other people can see them. Doing a good work seems insufficient: others need to know that I have done this good work! In this way I find my appetite for fame in contradiction to what Jesus taught. "But when you give alms," he says in the Gospel of Matthew, "do not let your left hand know what your right hand is doing, so that your alms may be done in secret; and your Father who sees in secret will reward you."

The burning desire for fame is of course a manifestation of pride, a pride that seeks not the hiddenness of the desert or the humility of the unseen act, but the adulation of others. Ultimately it is a destructive mind-set, since one can never receive enough acclaim to satisfy the craving for attention or fame or notoriety. Inexorably, it leads to despair and so must be resisted. But while the path to humility is necessary, it is a difficult one to tread. In Henri Nouwen's felicitous phrase, one strives to seek the freedom to be "hidden from the world, but visible to God."

And I wonder if the more hidden the act, the more valued it is by God. I am always reminded of the legend of a master sculptor in one of the great medieval cathedrals of France. The old man spent hours and hours carving the back of a statue of Mary, lovingly finishing the intricate curves and folds of her gown. But, someone asked the sculptor, what's the point? That statue will be placed in a dark niche against the wall, where certainly no one will ever see the back of it.

God will see it, he answered.

I long for that kind of holiness. But I am very far from it.

Still, I have seen many examples of the holiness of hidden lives. In my Jesuit philosophy community, I was sitting with a revered, older Jesuit at the dinner table when our middle-aged cleaning woman, an eastern European immigrant who visited our house once a week, passed by with her dust mop. She smiled at us.

"Do you know," he said to me after she had left, "that she has worked for us without complaint for ten years, and put three of her kids through college? And, you know, she is always cheerful, and she is always kind to me."

He paused and said, "When we get to heaven, I know that she'll be in line far ahead of me."

❦

The night before I left Nairobi, the Little Sisters threw me a farewell dinner. Once again it amazed me how well they did for themselves with the fewest of possessions and the simplest of things. Despite their poverty, it was a rich dinner, full of the hearty laughter I had come to identify with their community. And despite my sadness at leaving East Africa (and such friends), it was a joyful night.

After the dishes were cleared away, Sr. Monique asked the community to pray a blessing over me.

As they fell silent and bowed their heads, I knew that I had already received a special blessing from these women, whose hidden lives would always be lived in simple poverty, whose example demonstrated what it meant to preach the gospel, and whose abundant laughter had shown me the value of Christian joy.

"Please bless Jim," she began quietly, "who teaches us to live simply."

And when I heard that unexpected, unrehearsed, and undeserved compliment, it was, finally, my turn to laugh.

15

Who Trusts in God

The Ugandan Martyrs

Mwamini Mungu si mtovu.
Who trusts in God lacks nothing.
—Swahili proverb

One of the many ironies about my leaving the corporate world and entering the Jesuits was how much of my business background I would use during my two-year stay in East Africa. What I thought I had permanently left behind proved especially valuable in ministering to the refugees.

Essentially, my work with the Jesuit Refugee Service was helping refugees who had settled in Nairobi—so-called urban refugees—start small business projects. By earning money for themselves, indigent refugees were better able to support themselves and their families.

When I arrived in Kenya, JRS was already sponsoring a dozen of these little businesses, including backroom restaurants run by Ethiopian men, basket-making cooperatives run by Rwandese women, and carpentry workshops run by Ugandan men. The management of the program was straightforward. I worked alongside a friendly and energetic Austrian lay volunteer, a middle-aged woman named Uta. After completing a simple application for us, the refugees received a small amount of funds to purchase items necessary to begin their projects: wood for the carpenters, plastic plates and cups for the restaurant managers, straw for the basket makers.

On a regular basis Uta and I would visit the refugee businesses, located in their homes in the slums of Nairobi, to offer advice and support, help solve any problems, and in general make sure all was going well. During my stay in Kenya the program grew quickly. By the end of two years we were running more than sixty projects.

Consequently, I spent much of my time counseling the refugees about marketing, management, and, especially, accounting. I marveled at the way God had put my business education to good use. It also happened that many of the refugees came from Francophone, or French-speaking, Africa: countries such as Congo, Rwanda, and Burundi. So even my high school French was put to good use. At times it seemed as if God had planned it this way all along. When I mentioned this to my spiritual director, he smiled and quoted the old proverb: "God writes straight with crooked lines."

By far the most common projects were tailoring cooperatives run by women from nearly every East African country. Often the women would drop by our office and leave a sample of their product—dresses in boldly patterned *kitenge* cloth, children's shirts embroidered with lions and zebras, long lengths of fabric batiked in vibrant colors, and beautiful patchwork quilts fashioned from leftover fabric. Just as often, aid workers visiting our office would spy these wares and purchase them. In time, our little office became an excellent market for the tailoring groups.

One such cooperative was run by a remarkable woman named Alice Nabwire, a Ugandan refugee. Alice had migrated to Kenya several years before and now ran, along with two of her compatriots, a tiny dressmaking shop in a Nairobi slum.

Since Alice's shop was not far from the Jesuit community, I used to visit frequently, and over time we became friends. Though she worked in one of the poorest cities of the world and faced extreme difficulties, Alice remained optimistic. She was also a hardworking and clever businesswoman. If I asked to buy one of her dresses, she would usually try to convince me that it was better to buy two. (And usually she would succeed.) She personified one of my favorite lines from St. Paul: "We are afflicted in every way, but not crushed; perplexed, but not driven to despair; . . . struck down, but not destroyed."

Alice also had a dry sense of humor and a clear-eyed outlook on life in East Africa. I once told her that another Ugandan refugee had decided to name her baby after me, which I considered a signal honor. Just the other day, I said, the woman brought her baby into our office. Alice merely nodded. Continuing my story, I told her that the baby's baptism was a few months away.

"Brother Jim," said Alice, "who pays for his baptism clothes?"

"Gee," I said, "I assume the mother."

Alice nodded again.

A few days later the baby's mother visited our office and invited me to the baptism. Then she announced that not only did she need money for the baby's baptismal clothes, but they also had no place to have a reception, as is the custom. I offered to pay for the clothes from my own pocket and agreed to host a reception at my Jesuit community. The mother thanked me with enthusiasm. So on the appointed day, I joined their family in a local church and watched as a priest poured water over the head of James Martin Nakyobe. Afterward, the Jesuit community hosted a dozen members of her family for a reception of Fanta sodas, cookies, and cake.

The next week another woman told me that she was naming her son after me.

I mentioned this to Alice the next time I visited her shop. She shook her head back and forth.

"Brother Jim," she said, as if she were addressing someone particularly dense, "don't you see that if you keep paying for baptism clothes and receptions, soon there will be many, many babies named James Martin in Nairobi?"

⸭❖⸭

We were so successful selling refugee-made crafts from our office that Uta and I decided to open a small shop to cater to tourists, expatriates, and wealthy Kenyans. There we could sell not only the products from the tailoring cooperatives but also wood carvings, baskets, paintings, and reed mats from the rest of the refugee projects. After a few weeks of scouting around for a location, we settled on a little bungalow that we rented from a local Jesuit parish. It was located in a sprawling slum called Kangemi. Fortunately the house was situated on the outskirts of the slum, so our wealthier visitors wouldn't be too frightened to visit.

The shop was an instant success. In just six months' time we sold more than fifty thousand dollars' worth of merchandise, a princely sum in East Africa. The revenues were used to purchase more handicrafts to restock the shop and fund new businesses, which delighted the refugees. The shop also provided a place for the refugees to spend time with one another, catch up on news, and attend free classes, which we offered from time to time. (While I thought that my Introduction to Business Practices would be the most important, Introduction to Basket Making, taught by an elderly Sudanese woman, proved the most popular.)

Uta and I knew that to attract customers we would need to do some marketing. The first question concerned naming the shop.

What would we call it? I thought that we might name it after an African saint. Uta was undecided.

We decided to ask the refugees for advice. After all, the shop was for them. One morning I sat down with a group of refugees who were waiting to see Uta and me. In front of our bungalow was a wide porch, covered with a slate roof, which provided relief from the blazing equatorial sun. We had a few long wooden benches built (by people who worked in one of our carpentry projects), and the refugees took to passing time there, even after they had finished with their business. It heartened me to see women and men from different ethnic groups who were traditionally pitted against one another in their home countries sitting on our porch, seemingly at ease with one another as they traded news, exchanged business advice, looked after one another's children, and, in general, commiserated and laughed.

I brought up the subject: Uta and I think we should name this place so that it becomes more widely known and we can sell more products.

That is a good idea, they said.

What about naming the place for an African saint? I asked.

Just a few weeks before, a local Catholic magazine had carried a brief story of the Ugandan martyrs, a group of young men and boys killed by the *kabaka*, the king of the Baganda people, in the late nineteenth century. The young men had been baptized as Christians only shortly before their deaths.

"What about Kizito?" I asked, naming the youngest of the martyrs, killed at age fourteen. I had heard that a number of Catholic youth groups in Nairobi had taken Kizito as their patron. And I liked the name: it was easy to remember and, more important, would be easy for Westerners to pronounce.

Three Ugandan women who ran a quilt-making project smiled and nodded. "That is wonderful! Kizito is a good name."

I noticed a Sudanese woman seated on another bench, scowling. "Brother Jim, what about Bakhita?" she asked. Josephine Bakhita, originally a slave, later a member of the Canossian Sisters, had recently been beatified. "Bakhita would be better."

As if in reply, the Ugandans scowled. I began to perceive that choosing any African saint would mean, at least in the eyes of the refugees, honoring one country over another. So the shop would not be named after an African saint, to prevent divisiveness.

Maybe a simple Swahili word would be better. I located a Swahili dictionary.

How about *Mwangaza?* For "light." "That's the name of the Jesuit retreat house in Nairobi," one of my community members reminded me.

Tumaini? "Hope"? No, already taken by a women's religious order that ran a small community nearby.

Hekima? For "wisdom"? The Jesuit theology school in Nairobi.

I arrived at *imani*, the word for "faith." The Imani Centre had a nice ring to it. But Uta explained that the Kenyan president's political party used the word regularly for naming public buildings. I was running out of suitable Swahili words.

Finally, a refugee suggested something simpler: "What about *mikono?*" Hands. That sounded good: short, easy to remember, especially for American and European ears. I suggested it to the refugees a few days later.

"*Mikono?* Why are you calling it 'hands'?" I explained that the shop would showcase the work of their hands and that everyone would be working hand in hand. "Ah!" one of them said. "That is *very* good!"

But not everyone was pleased about the newly named Mikono Centre. "The Ugandan martyrs," said a Ugandan refugee, "would have been better." Indeed, for the rest of my stay, one Ugandan woman kept telling me that I had erred in not calling the place "Kizito Centre," since Kizito was such a powerful saint, and we were missing out on his intercession.

This was my first inkling of the importance of the martyrs for the Christians of East Africa.

⁂

Christian missionaries, both Catholic and Anglican, arrived in the interior of Africa during the late nineteenth century. The first of the Catholic missions was established by the White Fathers, a missionary society founded by the French cardinal Charles Lavigerie, the archbishop of Algiers and Carthage. (The White Fathers took their name not from the color of their skin but from the color of their long tunic.) As early as 1878, when he was asked by Pope Leo XIII to take charge of the missions in equatorial Africa, Lavigerie began a series of annual caravan journeys to central Africa as part of the Catholic evangelization of the area. The next year, a Catholic mission was founded in what is now Uganda.

The largest and most powerful of the local ethnic groups was the Baganda, a group in which European missionaries took particular interest. Edward Rice (a friend, incidentally, of Thomas Merton) offers an overview of the importance of the region and the Baganda people in his book *Captain Sir Richard Francis Burton*, a biography of the Victorian explorer and linguist. Rice recounts that the Baganda were among the richest and most advanced tribes in central Africa. Moreover, they "bore a certain patina of civilization that was to astound Europeans later, with well-organized bureaucracies, statesmanship of a superior order, finely developed arts and architecture, and unusual handicrafts." Yet the civilization also had a dark side, according to Rice, with both rulers and subjects having the reputation of being "unnaturally cruel."

Mutesa, the ruler of the Baganda, exemplified this cruel streak. When he took the throne in 1860, to ensure his own political survival he buried his brothers alive—all sixty of them. Yet he adopted a more or less benign approach to the Christian missionaries. (*Butler's Lives of the Saints* calls him a "not unfriendly ruler.") In essence, Mutesa allowed his subjects to choose among any of the faiths being imported into his kingdom—Catholic, Protestant, or Muslim. In turn, each group attempted to assert its influence on the king's court through the conversion of high-ranking officials. Mutesa, however, pointedly did not choose any one creed. In 1884 he died, still adhering to the local traditional religions.

Conversion to Christianity among the Baganda meant a rejection of the traditional religions. It also implied a setting aside of some of the traditional ways of life, an adherence to a new set of moral and religious standards, and, often, the establishment of a new set of alliances, based on religious belief. As a result, the group of new believers (called *abasomi*, or readers) came to be regarded with suspicion by other Baganda as a dangerous rebel faction. During the reign of Mutesa, however, these suspicions were kept under check.

With the accession of his son, Mwanga, the situation altered dramatically. As a young man, Mwanga had shown some favor to the Christian missionaries, but his attitude changed as soon as he took the throne. According to tradition, the *kabaka* was the center of all authority and power in the kingdom, and he could use his subjects as he wished. (An old Baganda saying is *Namunswa alya kunswaze*: "The queen ant feeds on her subjects.") But the presence of the missionaries was severely diminishing his authority among the converts. Mwanga was also a practicing pedophile, and upon discovering that the young men who had converted to Christianity were beginning to reject his

sexual advances, he grew enraged. As a result, the king sought to elim-
inate Christianity from his kingdom and began a violent persecution
of the missionaries and the new Christians.

In January of 1885, Mwanga had three Baganda Anglicans— Joseph Rugarama, Mark Kakumba, and Noah Serwanga—dis-
membered and their bodies burned. In October of that same year the
newly arrived Anglican bishop, James Hannington, was murdered
along with his caravan on their way to the region. In response, Joseph
Mukasa, a senior adviser to the *kabaka* and a recent Catholic convert,
reproached Mwanga for executing Bishop Hannington without having
offered him the customary opportunity to defend himself. Mwanga,
furious at what he saw as Mukasa's insolence, had him beheaded on
November 15, 1885. Mukasa became the first of the black Catholic
martyrs on the continent.

Among those now in obvious danger was the head of the royal
pages, Charles Lwanga, who had been instructed in Christianity by
the White Fathers and who was now Mukasa's successor in guiding the
young converts. The day of Joseph Mukasa's death, Lwanga went to
the Catholic mission with other catechumens (those who were receiving religious instruction), and together with them he was baptized by
Siméon Lourdel, one of the White Fathers. Among the pages was Kizito, age fourteen.

Their saga is retold by a current-day White Father, Aylward
Shorter, of the Catholic University of East Africa, in Nairobi. (Today
this order has reverted back to its official name, Missionaries of
Africa.) According to Fr. Shorter, the next day the pages were summoned into the royal court by the enraged *kabaka*. The king had
learned that one of the young pages in his court, Mwafu, had been
receiving religious instruction from another page, Denis Sebuggwawo.
The king demanded that the pages confess their allegiance. All but
three of the Catholic and Anglican pages did so. Mwanga, apparently

baffled by this solidarity, put off their executions. At one point Charles Lwanga—echoing the stance of another, earlier, martyr, St. Thomas More—stated his allegiance to the kingdom of Buganda, declaring his willingness to lay down his life for the king. He would not, however, abjure his faith.

In February, a fire in the royal palace impelled Mwanga to move his court to a lodge on the banks of Lake Victoria. While there, Charles Lwanga protected several of the pages against the king's violent sexual advances. Mwanga by this point had already obtained the consent from his chiefs to kill the Baganda Christians. Around this time, Lwanga secretly baptized five of the catechumens.

On May 26, the pages were called into the royal courtyard to hear their fate. From this point on, the story of the Ugandan martyrs closely resembles those of the early Christians. Fr. Lourdel, who had repeatedly pleaded for an audience with the king, was an unwilling witness. All of the men declared that they were prepared to remain Christians until death. In the end, Mwanga decreed that all of them—sixteen Catholics and ten Anglicans—be marched to Namugongo, eight miles away, where they would be burned. On their way to execution, bound by ropes and shackles, they were marched past Fr. Lourdel, who would later attest to their remarkably calm disposition.

They were marched to Namugongo, where, bound with ropes, shackles, iron rings, and slave yokes, they waited for one week. During that time the martyrs prayed and sang hymns; the Catholics among them recited morning and evening prayers, grace before and after meals, as well as the Angelus and the rosary, in preparation for their deaths. On June 3, before the execution of the rest of the young men, Charles Lwanga was put to death by the king's men. He was wrapped tightly in a reed mat, a yoke was hung on his neck, and he was thrown onto a pyre. Taunting his executioners, Charles is said to have shouted, "You are burning me, but it is as if you are pouring water over my body!" Before he died he cried out, "Katonda," or "My God."

His companions were killed in the same gruesome fashion. Aylward Shorter writes, "As the flames rose, their voices could be heard praying and encouraging one another." The last words of the young Kizito were "Good-bye, friends. We are on our way."

In all, forty-five Christians were martyred at Namugongo: twenty-two Catholics and twenty-three Anglicans.

Again the story brings to mind the tales of the early Christian martyrs and recalls a quote from the third-century Christian writer Tertullian: "As often as we are mown down by you, the more we grow in numbers; the blood of Christians is the seed." For after the White Fathers were expelled from the region, the Baganda Christians continued with the process of evangelization, translating the catechism into Luganda, offering secret instruction in the faith, and encouraging one another to persevere. Upon their return after Mwanga's death, the White Fathers discovered five hundred Christians and more than a thousand catechumens awaiting further instruction.

In 1964, Pope Paul VI canonized all twenty-two of the Catholic martyrs. Five years later, as the first pope to visit sub-Saharan Africa, he laid the foundation stone of the shrine to be built in Namugongo in honor of St. Charles Lwanga and his companions. The shrine was completed in 1975, on June 3, now the feast day of the Ugandan martyrs.

In the months following its opening, the Mikono Centre continued to do well. Our first Christmas sale proved encouraging: we sold nearly half our stock. Gradually the store was becoming known in Nairobi. But it was also a tiring time, for when the refugees discovered we had sold so many items, they also knew that we would need to purchase goods to replenish our stock, and the number of refugees who visited skyrocketed. At times, the porch was packed with dozens of men and women carrying all sorts of handicrafts, waiting to see us.

After several years with the Jesuit Refugee Service, Uta decided to return to Austria. Her replacement was Michael, a young and hard-working German Jesuit. One day Michael suggested, after we had seen fifty refugees (we counted), that we might take a week's break and travel to Uganda. The Jesuit Refugee Service team in a refugee camp in northern Uganda had long been asking us to visit them. Visiting the camp would also be a way for us to see what some of the refugees had experienced before arriving in Nairobi. I hoped, too, that we would be able to visit the shrine in Namugongo. So Michael and I purchased tickets for the overnight train journey from Nairobi to Kampala, the capital of Uganda. From there we would hitch a ride on a "Missionary Air Fellowship" plane, a tiny five-seater, to the refugee camp in the north, near the Sudanese border.

The next week we found ourselves on a crowded Kenyan Railways train slowly wending our way through the slums of Nairobi and the Kenyan highlands; over the famous "source of the Nile," at Jinja, Uganda; and finally arriving—twenty-six hours later—in Kampala.

Like the rest of Uganda, the capital city had suffered grievously under the dictatorship of Idi Amin and the brutal civil war that followed his overthrow. While Uganda was making a slow but steady economic recovery, the signs of the country's long struggle with poverty and violence were evident. The modest sandstone train station in the dusty city was pockmarked with bullet holes, its walls chipped from machine-gun fire.

The three Jesuits who met us at the station drove us through the dusty streets to Xavier House, a community of fifteen Jesuits who worked in various ministries in Kampala. One Jesuit physician worked at Makerere University, running an AIDS clinic and doing research on the disease. A few hundred meters away, two Jesuit novices worked in Nsambya Hospital, an institution almost entirely devoted to caring for AIDS patients. Even if I hadn't heard stories of how AIDS had decimated Uganda's population, the reality would have been underscored by the sight of coffin makers on nearly every street corner in Kampala. Plain wooden caskets were stacked up, sometimes ten high, along every roadside.

The day before Michael and I were to leave for the refugee camp, one of the Jesuits asked if we would like to visit Namugongo. The next morning we piled into his little jeep and drove to the shrine, located only a few kilometers away from the community. Our host told us that many African Jesuits, from all over the continent, come to Kampala to visit the shrine. Hundreds of lay pilgrims walk to the shrine from around Uganda, and from as far away as Kenya and Tanzania, for the celebration of the martyrs' feast day, on June 3. Each year a different one of the eighteen Catholic dioceses in Uganda is given the honor of planning the liturgy for the day. During the rest of the year, many other celebrations—for youth groups, "charismatic" groups, and missionary organizations—draw thousands of Ugandan Catholics to Namugongo to pray. Though Namugongo has remained a small town, it boasts a number of Catholic schools and parishes, a retreat house, and even novitiates for the Comboni Missionaries and Sisters, a Catholic order founded in Italy.

The Basilica Church of the Ugandan Martyrs is built in the traditional *kasiisira* style, mirroring the round wood-and-mud huts and palaces of the Baganda people. It is an immense conical structure, braced with metal struts, culminating in what looks like a gigantic metallic cap decorated with a large cross. The overall effect is that of a giant metal spaceship that has landed in the green hills of Uganda.

Nearby is a large open theater, surrounding a sort of lake, all of which was constructed for a Mass during the visit of Pope Paul VI in 1969.

The intricately carved wooden doors of the shrine depict scenes from the trials and deaths of the martyrs. The inside of the sparsely decorated chapel is airy and cool. Prominently displayed is a colorful portrait of the twenty-two Catholic martyrs. Michael and I knelt in the pews and prayed to Charles Lwanga and his companions. Yet I felt curiously unmoved. Though I was almost at the precise spot of their martyrdom, the Church somehow seemed too large and too modern for me to feel a connection to these nineteenth-century martyrs.

It was the Anglican shrine just a few kilometers down the road that I found more powerful.

The Anglican site at Namugongo is far simpler than the Catholic shrine. A small whitewashed chapel stands in an open grassy field. Just a few meters from the chapel, in the center of an open field, is a low circular wall that surrounds a shallow pit.

As Michael and the others explored the little church, I approached the wall. Lying at the bottom of the pit were clay replicas of the African martyrs. Each mannequin had been wrapped in a reed mat and bound with slim wooden stakes. They were stacked on top of one another and stared wide-eyed at me.

Though I had read the story of their martyrdom, the starkness of this representation shocked me. For all I had read about the way they had died, this plain display hammered home the point: a martyr's death, often represented on holy cards as ethereal, even beautiful, is typically gruesome, painful, and physically degrading. It was here that I felt closer to grasping the sacrifice of these Africans, and here that I felt their spirit more alive. It was here that I felt able to pray with them, and for them.

A few weeks later, I was wandering around the Catholic Bookstore in downtown Nairobi. Located just a few meters away from the Catholic cathedral, the bookstore boasted an admirable selection of books (in Swahili and English), as well as religious objects and cassette tapes. It was also the best place in town to run into other Catholic aid workers and catch up on the latest news.

Underneath a long glass counter in the rear of the store was an impressive display of holy cards. Pride of place was given to the Ugandan martyrs. I set my sights on a large, vivid poster similar to the painting I had seen at Namugongo. It depicted the Catholic martyrs in traditional dress holding elephant tusks, crucifixes, and Bibles. In the middle of the group was the tall figure of St. Charles Lwanga. Behind them rose an orange wall of flames. I thought the poster would be a fine addition to our shop and would also please my Ugandan friends, who were still disappointed about the name of the Mikono Centre. Unfortunately, I had little money and had to content myself with only three small holy cards.

I knew instantly which three to purchase. All were dark-skinned Ugandans standing atop lush vegetation before a rosy early-morning sky. St. James Buzabalyawo, pictured standing beside flames and offering two loaves of bread, was "Patron of traders and merchants." Perfect for all of the refugee projects. St. Mugagga, who carried a long length of orange cloth and held a jeweled chalice, was "Patron of tailors and community development." Perfect for the tailoring cooperatives that we sponsored, like Alice Nabwire's shop. Finally, St. Mbaga Tuzinde, "Patron of clerical and religious vocations." Perfect for me and the other Jesuits, priests, and sisters who worked with the Jesuit Refugee Service. I bought two sets of cards, one for me and one to post in our office.

I found myself praying to the three saints frequently. Something about their portraits on the holy cards spoke to me. Each martyr was pictured with the calm expression that I had seen on so many refugee faces—when they finished telling me of the appalling cruelty they had endured in their own countries, the degradation they had experienced in refugee camps, or the resentment they still faced in Nairobi. Though I had experienced none of the humiliations that the refugees or the African martyrs had faced, I wanted to emulate all of them, not only for their courage in the face of the severest persecution and for their implacable faith, but for another reason as well: the very hiddenness of their lives.

The Ugandan martyrs are not well known in the United States. If their story is known at all, it is known only in part; the one name that most Americans might have heard of is Charles Lwanga. The rest of those who suffered so intensely for their faith, such as Kizito, are merely listed as "companions." This makes their sacrifice more meaningful to me, holier, carried out as it was in obscurity. Their holiness was of the deepest sort—simple and hidden.

I recognized the same hiddenness in the refugees I knew. If the story of the plight of these men and women was known in the West, it was known dimly at best. The fact that Alice Nabwire and her companions labored in obscurity in the slums of Nairobi made her witness to optimism and her faith in the future even more inspiring.

In this way I saw the lives of the refugees reflected in the stories of the martyrs. And so I prayed frequently to the Ugandan martyrs: to Charles Lwanga, to James Buzabalyawo, to Mugagga, to Mbaga Tuzinde, and especially to Kizito, for their intercession in the lives of the refugees, and in my own as well.

16

The Most Precious
Thing I Possess

Aloysius Gonzaga

> He was tougher than his would-be admirers would have
> him, both tougher and more tender, enormously more
> complex, his heaven won by way of a detour
> through hell.
> —DANIEL J. BERRIGAN, SJ

Aloysius Gonzaga needs rescuing from the hands of overly pious artists. On holy cards and in countless reproductions, the young Jesuit is usually depicted clad in a jet black cassock and snowy white surplice, gazing beatifically at an elegant crucifix he holds in his slim, delicately manicured hands. For good measure, he is sometimes portrayed gently grasping a lily, the symbol of his religious chastity.

There is nothing wrong with any of those images per se, except when they obscure what was anything but a delicate life and prevent young Christians (and older ones, for that matter) from identifying with someone who was, in fact, something of a rebel.

On March 9, 1568, in the castle of Castiglione delle Stivieri, in Lombardy, Luigi Gonzaga was born into a branch of one of the most powerful families in Renaissance Italy. His father, Ferrante, was the marquis of Castiglione. Luigi's mother was lady-in-waiting to the wife of Philip II of Spain, in whose court the marquis also enjoyed a high position.

As the eldest son, Luigi was the repository of his father's hopes for the family's future. As early as age four, Luigi was given a set of miniature guns and accompanied his father on training expeditions so that the boy might learn, as Joseph Tylenda, SJ, writes in his book *Jesuit Saints and Martyrs*, "the art of arms." He also learned, to the consternation of his noble family and without realizing their meaning, some salty words from the soldiers. So anxious was Ferrante to prepare his son for the world of political intrigue and military exploit that he dressed the boy in a child-sized suit of armor and brought him along to review the soldiers in his employ. By the age of seven, however, Luigi had other ideas. He decided that he was less interested in his father's world and more attracted to a very different kind of life.

Nevertheless, Ferrante, mindful of Luigi's potential, remained enthusiastic about passing on to his son the marquisate. In 1577, he sent Luigi and his brother Ridolfo to the court of a family friend, the grand duke Francesco de'Medici of Tuscany, where the two were to gain the polish needed to succeed in court. But again, rather than being fascinated with the intrigue and (literal) backstabbing in the decadent world of the Medicis, Luigi withdrew into himself, refusing to participate in what he saw as an essentially corrupt environment. At ten, disgusted by his situation, he made a private vow never to offend God by sinning.

It was around this time that Luigi began the serious and often severe religious practices that strike contemporary observers as prudish at best and bizarre at worst, especially for a child. It is certainly the main reason that the life of St. Aloysius Gonzaga sometimes repels even devout Catholics today. He fasted three days a week on bread and water. He rose at midnight to pray on the stone floor of his room. He refused to let a fire be lit in his bedchamber even in the bitterest weather. And he was famously concerned with keeping his chastity and safeguarding his modesty. *Butler's Lives of the Saints* notes that from as early as age nine, Luigi maintained "custody of the eyes," as spiritual writers say. "We are told, for instance, that he kept his eyes persistently downcast in the presence of women, and that neither his valet nor anyone else was allowed to see his foot uncovered."

These practices, so admired by earlier generations, are what turn some contemporary believers away from Gonzaga and what appears to be his almost inhuman piety.

But when considering these aspects of his life, one must remember three things. First, the prevailing Catholic piety at the time, which warmly commended such practices, obviously exerted a strong influence on Luigi. The young nobleman was, like all of us, a person of his times. Second, Luigi adopted these practices while still a boy. Like some children even today, Luigi was given less to mature moderation and more to adolescent enthusiasm. Third, and perhaps most important, without any religious role models in his life, Luigi was forced, in a sense, to create his own spirituality. (There were no adults to say, "That's *enough*, Luigi.") Desperate to escape the world of corruption and licentiousness in which he found himself, Luigi, headstrong and lacking any adult guidance, went overboard in his quest to be holy.

Yet, in later years, even he recognized his excesses. When he entered the Society of Jesus, he admitted as much about his way of life. "I am a piece of twisted iron," he said. "I entered religious life to get twisted straight." (This famous saying of his, according to the Jesuit scholar John Padberg, may also have referred to the twisted character of the Gonzaga family.)

In 1579, after two years in Florence, the marquis sent his two sons to Mantua, where they were boarded with relatives. But unfortunately for Ferrante's plans, the house of one host boasted a fine private chapel, where Luigi spent much time reading the lives of the saints and meditating on the psalms. It was here that the thought came to the marquis's son that he might like to become a priest. Upon returning to Castiglione, Luigi continued his readings and meditations, and when Charles Cardinal Borromeo visited the family, the twelve-year-old Luigi's seriousness and learning impressed him greatly. Borromeo discovered that Luigi had not yet made his first communion and so prepared him for it. (In this way a future saint received his first communion from another.)

In 1581, still intending to pass on to Luigi his title and property, Ferrante decided that the family would travel with Maria of Austria, of the Spanish royal house, who was passing through Italy on her return to Spain. Maria was the widow of the emperor Maximilian II, and Ferrante saw an excellent opportunity for his son's courtly education. Luigi became a page attending the Spanish heir apparent, the duke of Asturias, and was also made a knight of the Order of St. James.

Yet these honors only strengthened Luigi's resolve not to lead such a life. While in Madrid, he found a Jesuit confessor and eventually decided to become a Jesuit himself. His confessor, however, told him that before entering the novitiate, Luigi needed first to obtain his father's permission.

When Luigi approached his father, Ferrante flew into a rage and threatened to have Luigi flogged. There followed a battle of wills between the fierce and intransigent marquis of Castiglione and his equally determined sixteen-year-old son. Hoping to change his son's mind, the marquis brought him back to the castle at Castiglione and promptly sent Luigi and his brother on an eighteen-month tour around the courts of Italy. But when Luigi returned, he had not changed his mind.

Worn out by his son's persistence, Ferrante finally gave his permission. That November, Luigi, at age seventeen, renounced his inheritance, which passed to his brother Ridolfo, a typical Gonzaga with all the bad habits thereof. His old life over, Luigi left for Rome.

On his way to the novitiate, Aloysius (as he is most often called today) carried a remarkable letter from his father to the Jesuit superior general, which read, in part, "I merely say that I am giving into your Reverence's hands the most precious thing I possess in all the world."

There is a colossal painting by Guercino hanging in the Metropolitan Museum of Art that shows, in allegory, the moment of Luigi's decision. From contemporary portraits we know a little of what Luigi looked like, and the painting depicts him with the long nose and slim face of the Gonzaga family. Covered by a marble arch and standing under a canopy of lute-playing cherubim and seraphim, Aloysius, in a black Jesuit cassock and white surplice, looks intently at an angel, who stands in front of an altar and points to a crucifix. Far in the distance under a blue Italian sky is his father's castle. At Aloysius's feet lies the symbol of chastity, a lily. Behind him, on the ground, is the crown of the marquis, which Aloysius has relinquished. A cherub hovers in the sky, holding above the young man's head a crown of another kind, the crown of sanctity.

Aloysius's determination to enter religious life, even in the face of his father's fierce opposition, filled me with admiration when I was a Jesuit novice. When I first announced to my parents my own intention to leave the corporate world and enter the novitiate, they too were, at least for a time, upset, and they pleaded with me not to join the Jesuits. (They did not, however, threaten to have me flogged.) After a few years, they came to accept my decision and cheerfully support my vocation. But in that interim period, when I was determined and so were they, Aloysius became my patron.

In his single-minded pursuit of God, and especially his willingness to give up literal riches, Aloysius perfectly emblemizes a key meditation of the Spiritual Exercises called the "Two Standards." In that meditation, St. Ignatius asks the retreatant to imagine being asked to serve under the banner, or "standard," of one of two leaders—Christ the King or Satan. If one does choose to serve Christ, it must necessarily be by imitating the life of Jesus, choosing "poverty as opposed to riches; . . . insults or contempt as opposed to the honor of the world; . . . humility as opposed to pride." There are few who have exemplified this as well as Aloysius. So to me he has been a great hero.

Because of the severe religious practices that Aloysius had already adopted, the Jesuit novitiate proved surprisingly easy. As Fr. Tylenda writes, "He actually found novitiate life less demanding than the life he had imposed upon himself at home." (The disappearance of the constant battles with his father must have given him some relief as well.) Fortunately, his superiors encouraged him to eat more regularly, pray less, engage in more relaxing activities, and in general reduce his penances. Aloysius accepted these curbs. In an essay entitled "On Understanding the Saints," Richard Hermes, SJ, noted that though Aloysius's single-minded pursuit of God's will had led him to embrace some of these extreme penances, "it was the same single-minded obedience which led him to moderate these practices as a Jesuit."

"There is little to be said about St. Aloysius during the next two years," says Butler, "except that he proved to be an ideal novice." He pronounced his vows of poverty, chastity, and obedience in 1587 and the next year received minor orders and began his theology studies.

At the beginning of 1591, a plague broke out in Rome. After begging alms for the victims, Aloysius began working with the sick, carrying the dying from the streets into a hospital founded by the Jesuits. There he washed and fed the plague victims, preparing them as best he could to receive the sacraments. But though he threw himself into his tasks, he privately confessed to his spiritual director, Fr. Robert Bellarmine, that his constitution was revolted by the sights and smells of the work; he had to work hard to overcome his physical repulsion.

At the time, many of the younger Jesuits had become infected with the disease, and so Aloysius's superiors forbade him from returning to the hospital. But Aloysius—long accustomed to refusals from his father—persisted and requested permission to return, which was granted. Eventually he was allowed to care for the sick, but only at another hospital, called Our Lady of Consolation, where those with contagious diseases were not admitted. While there, Aloysius lifted a man out of his sickbed, tended to him, and brought him back to his bed. But the man was infected with the plague: Aloysius grew ill and was bedridden by March 3, 1591.

Aloysius rallied for a time, but as fever and a cough set in, he declined for many weeks. He had an intimation in prayer that he might die on the Feast of Corpus Christi, and when that day arrived he appeared to his friends better than on the previous day. Two priests came in the evening to bring him communion. As Fr. Tylenda tells the story, "When the two Jesuits came to his side, they noticed a change in his face and realized that their young Aloysius was dying. His eyes were fixed on the crucifix he held in his hands, and as he tried to pronounce the name of Jesus he died." Like Joan of Arc and the Ugandan martyrs, Aloysius Gonzaga died with the name of Jesus on his lips.

He was twenty-three years old.

His unique sanctity was recognized, especially by his Jesuit confrères, even during his life. After his death, when Robert Cardinal Bellarmine would lead the young Jesuit scholastics through the Spiritual Exercises in Rome, he would say about a particular type of meditation, "I learned that from Aloysius."

Aloysius Gonzaga was beatified only fourteen years after his death, in 1605, and canonized in 1726.

It was in the novitiate that I was introduced to Aloysius Gonzaga. Actually, it would have been impossible to miss him there: he is one of the patron saints of young Jesuits and is, along with St. Stanislaus Kostka and St. John Berchmans, part of a trio of early Jesuit saints who died at a young age. Frequently they appear together as marble statues in Jesuit churches: Aloysius carrying his lily, John holding a rosary, and Stanislaus clasping his hands and looking piously heavenward.

As a novice, I found it natural to pray to the three—since I figured all of them understood the travails of the novitiate, of Jesuit formation, and of religious life. St. John Berchmans, in fact, was quoted as saying, "Vita communis est mea maxima penitentia": Life in community is my greatest penance. Now *there* was someone to whom a novice could pray.

On the other hand, one Jesuit friend commented, "Well, I wonder what the community thought of *him*!"

But it wasn't until two years after the novitiate, when I started working with refugees in East Africa, that I began to pray seriously to Aloysius. Even at the time I wondered why; my sudden devotion came as a surprise. Sometimes I think that one reason we begin praying to a saint is that the saint has already been praying for us.

In any event, I found myself thinking about Aloysius whenever life in Nairobi became difficult—which was frequently. When I was frustrated by a sudden lack of water in the morning, I would silently say a little prayer to St. Aloysius for his intercession. When the beat-up jeep I drove failed to start (once again), I would ask St. Aloysius for a bit of help. When burglars broke into our community and stole my shoes, my camera, and the little cash I had saved up, I asked St. Aloysius to help me hold on to the slender reed of my patience.

And when I was stuck in bed for two months with mononucleosis and wondered what I was doing in Kenya, I sought his intercession and encouragement. I figured he knew something about being sick. During my two years in East Africa, I had a feeling that St. Aloysius was in his place in heaven looking out for me as best he could. At the very least, I was keeping him busy.

☙❖❧

Before leaving for Africa, I had decided to make the trip to Kenya nonstop, without an overnight stay in Europe. Most of my Jesuit friends counseled that traveling without a break would be unnecessarily grueling. "You're insane," said a friend. But I thought that spending a night in a European hotel was needlessly extravagant, particularly for someone living under the vow of poverty and especially for a Jesuit planning to work with the poor. How could someone ministering to refugees—who in their flight from their own countries hadn't rested in hotels—justify such a choice?

Unfortunately, following my sleep-deprived, poverty-minded twenty-six-hour journey from Boston to New York to Amsterdam to Kilimanjaro to Nairobi, I felt like a zombie. Three days passed before I recovered fully.

Two years later, on my return trip from Nairobi, I decided to stop off in Rome for a few days and give myself a little vacation. Some Jesuit friends living there promised to fill my stomach with pasta and help me regain some of the fifteen pounds I had lost during my time in Africa. I also hoped to embark on a sort of mini-pilgrimage to the Jesuit sites in Rome.

I had visited Rome only once before, during that breathless, monthlong Eurail pass tour following graduation from college, and had completely missed all the Jesuit sites. (Since at the time I wasn't sure what a Jesuit was, I was blithely unaware that I was missing the Jesuit sites.)

I do, however, recall noticing the main Jesuit church in Rome on a map: "Il Gesù."

I remarked to the friend with whom I was traveling, "Il Gesù? What kind of a name is that for a church? 'The Jesus'?"

In my ignorance I missed one of the greatest examples of baroque architecture in Rome, and what art historians have called one of the most important buildings in the world. (Though referred to as "Il Gesù," its actual name is the Church of the Holy Name of Jesus.) It is a magnificent structure located on a famously windy piazza in Rome. Legend has it that when the devil and the wind were walking together in the plaza, the devil asked to drop into the church and left the wind outside waiting. The wind has been there ever since. Apparently, this is supposed to say something about the Jesuits and their diabolical ways, or their propensity to talk. Having first heard this tale in the novitiate, I was immensely pleased when I finally reached the piazza and was nearly knocked over by the wind.

In my headlong post-collegiate rush to see everything in Rome, I also skipped the sublime Church of St. Ignatius, and thus overlooked the place where St. Aloysius, St. John Berchmans, and St. Robert Bellarmine are buried. St. Robert Bellarmine—renowned cardinal, theologian, and scholar and one of the most influential and educated men of the sixteenth century—requested the privilege of being buried near the tomb of the holy young man he had once counseled.

Besides the Gesù and St. Ignatius, there were plenty of other Jesuit sites I wanted to visit, such as the rooms of St. Ignatius of Loyola (next to the Gesù), which had recently been renovated and restored to their original appearance. The rooms were spare and plain, furnished with a chair and the desk on which Ignatius labored over the Jesuit *Constitutions*. Also present was a small bronze bust of Ignatius on a plinth that replicated the saint's height and indicated that he was every bit as short as the biographers claim.

I also visited a tiny chapel at La Storta, a small town just outside of Rome. It was there that St. Ignatius received a vision in which God announced, "I will be propitious to you in Rome." And I also wanted to visit the Church of Sant'Andrea al Quirinale, a small baroque jewel designed by Gian Lorenzo Bernini and used as a chapel by Jesuit novices.

Upstairs in Sant'Andrea al Quirinale is a memorial to St. Stanislaus Kostka. His tomb is a marble representation of the saint reclining on his deathbed, which gave me a nasty shock when I entered the room. His cassock is done in black marble and his face and hands in white, lending the statue a creepily realistic look. The Jesuit art historian C. J. McNaspy, writing about the otherwise magnificent church, commented, "The statue of St. Stanislaus, upstairs in the sanctuary, however, I find deplorable. One would have thought that the young saint suffered enough in life."

But what I most wanted to see in Rome was the rooms of St. Aloysius, in a building attached to the Church of St. Ignatius. His rooms are housed in what was called the Roman College, the Jesuits' main educational institution in Rome, founded in 1551 and now a historical landmark.

Earlier in the day I had been told to ask a priest on duty for the keys to Aloysius's rooms. So I breezed through the nave of the Church of St. Ignatius, making sure to take in the jaw-dropping trompe l'oeil—literally, "fools the eye"—ceiling painted in the seventeenth century by Br. Andrea Pozzo, SJ. Its theme is the life of St. Ignatius, and, believe me, the details are so realistic and the perspective so convincing that it's difficult to believe you are staring at a painting. The ceiling appears to dissolve into a sunny Italian sky, complete with cottony white clouds, pink-faced angels, and airborne saints.

A bald-headed Jesuit stood in the nave reading his breviary. I mustered up some poor Italian, a sort of stew of the words *scusi, Luigi Gonzaga, camere,* and *grazie*. He smiled, nodded, handed me a set of keys, and pointed. After an ancient elevator rattled me to the third floor, I passed through a door and was surprised to find myself on the outside of the building. A rickety metal catwalk led over a courtyard to a contiguous building—the old Roman College. Another door opened onto an indoor hallway, and I spied a sign with small lettering: *Camere di S. Luigi Gonzaga.*

Excited, I fished out the keys from my pocket. Finally, after two years in Africa praying to St. Aloysius and feeling his intercession and encouragement, I would visit a place where I felt that I could say thanks in a special way. Standing before the door, I felt as though my pilgrimage was complete.

Suddenly a loud voice barked, "Hey! Hey!" (Or at least the Italian equivalent.)

With my hand just a few inches from the keyhole, I turned around in time to see a red-faced Italian Jesuit making his way toward me.

"É chiuso!" he shouted. It's closed!

He snatched the keys from my hand. I sputtered in Italian what I was trying to do. I was humiliated.

He turned on his heel and disappeared through the door.

Too stunned to do anything, I stood at the door for a few minutes and tried opening it. Locked. Now I noticed there were other doors—John Berchmans's was a few feet away. I realized I would now miss his room, too.

Glumly, I made my way back into the church and bumped into the first priest. He asked if I liked the rooms.

Flustered, I blurted out in English, "I couldn't go in. Someone took the keys from me!"

As it happened, the man was just then crossing the nave of the church, and I pointed him out.

Then I asked the first priest, "Is that the superior?"

The Italian Jesuit drew himself up and declared, "Io sono superiore qui!" I am the superior here! Then he pulled an identical set of keys from his pocket, smiled, and gave them to me.

I retraced my steps. This time when I reached the door, there was no one to stop me. I slipped the key into the keyhole.

Having already seen the austere rooms of St. Ignatius, I expected a similar scene. But the rooms of St. Aloysius were the opposite. The small chamber was dominated by a large marble baroque altar that occupied almost an entire wall; a murky oil painting of the saint hung over it. The walls were covered with heavy red damask and decorated with small framed pictures of scenes from the life of Aloysius. On one side of the room stood a dusty glass cabinet that held the cassock, clothes, and assorted possessions of Aloysius. Unlike the stripped-down rooms of Ignatius, this room bespoke centuries of piety and devotion to the saint that had slowly been built up, layer by layer.

Alone in the room, I knelt down on the *prie-dieu* in front of the altar. After a hectic two years of working in Nairobi, I found myself for perhaps the first time in a quiet and secluded setting. I thought of all the people who had prayed to Aloysius over the centuries. As the patron saint of youth he has doubtless heard millions of schoolchildren's prayers asking for help on an exam, on a difficult report, or with a hard-nosed teacher. He has certainly been prayed to by generations of Jesuit novices. And more recently, thanks to his work with plague victims, he has been embraced as patron by people living with AIDS. I thought of all of these men and women asking for his help. And I remembered the two years in East Africa I had spent praying for his intercession. Suddenly I was given what St. Ignatius called the "gift of tears"—another surprise.

I wondered where the sudden emotion came from: perhaps relief at having safely completed two years in Africa, perhaps sadness at having left my friends in Kenya, perhaps gratitude to Aloysius for his intercession. When I looked at my watch, an hour had passed.

Why is a person attracted to one saint and not another? Why do the stories of people whose lives have, at least on the surface, so little in common with ours speak to us? How is it that I feel so drawn to ask the help of someone who died centuries ago? What is it that moves me about the son of a sixteenth-century marquis? In many ways, an attraction or a devotion to a saint is, to use an overused expression, a mystery. But because of this, such devotions need to be reverenced for what they are—unexpected graces in the spiritual life and gifts from the God of surprises.

17

Full of Grace

Mary

Hail Mary, full of grace,
the Lord is with you.
—Traditional prayer

Like many Catholics, I would be hard-pressed to recall exactly when I was first introduced to Mary, so intricately woven is she into the tapestry of our religious culture.

One of my earliest memories is kneeling in the dark before a small reproduction of Michelangelo's *Pietà*, which sat atop my bedroom dresser. In 1964, the *Pietà* paid a special visit to New York City as part of the World's Fair, and my grandparents bought me a little cardboard image as a souvenir. Silhouetted against a dark blue background was a white image of the statue that glowed in the dark. It wasn't until years later that I saw a photograph of the real *Pietà* in one of the oversized art books my mother kept on our living room bookshelves. And it was only with some difficulty that I connected Michelangelo's marble depiction of Mary holding the dead Jesus with the white image that glowed brightly on my dresser at night. At the time, all I knew was that it was a holy picture and that I would do well to pray before it.

Our parish church, Epiphany of Our Lord, in Plymouth Meeting, Pennsylvania, boasted a number of images of Mary. Another reproduction of the *Pietà*, in fact, done in sugar-white marble and smaller than the original, stood in the sanctuary of the original church, which was temporarily located in the auditorium of the parish school. It was in this auditorium that I made my first Holy Communion and was confirmed. In 1966, when the growing parish was able to raise enough money to build a freestanding church, it erected an airy structure with tan bricks, vivid stained-glass windows, and a soaring, barnlike wooden ceiling. The parish *Pietà* was transferred into the sanctuary of the new church and stood to the left of the altar, on the gold wall-to-wall carpet. Over the entrance of the church was a towering stained-glass window depicting the Epiphany: Mary, robed in ruby red and navy blue, held a pink-faced infant Jesus while Joseph, dressed in orange and red, joined the three wise men in adoration.

To commemorate my first Holy Communion in the auditorium-cum-church, my parents gave me a rosary, as well as a booklet about how to pray the rosary. For many years the rosary hung on my bedpost, and at night its black beads would rattle every time I turned over in bed. When I couldn't sleep I would pray some Hail Marys until dozing off. And when I jumped out of bed in the morning, the rosary would often stay behind in a tangle of sheets. As a result, it was forever falling onto the floor when my mother made my bed after I had left for school. One day she was horrified to run over it with her vacuum cleaner, which snarled angrily, as if the good rosary had disturbed the evil spirits dwelling in that old Hoover.

Pulling it from the vacuum cleaner bag, my mother dusted it off and replaced it on my bedpost. In the process, however, three of the beads were lost. When I showed the abbreviated rosary to my sister, she said, "Now it won't take you so long to pray it."

But growing up, I had little, if any, devotion to Mary. While Mary was part of the larger religious culture, she did not play a large role in my own life or my family's. In high school, when my Jewish friends began wearing *chai* medals, depicting the Hebrew word for "life," I asked my parents for a Miraculous Medal, which I had noticed that other Catholic boys were wearing. It depicted Mary surrounded by the words "O Mary, conceived without sin, pray for us who have recourse to thee." I wasn't sure what *recourse* meant, but it seemed to promise some sort of help, and that sounded good enough to me.

That Christmas I received the silver medal, which I immediately hung around my neck, removing it only for weekly swimming classes. At night, when I rolled over in bed, the medal's chain would occasionally strangle and awaken me. I was proud to wear my Miraculous Medal and show it off to friends, but this sprang less from a devotion to Mary and more from a desire to fit in with my high school pals. Later I would learn that the Miraculous Medal was traditionally supposed to protect its wearer from any impure thoughts. (It hadn't worked.)

Still, whenever I prayed for something, I would always use the Hail Mary. If I wanted to do well on a test, I would ask God for this favor and then, as testimony to my desire, offer a string of Hail Marys. The more I wanted something, the more Hail Marys I prayed.

Looking back, I wonder why I didn't use instead the Our Father, the "perfect prayer" taught by Jesus. Perhaps, with its rhythmic cadence, the Hail Mary was easier to pray. On the morning of a big test or a solo during band practice I would pray dozens of Hail Marys on the way to school. My shoes hit the sidewalk to the beat of the prayer:

> *Hail* Mary,
> *full* of grace,
> the *Lord* is with thee . . .

I prayed my walking Hail Marys through elementary school, high school, college, and beyond.

Despite the prayers in her honor, Mary remained a distant presence in my life. Certainly she was the one to whom I would pray for favors, whose rosary helped me sleep peacefully at night, and whose prayer kept me company on the sidewalk. But the notion that Mary was a real person, someone who might provide me with a model of how to live my life—rather than a quasi-magical figure—would not come to me until years later, when I entered the Jesuit novitiate.

⚜

One of the few personal effects that I brought to the novitiate was my rosary: the battered set I had kept since my first Holy Communion. While I wasn't sure whether I would need it, it seemed reasonable to bring it along—once again an outward sign of my hoping to fit in. Still, I wondered whether any of the novices would think me overly pious, old-fashioned, or perhaps superstitious.

I needn't have worried. Most of the novices had brought rosaries with them, and all of them understood better than I did Mary's role in salvation history and in the life of believers. And as the liturgical year unfolded, I would hear a great deal about Mary in the homilies at daily Masses in our house chapel.

All the homilies about Mary surprised me. Rather than presenting her as a cool, distant presence, they revealed her to be a human being. In one homily we considered Mary as the "first disciple," the first one to receive the Word of God, Jesus, and the first to announce the good news of his coming birth to her cousin Elizabeth. In another, Mary offered the Magnificat, her song of praise, and in doing so acted as a prophetic voice announcing the deliverance of her people. In another homily we looked at her as the one who prayed: Mary the contemplative, who "treasured all these things in her heart," as the Gospel of Luke puts it. In still another, Mary was the resourceful young woman who bore a son at an early age, fled with her family into another country, raised her son in difficult circumstances, and lived with surprise, uncertainty, and mystery—and was able to do all of this because of her faith.

In my own reading I encountered other theological models of Mary as well, all flowing from her role in the life of her son: Mary the model for all who seek to "bring" Jesus into the world; Mary the one who "points" us to Jesus (her last words in Scripture are "Do whatever he tells you"); Mary the sign of God's continuing liberation at work in our world; and Mary the one who, in theologian Elizabeth Johnson's words, symbolizes God's "unbreakable love for the people of the covenant."

But for some reason, it was the story of the Annunciation in the Gospel of Luke—the tale of the angel Gabriel's visit to Mary—that led me to a real devotion to the mother of Jesus.

I had heard the story many times before entering the novitiate but had paid little attention to it. When I was in high school and college, Luke's story struck me as somewhat fanciful, hard to believe, and even harder to see as applicable to my life. But when I first heard the passage read during Mass in the novitiate, it was like hearing it for the first time. It had a startling urgency about it. Quite suddenly the Gospel story flooded into my morning prayer, invaded my thoughts during the day, and became the focus of my evening meditation.

For a long time I wondered: What is it about the Annunciation that is so captivating for me and for so many believers?

Why, for example, is this brief passage from the Gospel of Luke the subject of more artistic renderings—paintings, sculptures, mosaics, frescoes—than almost any other passage in the New Testament, save the Nativity and the Crucifixion?

One could argue that there are other incidents from the life of Jesus with greater *theological* importance—miracle stories, physical healings, sermons, and the like. There are passages from the New Testament with greater relevance to the life of the Church—the naming of Peter as the leader of the Church, the feeding of the five thousand. One could say that the Gospels contain stories of greater significance for the spiritual life of believers—just think of the Sermon on the Mount. So why do those few verses in the first chapter of Luke exert such a hold on so many believers? And why did they exert such a hold on me?

Perhaps it is because that event depicts the dramatic entrance of the divine into our everyday world: God greets a young girl in her simple home in a small town. Perhaps it is because the passage highlights the special role of women in the divine plan: Mary accomplishes something that no man could do. Perhaps Mary is someone whom many believers hope to emulate: humble, obedient, loving, trusting.

But the Annunciation drew me in for a different reason: it seemed that in this Gospel story Mary wonderfully exemplifies the role of the real-life believer. The Annunciation perfectly describes the growth of a personal relationship with God—something I was just discovering during those first months as a Jesuit. And in doing so, the story offers us a microcosm of the spiritual life.

To begin with, the initiative lies entirely with God. It is God, through the angel Gabriel, who begins the dialogue with Mary—"Hail Mary, full of grace"—as God does in our lives. God begins the conversation. God speaks to us, and in often unexpected ways. We are surprised to find ourselves moved to tears by catching a glimpse of a spectacular sunset on an otherwise cold and cloudy day, by getting an unexpected phone call from a good friend, by hearing a long-awaited word of forgiveness. In these things, and in our emotional responses to them, we are surprised to experience God's presence. To experience something we "know not what." Something outside of ourselves. Something transcendent.

But it is always *God* who takes the initiative and who surprises us with his presence, as God did with Mary.

When Mary first experiences the presence of God, she is fearful, or "perplexed," as some translations have it. How often this happens to us! When we first begin to wonder if God might be communicating with us, we can grow fearful or confused. Often we feel unworthy before the evidence of God's love, since the presence of the divine illuminates our own human limitations.

Many figures in both the Old and New Testaments experienced this sense of personal unworthiness. Consider Peter in the Gospel of Luke. After Peter and his companions have been fishing all night without success, Jesus asks them to throw out their nets again. When their nets miraculously fill to the point of breaking, Peter suddenly realizes who stands before him. In the presence of the Messiah, Peter feels intensely his own unworthiness. "Go away from me," he says, "for I am a sinful man!"

We stand in awe of the majesty of God, the *mysterium tremendum et fascinans*, as the theologian Rudolf Otto calls it: the tremendous and fascinating mystery that both attracts and frightens us.

Once, on a retreat, I was struggling with my vocation as a Jesuit. Walking along the New England shoreline, I wondered how, with a vow of chastity, I would ever experience love. Would I be lonely? Was chastity what I was meant for?

Suddenly I was flooded with memories from my years as a Jesuit: friends I knew and loved; caring spiritual directors; friendly community members; holy priests, brothers, sisters, and laypersons—all whom I had met through my life as a Jesuit, whom I had met only *because* I was a Jesuit. I understood this as a clear response to my questioning: my vocation is not only the way I love God but also the way God loves me. That realization was a resounding *yes* from God.

Not surprisingly, I was overwhelmed with gratitude. At the same time, the notion that the Creator was communicating with me in this direct way was disturbing and, yes, frightening. It was hard to reconcile the feeling of fear with that of gratitude.

That quintessential human experience—fear—is repeated frequently in Scripture. It is the experience of the shepherds in their fields in the narrative from Luke. "The glory of the Lord shone around them," says the New Revised Standard Version, "and they were terrified." Much better at conveying this is the King James Version: "They were sore afraid."

In light of this human fear, the angel offers the shepherds the message that God offers all who draw back: "Do not be afraid." Jesus, in the boat with a frightened and embarrassed Peter, says the same: "Do not be afraid; from now on you will be catching people." God sees and understands our fear.

At the Annunciation, God understands Mary's reactions as well. So Gabriel says, "Do not be afraid."

Significantly, the angel now offers Mary a more detailed explanation of what God is asking of her. (The word *angel*, by the way, is taken from the Greek *angelos* and simply means "messenger.") "You have found favor with God," says Gabriel. "And now, you will conceive in your womb and bear a son." Again, how similar to our own lives. As we reflect on our experience with God, it gradually becomes clearer what God is asking us to do. Holding a newborn child for the first time is for parents a vivid experience of God. Many parents have told me that one of their first reactions following the birth of a child, after gratitude, is a surprising one: fear. How will I ever care for this child? What will I do if my baby gets sick? But over time it becomes clear what God is asking them to do: Love your child.

Then, in Luke's telling, we hear Mary's question. This young, probably illiterate woman from a backwater town presses God's messenger for a further explanation. "How can this be," asks the practical Mary, "since I am a virgin?"

This is the facet of the story perhaps most familiar to us: Who hasn't questioned the will of God in their lives? Who, when confronted with dramatic change, hasn't questioned God's plan?

Who hasn't said to God, "How can this be?" Who hasn't said, "Why me?"

Gabriel responds in the way that God often responds to us. The angel reminds Mary to look for signs of God's promise *already* fulfilled in her life and in others' lives. Gabriel points to Mary's cousin: "Now, your relative Elizabeth in her old age has also conceived a son; and this is the sixth month for her who was said to be barren," he says. "For nothing will be impossible with God." Look at what God can do, and has done already.

Frequently in spiritual direction, I meet people doubting that God is accompanying them during a difficult time. Perhaps someone has lost a job. Or a friend or parent has grown ill. Or a relationship has ended. Even the devout begin to doubt the presence of God in their lives. And usually all it takes for them to regain their trust is a simple question: "Hasn't God been with you in the past?" Often they will think for a while and say something like "Now that you mention it, each time I thought I couldn't go on, I found that something or someone helped me do so. I really felt God was right there with me."

A few years ago I edited a book called *How Can I Find God?* in which I invited a number of contributors to answer the same question: If someone asked you how to find God, what would you say? The answer I found the most unexpected was from the superior general of the Society of Jesus, a Dutch Jesuit named Peter-Hans Kolvenbach.

What he said reminded me very much of the story of Mary and the angel.

From his office in Rome, Fr. Kolvenbach recounted the story of a holy abbot who used to speak frequently to his monks of finding God, searching for God, and encountering God. One day one of the monks asked if the abbot had ever encountered God. After a bit of embarrassed silence, the abbot admitted that he had never had a direct experience of God. Yet, he said, there was nothing surprising about that: God himself said to Moses in the book of Exodus, "You cannot see my face." But God also taught Moses that he could see God's back as he passed by: "You shall see my back." So looking back over his many days, the abbot could see very clearly the "passage of God" in his life.

Fr. Kolvenbach concluded his meditation this way:

> In this sense, it is less a matter of searching for God than of allowing oneself to be found by him in all of life's situations, where he does not cease to pass and where he allows himself to be recognized once he has really passed: "You will see my back."

More often than not, God is most easily found by simply looking back over your life, or your week, or your day, and saying, "Yes, *there* was God." Finding God is often a matter of simply being aware, or simply remembering.

Gabriel, in essence, says the same thing to Mary. Look at what God has already done. And look at what God is doing. Just look at Elizabeth. "In her old age [she] has also conceived a son; and this is the sixth month for her who was said to be barren." One scholar, Jane Schaberg, explains, "The reversal of Elizabeth's humiliation shows that nothing is impossible for God."

When Mary reflects on her own experience and on her knowledge of what has happened to Elizabeth, she is finally able to say yes to this strange request by God. "Let it be with me according to your word."

Mary answers this in perfect freedom. As do we. God invites us to join him, to follow him, to create with him, but the decision is always up to us. We are free to say yes or no.

With her yes, Mary partners with the Almighty and is empowered to bring Christ into the world. This world-changing yes is what St. Bernard speaks of in one of his sermons on Mary: "Answer with a word, receive the Word of God. Speak your own word, conceive the divine Word. Breathe a passing word, embrace the eternal Word."

With our own yes to God's voice in our lives, we are also asked to nurture the Word of God within us and bring Christ into the world—certainly not in the same way that Mary did, but in our own situations. Using our individual talents, we are called to bring Christ into the lives of others.

In describing the arc of Gabriel's conversation with Mary, the Gospel of Luke perfectly describes the arc of the spiritual life: God initiates the conversation; we are initially hesitant and fearful; we seek to understand God's word in our life; God reminds us of our experience; and if we choose to say yes to God, we are able to bring new life into the world.

But that's not the whole story. A few months ago I was discussing this passage with a friend named Sr. Janice. At the end of our discussion she said, "If you're thinking about the Annunciation as it relates to the spiritual life, you're forgetting the most important part of the story!"

I had no idea what Janice was talking about.

"Then the angel *left* her!" She laughed. "Isn't that always the way it is with us? After these encounters with God—however they happen in our lives—we are left alone to carry out what we are asked to do.

Though God is still with us, frequently it seems lonely. Who knows if Mary ever encountered God as deeply as she did before Jesus' birth?"

She was right. This is the hardest part: trusting in what God has told us. The part of faith.

⊱⊰

Speaking of faith, it is difficult to know how this encounter between Mary and Gabriel actually transpired. Indeed, the story of the Annunciation underlines an important challenge for the adult believer: the struggle to understand not just some of the incredible tales from the lives of the saints, but, more important, some of the more difficult passages from the Old and New Testaments.

There is, for example, a charming story of St. Augustine trying to make sense of the Trinity. One day, worn out from his long study of this mystery, he decides to take a walk on the beach and clear his mind. Along the way, Augustine comes across a little boy patiently pouring water into a hole in the sand. He cups seawater in his hands and empties it into the hole. Augustine watches him do this, run back to the shoreline, and repeat the process over and over.

After a while, Augustine asks the boy what he is doing.

"I'm trying to fill this hole with the ocean," the little boy is supposed to have said.

"But that's impossible," says Augustine. "You will never fit the ocean in that little hole!"

"Nor will you be able to fit the mystery of the Trinity in your mind," replies the boy, and Augustine realizes he is speaking with an angel.

What are we to make of this tale? Did an angel speak to St. Augustine? Did anything remotely like this ever happen? Does it matter if it happened at all?

Maybe it happened in precisely that way. Most likely, however, it is a pious legend. On the other hand, the story may be based on a kernel of fact; perhaps a friend of Augustine's said something similar to him about his quest to comprehend the Trinity. Certainly it conveys an important truth about the Trinity and Augustine's struggle to understand that mystery. But the question remains: what is legend and what is fact?

In the Jewish and Christian traditions, Scripture is one of the primary ways through which God is revealed to us, through the stories in the Old Testament of God's activity with the Jewish people, and through the story in the New Testament of God living among us as Jesus Christ. As theologians say, Scripture tells us about our "salvation history." In the New Testament, stories about the life, death, and resurrection of Jesus, originally based in oral traditions, were collected by four editors (Matthew, Mark, Luke, and John) into the four Gospels. Each *evangelist* (the word comes from the Greek for "good news") used slightly different material to emphasize different aspects of Jesus, much in the same way that four people telling a story about a single person will highlight different qualities and focus on different incidents. Much of the variance in the stories is an indication of the complexity of the person, not of any desire on the part of the storyteller to mislead.

So with the four Gospels we are offered a (nearly) complete picture of Jesus. One of my theology professors used to say that the New Testament provides us with "a general outline of Jesus' life."

But not an entirely complete or totally accurate one. There are some major continuity problems in the Gospels. In some places, the Gospel writers—who were not, after all, professional historians—do not agree on important details. Most notably, in the Gospel of John, Jesus makes at least five trips to Jerusalem during his ministry. In the other three Gospels, he makes only one. Which one is correct? In Luke and Matthew there are extended discussions of the birth of Jesus, passages often referred to as the "infancy narratives," while there are no stories like this in John or Mark at all. Why the absence? In some Gospels Jesus gives his parables without explanation, despite the disciples' inability to understand. In others, he seems to take pity on them and explain things a bit more. What did Jesus really do? Based on the four Gospels, it's difficult to say.

The New Testament can be difficult to grasp, even for the devout Christian. Overall, then, it's important to use both faith *and* reason when reading Scripture.

This is especially true in the case of the story of the Annunciation. For many years I've wondered about the accuracy of the story that Luke tells at the beginning of his Gospel. How did it *really* happen?

In this case, nearly every Scripture scholar points out that the sources of this Gospel passage are especially difficult to pin down. For one thing, who but Mary could have related the story of her meeting with the angel? Here is what the renowned New Testament scholar John Meier says about this in *A Marginal Jew*, his multivolume study of the "historical Jesus":

> While Mary might theoretically be the ultimate source for some traditions in the Infancy Narratives, grave problems beset the claim that she is the direct source of any narrative as it now stands. To begin with, Mary cannot be the source for all the infancy traditions in both Matthew and Luke; for, as we shall see, Matthew and Luke diverge from or even contradict each other on certain key points.

On the other hand, perhaps Luke was the one who got it exactly right, having heard the story from Mary, or maybe from Jesus. Perhaps, then, it happened exactly the way it was described. (Why not? Nothing is impossible with God.) Perhaps it happened somewhat differently, say, in a dream. (Again, why not? Why couldn't God communicate in this way?) Perhaps the story of the angel was the best way that Mary could communicate an otherwise unexplainable encounter with the divine. Or perhaps the drama of Mary's pregnancy happened gradually, over many months, with her understanding of God's request growing as the baby grew within her. Perhaps, too, Mary's understanding of her eventual role in salvation history deepened with the help of friends and family: her husband, Joseph; her cousin Elizabeth; and her parents, all of whom helped her reflect on God's activity in her life.

In her book *Truly Our Sister*, Elizabeth Johnson turns to another great Scripture scholar and concludes that "the angel does not answer Mary's objection with a satisfactory description of the mechanics of 'how shall this be.' Joseph Fitzmyer's judgment about what happened historically is the baseline from which all theologizing should proceed: 'What really happened? We shall never know.'"

After meditating on the passage from Luke for many years, I have come to believe that either Mary did meet Gabriel (more or less as the passage says) or she had a dramatic and unique encounter with the divine that could only be expressed in terms of a heavenly messenger—based on the Jewish tradition of angels and holy messages. Her experience, which she treasured in her heart, as Luke says, was communicated to the disciples after the death and resurrection of her son, when all these things could be more fully understood. These stories were passed orally from person to person but were especially treasured by the community that Luke wrote for, and so he included them in his Gospel.

But while my reason may not be able to tell me exactly how it happened, my faith tells me that the story is essentially true. Again I like what Elizabeth Johnson has to say: "We do not have access to

Mary's religious experience, but can simply say that by the power of the Spirit she encountered the mystery of the living God, the gracious God of her life, the saving Wisdom of her people. In that encounter, the die was cast for the coming of the Messiah."

Here is the story of the Annunciation, as told in the Gospel of Luke:

In the sixth month the angel Gabriel was sent by God to a town in Galilee called Nazareth, to a virgin engaged to a man whose name was Joseph, of the house of David. The virgin's name was Mary. And he came to her and said, "Greetings, favored one! The Lord is with you." But she was much perplexed by his words and pondered what sort of greeting this might be. The angel said to her, "Do not be afraid, Mary, for you have found favor with God. And now, you will conceive in your womb and bear a son, and you will name him Jesus. He will be great, and will be called the Son of the Most High, and the Lord God will give to him the throne of his ancestor David. He will reign over the house of Jacob forever, and of his kingdom there will be no end." Mary said to the angel, "How can this be, since I am a virgin?" The angel said to her, "The Holy Spirit will come upon you, and the power of the Most High will overshadow you; therefore the child to be born will be holy; he will be called Son of God. And now, your relative Elizabeth in her old age has also conceived a son; and this is the sixth month for her who was said to be barren. For nothing will be impossible with God." Then Mary said, "Here am I, the servant of the Lord; let it be with me according to your word." Then the angel departed from her.

After praying about the Annunciation, I found myself increasingly drawn to Mary, and I began to find her in my ministry. This would prove true in my work in the novitiate and in future ministries as well. I would encounter her through the devotion of many who suffered: an elderly woman struggling with illness in a hospital in Cambridge who clutched the rosary during episodes of pain; a homeless man in Boston who spoke of Mary as "my only mother"; an unemployed young woman in Chicago who talked of praying to her every night for a job.

Most especially, I would see her spirit reflected in the faces of the poor. While working with East African refugees in Nairobi, it happened that most of the refugees with whom I worked were women. In endless ways they brought to mind the story of Mary. I saw Mary during the flight to Egypt, in Rwandese women caring for their children in the face of enormous odds. I saw Mary in Nazareth, in Ugandan women eking out a living in a poor town in the midst of oppression. And I saw Mary at Calvary, in Ethiopian mothers mourning the loss of a child from AIDS, dysentery, malnutrition, or violence.

Toward the close of my Jesuit training, I would meet Mary in a far different type of ministry.

⚜

During theology studies, Jesuit seminarians spend roughly ten hours a week working in a ministry outside of the classroom. The purpose of these assignments is not only to prepare us for eventual full-time ministry, but also to encourage us to consider real-life problems as we reflect on theological questions such as the problem of evil, the nature of God, and the mystery of grace. Active ministry helps the Jesuits (and the lay students as well) ground theology in reality.

Some students opted to fulfill the requirement by working full-time for a few weeks during the summer. A few worked at a busy retreat house in Appalachia, where parishes would bring busloads of families for weekend retreats. One Jesuit in my community ran a basketball camp for poor neighborhood boys at a nearby parish. But most chose to complete their ministerial requirements during the school year. Some students worked at local parishes; others assisted at Catholic elementary schools in the area.

At the beginning of the school year, I decided to work as a chaplain in a local jail. One of my Jesuit friends, George, had worked in prison ministry for several years. George was the Dorothy Day fan from the novitiate. He carried his commitment to social justice intact all the way from his days as a novice to his work at the jail.

Though by now I had worked in a variety of ministries, the jail proved a shock. The Suffolk County House of Corrections is housed in a squat concrete-and-brick building not far from downtown Boston. (Technically, a jail is where prisoners are held until their trial or for short periods of time; if they are convicted they move into a prison.) Those incarcerated at Suffolk County were serving time for a variety of crimes—murder, theft, rape, child molestation—but mainly drug-related offenses. On my first morning, gathered in the gloomy concrete-and-tile lobby were scores of women—Anglo, African American, Hispanic, all poor—waiting to see their husbands or boyfriends during visiting hours. George accompanied me to the jail's employment office, where I filled out a lengthy questionnaire and had my photo taken. A few days later, after a background check was completed, I was given my ID badge.

The next week I began work. To enter the jail, I was buzzed past a bulletproof glass door and stood patiently inside a small enclosure while a guard carefully inspected my ID and inked my hand with the daily stamp. Another loud buzz opened a second glass door, which gave me access to the building's interior.

Inside, the building felt less like a jail and more like a cold, sterile hospital. Fluorescent lights threw harsh reflection on the whitewashed cinder-block walls and white terrazzo floors. On the way to George's small office, George and I passed a man wearing a standard-issue bright orange jumpsuit, led by a correctional officer, or CO. ("Don't call them *guards*," said George. "They don't like that.") The inmate's hands were cuffed behind his back. Once inside George's office, he and I discussed what kind of work I would do.

My ministry would be straightforward: leading weekly communion services (which included giving a homily), visiting the men in solitary confinement, and sometimes speaking with the inmates in "GP," or general population. Occasionally I would spend time one-on-one with inmates, offering counseling or spiritual direction.

I found the visits to solitary the easiest part of the job. The inmates in solitary were lonely and eagerly welcomed the chance to talk with anyone. This stood in stark contrast to other kinds of ministry I had done—like hospital work—where people were sometimes uninterested in, or incapable of, talking with me.

Since the inmates were confined to their cells, I would stand outside the cell and speak through a crack in the doorjamb. Or I would kneel and talk through the narrow metal slot through which their meals were passed. The cells were arranged in a V shape that opened toward the CO's desk. I would make my way slowly down one side of the V, talking in turn to each man, and progress up the other side. Usually I spent five or ten minutes with each person. Barring those sick or asleep, everyone was anxious to speak. If I passed too much time with one inmate, the others complained. "What about us, Father?" they would shout through the locked metal doors.

The lonely men in solitary would do almost anything to lengthen their conversations with me. I was puzzled that one man kept repeating the same questions about the Bible every week, until I realized that he figured that Scripture was a topic I would find interesting, and therefore would keep me by his door.

The inmates' knowledge of Scripture often surpassed mine. One afternoon, I spoke with an African American inmate about his life on the "outside." At the time, I was in the middle of a semester-long class on St. Paul's letter to the Romans. The inmate admitted sadly that no matter how much he tried, he seemed constantly to be living a sinful life.

"I want to be good," he said, "but somehow I just can't seem to do it. I just keep doing the bad stuff."

I told him that his situation sounded like something St. Paul said somewhere. Rather than doing the good he wanted to do, Paul did the evil he didn't want to do. But I couldn't remember where I had read that.

"That's from Paul's letter to the Romans," he said. "Chapter 7."

I made a mental note to pay closer attention in my New Testament class.

I looked forward to the weekly communion services even though they proved difficult to arrange. If there had been disciplinary problems on the floor that day (fights, for example), the guards forbade the inmates from attending, and so the services were canceled, and I spent more time with the men in solitary. But if the inmates had behaved well, at the appointed time the CO would shout in a deafening voice, "Catholic services!" In a few minutes twenty or thirty men from the floor would file in. Those in solitary of course were not permitted to join.

As the rite suggests, before distributing communion I said a few brief prayers and asked one or two of the inmates to read a passage aloud from Scripture. Then I would offer a short reflection and ask the men what they thought about the reading.

Because the Bible was often the only book allowed in their cells and they had so much time on their hands, the inmates had a lot to say. They grasped the Scriptures well, particularly—as had the man in solitary—St. Paul and his talk of sin and redemption. Many displayed an intuitive grasp of the darker side of human nature and the need for repentance and grace to help us along the way. Just as often, the inmates seemed to understand the inherent humanity of the figures from the Bible. Perhaps because they passed so much time in their cells with John the Baptist, Jesus, and Paul, the inmates saw these holy people as more real than many other Christians do. And perhaps spending so much time by themselves made the inmates more acutely aware of their own humanity.

One afternoon during Advent, we were discussing the passage from the Gospel of John focusing on John the Baptist. "He must increase, but I must decrease" says John of Jesus. I asked the men whether they thought it was difficult for John to say that. Was it difficult for John to be humble?

Several hands shot up in the air.

"No," said one. "It wasn't hard for him. John the Baptist was a man of God, and a man of God *knows* that he has to be humble!"

Another man called out, "No, man, it *was* hard for him. He was like everybody else—he wanted to be a big man. Everybody wants to be the big man!"

"Who's right?" another asked me.

To my mind, they both were. We realized that in our discussion we had stumbled onto two main requirements for the spiritual life—humility and confidence. John the Baptist was confident in his mission from God but humble enough to see that his place was in service to Jesus of Nazareth. It was confidence *in* God and humility *before* God.

Other questions were less helpful.

"Can snakes talk?" asked an inmate one day, apropos of nothing.

"What do you mean?"

"Well, there's that part in the book of Genesis where the snake talks to Adam and Eve."

Before I could respond, another inmate called out, "Aw, man, you don't believe in that bullshit!"

Finally, a third man said, "I think that if God *wanted* a snake to talk, it could talk!" Everyone nodded in agreement.

Many inmates enjoyed talking about Mary. Several sported colored plastic rosary beads around their necks, though it was difficult to tell if this was devotion, superstition, or something else entirely. Years earlier I had worked in Kingston, Jamaica, with the Missionaries of Charity in a hospice for sick and dying men. As I passed through the slums on my way to work in the morning, I was amazed at the numbers of poor young men who requested rosary beads. In time I learned that the various colors of the plastic beads were identification markers for gang members. It was that way for many of the men in the jail.

But not for all of them. A young Irish-Catholic man serving time for dealing drugs tentatively told me that he prayed to Mary because he never knew his mother. "Mary understands me," he said. Another kept rosary beads (or "rosemary beads," as he called them) under his pillow for daily use. We had a long discussion about the "mysteries" of the rosary, that is, the meditations on the lives of Mary and Jesus that make up the traditional rosary prayer.

After one communion service, an inmate who must have been six feet four and three hundred pounds confessed that he didn't think he was praying the rosary the right way.

I told him that there was no "right" way to pray; any prayer was pleasing to God. I asked if maybe he'd like to know a little more about the traditional way of using the rosary.

"Yeah," he said. "You know, the other guys say it takes them half an hour, but it only takes me a minute or so."

A minute? How did he manage that?

He pulled out a plastic rosary from his pocket and began fingering one of the small beads. "I pray a Hail Mary for each of these little ones here," he said, "and an Our Father for the big ones."

That was correct, of course, but I wondered how he could do it so fast.

"Why don't you show me how you say those prayers."

"Okay," he said. He closed his eyes and began fingering the beads rapidly. "Hail Mary, Hail Mary, Hail Mary, Hail Mary, Hail Mary . . ."

I grasped his dilemma. "You know," I said, "there's a whole *prayer* that goes with the Hail Mary. It goes 'Hail Mary, full of grace, the Lord is with thee . . .'" I finished the prayer.

His face fell. "Shit, that'll take the whole damn *day!*"

As Christmas approached and the rest of the world prepared for the holidays, little changed inside the jail. In fact, December was an especially sad time for the inmates, as they thought about their families on the outside or, more likely, how rarely they had passed a happy Christmas. A bright spot during the month, however, was provided for some inmates by Mary.

Near the beginning of the semester, I began a Bible study class for the women inmates at Suffolk County. In the afternoon, when the women were released from their cells into an open recreation area, I offered an opportunity to read and discuss the Old and New Testaments. The classes were nothing more than a few of us sitting on broken plastic chairs around a small Formica table. During our meetings, the other women hung around the floor or lounged nearby and watched trashy talk shows on a television mounted high on the wall.

One day near Christmas I decided that we would discuss two stories from the Gospel of Luke: Mary's encounter with the angel and her later meeting with Elizabeth, when she proclaims her Magnificat ("My soul magnifies the Lord, and my spirit rejoices in God my

Savior . . ."). The previous night I had prepared a few notes I could use if the women found the material uninteresting or difficult to understand. As I prepared my outline, I remembered that on a recent retreat I had come to understand these readings in a new way.

Usually I think of Mary as a model of patience and trust who accepted Gabriel's message after only a short period of doubt. But as I meditated on those passages from Luke during that year's retreat, my prayer led me to a different understanding. At the greeting of the angel, Mary might not have been calm and trusting, but frightened and confused. Even after the angel explained things to her, the meaning of his message might still have terrified her and only raised *more* questions in her mind: What does all this mean? What will become of me? Yet in the face of this uncertainty, Mary did what she needed to do. Though she could have had no idea what would happen to her or her family, she soldiered on. It helped me see that sometimes all we can do is live life on a daily basis, even in the midst of fear and confusion. And that sometimes, even in the spiritual life, it is okay to be a little frightened.

This also gave me new insight into the story of the Visitation, which follows the Annunciation. The Gospel of Luke says, "Mary set out and went with haste" to her cousin Elizabeth. Normally, Mary's visit is interpreted as the result of her desire to proclaim the good news to her cousin. But in my prayer I saw Mary setting out in haste because she was *afraid*, desperately in need of an older woman's counsel and wisdom to help her understand what to do.

Remembering these insights, I reviewed my retreat journal and diligently prepared my notes for the Bible study, ready to share my thoughts with the inmates.

I began our class the next day with a brief prayer. Then I started reading from the Gospel of Luke. The five women present, all new to the class, began giggling. One said, in heavily accented English, "Do you speak Spanish?"

To my horror, I realized that none of the women spoke any English. (And my Spanish is pretty elementary.) My first reaction was disappointment over all that time I had spent the night before. They wouldn't get to hear my fantastic reflections!

All I could do, in halting Spanish, was explain which passages I thought we might discuss. In response, one of the women opened her Spanish Bible and started reading the story of the Annunciation and the Visitation aloud, in a firm, clear voice: "En el sexto mes, el ángel Gabriel . . ."

After she finished, I asked only one question: "¿Qué piensan ustedes de la Virgen María?" What do you think about Mary?

Then, for a full hour, came an unbroken conversation about Mary. From what I could follow (at times the talk was rapid-fire, enthusiastic, emotional, and punctuated with laughter), the women talked of the hardships of giving birth in poverty, of the difficulties of raising children, of how hard it must have been for Mary to see her son die. Mostly they talked about how they loved Mary and felt that among all the saints in heaven, Mary understood them the best. They spoke about Elizabeth, too: how it was good to have an older woman in the family to whom you could go for advice, how older women were always wise—wiser than older *men*, they said—and how Mary was lucky to have someone to take care of her in her need. One of the inmates even knew an older woman who had a baby after a long time and told us how happy she was.

Though I sat with my carefully prepared notes on the tabletop before me, I said nothing for the entire hour. Listening to these women, I remembered the women from East Africa I had known, and I recognized again that I was in the presence of people who understood Mary far better than I ever could. So I just listened. What, really, could I add?

⧽✧⧼

My devotion to Mary, to the woman of the Annunciation, to the woman who brought Jesus into the world, centers on the human person she was. On how she responded to God's invitation. On how she shows us to live with faith in the impossible, how she persevered in the most difficult circumstances, how she trusted. How she loved. My devotion to Mary is very much to the *woman*, Miriam of Nazareth.

But it is also very much a devotion to the mother of God, to the Blessed Virgin, the woman who now enjoys new life with her son, the woman who listens to our prayers and intercedes for all of us. And it is a devotion to the woman of the rosary—my first rosary, which I still have, and which reminds me of my faith: occasionally broken and battered, frequently imperfect, and yet somehow whole, its roots deep in my childhood and continuing to grow in the present, in the sunlight of God's creating and renewing love.

18

Holy in a Different Way

A Conclusion

From the saints I must take the substance, not the
accidents, of their virtues. I am not St. Aloysius, nor must
I seek holiness in his particular way, but according to the
requirements of my own nature, my own character, and
the different conditions of my life. I must not be the dry,
bloodless reproduction of a model, however perfect. God
desires us to follow the examples of the saints by
absorbing the vital sap of their virtues and turning it into
our own lifeblood, adapting it to our own individual
capacities and particular circumstances. If St. Aloysius
had been as I am, he would have become holy in a
different way.
—POPE JOHN XXIII, *JOURNAL OF A SOUL*

During theology studies, I studied with a professor of church
history named John O'Malley, a distinguished Jesuit scholar
and author. Often at the end of a long and erudite lecture—say, on the
medieval papacy or the history of Western monasti-
cism—Fr. O'Malley would pause, turn to the class, and say,
"So what?"

Then he would explain how the historical development he had just described had affected the Church at the time and how it continued to influence the Church and the world. This was his way of summarizing the material and also showing its relevance to our lives.

"So what?" is a good question to ask now that we've reached the end of this journey with the saints. In the last few chapters, you've read how I met some holy men and women over the course of my life, enjoyed a fair share of interesting experiences, felt plenty of strong emotions, and even learned a few lessons.

So what?

Well, first of all, I hope that you've discovered a few saints you might like to get to know better. As I've mentioned, I think one reason we are initially attracted to a saint is that the saint is already praying for us—though I admit this is an impossible hypothesis to prove. Maybe you've been impressed by the contemporary saints in this book, such as Dorothy Day or Pedro Arrupe or John XXIII. Maybe you're beginning to see them as models for your own life.

For me, that's an important function of the saints; I see them as models and enjoy the benefits of their experiences. All the saints encountered suffering of some kind, and when we undergo similar difficulties it's consoling to know not only that there were Christians who underwent such trials, but also that, united with God, the saints are able to pray for us as we suffer.

For example, Thérèse of Lisieux and Bernadette Soubirous struggled with serious illnesses in their short lives, as did Pedro Arrupe in his long life. In the face of discouragement about sickness, you might take comfort in the admission of Thérèse that even she got discouraged, or in the stalwart trust of Bernadette, or in Pedro Arrupe's desire to place himself in "the hands of God." In knowing their lives, you can avail yourself of the saints' wisdom. Like an experienced traveler, a saint can guide you along the path of suffering. Benefiting from their insights is one reason to read the lives of the saints.

To take another example, for those struggling with their church, Catholic or otherwise, it's good to remember that some of the saints did the same. Dorothy Day, the devoted apostle of the church, liked to quote Romano Guardini's trenchant saying, "The church is the cross on which Christ is crucified today." Thomas Merton, when silenced by his religious superiors, wrote to a friend with undisguised anger that a monk would not be allowed to speak against war: "Man, I would think that it just might possibly salvage a last shred of repute for an institution that many consider to be dead on its feet . . ." St. Catherine of Siena, during a time of church scandals in the four-teenth century, wrote to a group of cardinals in Rome, saying, "You are flowers that shed no perfume, but a stench that makes the whole world reek." Even the saints—or, perhaps, *especially* the saints—faced disappointment, frustration, and anger with organized religion.

This has always been helpful to me. On my bedroom wall are posted holy cards of my favorite saints (basically, those in this book). When I feel discouraged about the Catholic Church, I recall that for all their problems with the Church, people like Day, Merton, and Catherine of Siena remained firmly within the Catholic community. During moments of frustration, I can say, "Well, they were smarter and holier than I am, and they stuck it out."

The saints offer us encouragement, like the runner just ahead of us in the race, urging us on and reminding us to pace ourselves. This is true not simply when we are sick or discouraged but also when we're leading healthy, active lives. When I'm busy, I remember Thomas Aquinas, the thirteenth-century multitasker; the man who employed three scribes to take down his notes simultaneously reminds me that prayer is as important as work. When I write, I remember Thomas Merton; the famous writer reminds me that fame is not the reason one writes. When I work with the marginalized, I remember Mother Teresa; the servant to the poor reminds me that it is Christ I am serving. When I'm fighting for something that I believe is just, I remember Joan of Arc; the lifelong fighter reminds me of the need to trust in God, not in results.

The saints are models of what our lives could be. In following the example of their lives, we can be formed by them. In the words of Lawrence S. Cunningham, "We hope to be what they are."

I feel their friendship, too. The more I get to know them, the more I feel that these men and women who enjoy life with God are pulling for me, that they are on my side, that they want me to succeed in the Christian life, that they want me to be a good Jesuit and a good priest. This is impossible to prove, but since first encountering them, I've believed that they are praying for me. "Don't give up," they say. "Don't worry," they remind me. Or, as Julian of Norwich said, "All will be well, and all will be well, and all manner of things will be well."

I also turn to the saints for their intercession. As Elizabeth Johnson says in her book *Friends of God and Prophets*, there are two traditional ways in which Christians have understood the saints: as companions and as patrons.

These two models overlap in my life. I turn to a saint in prayer (patron) because his or her story resonates with my own and I have sought out his or her company (companion). So while I look to Thérèse of Lisieux during illness, or to Thomas Merton during my struggles with the Church, or to Peter for faith in dark times, I also ask for their intercession at those times.

How does intercession work? For some Christians it seems a superstitious belief—all those candles and statues and medals and prayers that sound suspiciously like magical incantations. For others, intercession is one of the foundations of their faith. The Apostles' Creed says in part, "I believe in . . . the communion of saints," which includes the belief that they are praying for us. For me, the help of the saints makes sense on a practical and theological level: Why wouldn't those who are with God desire to help us here on earth? Why wouldn't they want to intercede for us? To me, it seems natural. But, again, it's impossible to prove.

All I know is that when I've received something for which I've prayed and for which I've asked some assistance from a saint, I am first grateful to God, but also grateful for whatever extra help the saint may have given me.

Just recently, for example, I was working with an acting company that produced an Off-Broadway play based on the life of Judas Iscariot. The play put Judas on trial in purgatory for his actions, to examine whether he deserved eternal damnation. Included in the play was testimony from "expert witnesses," such as St. Peter, St. Thomas, St. Matthew, Mother Teresa, and even Thomas Merton. As a result, I spent a good deal of time with the cast discussing some of the saints in this book. I even passed along early drafts of some chapters as a way of helping the actors come to know the lives of the saints.

The playwright, named Stephen, was something of a lapsed Catholic who nonetheless had an instinctive feel for important questions of faith. His play, for example, prominently featured St. Monica, the mother of the fourth-century saint Augustine. In real life, Monica had prayed fervently for the conversion of her young and wayward son, and she is sometimes considered the patron saint of persistent prayer. In Stephen's play, which he wrote in slangy, streetwise style, a fiery young St. Monica is a self-described nag whose famous persistence with God was the only thing that helped save her son.

"You know what?" she says to the audience. "I *am* a nag! And if I wasn't a nag, I wouldn't never made it to be no *saint*, and the Church wouldn't a had no father of the Church named St. Augustine!" Moreover, she encourages the audience to seek her intercession:

"You should try giving me a shout if ya ever need it, cuz my name is St. Monica, and I'm the mother of St. Augustine, and ya know what? My ass gets *results!*"

After one performance, a young Jesuit said to me, "You know what? I should pray to St. Monica more often."

The Sunday after the play closed, I was scheduled to celebrate Mass at a local Jesuit church, and I'd invited some of the cast members along. I very much hoped that Stephen would come, as he hadn't been to Mass for some time. Sunday morning, however, Stephen called with some bad news. "Hey, Jim," he said, "I guess I won't be able to come. There's like this *river* of water leaking into my apartment, and the superintendent isn't coming until 10:00."

I told him I would pray to St. Monica. So in my room, after I had hung up the phone, I knelt down, lit a few candles for good measure, and said a prayer to her: "So here I am, Monica, giving you a shout: Let Stephen be able to come to Mass."

On the way to church, I called Stephen from a cab and told him I was praying for a small miracle. "Well, I don't know," he said. "It doesn't look too good. The super's not here yet." Inside the church I lit another candle, in front of a statue of St. Aloysius Gonzaga.

By the time I reached the sacristy it was time for another call. "Any miracles yet?" I said.

"You know," he said, "I think it's going to be okay. It's just a radiator leaking upstairs. I turned it off myself."

The Mass began with no Stephen in sight. But as I stood up to read the Gospel, I saw the door in the church narthex open. Ambling in came Stephen, who took a seat in the last pew. A few minutes later he came up for communion.

Do I think Monica and Aloysius had something to do with it? Who can say for sure? But for me the answer is yes.

It reminds me of a line from the movie version of *The Song of Bernadette*. In response to the need for proof of Bernadette's vision and the subsequent miracles at Lourdes, one character says, "For those with faith no explanation is necessary; for those without faith no explanation is sufficient."

How do I feel about the variety of ways in which people relate to the saints today? What about the seemingly bizarre piety surrounding the cult of the saints? What of the tradition of burying statues of St. Joseph in the ground in order to get a house sold? Or those front-lawn shrines to the saints sometimes housed in overturned enamel bathtubs? Just a few weeks ago, I was walking through a heavily Italian section of Brooklyn and was amazed at the number of homemade shrines to Mary and St. Anthony and St. Jude, whose painted concrete statues were festooned with colorful plastic flowers and twinkling lights.

As a Catholic I am used to that. It's part of Catholic culture. It may disturb some progressive Catholics, and certainly many Protestants, but it's good to give people the benefit of the doubt when it comes to their faith. If such practices help people feel closer to their favorite saint, and that in turn helps them feel closer to God, then that's terrific—as long as people remember that it is God to whom they are praying and that devotion to a saint should never blind them to the centrality of Jesus in their lives.

But as with any friend, a saint should not be seen from a strictly utilitarian point of view: that is, we shouldn't see them simply as models, as intercessors, as ones who exist to encourage us. This is far too narrow an understanding of the saints. Too often we reduce their role to doing things for us. Or, worse, *getting* us things.

Recently, a friend told me that she prays to Mother Cabrini—or St. Frances Xavier Cabrini, the Italian nun canonized for her work with immigrants in New York City—when she wants to find a parking space. Apparently, Mother's urban sympathies make her the go-to woman for frustrated drivers. Her prayer is a variation on St. Anthony's:

> Mother Cabrini, Mother Cabrini,
> please find a spot
> for my little machine-y.

It's fun to imagine Mother Cabrini searching out parking lots for an open space. But if we reduce the saints to a purely *functional* role, we overlook the invitation simply to rejoice in the variety of gifts that they reveal in the kingdom of God. The saints are not just useful tools; they are people to celebrate. The stories of their lives on earth are gifts for which we can be grateful, as we are grateful for works of art. Someone once wrote that the saints are like actors in a play, and the script of that play is the gospel.

To borrow another metaphor, from Thérèse of Lisieux, loving the saints is like enjoying the marvelous variety of a garden. You don't love a flower for what it does, but for what it is. Now I know that the most common image of the saints is probably the "cloud of witnesses" that comes from St. Paul. And while I like that image for its notion of the saints as a hovering presence, it also seems a bit cold and impersonal. I much prefer the image of the garden, where each of the saints shows forth God's beauty in a different way.

Without a doubt, that's the most important aspect of the saints for me: they teach me about being who I am. Each of the saints has been, to quote John XXIII, "holy in a different way." Each was placed in a different situation and time. Each had a different personality and dealt with life differently. And each related to God a little differently.

Think of the variety of holy men and women just in these pages. Not only did they live in different times and places and speak different languages, but they also possessed their own personalities and followed their specific calls to holiness.

Some examples: Though both of their lives were rooted in God, Thomas Merton and Aloysius Gonzaga approached life in very different ways. Merton was forever questioning his vow of stability, his place in the monastery, and his vocation as a Trappist, almost until the end of his life. Aloysius, on the other hand, seemed to have known precisely what he wanted to do—that is, become a Jesuit—from childhood.

Or think about Thérèse of Lisieux and Dorothy Day. Thérèse realized that God had called her to spend life cloistered behind the walls of a Carmelite convent, while Dorothy Day understood that her invitation was to spend life on the "outside," working among the poor and marginalized in the big cities. Both grasped their respective calls. But both appreciated styles of sanctity that varied significantly from their own. Thérèse, for instance, greatly admired the Catholic missionaries working in Vietnam. And Dorothy Day admired Thérèse enough to write a little book about her.

The earliest example of the variety of ways to be Christian can be found in the story of the call of the first disciples. The Scripture scholar William Barclay, who was mentioned in the chapter on St. Peter, offered some provocative insights on why Jesus of Nazareth might have chosen fishermen among his first disciples: fishermen are patient, they are brave, they know how to fit the bait to the fish, they know how to stay out of sight, and so on.

But that only explains why Jesus chose the four disciples who were fishermen. What about everyone else? Why would Jesus call, say, a tax collector and a religious zealot and, among his wider circle of disciples, a prostitute?

One reason may have been that Jesus saw how each disciple contributed something unique to the community. The unity of the Church, both then and now, encompasses a tremendous diversity. As St. Paul says in his first letter to the Corinthians, "There are varieties of gifts, but the same Spirit. . . . To each is given the manifestation of the Spirit for the common good. . . . For just as the body is one and has many members, and all the members of the body, though many, are one body, so it is with Christ."

Each of us brings something to the table, and we each, through our own gifts, manifest a personal way of holiness that enlivens the community. We help build up the kingdom of God in ways that others cannot. Mother Teresa echoes this in her famous saying: "You can do something I can't do. I can do something you can't do. Together let us do something beautiful for God."

⚜

This diversity is an outgrowth of human desire, whose place in the spiritual life was illuminated by Ignatius of Loyola in *The Spiritual Exercises*. Put simply, the saints had different desires, and those desires led them to serve God in different ways. Such desires affected not only what they did but who they became. These natural inclinations are means by which God accomplishes his work in various places and in a variety of modes. When I was studying theology, my Jesuit community had a small poster in the living room that said:

> Bernardus valles,
> Colles Benedictus amavit,
> Oppida Franciscus,
> Magnas Ignatius urbes.

That is:

> Bernard loved the valleys,
> Benedict the hills,
> Francis the small towns,
> and Ignatius the great cities.

Each found his home in a place suited to his own desires, and so was moved to accomplish his own particular task. Their desires shaped their vocations. Ignatius, for example, would probably have felt his ambitious plans stymied in a small town. And Francis of Assisi would certainly have gone crazy trying to run a large religious order from an office in Rome!

God awakens our vocations primarily through our desires. At the most basic level, a man and a woman come together in love out of desire and discover their vocations as a married couple. Out of desire, a husband and a wife create a child and discover their vocations as parents. Desire works in a similar way in the lives of the saints, drawing them to do certain types of work, giving rise to special vocations, and leading to an individual brand of holiness. Angelo Roncalli became a priest because he desired it. Dorothy Day entered the Catholic Church because she desired it. Charles de Foucauld embraced a life of poverty in the desert because he desired it. Ultimately, one's deepest desires lead to God and to the fulfillment of God's desires for the world.

That insight lies behind one of my favorite passages in *The Seven Storey Mountain*. Shortly after his baptism, Thomas Merton is speaking with his good friend Lax. Merton tells his friend that he wants to be a good Catholic. "What you should say," says his friend, "is that you want to be a saint." Merton tells the rest of the story:

A saint? The thought struck me as a little weird. I said:

"How do you expect me to become a saint?"

"By wanting to," said Lax, simply. . . . "All that is necessary to be a saint is to want to be one. Don't you believe God will make you what He created you to be, if you consent to let him do it? All you have to do is desire it."

The next day Merton speaks with his mentor, Mark Van Doren, the esteemed professor of English at Columbia University, and mentions his confusing conversation with Lax. Van Doren's response is both direct and disarming:

"Lax is going around telling everyone that all a man needs to be a saint is to want to become one."

"Of course," said Mark.

Following these individual desires led each of the saints to a special kind of holiness. Grace builds on nature, as Thomas Aquinas said. Ignatius of Loyola gave up a military career to follow God, while Joan of Arc began one. Dorothy Day worked in a newspaper to spread the gospel, while Bernadette Soubirous shrank in horror from the idea of her story being published. Thomas Aquinas spent his life surrounded by books, while Francis of Assisi told his friars not to own even one lest they become too proud. The multiplicity of desires leads to a multiplicity of paths to God.

But there is a potential problem with this variety. It's a challenge to appreciate another person's path when it is different from your own. If you're an active person, you might wonder about the sedentary life of the contemplative. ("All that prayer when there's so much to be done?") If you're of a contemplative bent, you might question the frenetic life of the activist. ("All that activity when all God wants is for you to be with him in prayer?") You can easily imagine Peter looking at Paul and saying to himself, "I'm supposed to work with a former Pharisee?"

It can be especially difficult to accept another's way of discipleship if we are unsure of our own. The resulting misunderstanding can lead to disagreement and strife within the Christian community.

But it's good to remember that even the saints disagreed with one another—often strongly. Quarrels between the saints have a venerable tradition in the Christian church, going all the way back to Peter and Paul.

So what holds things together in the midst of this diversity? What keeps the communion of saints in communion?

The unity of the Christian saints rests on their commitment to Jesus Christ. Like the early disciples who trusted the judgment of their master, we must trust God's reasons for calling people quite different from us, even though those reasons may remain mysterious to us. As a Jesuit I have frequently met people who have sung the praises of another Jesuit whom I had quickly written off as too quiet or too cerebral or too ornery to do any good. It's a reminder of the wisdom of the One who calls us together and sends us on a mission.

Perhaps, in fact, all that kept the fractious disciples together was Jesus himself—not so much their reliance on him to settle disagreements, but their fundamental trust in him. They may have said, "Okay, Lord, I don't like that other fellow very much, and I don't really understand him, but if you say he's part of our group, that's good enough for me."

Even at this point, you still may be thinking, "Well, I'm not like *any* of the people in this book. I'm not a social activist like Dorothy Day or a contemplative like Thomas Merton or a great scholar like Thomas Aquinas or a visionary leader like Pedro Arrupe, and I'm certainly not an *actual* visionary like Bernadette Soubirous. Holiness is beyond me."

I disagree. I think that sanctity is God's goal for each of us, our endpoint. As Mother Teresa said, "Holiness is not the luxury of a few. It is everyone's duty: yours and mine."

Despite the recent emphasis on every person's call to holiness, some Christians still believe that sanctity is reserved only for saints who are long dead, such as Peter or Joan of Arc, or, once in a while, for the professionally religious person—a priest or sister or brother, Ignatius of Loyola or John XXIII. And those like the Ugandan martyrs or Charles de Foucauld, who died for their faith. And maybe, just maybe, the extraordinary layperson: the unknown parent who dedicates his entire life to caring for the poor, or the more well-known Dorothy Day. But the idea of the holy person *in everyday life* still strikes many people as a bit strange.

Let's imagine, for example, a young married woman with two little children, ages four and six. When the alarm clock jolts her awake in the early morning, she's still weary from the day before. As usual, her two children are already awake. One is crying her eyes out because she's had a bad dream. The other child is already calling for a drink of water and for his favorite stuffed animal, which he tossed out of his bed last night. And let's say that her husband is away on a business trip and can't help her with the kids this morning. Let's say that she has a job outside the home as well and has to make breakfast and get the kids ready for school before leaving for another hectic day at the office.

As she lies in bed for a few seconds, staring at the ceiling, she thinks about all the things she has to do for her family today, all the things she has to do for her boss at the office, and none of the things she can do for herself. She wonders how she'll be able to accomplish even half of what she needs to do today. Sometimes, during these early morning moments, she laments the fact that she doesn't have time for things such as prayer and meditation. The young mother wishes she lived a holier life, a more *religious* life. Recently she read a magazine article about her favorite contemporary saint, Mother Teresa.

And she says to herself, sadly, "I'll never be like her."

But that's the problem. She is not meant to be Mother Teresa; she's meant to be herself.

Thomas Merton often distinguished between the "false self" and the "true self." The false self is the person we present to the world, the one we think will be pleasing to others: attractive, confident, successful. The true self, on the other hand, is the person we are before God. Sanctity consists in discovering who that person is and striving to become that person. As Merton wrote, "For me to be a saint means to be myself."

In other words, the working mother is not *meant* to be Mother Teresa. She is meant to be a woman who loves her children, her husband, her friends and coworkers, and finds meaning in her own world. She is meant to experience the presence of God in her life and in the lives of the people with whom she lives and works. Sometimes this means doing big things with love—raising children, for example. And sometimes it means doing smaller things with love. That's the Little Way that Thérèse of Lisieux wrote about. For the young working mother, this could mean keeping a lid on her temper at work (no matter how justified it may be).

Part of this process means that this young woman has to let go of her desire to be someone else. Because, in reality, she might be lousy at the type of work that Mother Teresa used to do. To underline this point, Mother Teresa might have been lousy at the work that this working mother is doing!

God's invitation to live out our unique vocations is part of what makes the world so rich. "How gloriously different are the saints," wrote C. S. Lewis. Problems arise when we begin to believe that we have to be someone *else* to be holy. We try to use someone else's map to heaven when God has already planted in our soul all the directions we need. In that way, we ignore our own call to sanctity. When admirers used to visit Calcutta to see Mother Teresa, she would tell many of them, "Find your own Calcutta."

This is not to say that we aren't called to emulate the saints or, more to the point, Jesus. Reading the Gospels and the lives of the saints are fine ways of discovering new paths to holiness. That is part of the discovery process Merton speaks of. After all, it was in reading about Merton's journey that I discovered something of what my own journey must be. Through reading, conversation, and prayer, I grow gradually into the person I am meant to be. My life with the saints helps me see more clearly and embrace more eagerly whatever God has in store for me.

In order to continue on our journey to sanctity, we have to hold lightly others' interpretation of holiness. Not only that, once we set aside the notion that we're supposed to be someone else, we must begin the long process of discovering who we really are and what we are meant to do.

At the heart of this understanding is accepting who we are before God. "For it was you who formed my inward parts; you knit me together in my mother's womb," says Psalm 139. "I praise you, for I am fearfully and wonderfully made." The beginning of sanctity is loving ourselves as creations of God. And that means *all* of ourselves, even the parts of us that we wish weren't there, the parts of us that we wish God hadn't made, the parts of us that we lament. God loves us as a parent loves a child—often more for the parts of the child that are weaker or where the child struggles and falters. Those weaknesses are often the most important paths to holiness, because they remind us of our reliance on God.

"So, I will boast all the more gladly of my weaknesses," wrote Paul in his second letter to the Corinthians, "so that the power of Christ may dwell in me. Therefore I am content with weaknesses, insults, hardships, persecutions, and calamities for the sake of Christ; for whenever I am weak, then I am strong."

❦

Believing that God wants us to be ourselves has been liberating for me. While I'm always called to grow, God asks only that I be myself, no matter what the situation. So when I'm listening to a friend tell me his problems, or hearing someone's confession, or standing before a homeless man in the street, I don't have to say, "What would Peter or Francis or Thérèse or John XXIII do?" Certainly they are models of Christian action for me. But God has not placed them in this particular situation. God, in his mysterious wisdom, has placed *me* here, with my talents and skills, as well as my weaknesses and limitations. Therefore, a better question is, "What should *I* do?"

As Gerard Manley Hopkins wrote,

> For Christ plays in ten thousand places,
> Lovely in limbs, and lovely in eyes not his.

In other words, in *your* eyes and in *your* limbs.

Believing that all of us are called to be saints has profound implications for daily life. An acceptance of what the Second Vatican

Council termed the "universal call to holiness" imbues even the most hidden moments of one's life with a special grace.

The universal call to holiness is an invitation to be ourselves. It's also an invitation to remember the sacramentality of everyday life and to realize the great goal that God has set for us: sanctity. It is what the saints came to realize, sometimes in an instant, sometimes over the course of many years, whether they were born in first-century Palestine, thirteenth-century France, or twentieth-century America. Whether they lived in a quiet cloistered monastery in Lisieux, in a lonely desert tent in Morocco, or in the grand papal palace in the Vatican. Whether they worked alongside the poorest of the poor in Calcutta, with the plague victims in Rome, or with the gentiles of Asia Minor. Whether they succumbed to illness early in life, were martyred in middle age, or died after a long life of perfect health.

The call to sanctity is an invitation to friendship with God. It is a call that transformed the lives of the saints into gifts to the One who loved them into being. The invitation to holiness is a lifelong call to draw closer to God, who wants nothing more than to encounter us as the people we are and the saints we are meant to be.

⊰◊⊱

Though we've reached the final chapter, I don't consider this book finished. There are still many saints I am just getting to know. Posted on my wall a few years ago was a holy card of St. Katharine Drexel, who gave up a fabulous fortune in nineteenth-century Philadelphia to become a missionary sister working among African Americans and Native Americans. I prayed to her a great deal during my father's final illness. (He was inordinately proud of the fact that she was not only an American saint, but a Philadelphian saint.) And a few months ago, on a return flight to Lourdes, I saw the film *A Man for All Seasons* again and remembered how much I liked reading about Thomas More when I was in the novitiate. And here's a saint whom I know very little about, other than that he was a joyful man who liked a good laugh: St. Philip Neri. (He was also a friend of St. Ignatius.)

I would like to get to know each of these saints soon. So, in a sense, this book marks a beginning for me.

I hope this book is also a beginning for you, and that it has offered encouragement in your own journey with the saints. The saints in this book are those for whom I feel the most affection, those who have afforded me courage, and those who I believe have prayed for me during some tough times. I hope that some of them will become your companions, too. Then one day, united in heaven, we will be able to thank God for these men and women who have been our models, our intercessors, and our friends.

19

Still Trying to Become a Saint

An Epilogue

From time to time, after a lecture or during a book signing, some-one will smile, reach into a backpack or a plastic bag, and pull out a copy of *My Life with the Saints*. It's both gratifying and humbling to see the dog-eared pages and underlined passages, and to realize that someone may have found this book helpful.

It's even more of a treat when the person asks, "Do you know who my favorite saint is?"

Because then, invariably, the person's face will brighten as they name the saint and describe the influence that he or she has had in their life. Often they will recount a story from the saint's life that was wholly unknown to me, which is another delight. It's like hearing something surprising about a mutual friend. Just as often, people will scold me—good-naturedly—about my having left out *their* saint from my book, and will then try to convince me why he or she should have been included.

In the ten years since this book was first published, I've noticed that the same questions pop up over and over again. This is the case whether I'm speaking at conventions, parishes, retreat centers, book-stores, colleges or high schools. So I thought I might answer them here and then reflect on where my journey has taken me since I finished this book, and share what I've learned about sanctity.

⚜

By far the most common question is, "Why didn't you include [a particular saint]?"

Once, at a dinner before a lecture in the Midwest, a Catholic bishop carefully pushed aside the pitcher of water that stood between us on the table, fixed me with a stern gaze, and said, "I have one question: Where is St. John Paul II?" A Catholic columnist publicly (but lightheartedly) took me to task for not including St. Patrick, because he knew that I was of Irish descent. One woman on a radio call-in show was vocal about my neglect of St. Gertrude, which was particularly embarrassing because I knew almost nothing about her life. A young woman after a parish talk in Boston said that leaving out St. Mary Magdalene was "unforgiveable," given how important she is to so many women—and men for that matter.

Other saints whose noninclusion have been lamented frequently include Philip Neri, Augustine, and Monica, to name a few, as well as pretty much every Jesuit saint. One Jesuit said to me, with a smile, "No Francis Xavier? What are you going to say to *him* when you get to heaven?"

The answer to that overall question is simple: I wrote about the saints to whom I had the strongest personal devotion. Needless to say, I have nothing against any of the other saints that people mention, but I'm not as captivated by their lives, nor do I find myself praying to them as frequently. So while I admire the saints that people suggest for inclusion, they are not as dear to me as they may be for them. This is no doubt the working of grace: some saints appeal to us in a particular way.

Perhaps, as I mentioned in this book, this is because they are praying for us.

Any book about "my" life with the saints, then, was bound to be personal. Leaving out a particular saint was not a slight, far less a judgment, but simply a reflection of my personal journey. In the end, I'm not sure why I don't have as hardy a devotion to St. Patrick as I do to St. Peter. (Except on March 17, that is.) But if I asked you to enumerate your favorite saints, your own list would be no doubt different from my own.

That may also help answer the second most common question, which is, "Why don't you write a sequel?"

That is also is easy to answer. Because I focused on the saints about whom I was the most passionate, any sequel would necessarily mean highlighting saints for whom I don't have as much affection. That lesser enthusiasm would surely make for a less lively book. Who would want to read a book called *My Life with the Saints I'm Not Quite So Devoted To*? Far better, I think, to let this book stand on its own, circumscribed as it is by my own inclinations, and let other authors write about the saints they love.

There is, however, one exception. There is a group of saints to whom I feel intense devotion but who were omitted from the book: the North American Martyrs, a group of French Jesuits who worked among the Huron peoples in northern New York and Canada during the seventeenth century. (Those martyred in Canada are often called the Canadian Martyrs.)

I have an intense devotion to the North American Martyrs, and I'm deeply moved by the way they left everything they knew to come to minister, amidst great dangers, to a group of peoples considered by many in Europe at that time to be "less than human." In fact, I've traveled several times to Auriesville, New York, and once to Midland, Ontario, Canada, to pray at the shrines that commemorate their ministry and martyrdoms. I never leave unmoved. But ten years ago, I felt that this book already included enough Jesuits—St. Aloysius Gonzaga, St. Ignatius of Loyola and Pedro Arrupe—so I decided to omit the North American Martyrs.

You might be surprised by this devotion to these missionaries, which may seem old-fashioned. Today there is a tendency to downplay, criticize, or even condemn missionaries of old. The argument goes like this: Missionaries came to impose their Eurocentric ways on an unsuspecting people who would have been happier without Christianity. As tools of the brutal colonialist oppressors, the legacy is one of domination. As a result, as Emma Anderson, a history professor, opines in her highly critical book *The Death and Afterlife of the North American Martyrs*, Catholic martyrs in the United States have become mainly "symbols of Catholic doctrinal purity and intransigence."

Some of that reading is true. Sometimes missionaries supported, either wittingly or unwittingly, some of the more baneful practices of the colonial powers. But much of that reading is inaccurate. *The Jesuit Relations*, the collection of letters sent to France by the missionaries of the time, paints a striking portrait of the lengths to which the Jesuits went to enculturate themselves. Learning the local languages was only the first hurdle. The French Jesuits also needed to eat what to them was unpleasant food, sleep tightly packed next to one another in longhouses, and endure uncomplainingly the biting cold and, later, torture. (One letter notes that one must never flag when paddling in a canoe with the Hurons.)

From the *Relations* one also receives a vivid picture of the Jesuits' deep love for the people among whom they lived: "We see shining among them some rather noble moral virtues," wrote St. Jean de Brébeuf in one of my favorite passages. "You note, in the first place, a great love and union, which they are careful to cultivate. . . . Their hospitality to all sorts of strangers is remarkable; they present to them, in their feasts, the best of what they have prepared, and, as I said, I do not know if anything similar, in this regard, is to be found anywhere."

The North American Martyrs suffered the severest privations to minister to people they both loved and admired. St. Isaac Jogues had his fingers either chewed or burned off, returned to France, and then asked to *return* to what was then called "New France." Indeed, at the time, there was a controversy over whether a priest whose fingers had been so mutilated could "validly" celebrate the Mass. Pope Urban VII swept aside any canonical restrictions by saying, "It would be shameful if a martyr of Christ should not be allowed to drink the blood of Christ."

When people criticize missionaries, I want to ask: Would you be willing to leave everything you know and travel across the world to live among people you've never met to share the good news of the gospel with them?

So to make up for their omission in the first edition of this book, I would like to urge you to read more about: St. Isaac Jogues, St. Jean de Brébeuf, St. Rene Goupil, St. Jean de la Lande, St. Antoine Daniel, St. Noël Chabanel, St. Charles Garnier, and St. Gabriel Lalemant. A fine place to start is *Jean de Brébeuf*, by Joseph Peter Donnelly (published by Loyola Press).

Readers also frequently ask this question: "Why did you include people who aren't official saints?" Although I answer that question in the book, it may be helpful to address it more specifically, since it comes up so often.

A few people in this book were not, at the time, "official" saints. But my aim wasn't simply to introduce you to officially canonized men and women but to point to examples of holiness. Besides, in the early years of the Church, there wasn't an official process of canonization. St. Peter and St. Mary Magdalene, for example, weren't canonized in the same way that men and women are today. There wasn't a Vatican process because there wasn't a Vatican, at least as we know it today. Rather, there was the general opinion held by the people of the time that a person was a saint—particularly when it came to the apostles or the disciples. If you spent any time around Jesus and are mentioned in the Gospels, being called a saint is almost a given, unless you're, say, Judas. (By the way, if you'd like to know more about him, you might check out a book I've written called *A Jesuit Off-Broadway*.)

This is true not simply for apostles such as Peter; saints in the early Church became saints by popular acclamation or with the approval of local bishops.

Back to that original question, about the saints featured in this book. Ironically, two who were not saints then are now: Mother Teresa is now St. Teresa of Calcutta; and Pope John XXIII is now St. John XXIII. Two others are on their way: Pedro Arrupe and Dorothy Day are, as of this writing, now declared by the Church to be "Servants of God," the first step on the official road to canonization.

But another is far from being declared an official saint: Thomas Merton. In my book, though, I use the word *saint* in a more general way, as when St. Paul wrote, "Greet every saint [*hagion* is the Greek] in Christ Jesus" (Philippians 4:21). This more expansive way of understanding the saints is as holy persons, faithful members of the great community of believers. Besides, I do think Thomas Merton—even with his late-in-life, and very serious, breaking of his vow of chastity—is a saint. Or at the very least, he's saintly. Some may disagree, but I feel that he is a saint and may one day be declared as one. Remember, sanctity does not mean perfection.

Now for an update.

In the past ten years, a great deal has changed in my life. Of course, I'm ten years older—with the aches and pains that go along with that. Also, my Jesuit formation has ended: I pronounced my Final Vows as a Jesuit in 2009—on All Saints Day, as it happened.

It's harder to explain Final Vows than it is to explain getting older. Relatively few of us take Final Vows; all of us grow older. Basically, it means that I completed my Jesuit training, which took twenty-one years.

To explain further: as you've read in an earlier chapter, I pronounced my First Vows of poverty, chastity, and obedience in 1990, after two years of novitiate in Boston. After that came philosophy studies (at Loyola University in Chicago, where I worked with Brother Bill Tomes and the street-gang members in the housing projects that have since been torn down); regency (when I worked with the wonderful refugees in the Jesuit Refugee Service in Nairobi, as well as at *America* magazine); and theology (when I studied at the Weston Jesuit School of Theology in Cambridge, Massachusetts, now located at Boston College). I was ordained a priest in 1999.

After that, however, there was still one more phase of formation: *tertianship*, the so-called "third year of the novitiate," as prescribed by St. Ignatius of Loyola. Part of tertianship was "making" the Long Retreat for the second time, not at Eastern Point Retreat House in Gloucester, Massachusetts, but at the Jesuit novitiate in Culver City, California, a suburb of Los Angeles. So instead of praying by walking along the Atlantic, I prayed by walking along the Pacific, which is something I'm realizing just now as I write these lines.

Final Vows, which come after the completion of tertianship, is the Society of Jesus's final acceptance of the Jesuit. It's somewhat akin to getting tenure in a university (you're already a professor, but now your place in the school is more secure) or becoming a partner in a law firm (you're already an attorney, but now you're more fully in the fold). So, after twenty-one years, I became a fully professed Jesuit. One of my college friends said at the time, having attended my First Vow Mass in Boston, my Ordination Mass in Chestnut Hill, and my Final Vows in New York, "Do I have to come to anything else?"

My life has also grown busier in the past decade, because I've written more books and have therefore been asked to do more speaking engagements and also to help the media in their coverage of religion and spirituality. This has meant that I've had to deal more seriously with a particular temptation: pride.

The temptation comes not so much from writing books, which prompts some people to tell you how much they appreciate your writing. For some reason I always find that humbling, mainly because these are such personal interactions—a letter, an e-mail, a phone call, a one-on-one encounter—and very beautiful. No, it is the media appearances and interactions with "famous people" that tempt me more. This is not to say that the people themselves—reporters, journalists, and so on—tempt me to anything. Rather, the limelight can be seductive.

It may have even tempted Jesus. Remember that one of the three tests he faces in the desert comes when Satan invites him to throw himself down from the top of the Temple in Jerusalem, so that the angels may come to rescue him (Luke 4:9; Matthew 4:5). It can be seen, say many New Testament scholars, as not simply the temptation to perform showy miracles, but for fame itself. Later, in John 6:15, we read that the surging crowds wanted to make Jesus their king, and so he escaped from their midst.

Indeed, after the testing in the desert, Luke says that reports of Jesus spread throughout all of Galilee (4:14). The original Greek word used for "report" is *phēmē*, which means, quite simply, "fame." Jesus was fully human and fully divine, after all, and I would imagine that the fully human part of him may have struggled with this, at least at some point in his life. For it is an utterly human temptation.

Let me share a story about that temptation in my life. A few years ago, I was spending time with some well-known people on a regular basis. Around that time, while directing a weekend retreat, I was dismayed to find myself thinking that I preferred to be with my "more famous" friends. Isn't that terrible? I was disappointed to discover in myself that residual desire for fame at the expense of other people. So it is something that I must attend to.

It's the same kind of temptation that impels many of us to want to spend time with people who are more popular or attractive or influential. If you have ever been at a social gathering and have been in conversation with someone who continually looked over your shoulder to see if anyone more "interesting" or "important" has arrived, you know what I mean.

This temptation is insidious for a few reasons. First, it assumes that one person is more important than another. How this goes against what Jesus calls us to do and what the saints did! Imagine Mother Teresa saying, "Now that I have my Nobel Prize, I'm going to spend my time with people who are more important than the poor." Absurd! It denies everyone's essential value and also assumes that the lives of people who are more successful, popular, or well-known are necessarily more satisfying, which is not the case. I've discovered that well-known people are often unhappy. Fame itself is an empty husk.

So I need to be vigilant about this. I share this to remind you, once again, that members of religious orders and priests are not perfect. Neither am I. The quest for holiness includes a healthy understanding of your own flaws.

But overall, the basics of my life have not changed in the ten years since I wrote this book. I'm still a Jesuit (naturally: those were vows to

God after all). I'm still a priest. I'm still an editor at *America* magazine (now known as America Media) in New York City. And I still write books, which I very much enjoy doing.

Likewise, some things have remained the same about my relationship with the saints. I still enjoy reading the lives of the saints. Just last summer, on my annual retreat, I read a marvelous biography about Catherine of Siena, by Don Brophy, which filled me in on the life of someone I knew little about other than the few things I recounted in my chapter on Pedro Arrupe. That means that I've started to pray to some new saints as well. The one follows the other, at least in my experience.

I'm also still trying my best to live a holy life. Trying to follow Jesus, trying to be kind, and trying to help the poor. Basically, I'm trying to be a good Christian. So all those things are still the same.

⁂

Let me return to something else that *has* changed. I've gained a bit more wisdom on the Christian life. This has come as the result of some hard knocks, some retreats, some conversations with insightful friends, some experiences in prayer, and some counsel from spiritual directors, mentors—and even psychologists. For me, this wisdom comes mainly as insights. Suddenly I see an aspect of the Christian life more clearly than I had before. Then I try my best to put those insights into practice. I'm by no means a saint—you can ask my friends if you doubt that!—but I'm trying.

One of those insights, which I'd like to share with you, came around the time of my Final Vows.

A few weeks before the big day, I was given a wonderful gift. And since it wasn't cash, I didn't have to hand it in to my Jesuit superior. It was more of a spiritual gift.

There is a church in New York City run by the Jesuits called St. Francis Xavier. (The other one is called—no surprise—St. Ignatius Loyola). Until a few years ago, the interior of the church was depressingly dark. Decades of grimy soot from passing cars, smoke from thousands of candles and countless grains of incense, along with a very high ceiling that was probably never well lit made it a gloomy place. You could barely even *see* the ceiling.

But around the time of my Final Vows, in 2009, the church began an extensive restoration. And ever since I heard about the project, I was longing to peek inside.

For one thing, I hoped that the saints would be easier to see. St. Francis Xavier Church has dozens of wonderful statues of the saints. But unlike in other churches, where the saints are more or less at eye level, at Xavier the saints are perched high above the congregation, on ledges overlooking the pews; in the gloom, you could hardly make out who was who. In the back of the church, in the apse, so high that you can barely see them at all, are five statues of saints, larger than the rest. And I never knew who they were; the saints seemed so far away.

Around that time, I was visiting a Jesuit friend who lives in the Jesuit community, for dinner. "If you come early," he said, "maybe we could get into the church." Providentially, we ran into the pastor, who pointed us to a side door that opened into the interior of the church, which was completely empty and utterly quiet.

It was breathtaking. The newly cleaned church glowed with glorious colors: whites and creams and yellows and golds. Funny enough, the overall color of the interior is a kind of butterscotch.

And the first thing I saw, perched above the aisles on both sides, were the gleaming white statues of the saints. The church had made it easier to see them.

"But oh," my friend said, "let's climb up the scaffolding. I *really* want to show you something."

The back half of the church was completely filled with a complicated matrix of metal scaffolding, from floor to ceiling. So we ducked under the intricate framework and stepped onto a flimsy staircase, which was the reason they coined the word *rickety*. When we took that first step, the whole staircase shook loudly.

"Uh, I don't think so," I said to my friend.

"No, really," he said, "you have to see this."

We started to climb. Soon we were halfway up the full height of the church, and I didn't dare look down or up. I confess to experiencing some real fear.

"Um, I think this is fine here," I said, grabbing tightly onto the railings.

"No," he said, "It's worth it."

Just then, the pastor came into the church and said, "Hey, you're going up! Let me help." He turned on a switch, flooding the space with light.

We kept climbing, and soon I saw the underside of a makeshift wooden floor, just above us. We got closer, and I poked my head through a small opening in the floor.

When we emerged into the small space, I was amazed. We were in the very rear of the church, way up in the apse, in front of those five saints that had always seemed, at that great height, not only small but also far removed. We were impossibly high up, only a few feet away from the ceiling of the church, which glowed in yellows and golds.

Now I could see clearly the life-sized statues of saints, who stood silently before us: St. Ignatius of Loyola, St. Francis Xavier, and St. Joseph.

Toward the center was Mary. And in the very center was Jesus.

It was hard to say why it was so moving, so "consoling," as St. Ignatius would say. Maybe because of the sheer beauty of the statues and the church itself. Maybe because I was so close to the statues of five people I love so much. Maybe because I remembered a line from the Jesuit Vow Formula, which I was about to pronounce again, about standing before the "entire heavenly court." Maybe all those things.

Then I had an insight.

It dawned on me, as I stood on that temporary platform, that the Christian journey is something like this climb. Sometimes the saints can seem like their statues in many churches: obscure, hard to identify, far off. But once you get to know them, by learning more about their real lives, that vision changes: you see them clearly, and you see how close their lives can be to yours, if you're willing to begin that climb.

Interestingly, that same year, something similar happened in the other Jesuit church in New York—the Church of St. Ignatius, where I regularly celebrate Mass. It, too, was undergoing a restoration, and that restoration also revealed something about the saints.

In the rear of the church is a lovely altar dedicated to three young Jesuit saints, each of whom is depicted in a beautiful statue. When the marble was cleaned and the brass polished, that altar gleamed, and it was easier to see Aloysius Gonzaga, Stanislaus Kostka, and John Berchmans. Each of them had died young, after leading heroic lives. St. Aloysius, as you know from this book, was the scion of a wealthy family who renounced his fortune and died at age twenty-one, after becoming infected in his work with plague victims. St. Stanislaus Kostka, who was beaten by his brother over his desire to live a more charitable life, walked 450 miles to enter the novitiate and died at age eighteen. St. John Berchmans, a model Jesuit who, like St. Thérèse of Lisieux, did small things with great love, died at age twenty-one.

After the church was cleaned, a parishioner said to me, "I didn't know those saints were even *there*!"

And I thought, *That's true for many of us.*

We can overlook these incredible saints and forget about their astonishing stories, which is a sad thing. Because underneath the years of grimy forgetfulness lies a great beauty.

The climb up that staircase in the Church of St. Francis Xavier was like the Christian journey in another way, too. As I climbed, I realized something about Christianity, something you may have figured out long ago: it's hard.

That might sound obvious, but it took me a long time to realize that. In fact, I don't think I understood it that clearly when I wrote this book. When I entered the Jesuits, I figured that if I understood the gospel, prayed hard, and got my act together—spiritually, psychologically, emotionally—I could live the Christian life with ease.

Once I figured it all out, I thought, it would become easy, something I wouldn't even have to think about, like riding a bike.

But that's not true all. It's an effort. It takes work. It's hard.

Forgiving people is hard. Loving is hard. And, like climbing those steps, it can be frightening, too. Working with the poor can be frightening. Caring for someone who is ill can be frightening. And you start to doubt that you'll make it. You think, *I'll never be able to do this. I'll never be able to climb this far.* But you can. You can with the help of friends who urge you on, saying, "Come on, just a little further." You can climb that ladder within the church. You can walk toward Jesus.

You can climb that ladder with the help of the saints, who encourage you from their posts in heaven as our patrons and our companions. It's wonderful when churches renew the statues of the saints because the saints do the same thing for the Church.

One of the old Preface prayers in the Mass included a magnificent line in praise of God, which says, "You renew the church in every age, by raising up men and women outstanding in holiness."

The saints clean the Church with their holiness, coming precisely when we need them most. St. Francis of Assisi came preaching simplicity when people needed relief from corruption and scandal. St. Ignatius of Loyola came when people needed a new way to find God in all things. St. Teresa of Calcutta came when we needed to be reminded of the call to care for the poor and forgotten.

But it wasn't easy for them either. The saints knew best of all that, like that rickety staircase, the path to God is frightening and can tempt us to doubt. But they knew something else too: it's worth it.

Now, sometimes in our daily life, or in our prayer, we take that path and we feel so close to God. When I was standing in front of those statues, I said to my friend, "You know, we'll never be here again. We'll never get this high again. The scaffolding will come down and we'll only look up at them."

And my friend said, "Don't forget to touch one before you leave."

So I reached out and touched the foot of St. Ignatius. And then the hem of the Jesus' robe. And I thought, *Well, I'll remember that the next time I'm in here and look up at them.*

How like our lives! We have a deep experience of God, we feel lifted up, or close to the divine, and may not have another experience like that for years. We must look from below, remembering. Think of Mother Teresa, who had a profound spiritual experience early in life, which led her to care for the poor, and then faced silence from God for the rest of her life.

I was thinking about all these things at the top of the ladder.

What is that ladder? How do we get closer to Jesus, Mary, and the saints? How do we travel to God? Well, the ladder is the gospel. And each rung, you might say, is one of the Beatitudes, from the Gospels of Matthew (5:3–12) and Luke (6:20–22). "Blessed are the poor in spirit," begins Jesus in Matthew's Gospel. Then he lists the path to holiness by laying out all the characteristics of the disciple.

That's the climb the saints made. Each beatitude is a step on the staircase. Poverty of Spirit. Mercy. Meekness. Righteousness. Purity of Heart. Peacemaking. And the willingness to suffer persecution.

Each of those steps may seem hard, even dangerous, to step on, and it may seem that we can't do it, but that's the path we're invited to climb. And it is Jesus himself who urges us on, saying, "Come on. It's worth it. I know it looks hard. I know you think you can't do it. I know you think you can't strive for holiness, but you can. Wait until you see what I have in store for you."

At the end of the climb is something that may seem hard to see, something that God calls us to: sanctity. Blessedness. For blessed are the merciful. Blessed are the peacemakers.

Sanctity is God's goal for us. But there is something else waiting for us, something that the saints show us with their lives. And it's something you don't hear much about in religious circles: happiness.

For there is another meaning to the word normally translated as "blessed" in the Beatitudes. *Makarioi* is the original Greek word, and it has another meaning: happy. So happy are the peacemakers. Happy are the merciful. Happiness awaits those on the road to sanctity.

So why not step onto the Christian ladder with your eyes fixed on the heavenly court, confident in the prayers of our patrons and companions—the saints—knowing that you can make it, no matter how difficult or how frightening it may seem. Knowing that, at the end of the climb, both now and in the time to come, you will be near the saints; you will touch Jesus, and you will be blessed.

And happy.

New York City
March 3, 2016
Feast of St. Katharine Drexel

FOR FURTHER READING

I hope that the reflections in this book will encourage readers to learn more about these saints, blesseds, holy persons, and companions. There are few things more satisfying, I think, than reading the lives of the saints and seeing how God's grace manifests itself in different ways and in different lives. To that end, I've listed a few books that may be helpful in coming to understand and appreciate these holy men and women. I drew heavily on all these books in my research and thank the authors for their work.

The standard reference for the lives of the canonized saints (that is, those officially recognized by the Church) remains *Butler's Lives of the Saints*. Its original form is a colossal, multivolume work organized according to the saints' feast days, with each volume corresponding to a month. There is also a shorter version, called *Butler's Lives of the Saints: Concise Edition, Revised and Updated*, edited by Michael Walsh of Heythrop College, in London (HarperSanFrancisco, 1991). Though it is, like the original work, heavily oriented toward the English saints (such as St. Michael of Wyche, bishop of Chichester, and St. Cuthbert, bishop of Lindisfarne), its concise descriptions are models of clarity.

Fr. Richard McBrien's more recent *Lives of the Saints: From Mary and St. Francis of Assisi to John XXIII and Mother Teresa* (HarperSan-Francisco, 2001) is similarly lucid, helpful, and wide-ranging, and not quite so Anglocentric. It is a worthy successor to Butler's *Lives* and even improves on the original by including chapters on the history of Christian spirituality and the particulars of the canonization process. (It is also, like Walsh's revision, more readable than the original.)

Robert Ellsberg's *All Saints: Daily Reflections on Saints, Prophets, and Witnesses for Our Time* (Crossroad, 1997) is a rich compendium of traditional saints (Thérèse, Joan of Arc), as well as other, less traditional holy individuals (Mozart, Gandhi), organized day by day: it's a perfect companion to prayer and reflection. So is *Blessed among All Women: Women, Saints, Prophets, and Witnesses for Our Time*, by the same author (Crossroad, 2005). Ellsberg's *The Saints' Guide to Happiness: Everyday Wisdom from the Lives of the Saints* (Farrar, Straus & Giroux, 2003) is a look at the way the saints viewed our quest for joy in life and is a sort of narrative version of *All Saints*. Lawrence S. Cunningham's *The Meaning of Saints* (HarperSanFrancisco, 1980) is a more theological look at the place of saints in the life of faith. And Cunningham's *A Brief History of Saints* (Blackwell, 2005) is perhaps the best short introduction to the historical development of devotion to the saints. Kenneth Woodward's fascinating book *Making Saints: How the Catholic Church Determines Who Becomes a Saint, Who Doesn't, and Why* (Touchstone, 1996) offers a detailed look at the making of saints in the Catholic Church. Finally, *Saints and Feasts of the Liturgical Year*, by Joseph Tylenda, SJ (Georgetown University Press, 2003), is a perfect pocket-sized overview, arranged according to the liturgical calendar of the Roman Catholic Church.

Other books on individual saints are listed on the pages that follow. The saints are listed in alphabetical order by first name.

ALOYSIUS GONZAGA

The best short version of Aloysius's life can be found in *Jesuit Saints and Martyrs: Short Biographies of the Saints, Blessed, Venerables, and*

Servants of God of the Society of Jesus, by Joseph Tylenda, SJ (Loyola Press, 1998). Also, *Aloysius*, edited by William Hart McNichols, SJ, and Clifford Stevens (Our Sunday Visitor, 1993), is a quirky and fascinating collection of essays, reflections, and drawings by a variety of authors about the young Jesuit saint. There you will find the essays by Daniel Berrigan, SJ, and Richard Hermes, SJ, quoted from in this book.

BERNADETTE SOUBIROUS

There are at least three superb books about St. Bernadette and what transpired at Lourdes. The first is *Lourdes: Body and Spirit in the Secular Age* (Penguin UK, 2008), a fascinating study by Ruth Harris, an Oxford University historian, that looks at the life of Bernadette, the history of the apparitions, the religious traditions of the region, the documentation behind the healings, and the sociological and ecclesial factors that helped popularize pilgrimages to Lourdes in the late nineteenth century. It is an exhaustive, scholarly, and sympathetic study. René Laurentin's *Bernadette of Lourdes: A Life Based on Authenticated Documents* (Winston Press, 1979) is widely acknowledged as the best individual biography of the saint (though the English translation is clunky in places). Laurentin uses numerous original documents to give an accurate portrayal of her life. And, of course, *The Song of Bernadette*, by Franz Werfel (St. Martin's, 1989), is the often sentimental but finally touching book that brought the story to millions and inspired the movie of the same name.

CHARLES DE FOUCAULD

The most comprehensive biography is *The Sands of Tamanrasset: The Story of Charles de Foucauld*, by Marion Mill Preminger (Linden Books, 2002). For his own writings, you might try *Charles de Foucauld*, edited by Robert Ellsberg (Orbis, 1999), whose introduction offers a concise overview of the life of this remarkable man. (The book is one in the publisher's series Modern Spiritual Masters.) You might also want to read a beautiful book by one of Charles de Foucauld's latter-day followers, Carlo Carretto, called *Letters from the Desert* (Orbis, 2002). In the 1960s, Carretto, an Italian, left behind a prominent career as a Catholic activist for a life in North Africa with the Little Brothers of Jesus. It is a magnificent book, deeply moving, that perfectly illustrates the notion of "the hidden life."

DOROTHY DAY

Dorothy's autobiography *The Long Loneliness* (HarperSanFrancisco, 1997) is the best way to meet one of the most extraordinary Catholics of the twentieth century. Her book *On Pilgrimage* (Eerdmans, 1999) is also lovely and fills in some of the gaps of *The Long Loneliness*. Also, *The Duty of Delight: The Diaries of Dorothy Day* (Random House, 2011) and *All the Way to Heaven: The Selected Letters of Dorothy Day* (Random House, 2012), both edited by Robert Ellsberg, are both essential reading.

Robert Coles's book *Dorothy Day: A Radical Devotion* (Perseus, 2000) provides an admiring and personal introduction to the cofounder of the Catholic Worker movement by someone who knew her well. The most comprehensive anthology of her works, including articles from the *Catholic Worker*, is *Dorothy Day: Selected Writings*, edited by Robert Ellsberg (Orbis, 2005), which includes a précis of her life and a short history of the Catholic Worker movement. Also, Paul Elie's book *The Life You Save May Be Your Own: An American Pilgrimage* (Farrar, Straus & Giroux, 2003) is a brilliantly realized history of the interwoven lives of Dorothy Day, Thomas Merton, Flannery O'Connor, and Walker Percy. You will get to know these four American Catholics better, and you will find few books that better describe what it means to live a holy life in the modern world.

FRANCIS OF ASSISI

There are probably hundreds of books about St. Francis. *The Little Flowers of St. Francis of Assisi*, edited by William Heywood (Vintage, 1998), is a compendium of beloved stories about the saint (preaching to the birds, converting the wolf of Gubbio, and so on) compiled by some of his earliest admirers. Adrian House's *Francis of Assisi: A Revolutionary Life* (Paulist, 2001) is a successful account that considers both the facts and the fictions of his life. Nikos Kazantzakis, in *Saint Francis* (Touchstone, 1971), offers a compelling (though fictionalized) portrait of the saint as a lively and fearless young man. Valerie Martin's *Salvation: Scenes from the Life of St. Francis* (Knopf, 2001) is a marvelously poetic retelling of his life. Lawrence S. Cunningham does an exceptional job in *Francis of Assisi: Performing the Gospel Life* (Eerdmans, 2004) of situating Francis within the Catholic tradition that he rejoiced in. A fascinating treatment of his mission to the sultan is contained in Paul Moses's *The Saint and the Sultan: The Crusades, Islam and Francis of Assisi's Mission of Peace* (Random House, 2009). Finally, Julien Green's *God's Fool: The Life and Times of Francis of Assisi* (Harper & Row, 1985) is, to me, the most successful at capturing the overall appeal of Francis, as well as his radiant personality. Sadly, Green's book can be hard to find, but it is worth the effort of tracking down a used copy. (And Francis, no doubt, would be happier if you bought used books!)

IGNATIUS OF LOYOLA

Instead of the dry books I plowed through in the novitiate, I wish I had first read *The First Jesuits*, by John W. O'Malley, SJ (Harvard University Press, 1993). It is simply the best introduction to the early Jesuits, with a focus on St. Ignatius. It shows how, contrary to popular belief, the Society of Jesus was not founded to "counter" the Protestant Reformation but for the purpose of "helping souls." The detailed work of an eminent scholar, the book is superbly written and in places even witty. For a more focused look at Ignatius, Philip Caraman's book *Ignatius Loyola: A Biography of the Founder of the Jesuits* (Harper & Row, 1990) is a good resource. *The Autobiography of St. Ignatius Loyola*, translated by Joseph F. O'Callaghan and edited by John C. Olin (Fordham University Press, 1992), is the saint's story as told to his fellow Jesuit Gonçalves da Câmara. (But remember, when it comes to prose, Ignatius is no Thomas Merton.)

For a better understanding of Jesuit spirituality and the "tensions" inherent in Jesuit life, you will do no better than a short book called *Contemplatives in Action: The Jesuit Way*, by William A. Barry, SJ, and Robert G. Doherty, SJ (Paulist, 2002). *Eyes to See, Ears to Hear: An Introduction to Ignatian Spirituality*, by David Lonsdale (Orbis, 2000), is a much longer treatment but an excellent place to begin one's study of Ignatian spirituality. More of a how-to book on the same topic, covering contemplation, meditation, and the examination of conscience, is *Inner Compass: An Invitation to Ignatian Spirituality*, by Margaret Silf (Loyola Press, 1999).

There are many good resources on the Spiritual Exercises themselves. Two of the most useful translations are *The Spiritual Exercises of Saint Ignatius: A Translation and Commentary*, by George E. Ganss, SJ (Institute of Jesuit Sources, 1992), which provides an analysis of key words and phrases, and *Draw Me into Your Friendship: A Literal Translation and a Contemporary Reading of the Spiritual Exercises*, by David Fleming (Institute of Jesuit Sources, 1996, from which I've taken some excerpts for this book), which offers an alternate (and very helpful), modern translation alongside the traditional one. (Remember, however, that the Exercises are more appreciated in their doing.) A very fine and very brief book discussing the spirituality of the Exercises is *Letting God Come Close: An Approach to the Ignatian Spiritual Exercises*, by William A. Barry, SJ (Loyola Press, 2001). For those interested in directing the Exercises, an expert's handbook is *Understanding the Spiritual Exercises*, by Michael Ivens, SJ (Gracewing, 1998). For an understanding of the tradition of making the Exercises in everyday life, that is, without having to go to a retreat house for thirty days, you would do well to pick up *The Ignatian Adventure: Experiencing the Spiritual Exercises of St. Ignatius in Daily Life*, by Kevin O'Brien, SJ (Loyola Press, 2011). Finally, Paul Mariani wrote a compelling journal of his long retreat at the Jesuit retreat house in Gloucester, Massachusetts, entitled *Thirty Days: On Retreat with the Exercises of St. Ignatius* (Viking, 2002).

JOAN OF ARC

Donald Spoto's superb biography *Joan* (HarperSanFrancisco, 2007), which uses all the tools of modern historical research, is the best contemporary introduction to the Maid of Orléans. Vita Sackville-West's *Saint Joan of Arc* (Grove, 2001), first published in 1936, is a lively retelling of her story. *Joan of Arc: Her Story*, the classic biography by Régine Pernoud and Marie-Véronique Clin, has been revised and translated by Jeremy duQuesnay Adams and published by St. Martin's (1999). Written by two distinguished French scholars, it is a model of careful historical research. It also has great appendixes. And no one should miss *Joan of Arc: In Her Own Words*, translated by Willard Trask (Books & Company, 1996), an exceptional book that takes Joan's trial testimony and arranges it chronologically so that the reader feels as if Joan is telling her life story from inspiring start to moving finish.

JOHN XXIII

Deeply moving in places (though slow going in others), John's autobiography, *Journal of a Soul: The Autobiography of Pope John XXIII* (Doubleday, 1999), is a compendium of his diary entries from his seminary days to his years as pope and is readily available. Just as moving (and even exciting in places) is Peter Hebblethwaite's highly readable biography *John XXIII: Pope of the Century* (Continuum, 2000), which gives an overview of not only the man but also his influence on the Church and the world.

Pope John XXIII: A Spiritual Biography, by Christian Feldman (2000), is part of the Lives and Legacies series from Crossroad and provides an overview of the spirituality of Angelo Roncalli. *A Retreat with John XXIII: Opening the Windows to Wisdom*, edited by Alfred McBride, O. Praem (St. Anthony Messenger, 1996), is also part of a series (A Retreat With) and uses John's writings as a way to foster prayer and reflection.

The little book that initially drew me to John is called *Wit and Wisdom of Good Pope John*, collected by Henri Fesquet (P. J. Kenedy & Sons, 1964). It is out of print but worth the effort to track it down.

JOSEPH

Since there is little known about the life of Joseph, it is not surprising that there are comparatively few books on the saint. For an exegesis of his brief appearances in the New Testament, you will do no better than Raymond E. Brown's landmark work *The Birth of the Messiah: A Commentary on the Infancy Narratives in the Gospels of Matthew and Luke* (Doubleday, 1993). There is also a description of the carpentry skills Jesus might have learned from Joseph in Nazareth in the first volume of John Meier's magisterial study of the "historical Jesus," *A Marginal Jew: Rethinking the Historical Jesus*, called *The Roots of the Problem and the Person* (Doubleday, 1991).

There are, however, two short books that attempt to construct a tentative portrait of Joseph and trace the history of Christian devotion to him. They are *Saint Joseph: Shadow of the Father*, by Andrew Doze (Alba House, 1992), the more serious and pious approach, and *Saint*

Joseph: His Life and His Role in the Church Today, by Louise Bourassa Perrotta (Our Sunday Visitor, 2000), a book written in a rather more accessible style.

JUDE

Thank You, St. Jude: Women's Devotion to the Patron Saint of Hopeless Causes (Yale University Press, 1996), by the historian Robert A. Orsi, is a study of devotion to the saint in the United States. Also, *Jude: A Pilgrimage to the Saint of Last Resort*, by Liz Trotta (HarperCollins, 1998), is the author's personal journey (literally: she travels to the reputed place of his birth) to come to know what you could call the "historical Jude."

MARY

Elizabeth Johnson's book *Truly Our Sister: A Theology of Mary in the Communion of Saints* (Continuum, 2003) is a magnificent theological reflection on the mother of God by a leading American theologian who is acutely sensitive to the place of Mary in the Catholic world. After *Truly Our Sister* was published, the author excerpted essays on Mary's appearances in Scripture from the work and collected them in a short book called *Dangerous Memories: A Mosaic of Mary in Scripture* (Continuum, 2004). In Jaroslav Pelikan's *Mary through the Centuries: Her Place in the History of Culture* (Yale University Press, 1996), a Lutheran scholar looks at how the image of Mary has changed and grown over the years. Sally Cunneen's book *In Search of Mary: The Woman and the Symbol* (Ballantine, 1996) is similarly helpful in tracing the influence of and devotion to Mary throughout Christian history. *Meditations on Mary* (Viking, 1999) is a collection of fascinating essays by the always insightful Kathleen Norris, illustrated with lavish full-color reproductions of Old Master portraits of Mary.

PEDRO ARRUPE

An excellent introduction to Fr. Arrupe is *Pedro Arrupe: Essential Writings*, selected by Kevin Burke, SJ (Orbis, 2004), who also included a short biographical introduction in the book. Just as good is a book published by the Institute of Jesuit Sources called *One Jesuit's Spiritual Journey: Autobiographical Conversations with Jean-Claude Dietsch, SJ* (1986), a series of lively and moving interviews. If you want a greater understanding of Arrupe's thoughts on social justice, religious life, education, culture, and a host of other topics, the Institute of Jesuit Sources offers a series of Arrupe's major talks, essays, and letters in *Challenge to Religious Life Today* (1979), *Justice with Faith Today* (1980), and *Other Apostolates Today* (1981).

PETER

Perhaps the best recent study on Peter is Pheme Perkins's book *Peter: Apostle for the Whole Church* (Augsburg Fortress, 2000), an investigation into the "historical Peter," with an emphasis on his role in the early Christian community. Richard McBrien's book *Lives of the Popes: The Pontiffs from St. Peter to John Paul II* (HarperSanFrancisco, 2000) gives a good brief summary of the life of the "first pope." Finally, Richard Rohr's book *Soul Brothers: Men in the Bible Speak to Men Today* (Orbis, 2004), which is illustrated with portraits by Louis Glanzman, includes a touching meditation on how Peter came to God not by doing right, but by "doing wrong."

MOTHER TERESA

Kathryn Spink's *Mother Teresa: A Complete Authorized Biography* (HarperSanFrancisco, 1998) makes for an engrossing read and details especially well the struggles of St. Teresa of Calcutta's early efforts to found the Missionaries of Charity. Because it was published shortly after her death, however, it does not include some of the more recently published information about St. Teresa's "call within a call" and her struggles with prayer. For that, you can read Carol Zaleski's article "The Dark Night of Mother Teresa," in *First Things* magazine (May 2003), which is based on the research of the Reverend Brian Kolodiejchuk, MC. Malcolm Muggeridge's book *Something Beautiful for God: The Classic Account of Mother Teresa's Journey into Compassion* (HarperSanFrancisco, 1986), though first published in 1971, remains an illuminating look at her ministry and, incidentally, her effect on even nonbelievers, like the author. A helpful book of her writings and prayers is *Mother Teresa: In My Own Words*, compiled by José Luis González-Balado (Liguori, 1996).

THÉRÈSE OF LISIEUX

The Autobiography of Saint Thérèse of Lisieux: The Story of a Soul, translated by John Beevers (Image Books, 1987), is Thérèse of Lisieux's remarkable story told in her own words, from the simple beginning to the difficult end of her rich life. You might also turn to two critical biographies to better understand the Little Flower: Monica Furlong's *Thérèse of Lisieux* (Orbis, 2001) and Kathryn Harrison's *Saint Thérèse of Lisieux* (Penguin, 2003). Dorothy Day also wrote a warm and loving portrait of the saint, called *Thérèse* (Templegate, 1979). Kathryn Harrison's book is especially good at focusing on some of Thérèse's ascetical practices and exploring what led to her austere life. However, when I recently asked a Carmelite scholar about his favorite biography of the saint, he suggested Guy Gaucher's *The Story of a Life: St. Thérèse of Lisieux* (HarperSanFrancisco, 1993).

THOMAS AQUINAS

G. K. Chesterton's affectionate biography *Saint Thomas Aquinas: "The Dumb Ox"* (Image, 1974) is a fine introduction to the life of the Angelic Doctor. Focusing more on Thomistic theology is *Knowing the*

Love of Christ: An Introduction to the Theology of St. Thomas Aquinas, by Michael Dauphinais and Matthew Levering (University of Notre Dame Press, 2002). And Aidan Nichols's book *Discovering Aquinas: An Introduction to His Life, Work, and Influence* (Eerdmans, 2003) is exactly what its subtitle says.

There is also a fine, brief introduction to St. Thomas and Thomistic philosophy in *The HarperCollins Encyclopedia of Catholicism*, edited by Richard McBrien (HarperCollins, 1995). The great Jesuit scholar Frederick Copleston, author of the huge, multivolume *History of Philosophy* (Image, 1993), has an extensive chapter on Aquinas and his writings in the second volume of his magnum opus. The chapter is also available as a single work called *Aquinas: An Introduction to the Life and Work of the Great Medieval Thinker* (Penguin, 1955). Another scholarly treatment of Aquinas is Étienne Gilson's *The Christian Philosophy of St. Thomas Aquinas* (Random House, 1956).

St. Thomas's major work, the *Summa Theologica*, while long, is often surprisingly accessible, thanks in great part to the author's clear and highly readable style. It is also readily available, and you will look very learned carrying it around. Also, *Summa of the Summa*, edited by Peter Kreeft (Ignatius Press, 1990), is a summary of the most important themes in Thomas's work.

THOMAS MERTON

Thomas Merton's popular autobiography *The Seven Storey Mountain* (Harcourt Brace, 1999) takes the reader from Merton's birth in France up to his first few years in the monastery. *The Sign of Jonas* (Harcourt Brace Jovanovich, 1979) can be in many ways even more captivating for the reader; it continues the tale of Merton's early years as a Trappist. For the truly ambitious, the multivolume *Journals of Thomas Merton* (HarperSanFrancisco, 1995–98) provides the rest of the story in Merton's own words. There is also an abbreviated version of these same journals, entitled *The Intimate Merton: His Life from His Journals* (HarperSanFrancisco, 2001), edited by Patrick Hart and Jonathan Montaldo. The excerpt included on page 57 is from *No Man Is an Island* (Harcourt Brace Jovanovich, 1955, p. 126).

Moving from autobiography to biography, *Thomas Merton, Brother Monk: The Quest for True Freedom* (Continuum, 1997) is a splendid treatment of the monastic roots of Merton's spirituality, written by a fellow Trappist (and writer), M. Basil Pennington, OCSO. Monica Furlong's *Merton: A Biography* (Ligouri, 1995) is also a good brief introduction. Henri Nouwen, the contemporary spiritual writer, offers a series of perceptive meditations in his very short book *Encounters with Merton* (Crossroad, 2004). Finally, for a more complete and more scholarly (but no less interesting) telling of the tale, you should try Michael Mott's utterly fascinating biography, *The Seven Mountains of Thomas Merton* (Harcourt Brace, 1993). It's very long and very worth it.

UGANDAN MARTYRS

As a measure of how little they are known in the West, it is difficult to find books about the Ugandan martyrs. *African Saints: Saints, Martyrs, and Holy People from the Continent of Africa*, by Frederick Quinn (Crossroad, 2002), includes a brief discussion of their story, as do a number of other general books on the saints. The story of Mutesa, the ruler of Buganda, can be found in Edward Rice's *Captain Sir Richard Francis Burton* (Scribners, 1990). The general interest book about Charles Lwanga and his companions, however, has yet to be written, and their lives still remain largely hidden from many of us.

ACKNOWLEDGMENTS

T his book was a lengthy project that could not have been accomplished without the intercession of the saints as well as the help of many friends a little closer to home.

Since I am not an academic, I was worried that despite my efforts at research, I might make some inadvertent mistakes in retelling the lives of the saints. (In telling stories from my own life, however, I felt on firmer ground!) So toward the end of my writing, I mailed each chapter to an "expert" on each saint for a more scholarly review. The letters and comments I promptly received in reply (which did in fact correct some errors) were always full of the most insightful comments and suggestions. So I am enormously grateful for the time and effort of my saintly experts: Janice Farnham, RJM (Joan of Arc, Bernadette Soubirous); Steven Payne, OCD (Thérèse of Lisieux); Lawrence S. Cunningham (Thomas Merton, Francis of Assisi); Daniel J. Harrington, SJ (Peter); John Padberg, SJ (Ignatius of Loyola, Aloysius Gonzaga, Pedro Arrupe); Robert Ellsberg (Dorothy Day, Joseph); Kathryn Spink (Mother Teresa); John W. O'Malley, SJ (John XXIII); Joseph Koterski, SJ (Thomas Aquinas); Aylward Shorter, MAfr (the Ugandan martyrs); and Elizabeth Johnson, CSJ (Mary). There is no way I could have completed this book without their generous help and learned insights. I am so fortunate to know them and count them as "friends of God and companions."

In addition, John Donohue, SJ, and Janice Farnham, RJM, read a very early draft of this book and offered suggestions and advice that helped me determine which path the book should take. And as the manuscript continued to take shape, Richard Leonard, SJ, provided a detailed list of comments that improved the focus of the book immeasurably. I am also grateful to George Lane, SJ, Jim Manney, Matthew Diener, and Joe Durepos at Loyola Press for their enthusiasm about this book, as well as Vinita Wright for her amazingly astute edits, and Heidi Hill, for her superb fact checking, a colossal effort for a book like this one. One hears many complaints these days from writers about the supposedly lost art of copyediting and fact checking: I have none. Vinita and Heidi were exceptionally good.

Thanks also to those who helped with some very specific parts of the manuscript: Michael Hilbert, SJ, of the Pontifical Gregorian University, in Rome, read the chapter on St. Aloysius and ensured that my memory of the Ignatian sites in Rome was accurate. Julie Sosa Meza corrected my poor Spanish. Peggy Pennacchi, who traveled with me throughout Europe all those years ago, kept a diary of our trip and reminded me of many details I had forgotten. (And we did, believe it or not, arrive in Orléans on All Saints Day.) Tony Wach, SJ, in Kampala, Uganda, helped refresh my memory of the physical layout of the martyrs' shrine in Namugongo. James Carr, SJ, then serving as assistant novice director in the Jesuit novitiate in Boston, Massachusetts, tracked down the titles of the (numerous) biographies of Ignatius that we read in the novitiate. Drew Christiansen, SJ, of *America* magazine, helped inform my discussion of John XXIII's encyclical *Pacem in Terris*. Thanks also to Kevin O'Brien, SJ, and Dave Nantais for cheerfully accompanying me on the hottest weekend of the year to the Abbey of Gethsemani, in Kentucky, in the summer of 2003. And to George Williams, SJ, and Brian Frain, SJ, for their company on our pilgrimage to Lourdes the next summer—as well as to Rob Lively of the Order of Malta for his kind invitation.

There were many others who read the book at various points or otherwise offered helpful suggestions or encouragement on the project. Happily, the list of Jesuits who have been companions during this project is a long one, so just assume an "SJ" after the following names, presented in no particular order: David Donovan, Bill Barry, Damian O'Connell, George Williams, Kevin White, Jim Hayes, Myles Sheehan, Dave Godleski, Ross Pribyl, Jim Bowler, Bill Clarke, Bob Reiser, Chris Derby, Mike Bayard, Jim Keegan, John Long, Vinnie O'Keefe, Dennis Linehan, Roger Haight, George Collins, Rick Curry, Chris Devron, Steve Schloesser, Howard Gray, Jim McDermott, Dan Berrigan, Bob Levens, Bob Gilroy, Matt Malone, Jim Keane, Phil Ganir, Brad Schaeffer, David McCallum, Richard Leonard, Steve Katsouros, Matt Cassidy, Tom Reese, Walter Modrys, Cardinal Avery Dulles, Jack McLain, Kevin O'Brien, and Rick Deshaies. To them and to all my brother Jesuits this book is dedicated. I am also very grateful to James Alison, Joan Chittister, Bishop Tom Gumbleton, Robert Ellsberg, Jeremy Langford, Bill McNichols, John Jones, Frank Oveis, Paul Elie, Paul Mariani, Ron Hansen, Maddie Tiberii, Dave Gibson, Bill McGarvey, Tim Reidy, and Grant Gallicho for their advice and prayers. Thanks also to my family—my mother, sister, brother-in-law, and nephews—for their continuing love and support.

In the space of the writing of this book, five editorial interns at *America* magazine have come and gone, and all helped with the editing and typing (and retyping) process. So I would like to thank Joseph McAuley, Shaila Dani, Brian Pinter, and Jackie Finlan for their always cheerful assistance and willingness to read my lousy handwriting. A special thanks to Casie Attardi, who lent me enormous help as the manuscript neared completion, including making endless copies to send out to readers.

Finally, thanks to all the holy men and women whom I've written about in these pages—for their lives, their examples, and, especially, their prayers.

A GUIDE FOR READING GROUPS

For the past several years, I have run two book clubs at a local parish in New York, and if I've learned anything, it's that the discussions of longer books sometimes need to be spread out over two meetings. Otherwise, people may feel daunted by a book's length. For reading groups, then, *My Life with the Saints* can be read all at once or divided into two sections: from the introduction to chapter 9, and from chapter 10 to the conclusion. I hope that these questions might stimulate good discussion and, also, fruitful personal reflection.

1. The first saint mentioned in this book is Jude. Who was the first saint to whom you felt drawn? How did you "meet" him or her? If you've been unfamiliar with the saints until now, which person in *My Life with the Saints* did you find most appealing?

2. Joan of Arc stayed true to her decision to follow God even in the midst of persecution. Have there been times when your faith put you in conflict with others? How did you deal with this?

3. The "Little Way" of Thérèse of Lisieux stresses not only doing small things with love but also adopting a stance of "littleness" before God. Does this kind of humility appeal to you? How does humility fit into your spiritual life?

4. Like even the holiest of persons, Thomas Merton was not perfect, and, like many saints, he could be disagreeable at times. Do you think imperfections make a saint less likable or more accessible?

5. The spirituality of Ignatius of Loyola can be summed up as "finding God in all things." What things enable you to find God in your life?

6. In the 1960s and 1970s, Pedro Arrupe challenged the Jesuits to promote "the faith that does justice." Where does work with the poor and on behalf of justice fit into your religious beliefs?

7. Do you believe the story of the visions of Bernadette Soubirous at Lourdes? What role do miracles play in your faith?

8. Were you surprised to read about Mother Teresa's "dark night"? Have you ever experienced anything similar? She eventually understood her desolation as a way of identifying with Jesus. How did you deal with your desolation?

9. Pope John XXIII was a joyful person with a good sense of humor. Do laughter and playfulness play a part in your spiritual life? How might humor lead people closer to God?

10. Dorothy Day is one of the few people mentioned in *My Life with the Saints* who raised a child. Has the notion of the parent as a holy person been overlooked in religious traditions?

11. Do you think it's true that Jesus chose Peter as an apostle as much for his weaknesses as for his strengths? Are there ways that your weaknesses have moved you closer to God?

12. In the life and writings of Thomas Aquinas, reason and faith were closely linked. Why do you think that some believe that religious people are not able to use their minds?

13. Like many saints, Francis of Assisi challenges us to live more simply. What role does a simple lifestyle play in your spiritual life?

14. The idea of the "hidden life" of Jesus of Nazareth, and of Joseph, is that sanctity can be found, with God's help, in everyday life. What aspects of your life, which may be hidden from others, serve to make you a more faith-filled person?

15. The Ugandan martyrs are a key symbol of faith for the people of Uganda and other African countries. Which saints are most popular in your locale? What are their stories?

16. Some saints, like Aloysius Gonzaga, followed religious practices that can seem foreign or even repellent to us. Does this make it more difficult for you to appreciate their lives?

17. The story of the Annunciation shows that we are free to accept or reject God's invitation in our lives. During what times have you, like Mary, listened well to God?

GENERAL QUESTIONS

18. In Elizabeth Johnson's formulation, there are two traditional ways of relating to the saints: as patrons and as companions. How do you relate to the saints?

19. One underlying theme of *My Life with the Saints* is Thomas Merton's adage "For me to be a saint means to be myself." How could Merton's insight be applied in your life?

20. Have you ever met any "saints" in your life? What made them holy in your eyes? How did their lives influence you?

21. Mother Teresa said, "In order to be a saint, you have to seriously want to be one." Thomas Merton's professor, Mark Van Doren, said roughly the same thing. What might this mean in your life?

ABOUT THE AUTHOR

James Martin, SJ, is a Jesuit priest, editor at large of *America*, the national Catholic review, and the author of many books. A graduate of the University of Pennsylvania's Wharton School of Business, Father Martin worked for six years in corporate finance at General Electric before entering the Society of Jesus in 1988. As part of his Jesuit training, he worked in a hospice for the sick and dying in Kingston, Jamaica; with street-gang members in Chicago; as a prison chaplain in Boston; and for two years in Nairobi, Kenya, where he helped East African refugees start small businesses to support themselves. After completing his philosophy studies at Loyola University Chicago and theology studies at the Weston Jesuit School of Theology in Cambridge, Massachusetts (now part of Boston College), he was ordained a priest in 1999. Father Martin's writing has appeared in many newspapers, magazines, and websites, both religious and secular, including *The New York Times*, *The Wall Street Journal*, and many others venues. He has commented on religion and spirituality on all the major radio and television networks, both nationally and internationally. His recent books include *Jesus: A Pilgrimage* and *The Jesuit Guide to (Almost) Everything*, both of which were *New York Times* best sellers, as well as *Seven Last Words*, *Between Heaven and Mirth*, *The Abbey*, and *A Jesuit Off-Broadway*, which is published by Loyola Press.